More Language Arts, Math, and Science for Students with Severe Disabilities

More Language Arts, Math, and Science for Students with Severe Disabilities

edited by

Diane Browder, Ph.D.

and

Fred Spooner, Ph.D.

University of North Carolina at Charlotte

·P A U L·H·
BROOKES
PUBLISHING C⁰ ®

Baltimore • London • Sydney

Paul H. Brookes Publishing Co.
Post Office Box 10624
Baltimore, Maryland 21285-0624
USA

www.brookespublishing.com

Typeset by Auburn Associates, Inc., Baltimore, Maryland.
Manufactured in the United States of America by
Sheridan Books, Inc., Chelsea, Michigan.

Cover images © iStockphoto.com/guter, aprott, ostrinka, fstop123, claylib, SarahLundPhotography,
VickyLeon, nittram, paulaphoto, Thorr, yaruta, AVAVA, Inventori.

Library of Congress Cataloging-in-Publication Data

More language arts, math, and science for students with severe disabilities / [37 authors]; edited by
  Diane Browder and Fred Spooner.
    pages   cm
  Includes index.
  ISBN 978-1-59857-317-6 (pbk.: alk. paper)
  ISBN 978-1-59857-647-4 (epub e-book)
  1. Children with mental disabilities—Education—United States.   2. Language arts—United
  States.   3. Inclusive education—United States.   4. Academic achievement—United States.
  I. Browder, Diane M., editor of compilation.   II. Spooner, Fred, editor of compilation.
  LC4616.M67 2014
  371.9—dc23   2013042112

British Library Cataloguing in Publication data are available from the British Library.

2018   2017   2016   2015   2014

10   9   8   7   6   5   4   3   2   1

Contents

About the
Reproducible Materials

Purchasers of this book may download, print, and/or photocopy the forms in Figures 9.2 and 13.1 for educational use. These materials are included with the print book and are also available at **www.brookespublishing.com/browder/eforms**

Also, for instructors, study questions and extension activities for every chapter are available to help you teach a course using ***More*** *Language Arts, Math, and Science for Students with Severe Disabilities*. Please visit **www.brookespublishing.com/browder**

About the Editors

Diane M. Browder, Ph.D., Professor, Department of Special Education and Child Development, University of North Carolina at Charlotte, 9201 University City Boulevard, Charlotte, NC 28223

Dr. Browder is the Lake and Edward P. Snyder Distinguished Professor of Special Education and has over two decades of research and writing on assessment and instruction for students with severe developmental disabilities. She received the 2009 Distinguished Researcher Award from the AERA Special Education SIG and the 2009 First Citizens Bank Scholar at the University of North Carolina at Charlotte. In 2011 Dr. Browder was recognized by the state of North Carolina with the O. Max Gardner Award for research that has made a contribution to humanity.

Fred Spooner, Ph.D., Professor, Department of Special Education and Child Development, University of North Carolina at Charlotte, 9201 University City Boulevard, Charlotte, NC 28223

Dr. Spooner is Principal Investigator on a personnel preparation project involving distance delivery technologies at the University of North Carolina at Charlotte and Co-principal Investigator on a U.S. Department of Education, Institute of Education Sciences (IES) Project to teach students with moderate and severe intellectual disability to solve mathematical problems. He has also served as a Co-principal Investigator with Diane Browder on a project for determining evidence-based practices in the area of intellectual disability and Co-principal Investigator on a project focusing on high-quality mathematics and science instruction for students who participate in alternate assessments judged against alternate achievement standards. Dr. Spooner has held numerous editorial posts, including Co-editor of *TEACHING Exceptional Children,* Co-editor of *Teacher Education and Special Education,* Co-editor for *The Journal of Special Education,* and Associate Editor for *Research and Practice for Persons with Severe Disabilities.* His research interests include instructional procedures for students with severe disabilities, alternate assessment, and validating evidence-based practices.

About the Contributors

Lynn Ahlgrim-Delzell, Ph.D., Assistant Professor of Research, University of North Carolina at Charlotte, College of Education, 9201 University City Boulevard, Charlotte, NC 28223

Dr. Ahlgrim-Delzell's research interests include literacy instruction and assessment and research methods for low-incidence populations. She has over 30 years of experience working with individuals with severe disability in various capacities.

Stephanie Al Otaiba, Ph.D., Professor, Southern Methodist University, Department of Teaching and Learning, P.O. Box 750455, Dallas, TX 75275

Dr. Al Otaiba conducts research on response to intervention, early literacy intervention, and teacher training. As a professor, she also teaches related graduate courses. She has published numerous articles and chapters related to her research interests and serves on editorial boards.

Jill Allor, Ed.D., Professor, Southern Methodist University, Department of Teaching and Learning, P.O. Box 750455, Dallas, TX 75275

Dr. Allor conducts research in early literacy instruction for students with and without disabilities. She is an author of curricular materials for both general and special educators. She has published numerous research articles and chapters.

Keri S. Bethune, Ph.D., BCBA-D, Assistant Professor, James Madison University, Department of Educational Foundations and Exceptionalities, 395 South High Street (MSC 6908), Harrisonburg, VA, 22807

Dr. Bethune's research focuses on applied behavior analysis, single-subject research design, teacher education (including coaching), and general curriculum access for students with severe disabilities and autism.

Heidi B. Carlone, Ph.D., Associate Professor, The University of North Carolina at Greensboro, School of Education, 404 SOE Building, Greensboro, NC 27412

Dr. Carlone studies the culture of science learning settings to better understand how science can be accessible for all learners.

Monica Delano, Ph.D., Associate Professor, University of Louisville, Department of Special Education, College of Education and Human Development, Louisville, KY 40292

Dr. Delano teaches in the program in moderate and severe disabilities as well as the program in autism and applied behavior analysis. Her research focuses on literacy interventions for students with autism spectrum disorders.

Jennifer C. Fischer-Mueller, Ed.D., Deputy Superintendent for Teaching and Learning, Public Schools of Brookline, Brookline Town Hall, 5th Floor, 333 Washington Street, Brookline, MA, 02445

Dr. Fischer-Mueller taught science in several New Hampshire schools including Souhegan High School, Hollis/Brookline High School, and Spaulding Junior High School. She received a variety of honors including the Tandy Technology Excellence in Science Teaching Award and was named CitiBank National Faculty.

Claudia Flowers, Ph.D., Professor, University of North Carolina at Charlotte, 9201 University City Boulevard, Charlotte, NC 28223

Dr. Flowers's research has focused on assessment and transition issues for students with disabilities. She is a partner with the federally funded National Centers and State Collaborative 28-state consortium that is developing a new alternate assessment for students with significant cognitive disabilities and Co-principal Investigator for the IES-funded Communicating Interagency Relationships and Collaborative Linkages for Exceptional Students.

Jessica Folsom, Ph.D., Research Associate, Florida Center for Reading Research, Florida State University, 2010 Levy Avenue, Suite 100, Tallahassee, FL 32310

Dr. Folsom is a former classroom teacher of adolescents with significant cognitive disabilities. She received her Ph.D. in special education with a focus in educational research.

Ellen Forte, Ph.D., President, edCount, LLC, 5335 Wisconsin Avenue NW, Suite 440, Washington, DC 20015

Dr. Forte holds several leadership positions on large-scale, federally funded research and assistance initiatives, including directing the validity evaluation component of the National Centers and State Collaborative 28-state consortium that is developing a new alternate assessment for students with significant cognitive disabilities. She serves as the chief policy advisor to the National Deaf Education Center at Gallaudet University on its implementation of standards, assessments, and accountability mechanisms, and serves as the chief standards and assessment policy advisor to the current National Evaluation of Titles I and II.

J. Mathew Jameson, Ph.D., Assistant Professor, University of Utah, 1705 E. Campus Center Drive, MBH112, Salt Lake City, UT 84112

Dr. Jameson's primary research interests include instructional strategies and inclusive educational procedures for students with significant cognitive disabilities. He has authored and coauthored articles focused on the provision of a free and appropriate public education, instructional strategies used to support students in inclusive settings, and evaluations of distance education and teacher preparation programs.

Bree A. Jimenez, Ph.D., Assistant Professor, The University of North Carolina at Greensboro, School of Education, 421 SOE Building, Greensboro, NC 27412

Dr. Jimenez studies general curriculum access and assessment for students with moderate and severe intellectual disabilities. Specifically, she investigates math and science instruction aligned to grade-level standards.

Cheryl M. Jorgensen, Ph.D., Affiliate Faculty, University of New Hampshire, Institute on Disability and Education Department, P.O. Box 8, South Acworth, NH 03607

Dr. Jorgensen is a founding member of the National Center for Inclusive Education at the Institute on Disability at the University of New Hampshire. Since 1985, she has worked with parents, teachers, and administrators to increase their commitment to and capacity for including students with disabilities in general education classes. Her research has focused on how presuming competence influences all aspects of students' educational programs and on the restructuring of policies, organizational structures, and teaching practices that naturally facilitate inclusion and learning for all students.

Victoria Knight, Ph.D., Assistant Professor, Vanderbilt University, Department of Special Education, GPC 228, 230 Appleton Place, Nashville, TN 37203

Dr. Knight's research has focused on general curriculum access for students with significant disabilities and autism and evaluating and disseminating evidence-based practices. She is the author of book chapters and peer-reviewed publications on these topics.

Angel Lee, M.Ed., Research Associate, University of North Carolina at Charlotte, 9201 University City Boulevard, Charlotte, NC 28223

Ms. Lee works with the National Center and State Collaborative on a General Supervision Enhancement Grant focusing on the development of curriculum and instruction aligned to the Common Core State Standards for students with significant disabilities. She is coauthor of three literacy curricula developed for students with significant disabilities: *The Early Literacy Skills Builder*, *Pathways to Literacy*, and *Teaching to Standards: English Language Arts*.

Ya-yu Lo, Ph.D., Associate Professor, University of North Carolina at Charlotte, Department of Special Education & Child Development, 9201 University City Boulevard, Charlotte, NC 28223

Dr. Lo's research focuses include applied behavior analysis, social skill instruction, effective academic and behavioral interventions, urban students with culturally and linguistically diverse backgrounds, functional behavioral assessment, and positive behavior support. She is a co-principal investigator of an IES grant, The solutions project: Teaching students with moderate/severe intellectual disability to solve mathematical problems (2013–2016).

John McDonnell, Ph.D., Associate Dean for Faculty Research Support, College of Education; Professor, University of Utah, Department of Special Education, 1705 E. Campus Center Drive, Room 221, Salt Lake City, UT 84112

Dr. McDonnell's research focuses on curriculum and instruction, inclusive education, and transition programs for students with intellectual and developmental disabilities. He has published extensively in these areas and has been actively involved in the development of innovative school programs for more than 25 years.

Bethany R. McKissick, Ph.D., Assistant Professor, Mississippi State University, Department of Curriculum, Instruction, and Special Education, 310 Allen Hall, Mail Stop 9705, Mississippi State, MS 39762

Dr. McKissick's research focuses on providing general curriculum access for students with disabilities. Additional research interests include evidence-based practices for teaching students with disabilities, students with severe challenging behaviors, inclusive education, and students with autism spectrum disorders.

Pamela J. Mims, Ph.D., Assistant Professor, East Tennessee State University, 807 University Parkway, Johnson City, TN 37614

Dr. Mims received her Ph.D. in special education in 2009 from the University of North Carolina at Charlotte. Her research interests include systematic instruction strategies and access to the general curriculum for students with significant disabilities. She has published multiple journal articles and book chapters and presents her work nationally.

Maryann Mraz, Ph.D., Professor, University of North Carolina at Charlotte, College of Education, Reading and Elementary Education Department, 9201 University City Boulevard, Charlotte, NC 28223

Dr. Mraz earned her Ph.D. from Kent State University and her M.Ed. and B.A. from John Carroll University. She has served as a board member of the Association of Literacy Educators and Researchers (ALER) and is the author of more than 60 books, articles, and chapters on literacy education.

Miriam Ortiz, M.S., Doctoral Student and Research Assistant, Southern Methodist University, Department of Teaching and Learning, P.O. Box 750455, Dallas, TX 75275

Ms. Ortiz is currently working on her Ph.D. in education at Southern Methodist University (SMU). Her current research interests include improving academic outcomes for children with, or at risk for disabilities as well as assisting struggling readers of all ages. She has been coauthor on several peer-reviewed journal articles and book chapters on the topic of reading instruction for students with varying disabilities.

Robert Pennington, Ph.D., Assistant Professor, University of Louisville, Department of Education, College of Education and Human Development, Louisville, KY 40292

Dr. Pennington is a Board Certified Behavior Analyst and has more than 20 years of experience working with students with intellectual disabilities and autism spectrum disorders. His research interests are writing and communication, computer-assisted instruction, and the application behavior analytic instructional procedures.

Drew Polly, Ph.D., Associate Professor, University of North Carolina at Charlotte, Department of Reading and Elementary Education, 9201 University City Boulevard, Charlotte, NC 28223

Dr. Polly's research interests include examining the best way to support teachers' use of standards-based mathematics pedagogies and digital technologies in their classroom.

Shamby Polychronis, Ph.D., Special Education Program Director, Westminster College, 1840 South 1300 East, Salt Lake City, UT 84105

Dr. Polychronis has experience teaching students with low-incidence disabilities in post–high school programs with an emphasis on community-based programs. Her scholarly interests include inclusive education, individual rights for people with disabilities, family support services, and collaborative partnerships between general and special educators.

Holly Prud'homme, M.Ed., Teacher, Maplewood Elementary School, 184 Maple Street, Somersworth, NH, 03878

From 2002–2006, Ms. Prud'homme participated in an Office of Special Education Programs–funded model demonstration project that developed the Beyond Access Model, an instructional planning process that supports valued membership, full participation, reciprocal social relationships, and learning of the general education curriculum in the general education classroom for students with the most significant disabilities. Ms. Prud'homme is featured in filmmaker Dan Habib's film *Who Cares About Kelsey?* that explores inclusive education for students with autism and emotional/behavioral disabilities.

David K. Pugalee, Ph.D., Director/Professor, University of North Carolina at Charlotte, Center for Science, Technology, Engineering, and Mathematics Education, College of Education Building, Suite 222, 9201 University City Boulevard, Charlotte, NC 28223

Dr. Pugalee has done extensive research on the role of language in teaching and learning of mathematics. He has published extensively in this area as well as articles and books on mathematics and technology and mathematics and special education.

Rachel Quenemoen, M.S., Project Director/Senior Research Fellow, National Center and State Collaborative, National Center on Educational Outcomes, University of Minnesota, 207 Pattee Hall, 150 Pillsbury Avenue SE, Minneapolis, MN 55455

Ms. Quenemoen conducts research and consultation/technical assistance on educational change processes to ensure that students with disabilities are included in and benefit from reform efforts. She has written numerous articles, chapters, research briefs, and presentations on improving outcomes for students with disabilities, including coauthoring a book on alternate assessment. She has worked for 35 years as an educational sociologist and currently serves on the assessment and accountability technical advisory committees for Idaho, Partnership for Assessment of Readiness for College and Careers, Puerto Rico, South Dakota, and Washington, DC.

Timothy Riesen, Ph.D., Research Assistant Professor, Utah State University, Salt Lake Center, 2500 South State Street, Salt Lake City, UT 84115

Dr. Riesen's research interests include transition to employment and inclusion of individuals with moderate to severe disabilities in education, employment, and community environments.

Alicia F. Saunders, Ph.D., Research Associate, University of North Carolina at Charlotte, Department of Special Education and Child Development, 9201 University City Boulevard, Charlotte, NC 28223

Dr. Saunders is the project coordinator for the Solutions Project, an IES grant, developing a mathematics word problem–solving curriculum for students with severe disabilities. She has helped design and conduct research in the area of general curriculum access, specifically in science, English language arts, and mathematics. Additionally, she has published multiple peer-reviewed journal articles, developed and conducted professional development webinars on aligning instruction to the Common Core State Standards, and is a coauthor of *Early Numeracy*, a mathematics curriculum for students with severe disabilities.

Julie L. Thompson, Ph.D., Graduate Research Assistant, University of North Carolina at Charlotte, 9201 University City Boulevard, Charlotte, NC 28223

Prior to pursuing a Ph.D. in special education, Dr. Thompson taught students with autism spectrum disorder (ASD) for 6 years. Her current research focuses on teaching academics to students with ASD, direct instruction, and applied behavior analysis. She is a National Board Certified teacher in severe and multiple disabilities and a Board Certified Behavior Analyst.

Jean Vintinner, Ph.D., Clinical Assistant Professor, University of North Carolina at Charlotte, College of Education, 9201 University City Boulevard, Charlotte, NC 28223

Dr. Vintinner is a former high school English and reading teacher whose academic interests include adolescent literacy, content area reading, and motivating struggling readers.

Shawnee Y. Wakeman, Ph.D., Clinical Assistant Professor, University of North Carolina at Charlotte, Department of Special Education and Child Development, 9201 University City Boulevard, Charlotte, NC 28223

Dr. Wakeman's research interest includes the relationship of the principal to the education of students with disabilities, access to the general curriculum and how it is enacted for students with significant cognitive disabilities, alignment of the educational system and the policy implications of those alignment issues, and alternate assessment. Dr. Wakeman is currently involved in several federally funded projects and publications related to alternate assessment and curriculum alignment.

Ryan Walker, Ph.D., Assistant Professor, Mississippi State University, Box 9705, 310 Alan Hall, Mississippi State, MS 39762

Dr. Walker has established an active research agenda investigating the teaching of science process skills, the relationship between art and science instruction, and the importance of authentic science experience for teachers.

Leah Wood, Ph.D., Snyder Fellow and Graduate Research Assistant, University of North Carolina at Charlotte, 9201 University City Boulevard, Charlotte, NC 28223

Ms. Wood is a third-year doctoral candidate pursuing a Ph.D. in special education. Prior to returning to school full-time, Ms. Wood taught students with moderate to severe intellectual disability for 6 years. She is the lead graduate research assistant for the GoTalk Phonics IES grant, and coauthor of the GoTalk Phonics Curriculum, which is in development.

Charles L. Wood, Ph.D., Associate Professor, University of North Carolina at Charlotte, Department of Special Education and Child Development, 9201 University City Boulevard, Charlotte, NC 28223

Dr. Wood's research focuses on instructional design, computer-assisted instruction, explicit instruction, and applied behavior analysis.

Foreword

Although there was ample evidence that students with severe disabilities could learn academic skills, many teachers initially had great difficulty understanding how to provide their students access to the general education, despite federal mandates to do so (i.e., Individuals with Disabilities Education Improvement Act [IDEA] of 2004 [PL 108-446]; No Child Left Behind Act of 2001 [PL 107-110]). Such teachers may have felt that providing access would preclude the functional (and social) skill development their students needed and that academic instruction per se had limited practical (or social) value (Agran, Alper, & Wehmeyer, 2002). Also, providing academic instruction would only result in failure for their students and serve to alienate them. Increasing the academic competence of typical students and, by extension, students with mild disabilities is a primary goal of education and one that is universally acknowledged, but for students with severe disabilities the value of such instruction was open for question. To complicate matters, ambivalence about this issue was due to the fact that many teachers of students with severe disabilities did not know how to teach academics—it was not part of their professional development, and there was not much in the research about how to teach these skills. They were familiar with the functional curriculum and easily understood its value. Furthermore, there was a sound curricular and methodological justification for functional skills instruction but not yet one of sufficient strength and soundness to justify academic instruction. Having two curricula—one for typical students and one for students with more extensive support needs—contradicted inclusive practices in a sense but was understandable in a way because the functional approach was aimed at increasing students' independence and competence—goals that special educators commonly shared. As a consequence, many teachers felt that it was an either/or situation in which they had to choose between academic or functional skills instruction, even though districts were pressuring them to provide more academic instruction.

Fortunately, educators have learned a great deal in the last decade and a half about the capacity of students with severe disabilities, and there is growing (and convincing) evidence that students with severe disabilities can learn many academic skills previously thought to be beyond their capacity. To a large extent this shift has been due to the research that Browder, Spooner, and colleagues have done in this area. *Teaching Language Arts, Math, and Science to Students with Significant Cognitive Disabilities* (Browder & Spooner, 2006) served to inform teachers that students with severe disabilities can indeed benefit from academic instruction. This sequel continues to call teachers to ensure that students with extensive support needs receive academic instruction, and to demonstrate that students in fact can learn advanced academic skills in core skills areas: literacy, mathematics, and science. Special education instructional models—particularly those designed for students with severe disabilities—typically include three phases. First, there is a demonstration that students with extensive support needs can indeed perform the desired skill (i.e., have the capacity to perform the skill—in this case, academic skills). Second, there is a large number of replications to demonstrate acquisition of the desired skills across students with varying needs and in varied situations. Third, there is a commitment to investigate and better understand factors that facilitate (or impede) skill development. Clearly educators have achieved the first phase, as evident in the existent research. *More Language Arts, Math, and Science for Students with Severe Disabilities* sets out to provide and achieve the second and third phases, and, ultimately, to reassert that academic instruction should be a top curricular priority for students with severe disabilities.

The term *state-of-the-art* is much overused in the educational literature, depriving it of much meaning. That being said, this book is truly state-of-the-art as it both demonstrates what students are capable of achieving and how to achieve these outcomes in a systematic way. It is arguably the most current summary of research about academic instruction for students with severe disabilities. In this respect, although its primary purpose is to describe replicable practice so that teachers know how to teach their students a variety of academic skills, the book also serves a second purpose—to reiterate that the education for students with severe disabilities can be distinguished by academic skills instruction and not its exclusion, and, in doing so, minimize the difference and separateness of special and general education.

Teachers may continue to struggle with the value they assign to academic skills instruction but this book makes it increasingly clear that the excuse of not knowing how to teach them becomes highly implausible, given that academic skills instruction does not involve a new set of instructional strategies. Several chapters in this book reiterate that the instructional strategies used to teach academics are behavior analytic strategies that have been commonly used and validated over the last 60 years. These are subsumed under the general practice of systematic instruction and include embedded instruction, system of least prompts, time delay, peer instruction, and student-directed learning strategies, among others. Academic instruction does not demand that teachers need to learn a new repertoire of skills but that they need to use existing skills in their teaching repertoires conscientiously, diligently, and innovatively. Reminding teachers of this may serve to lessen their anxiety about teaching academic skills.

In an effort to ensure that students receive academic instruction teachers may select academic content that is very different than the content same-aged peers are learning (e.g., different grade level, different content area). They justify this incongruity by asserting that the goal is based on the student's individualized education program, it addresses the need for academic instruction, and it facilitates inclusive practice. But because it is "different" content it may inadvertently suggest a difference that will separate them from other students. To minimize such a difference, Browder and Spooner encourage teachers to provide *grade-aligned instruction*. Grade-aligned instruction seeks to maximize the extent to which the academic instruction for the targeted student is aligned to the student's chronological age and grade level. This does not mean that the target student will be learning the same content at the same time as other students—although, hopefully, some students will—but grade-aligned instruction provides a means to maximize age-appropriate learning and social acceptance. It ups the ante for teachers and requires that they collaborate with regular educators to better understand grade-level standards and expectations, and, in doing so, further promote inclusive practice and access.

Academic competence has been positively associated with better postschool work outcomes and overall adult functioning (Benz, Lindstrom, & Yovanoff, 2000), and employers repeatedly call for graduates to enter the work force with higher academic competence. Furthermore, there has been an increase in the number of individuals with intellectual disability participating in postschool educational programs, and increased academic competence has been found to be of value for these students. Understanding this relationship has no doubt influenced teachers to have higher academic expectations for their students—particularly for students with mild disabilities. But the reasoning for this equally applies for students with severe disabilities: higher achievement in reading, mathematics, and problem solving, among other curricular areas, should enhance their future employability. However, this proposition, although appealing, is, as Browder and Spooner discuss, remains unproven. The assumption is that higher academic achievement will produce greater competence and functioning in adult life but this remains an empirical question and one that warrants further investigation. Hopefully this book will motivate researchers to address this question.

In the 40-plus years educators have sought to promote full inclusion of people with severe disabilities into school and the community, they have approached this challenge in different ways. At first, focus was guided by an emphasis on proximity—having students with severe disabilities in the same setting as typical students—a great first step but only that. Finding this approach insufficient they became aware of and concerned about the quality of social interactions. To be accepted by their peers, educators realized that they needed to facilitate and support valued, meaningful, and mutually beneficial social exchanges. Nevertheless, because students had different instructional goals, based on different standards and curricula, a separation still existed. The access to the general curriculum initiative represents a logical, next step to promote inclusive practice—curricular integration, as it were. Not only will students be in the same classrooms and have the opportunity to socially engage, but their learning will be based on the same standards and subjects taught to other students, commensurate with their individual needs. Perhaps this will minimize the long existing separation between students with and without disabilities. As Browder and Spooner emphasized, educators must endeavor to "have more inclusion, better content, and more learning." This book will no doubt help us achieve these goals.

Martin Agran, Ph.D.
University of Wyoming

REFERENCES

Agran, M., Alper, S., & Wehmeyer, M. (2002). Access to the general curriculum for students with significant disabilities. *Education and Training in Mental Retardation and Developmental Disabilities, 37,* 123–133.

Benz, M., Lindstrom, L., & Yovanoff, P. (2000). Improving graduation and employment outcomes of students with disabilities: Predictive factors and student perspectives. *Exceptional Children, 66,* 509–529.

Browder, D.M., & Spooner, F. (2006). *Teaching language arts, math, and science to students with significant cognitive disabilities.* Baltimore, MD: Paul H. Brookes Publishing Co.

Individuals with Disabilities Education Improvement Act (IDEA) of 2004, PL 108-446, 20 U.S.C. §§ 1400 *et seq.*

No Child Left Behind Act of 2001, PL 107-110,115 Stat. 1425, 20 U.S.C. §§ 6301 *et seq.*

Preface

"Something radically different is happening in educational services for students with severe disabilities" (Spooner & Browder, 2006, p. 1). When we edited *Teaching Language Arts, Math, and Science to Students with Significant Cognitive Disabilities* almost a decade ago, curricular expectations were rapidly changing, fueled by the No Child Left Behind Act of 2001 (PL 107-110). Schools had to assess every student on state standards in mathematics and language arts. Students with significant cognitive disabilities who could not participate in the state's general assessment were given an alternate assessment. Although alternate achievement standards could be used for reporting up to 1% of students as making adequate yearly progress, these standards were to be aligned with the state's academic content standards. In our prior book, we collaborated with many excellent thinkers about how educators could respond to this increased expectation for students with severe disabilities. We propose that many of those guidelines continue to be useful in creating high quality academic instruction. This book is offered as a sequel rather than as a second edition. As a sequel, we purposefully chose many new authors to expand the thinking about general curriculum access.

In the first edition, because the expectation was new, we offered more information on the rational for teaching general curriculum. Many of the chapters described how to bridge prior functional academic instruction to the newer options of teaching to state standards. Some chapters distinctly focused on teaching the content in inclusive settings. Most chapters had at least one general educator as a coauthor so we could build on the rich content knowledge of these curriculum experts. These chapters continue to provide a foundation for building academic instruction.

As we describe in the first chapter of this book, much has changed in the last decade. We know more about teaching instruction that aligns with grade-level content standards and we need to know more to be changing expectations of school accountability systems. Like the prior book, we encouraged authors to include at least one general educator on their writing teams. Our contributors' page will help you know who these experts were as well as the special educators who formed these teams. We then built the chapters using directions gleaned from research. For example, we have been learning about the importance of both the process of inquiry and conceptual knowledge in science, so we have a chapter that emphasizes each. There is much more research on teaching reading to students with moderate and severe disabilities than there was a decade ago, and we have tried to capture this cutting edge work. We are excited to have our first chapter on writing. In mathematics, there is more conceptual understanding about how students acquire a foundation of numeracy and much more on how to address upper level problem solving. Educators' approaches to assessment and state standards also have changed dramatically in the last decade, and so we have included chapters on alternate assessment and Common Core State Standards. One of the disappointments of the last decade is that opportunities for inclusion have not increased concurrently with the expansion of opportunities to learn academic content. We hope that chapters on embedding instruction and planning for inclusion will help educators envision how more students with severe disabilities can learn general curriculum in general education settings.

We would like to offer an explanation for our choice of terminology for the population in the title and content of this book. The term *significant cognitive disabilities* has been used in policy to describe students who take alternate assessments based on alternate achievement standards (AA-AAS). In the last decade (since our prior book was published), the term *intellectual disability* has replaced *mental retardation*. We do not think the term *cognitive disability* is synonymous with intellectual disability; nor does the policy restrict the use of AA-AAS to those with intellectual disability. To avoid confusion, between the two terms, we have begun to confine our use of *significant cognitive disability* to references to alternate assessment policy so as not to introduce a term that competes with *intellectual disability*. For decades the term *severe disability* has been used as shorthand for individuals with moderate and severe developmental disabilities including intellectual disability, autism spectrum disorders, and multiple disabilities that include some intellectual disability. We find that we continue to prefer this term to significant cognitive disability. We recognize that there is not professional consensus on this point and have honored contributors preferences for how they wished to refer to the population.

Finally, we want to provide a brief explanation about the vignettes that lead into each chapter. We have asked all authors to write a brief story that helps the reader envision the major themes of the chapter. All of the vignettes and characters described are fictional, but based on the authors' real life experiences and creative imagination. We hope that the vignettes help the readers envision how applying the guidelines in the chapter could appear in practice.

We hope you will find that this sequel offers ideas to you for taking the next step in academic planning. Now that the language arts lessons are in place, the next step is teaching more students to read and to gain more advanced comprehension. Now that mathematics and science have begun, it is time to deepen conceptual understanding. Now that students are learning some academics, it is time to delve deeply into age-appropriate, grade-aligned standards while demonstrating their use in students' lives. Now it is time to find new ways to align instructional contexts as well a s content; for example, by embedding systematic instruction in general education classrooms. It is time to let students once again surprise us by what they can do.

REFERENCES

Browder, D.M., & Spooner, F. (2006). *Teaching language arts, math, and science to students with significant cognitive disabilities*. Baltimore, MD: Paul H. Brookes Publishing Co.

No Child Left Behind Act of 2001, PL 107-110,115 Stat. 1425, 20 U.S.C. §§ 6301 *et seq.*

Acknowledgments

We would like to thank all the authors for their excellent contributions under tight deadlines and appreciate them for recruiting general educators as coauthors. We owe a debt of gratitude to Amy Kemp-Inman, a doctoral student in our special education program at the University of North Carolina at Charlotte, for her assistance with chapter references. We would like to also recognize Rebecca Lazo, Senior Acquisitions Editor at Paul H. Brookes Publishing Co.; Steve Plocher, Associate Editor; and Lisa Koepenick, Project Manager, who were assigned to our book. These three individuals expended a lot of hours to make this a highly successful manuscript.

SECTION I

Greater Access to General Curriculum

CHAPTER 1

More Content, More Learning, More Inclusion

Diane M. Browder and Fred Spooner

The bell rings and school begins. We have been invited to visit two of our neighborhood schools. We meander through the chattering students making their way from the buses to their classes. The artwork on the wall includes illustrations and pictures of Little Red Riding Hood told from the Big Bad Wolf's perspective. Although we know the purpose is to teach the students the character's point of view, the pictures and stories make us smile. One of the pictures belongs to Simone, a student with an autism spectrum disorder who participates in the alternate assessments based on alternate achievement standards (AA-AAS). She selected her wolf picture from the Internet and filled in sentences by selecting words and pictures. One of my favorite sentences is, "The wolf said, 'I was hungry!'" Today, along with other fourth graders, Simone is going to be working on reading paragraphs with fluency and answering comprehension questions about the characters in the story. At first, it may not be clear that Simone is a reader because she is nonverbal except for some echolalic speech. She reads silently and then uses her response board with phrases and pictures to answer each question. Sometimes her teacher or a peer reads the passage aloud if it is more complicated. Math is harder for Simone, and she continues to learn to count the objects she uses to solve problems, but that does not prevent her from doing today's lesson on finding the perimeter of a rectangle. Her math group has been given the challenge of deciding how much ribbon is needed for picture frames they will create by computing the perimeter. Simone really enjoys her cooperative learning group in social studies in which she helps fill in the graphic organizer with key facts using cards she practices reading with a peer before the group begins their work. Science is by far Simone's favorite subject because the teacher nearly always has the class discover the concept with an experiment. Yesterday they were discovering the process of erosion using water and a sand model. Simone has words such as *weather, erosion,* and *landforms* in her communication system. Ten years ago Simone might only have had pictures for *eat, restroom,* and *break,* but those she has learned easily through daily use. What she really wants to communicate today is what happened to the sand. Erosion, she says with her voice output response board.

We have just enough time to get to the high school where students hoard by us when the bell rings. It has been awhile since we were in a high school, and the students' energy, conversations, and clothes all amaze us. Lucas is a 10th grader with intellectual disability who also will participate in his school's alternate assessment. When we arrive in his language arts class, Lucas has just finished a read-aloud with a peer from a chapter in the novel the class is reading. The teacher is asking about the main character, a young man who has to decide if he is going to be loyal to a friend who tries to manipulate him to do the wrong things. Along with his classmates, Lucas's goal is to form an opinion about whether the main character should trust this friend. Everyone must support their answers using facts from the text. For Lucas, writing will involve selecting some answers from a list of quotes from his chapter summary and dictating others. In math, Lucas is working on transformations on a coordinate plane. The content made no sense to him (or to a lot of his classmates) in the prior day's lesson. Today the teacher had the idea to show how characters in video games can be rotated, inverted, and so forth using the coordinates on a plane. The class had fun giving coordinates (e.g., -10, +2) and seeing what happened to their characters. Because Lucas can recognize numbers and understands that there can be both positive and negative numbers, he is able to do some of the transformations with his partner. At lunch, he has to make sure that he does not overspend his daily limit for his lunch card, and that was how his teacher helped him understand negative numbers. After science and social studies, Lucas will be heading to his job tryout site. He helps stock shelves at an office supply store. Lucas is proud that his supervisor can give him a list with names and numbers of supplies and he has the reading and math skills to follow it. On his break the other day, some of Lucas's coworkers were talking about the economy and the president. Lucas knew enough from a report he did in social studies on the economy to join the conversation.

Our school tour has ended, and frankly we are impressed by how much more Simone and Lucas can do than we ever thought possible.

In each chapter of this book, the authors will begin with a fictitious description of how their guidelines would appear in practice. These vignettes will help the reader envision how to make the ideas real for students with severe disabilities. Although the vignettes are fictional, they are derived from the authors' actual experiences collaborating with practitioners to enhance educational services. The authors have worked closely with the Charlotte Mecklenburg School System for the last 15 years and have seen students with moderate and severe intellectual disability or autism spectrum disorders engaged in the types of academic activities previously described. Working in partnership with teachers and other professionals helped to generate new options for teaching state standards through both research and practice. The rest of this chapter, like those to follow, will provide the research and thinking that forms the foundation for providing more and better academic instruction for students with severe disabilities.

Why do we need more information on teaching language arts, mathematics, and science to students with severe disabilities? Some would argue that we need less, not more, academics for these students. Is it possible educators have gone too far? Maybe academics should be limited to skills with direct ties to everyday activities such as reading a menu or counting money to make a purchase. Will students benefit from engaging with novels, using linear equations, and understanding tectonic plates? In fact, who does benefit from these skills?

Sometimes it is easier to evaluate a practice such as academic instruction using what is known and familiar. If an educator is not familiar with what causes earthquakes, it may be difficult to perceive how a student with severe disabilities will benefit from this information. If an educator's job does not require algebra, it may not be obvious that some entry-level technical jobs use these principles. If an educator does not particularly enjoy leisure reading, it may not seem important for someone else to do so. If educators have never seen a student with moderate and severe developmental disabilities acquire and apply any of this knowledge, it may seem to be an absurd goal or one aimed at students with milder disabilities.

One of the exciting outcomes to occur since our earlier book on this topic (Browder & Spooner, 2006) is that it is now clearly possible to teach more advanced academic content to students with significant cognitive disabilities as educators translate longstanding evidence-based practices into use with core curriculum. Students themselves have taught us that they can learn these skills (Browder, Trela, et al., 2012; Browder, Trela, & Jimenez, 2007; Knight, Spooner, Browder, & Smith, 2012). What we do not yet know, however, is how such learning will have an impact on students' lives as adults. Given that the expectation for increased academic outcomes was fueled by the No Child Left Behind Act of 2001 (PL 107-110), students with severe disabilities who benefited from increased academic opportunities for their entire school career are only now beginning to graduate from school and take on adult responsibilities. How might their lives be different from earlier generations of students? For example, consider that many of these students will now graduate not only knowing just lists of everyday sight words but also with skills to access and comprehend text. Unlike older generations of students, they may be able to apply these skills to one of the most critical everyday activities in the 21st century: using the Internet. Because they have a wider range of literacy skills—such as some decoding, listening to passages with text-to-speech features, and applying comprehension skills—the Internet may be more accessible than ever. In fact, many students with moderate and severe disabilities are already using the Internet in their daily classroom activities.

Employment is another example of how increased academic skills may promote quality of life. Evidence suggests that students who graduate from high school have better postschool outcomes than those who do not (Sanford et al., 2011), as additional time in school provides increased academic competence. This opportunity to increase academic competence has not traditionally been available for students with severe disabilities, however. Although students with severe disabilities often stay in school until age 21, their postschool outcomes have been poor with notably low rates of employment (Wagner, Cadwallader, & Marder, 2003). In other words, despite the fact that many students with severe disabilities and their families have invested extra years in schools, their educational programs have not always invested in their increased academic competence. Although the priority of these final years may be preparing for jobs and the community, students with disabilities who have a greater array of academic skills at age 18 have more options after graduating. Students who have some generalized mathematical skills, for example, have more options for jobs that require working with numbers or computations. Those that can work with text have more options for jobs that require literacy. Students who know more about their worlds because of science and social studies can be more informed participants in a wide variety of community events (e.g., supporting clean water initiatives).

With this increased focus on academics, will students fail to acquire functional life skills? As we have argued elsewhere (Courtade, Spooner, Browder, & Jimenez, 2012), teaching more academic content does not need to replace or even compete with critical life skill instructional priorities. Hunt, McDonnell, and Crockett (2012) have noted that educational teams can focus on quality of life outcomes in ways that incorporate both academic and functional skills. These need not be competing goals. Not all academic goals have immediate functional use. Learning to read or solve mathematical problems requires a progression of skills, some of which are not as useable by themselves as they will be when applied to later learning (e.g., decoding to comprehend text). And not all functional goals have an academic link. Self-care continues to be a valid goal for some students with severe disabilities but does not typically have a direct academic tie. What educators are increasingly learning is how to incorporate both priorities. For example, everyone in a mathematics class can be motivated to apply their emerging skills in converting fractions to increase the servings in a recipe that they then get to prepare. For all students, making content meaningful will enhance both the motivation to master the content and the likelihood that new information will be retained.

In this book we promote teaching academic content aligned with the student's chronological age and grade placement. We call this *grade-aligned instruction.* Because grade-aligned academics are derived from the state standards for a given grade, this is also called *standards-based instruction.* Older students with severe disabilities may not have had opportunities for foundational academic learning in prior years, so they may come to the upper grades lacking basic literacy and numeracy. It is possible to promote this foundational academic learning while engaging students in the same content as their same-age peers. For example, a student who does not read may still learn to analyze text to compare characters in a novel through a read-aloud of a chapter summary and a graphic organizer to make this comparison. Concurrently, the student also may continue to develop early reading skills such as decoding and sight word recognition using some regulated text in headings, captions, and repeated story lines.

Since our prior book (Browder & Spooner, 2006), there have been several landmark articles on understanding access to general curriculum content and teaching state standards. This writing has tended to focus on two major debates in planning access: 1) Should the focus remain on individualized, functional goals rather than standards-based academic content? And, 2) How does inclusion intersect with access? Ayres, Lowrey, Douglas, and Sievers (2011) sounded a strong caution that curriculum that focuses on academic standards to the exclusion of individually determined functional goals risks poor postschool outcomes. Courtade and colleagues (2012) responded with seven reasons to promote standards-based instruction. Ayres, Lowrey, Douglas, and Sievers (2012) held their original position. In contrast, Hunt and colleagues (2012) offered a middle ground, urging educators to use ecological considerations of a student's individual needs to select academic goals, along with functional skills, for a well-balanced educational plan.

Every individualized education program (IEP) team has the challenging goal of planning this balance. Prioritization of state standards can be an arduous task that may exceed the time and resources of many IEP teams. In contrast, states often have curricular frameworks and other resources in which their standards have been prioritized for students who take AA-AAS. What the IEP team can focus on is how to make these priorities teachable and relevant for the individual student. Caution is needed not to omit content without actually giving students the opportunity to discover their interests and abilities. In the example at the beginning of this chapter, the concept of geometric transformations seems irrelevant to Lucas on the surface, but it actually may help him better understand one of his favorite leisure activities (video games). Omitting too much content also can leave gaps in priorities for inclusive contexts. Burdge, Clayton, Denham, and Hess (2010) recommended that educators target at least one goal per major curricular unit so that students with disabilities have a focus during all general education instruction.

The second area of debate is the relationship between general curriculum access and inclusion. Jackson, Ryndak, and Wehmeyer (2009) described the three components of access as context, curriculum, and learning. They proposed that access to general curriculum is only complete when it occurs in general curriculum classrooms (context) where students *learn* the curriculum (content) of their grade level. Educators are often challenged by realities of self-contained classrooms, watered down curriculum, and participation without learning. In this book we want to help educators move beyond these challenges to have more inclusion, better content, and more learning. In our prior book we noted that students must have the opportunity to learn the academic state standards on which they will be assessed regardless of their educational placement. This does not mean inclusion is not needed for full access to the general curriculum. What it does mean is that teachers can begin promoting content and learning while continuing to work toward more inclusive opportunities. We encourage teams to begin planning by asking how a student can access general curriculum content in a general education setting. To promote this planning, we've included the following sections to briefly describe advances in the literature on promoting more inclusion, more content, and more learning.

MORE INCLUSION

Over the past 10 years, educators have learned important lessons about the benefits of promoting academic learning for students with severe disabilities in general education classrooms. Wehmeyer, Lattin, Lapp-Rincker, and Agran (2003) found that middle school students with intellectual disability were more likely to receive instruction related to the academic content standards in general education compared with self-contained settings. Soukup, Wehmeyer, Bashinki, and Bovaird (2007) found similar differences four years later. Although this outcome might change as special educators intensify their focus on academic standards, the general education class will always be the context in which a content expert provides full coverage of the curriculum. It is difficult for special educators to replicate this full content coverage especially when their students range across multiple grades. In addition to the greater access to content general education contexts provide, students also receive social benefits through inclusion (Carter, Sisco, Brown, Brickham, & Al Khabbaz, 2008).

Although the literature provides research support for the overall benefits of inclusion (e.g., Carter et al., 2008; Wehmeyer et al., 2003), it also offers guidance for how to promote academic learning in this context. Copeland and Cosbey (2009) recommend beginning with practices that are typical of general education including cooperative learning groups, inquiry learning, and universal design for learning. Students will also likely need some systematic instruction in which target skills are taught with systematic prompting and feedback across trials. Hudson, Browder, and Wood (2013) applied criteria to evaluate experimental studies in which students with moderate and severe developmental disabilities learned academic content in general education classrooms. Hudson and colleagues found 17 experimental studies. The studies varied across instructional strategies (e.g., embedded trial instruction, system of least prompts, multiple exemplars, graphic organizers), modes of delivery (e.g., peer tutors, paraeducators, general educators), and content (e.g., science, mathematics, literacy). Despite these variations, the results indicated that students with moderate and severe intellectual disability could learn academic content in general education settings. Although more research is needed, especially on more complex academic content, these studies provide an evidence base for effective academic instruction in general education settings.

MORE CONTENT

Until the early 2000s, research in reading for students with severe disabilities was primarily focused on functional sight word instruction (Browder, Wakeman, Spooner, Ahlgrim-Delzell, & Algozzine, 2006), in mathematics on money and simple computation (Browder, Spooner, Ahlgrim-Delzell, Harris, & Wakeman, 2008), and in science primarily on daily living tasks (Spooner, Knight, Browder, Jimenez, & DiBiase, 2011). When our prior book was published, there were almost no experimental studies on how to teach academic content that linked to the student's grade. Some important advances have occurred since then.

In the area of language arts, an evidence base has emerged for the use of read-alouds to promote understanding of text (Hudson & Test, 2011). In this strategy, the teacher uses either excerpts from the original text or an adapted summary of book chapters. The student is engaged with the theme of the book through some attention-getting activity. Then the teacher reads the material aloud, pausing to give the students a variety of ways to engage with the text. For example, the student might make a prediction, help to read a line with assistive technology, point to text as it is read aloud, or locate a picture. During or after the read-aloud, the teacher asks comprehension questions that the student may either answer verbally or by using a picture response communication board. Browder and colleagues (2007) provided an example of using this strategy with adapted middle school novels. In Shurr and Taber-Doughty's (2012) read-aloud study, students with moderate intellectual disability conversed about pictures related to the passages prior to the reading.

Although read-alouds provide an important method to engage students with grade-level text, research also provides evidence that some students with moderate and severe disabilities can gain reading skills (Allor, Mathes, Roberts, Jones, & Champlin, 2010; Browder, Ahlgrim-Delzell, Flowers, & Baker, 2012). The pace of instruction may be slow for some students, so it is important to augment this instruction with read-alouds of grade-level text so that students can develop comprehension through listening while learning to read. Once students gain even entry-level skills for reading connected text, they can begin to learn to answer comprehension questions about what they learn (Hudson et al., 2013). Students also can learn writing skills concurrent with reading. For students who do not read, "writing" may involve developing printed communication through selecting pictures or phrases to fill in a template or through dictating a composition. Other students may begin to develop written text using emerging spelling and composition skills (see Chapter 7).

Stories also may provide a meaningful framework for learning mathematical problem solving. Browder, Trela, and colleagues (2012) used stories of everyday activities to teach grade-aligned mathematical standards to students with moderate and severe developmental disabilities. After a read-aloud of the story, the students filled in a graphic organizer with the numerical facts. Through task analytic instruction, the students learned the step-by-step process to solve the problem. One of the challenges students may face is the lack of basic numeracy skills. Skibo, Mims, and Spooner (2011) found students with severe disabilities could learn number identification through using response cards (e.g., "Show me *2*"). Students also need to learn the meaning of numbers through creating and manipulating sets (e.g., combining sets to add). Through manipulation of sets, students may progress to learn operations such as multiplication (Zisimopoulos, 2010).

One of the most important outcomes for science is that students learn to engage in the process of inquiry. Jimenez, Browder, Spooner, and DiBiase (2012) trained peers without disabilities to support students with moderate intellectual disability learning science concepts during a middle school inquiry-based lesson in general education. The students learned both to identify vocabulary for the science concepts and to complete a KWHL chart (Know, Want to know, How to find out, what is Learned). Science also involves learning generalized concepts such as the water cycle and chemical reactions. Knight and colleagues (2012) found that students with autism spectrum disorder could acquire concepts with the use of a graphic organizer.

There certainly is more to the general curriculum than language arts, mathematics, and science, but unfortunately the research to date is still limited primarily to these topics. In doing a dissertation on social studies, Zakas (2011) found almost no studies with students with developmental disabilities. One option for social studies is to use the read-aloud format for this content with a focus on comprehension. Zakas used graphic organizers to help students with autism spectrum disorders summarize key facts from a social studies passage.

One of the trends having a major impact on the content targeted for instruction is the implementation of Common Core State Standards (CCSS; National Governors Association Center for Best Practices, Council of Chief State School Officers, 2010). When our prior book was written, nearly all states had their own set of language arts and mathematics standards. Most states now have adopted the CCSS. The new generation of alternate assessments for students with significant cognitive disabilities is being written for inclusion in the CCSS. These standards are shaping how educators approach language arts and mathematics. The Next Generation Science Standards (NGSS; http://www.nextgenscience.org), developed by 26 states, are also now available. With this common understanding of learning outcomes, it becomes possible to develop curricular resources with direct links to standards across states (see Chapter 3 for examples).

MORE LEARNING

Although well-developed content and inclusive contexts are important goals for students with severe disabilities, neither will promote a student's quality of life unless meaningful learning occurs. Spooner, Knight, Browder, and Smith (2012) conducted a review of research on teaching academic content to students with moderate and severe disabilities to identify evidence-based practices. Spooner and colleagues found strong evidence for using time delay to teach vocabulary and sight words. Time delay is an errorless learning procedure. On the initial trials, the teacher presents the cue to respond (e.g., "Find *evaporation*") and the target stimulus (e.g., vocabulary word in an array with distractors) concurrently with a prompt (e.g., points to *evaporation*). Because the teacher indicates the correct answer with no delay, the student can respond without an error. These zero-delay trials will only be effective if the prompt already has stimulus control for the student (i.e., will imitate a pointing response) and if they are actually provided at no delay (compared with one second delay when a quick student could give an incorrect answer). After some predetermined number of zero-delay trials, the teacher delays the prompt by a few seconds (e.g., 4 seconds) so that the student can anticipate the correct response. The student receives feedback after each trial (e.g., praise for a correct response, correction of errors).

Some researchers have used a system of least intrusive prompting for academic learning. For example, Colyer and Collins (1996) used a hierarchy of prompts to teach students to use a next dollar strategy (rounding up to the nearest dollar when making a purchase). Mims, Hudson, and Browder (2012) used an adaptation of a prompt hierarchy to teach comprehension in a read-aloud. After asking the comprehension question, if the student did not answer correctly, the teacher reread the paragraph containing the answer. The next prompt was the sentence containing the answer and finally the one word answer combined with pointing to the answer on a response board.

Another important innovation in the last decade has been an increase in the use of technology to promote instructional learning. This may include video modeling, computer-assisted instruction, and the use of interactive white board technology. Mechling, Gast, and Krupa (2007) demonstrated how an interactive white board (SMART Board) could be used in teaching sight words. Cihak, Alberto, Taber-Doughty, and Gama (2006) compared picture and video prompting and found both to be effective.

GETTING FROM WHERE WE ARE TO WHERE WE WANT TO BE

If more content, learning, and inclusion are the targets for students with severe disabilities, the question is how to get from current challenges to this goal of full general curriculum access. One potential way is to give teachers more models for how to create access. In planning content, teachers need examples of prioritized content such as state web sites with curricular resources (e.g., those described in Chapter 3). Teachers also need to know processes for how to prioritize content. For example, to select the most important standards to address in fifth-grade science, the teacher can confer with the science teacher to target selected standards for each instructional unit to be covered that year. Consideration also needs to be given to any priorities the state publishes about what must be mastered for students who take AA-AAS. These two steps may still not be enough prioritization to write a measurable objective. The teacher also may need to pinpoint within these standards the specific learning target for the student. That is, what is the observable, measurable behavior the student is to acquire? During this pinpointing process is when consideration also can be given to making content personally relevant to the student. For example, although it may be important for the student to learn something in the chemistry unit, understanding the potential danger of chemical reactions may be especially relevant. Through this process, the educational team generates a standards-based IEP. Additional functional skills can be added to the IEP that are critical to the student but that do not necessarily have a link to state standards. Special education teachers also will need to gain more content expertise for making adaptations to teach these skills.

To promote learning, teachers need strong skills in systematic instruction. Rather than simply learning to use terms such as *time delay*, teachers need to be able to demonstrate competence in applying evidence-based procedures. To foster inclusion, teachers also need to know how to embed this instruction in general education and how to teach peers and other professionals to use these methods. Not all content needs to be addressed with systematic instruction. An important rule of thumb is to provide no more adaptation than necessary. An important skill special educators will need is to differentiate when to include the student with severe disabilities in typical general education instruction and when to make adaptations.

Finally, to promote inclusion, systems change will need to occur at the school and school system level. Sometimes students have been excluded from general education because they were viewed as having different curricular goals. The need to provide increased access to general curriculum may serve as a starting point for discussions about including students for content area instruction.

SUMMARY

Much has changed in the last decade for students with severe disabilities. Educators have discovered that students with severe disabilities can learn much more academic content than ever believed possible. Legislation such as the No Child Left Behind Act promoted major movement toward teaching the content that would be the focus of alternate assessments. In the rush to comply with this legislation, and encouraged by increased learning, the educational goals targeted were sometimes neither solid content nor relevant to the students. This outcome opened the door for critics to question whether standards-based instruction itself was unfounded (e.g., Ayres et al., 2011).

In contrast, there have been monumental achievements in this same decade. Some of the first studies on comprehensive reading programs for students with moderate and severe disabilities emerged (e.g., Allor et al., 2010). Students demonstrated that they could learn content aligned with their grade level in general education classes (e.g., Jimenez et al., 2012). Students themselves not only learned but also wanted to learn.

This book was developed with the premise that this grade-aligned, standards-based academic instruction holds strong promise for promoting competence for students with moderate and severe disabilities that can enhance quality of life. We agree with the critics, however, that we need to find ways to do it better. We are pleased to offer writing from a collection of experts to help us in this endeavor. Their chapters show us how to have more and better content, inclusion, and learning.

REFERENCES

Allor, J.H., Mathes, P.G., Roberts, J.K., Jones, F.G., & Champlin, T.M. (2010). Teaching students with moderate intellectual disabilities to read: An experimental examination of a comprehensive reading intervention. *Education and Training in Autism and Developmental Disabilities, 45*, 3–22.

Ayres, K.M., Lowrey, K.A., Douglas, K.H., & Sievers, C. (2011). I can identify Saturn but I can't brush my teeth: What happens when the curricular focus for students with severe disabilities shifts. *Education and Training in Autism and Developmental Disabilities, 46*, 11–21.

Ayres, K.M., Lowrey, K.A., Douglas, K.H., & Sievers, C. (2012). The question still remains: What happens when the curricular focus for students with severe disabilities shifts? A reply to Courtade, Spooner, Browder, and Jimenez (2012). *Education and Training in Autism and Developmental Disabilities, 47*, 14–22.

Browder, D.M., Ahlgrim-Delzell, L., Flowers, C., & Baker, J.N. (2012). An evaluation of a multicomponent early literacy program for students with severe developmental disabilities. *Remedial and Special Education, 33*, 237–246.

Browder, D.M., & Spooner, F. (2006). *Teaching language arts, math, & science to students with significant cognitive disabilities.* Baltimore, MD: Paul H. Brookes Publishing Co.

Browder, D.M., Spooner, F., Ahlgrim-Delzell, Harris, A., & Wakeman, S. (2008). A meta-analysis on teaching mathematics to students with significant cognitive disabilities. *Exceptional Children, 74*, 407–432.

Browder, D.M., Trela, K., Courtade, G.R., Jimenez, B.A., Knight, V., & Flowers, C. (2012). Teaching mathematics and science standards to students with moderate and severe developmental disabilities. *The Journal of Special Education, 46*, 26–35.

Browder, D.M., Trela, K., & Jimenez, B.A. (2007). Training teachers to follow a task analysis to engage middle school students with moderate and severe developmental disabilities in grade-appropriate literature. *Focus on Autism and Other Developmental Disabilities, 22*, 206–219.

Browder, D.M., Wakeman, S.Y., Spooner, F., Ahlgrim-Delzell, L., & Algozzine, B. (2006). Research on reading instruction for individuals with significant cognitive disabilities. *Exceptional Children, 72*, 392–408.

Burdge, M., Clayton, J., Denham, A., & Hess, K.K. (2010). Ensuring access: A four step process for accessing the general curriculum. In H.L. Kleinert & J.F. Kearns (Eds.), *Alternate assessment for students with significant cognitive disabilities: An educator's guide* (pp. 109–148). Baltimore, MD: Paul H. Brookes Publishing Co.

Carter, E.W., Sisco, L.G., Brown, L., Brickham, D., & Al-Khabbaz, Z.A. (2008). Peer interactions and academic engagement of youth with developmental disabilities in inclusive middle and high school classrooms. *American Journal on Mental Retardation, 113*, 479–494. doi:10.1352/2008.113:479-494

Cihak, D.F., Alberto, P.A., Taber-Doughty, T., & Gama, R.I. (2006). A comparison of static picture prompting and video prompting simulation strategies using group instructional procedures. *Focus on Autism and Other Developmental Disabilities, 21*, 89–99. doi:10.1177/10883576060210020601

Colyer, S.P., & Collins, B.C. (1996). Using natural cues within prompt levels to teach the next dollar strategy to students with disabilities. *The Journal of Special Education, 30*, 305–318.

Copeland, S.R., & Cosbey, J. (2009). Making progress in the general curriculum: Rethinking effective instructional practices. *Research and Practice for Persons with Severe Disabilities, 33-34*, 214–227.

Courtade, G., Spooner, F., Browder, D.M., & Jimenez, B. (2012). Seven reasons to promote standards-based instruction for students with severe disabilities. *Education and Training in Autism and Developmental Disabilities, 47*, 3–13.

Hudson, M.E., Browder, D.M., & Wood, L. (2013). Review of experimental research on academic learning by students with moderate and severe intellectual disability in general education. *Research and Practice for Persons with Severe Disabilities, 38*, 17–29.

Hudson, M.E., & Test, D.W. (2011). Evaluating the evidence base for using shared story reading to promote literacy for students with extensive support needs. *Research and Practice for Persons with Severe Disabilities, 36*, 34–45.

Hunt, P., McDonnell, J., & Crockett, M.A. (2012). Reconciling an ecological curricular framework focusing on quality of life outcomes with the development and instruction of standards-based academic goals. *Research and Practice for Persons with Severe Disabilities, 37*, 139–152.

Jackson, L.B., Ryndak, D.L., & Wehmeyer, M.L. (2008–2009). The dynamic relationship between context, curriculum, and student learning: A case for inclusive education as a research-based practice. *Research and Practice for Persons with Severe Disabilities, 33-34*, 175–195.

Jimenez, B., Browder, D., Spooner, F., & DiBiase, W. (2012). Inclusive inquiry science using peer-mediated embedded instruction for students with moderate intellectual disability. *Exceptional Children, 78*, 301–317.

Knight, V., Spooner, F., Browder, D.M., & Smith, B.R. (2012). Teaching science concepts using graphic organizers to students with autism spectrum disorder. *Journal of Autism and Developmental Disorders, 42*, 378–389.

Mechling, L.C., Gast, D.L., & Krupa, K. (2007). Impact of SMART Board technology: An investigation of sight word reading and observational learning. *Journal of Autism and Developmental Disorders, 37*, 1869–1882. doi:10.1007/s10803-007-0361-9

Mims, P., Hudson, M., & Browder, D. (2012). Using read alouds of grade-level biographies and systematic prompting to promote comprehension for students with moderate and severe developmental disabilities. *Focus on Autism and Other Developmental Disabilities, 27*, 67–80.

National Governors Association Center for Best Practices, Council of Chief State School Officers. (2010). *Common Core State Standards*. Washington, DC: Authors. Retrieved from http://www.corestandards.org/

No Child Left Behind Act of 2001, PL 107-110, 115 Stat. 1425, 20 U.S.C. §§ 6301 *et seq.*

Sanford, C., Newman, L., Wagner, M., Cameto, R., Knokey, A.M., & Shaver, D. (2011). *The post-high school outcome of young adults with disabilities up to 6 years after high school. Key findings from the National Longitudinal Transition Study-2 (NLTS2)* (NCSER 2011-3004). Menlo Park, CA: SRI International. Retrieved from http://www.nlts2.org/reports/2011_09/index.html

Shurr, J., & Taber-Doughty, T. (2012). Increasing comprehension for middle school students with moderate intellectual disability on age-appropriate texts. *Education and Training in Autism and Developmental Disabilities, 47*, 359–372.

Skibo, H., Mims, P., & Spooner, F. (2011). Teaching number identification to students with severe disabilities using response cards. *Education and Training in Autism and Developmental Disabilities, 46*, 124–133.

Soukup, J.H., Wehmeyer, M.L., Bashinki, S.M., & Bovaird, J.A. (2007). Classroom variables and access to the general curriculum for students with disabilities. *Exceptional Children, 74*, 101–120.

Spooner, F., Knight, V., Browder, D.M., Jimenez, B., & DiBiase, W. (2011). Evaluating evidence-based practice in teaching science content to students with severe developmental disabilities. *Research and Practice for Persons with Severe Disabilities, 36*, 62–75.

Spooner, F., Knight, V., Browder, D., & Smith, B. (2012). Evidence-based practices for teaching academics to students with severe disabilities. *Remedial and Special Education, 33*, 374–387.

Wagner, M., Cadwallader, T., & Marder, C. (with Cameto, R., Cardoso, D., Garza, N., Levine, P., & Newman, L.). (2003). *Life outside the classroom for youth with disabilities. A report from the National Longitudinal Transition Study-2 (NLTS2)*. Menlo Park, CA: SRI International. Retrieved from http://www.nlts2.org/reports/2003_04-2/nlts2_report_2003_04-2_complete.pdf

Wehmeyer, M.L., Lattin, D.L., Lapp-Rincker, G., & Agran, M. (2003). Access to the general curriculum of middle school students with mental retardation: An observational study. *Remedial and Special Education, 24*, 262–272.

Zakas, T. (2011). *Teaching social studies content to students with autism using a graphic organizer intervention* (Doctoral dissertation). Retrieved from ProQuest.

Zisimopoulos, D.A. (2010). Enhancing multiplication performance in students with moderate intellectual disabilities using pegword mnemonics paired with a picture fading technique. *Journal of Behavioral Education, 19*, 117–133.

CHAPTER 2

Embedded Instruction in Inclusive Settings

John McDonnell, J. Mathew Jameson, Timothy Riesen, and Shamby Polychronis

Hannah is a fifth-grade student with severe disabilities who is included full time in a general education class in her neighborhood school. During the development of her individualized education program (IEP), the team identified several quality-of-life goals based on a person-centered planning process. Two of the goals included 1) expanding her knowledge of the community, nation, and world through increased access to literature and media, and 2) increasing her independence in participating and completing assignments and activities at school and at home. Using these goals as context, the team determined that Hannah's ability to achieve these goals would be improved if she was able to learn how to read and define new words that she encountered in reading materials. They reviewed the Common Core State Standards (CCSS) in language arts and determined that the Literacy.L.5.4c standard—"Consult reference materials (e.g., dictionaries, glossaries, thesauruses), both print and digital, to find the pronunciation and determine or clarify the precise meaning of key words and phrases" (Common Core State Standards Initiative, 2012) would provide a logical basis not only for meeting her quality-of-life goals but also for meeting the requirements for her to participate in the general education curriculum in language arts and science.

Hannah uses an iPad to play games, music, and movies, so her IEP team thought they could build on her use of this technology to allow her to use an online dictionary to look up new words. Hannah's iPad was configured with a common dictionary application and was set so that displayed text is played aloud on her iPad when it is highlighted. The sensitivity of the cursor for highlighting words was adjusted to accommodate her fine motor abilities. The team developed a task analysis that required Hannah to type a new word into the look-up screen, highlight the word and the definition of the word, and repeat the word and the definition after it was played on her iPad. They developed an IEP goal that targeted Hannah's use of this strategy at school and at home.

The team decided that the best way to teach this skill was through embedded instruction. Hannah's special education teacher observed lessons in the general education class and identified a number of opportunities to provide embedded instruction

This chapter draws heavily from McDonnell, J., Johnson, J.W., & McQuivey, C. (2008). *Embedded instruction for students with developmental disabilities in general education classrooms.* Arlington, VA: Division on Developmental Disabilities, Council for Exceptional Children.

to Hannah on the skill. Her teacher developed a written teaching plan and trained the general educator and several peers that sat next to Hannah during language arts and science to implement the embedded instruction procedure. Hannah's teacher collects data on her ability to use the strategy through biweekly probes. Her general and special education teachers regularly review the performance data and adjust the instructional procedures as necessary to ensure that she continues to make progress toward her IEP goal.

The percentage of students with severe disabilities being educated in general education classes for at least a portion of the school day has increased steadily since the 1990s (U.S. Department of Education, 2012). This trend has been driven by strong advocacy efforts focused on achieving equal access and opportunity for students (Lipsky & Gartner, 1997) and research supporting the positive education and social benefits of inclusive education (Hunt & McDonnell, 2007). The initial focus of inclusion was on promoting social acceptance of students with disabilities by peers without disabilities. However, researchers realized that achieving this goal required that students with severe disabilities actively participate in the instructional activities of the class with their peers and have opportunities to learn the same content as other students (Giangreco, Dennis, Cloninger, Edelman, & Schattman, 1993).

The emphasis on students with severe disabilities learning rigorous academic content has also been driven by the ongoing standards-based reform movement in education that resulted in the enactment of the No Child Left Behind Act of 2001 (PL 107-110) and the Individuals with Disabilities Education Improvement Act (IDEA) of 2004 (PL 108-446). Under IDEA 2004, students with severe disabilities must be involved and progress in the general education curriculum and participate in the state's assessment or an alternate assessment in order to track their progress toward achieving state standards (Yell, Shriner, & Katsiyannis, 2006). Subsequently, 45 states have adopted CCSS, which provide clear and rigorous academic standards outlining what all students need to know to be college and/or career ready (Saunders, Bethune, Spooner, & Browder, 2013).

The changes in where students are educated and what they are taught has led to the development of a number of empirically validated instructional approaches and strategies that support students' acquisition of academic content in inclusive general education classrooms (Hunt & McDonnell, 2007). These interventions can be roughly divided into classroom- and student-based interventions.

Classroom-based interventions encompass a broad range of procedures designed to improve learning and social outcomes for all students in the class (Hemmeter, 2000). The interventions may often have one or more purposes related to enhancing instruction and learning for students with severe disabilities. For example, the interventions may focus on improving social development or social skills (Carter & Hughes, 2007), improving academic learning (Knight, Browder, Agnello, & Lee, 2010), and preventing behavior problems (Conroy, Sutherland, Snyder, & Marsh, 2008). Examples of validated classroom-based interventions for students with severe disabilities include universal design for learning (Dymond et al., 2006), cooperative learning (Hunt, Staub, Alwell, & Goetz, 1994), peer-mediated instruction (McDonnell, Thorson, Allen, & Mathot-Buckner, 2000), and professional teaming (Hunt, Soto, Maier, & Doering, 2003).

Student-based interventions are focused on individual student supports that will promote learning and social outcomes. Examples of these strategies include student-directed learning (Wehmeyer, Yeager, Bolding, Agran, & Hughes, 2003), curriculum modifications and adaptations (Fisher & Frey, 2001), peer supports (Carter, Cushing, Clark, & Kennedy, 2005), and embedded instruction (McDonnell, Johnson, & McQuivey, 2008).

This chapter focuses on the use of embedded instruction as a strategy for teaching academic content to students with severe disabilities in inclusive general education classes. This chapter defines embedded instruction, reviews the research on the use of embedded instruction with students with severe disabilities in general education classes, and outlines the steps for successfully designing and implementing embedded instruction.

DEFINITION OF EMBEDDED INSTRUCTION

Systematically embedding instruction into the ongoing activities of the general education class enables teachers to deliver instruction on core academic content that is compatible with the class schedule and organization and that enhances the learning experience by creating opportunities for a student to practice skills throughout the day. In embedded instruction, the instructional trials presented to a student are distributed within and across instructional and classroom management activities. This is different from more traditional teaching formats in which instruction trials are massed and presented one after another in a single teaching session. McDonnell and colleagues (2008) suggested that embedded instruction is characterized by several key features:

1. *The expected learning outcomes for the student in general education class are clearly delineated.* Embedded instruction should be based on explicit goals and objectives developed by the student's IEP team that are directly linked to the core curriculum.

2. *The timing for the delivery of instructional trials are planned and scheduled within each instructional lesson or class period.* Embedded instruction is based on a systematic analysis of the typical schedule and organization of the general education classroom. The analysis is focused on identifying specific contexts in which embedded instructional trials can be delivered seamlessly to the student. This information is used to develop a distributed trial schedule that assists instructors to determine when to present trials to the student. The primary goal of embedded instruction is to provide systematic instruction to the student within the natural flow of class activities.

3. *Instruction is based on empirically validated instructional procedures.* Embedded instruction teaching plans rely on validated instructional procedures that control the instructional examples, response prompting and fading procedures, error correction procedures, and reinforcement procedures used with students. Embedded instruction teaching plans should be designed to enhance the rate of student learning by minimizing student errors during acquisition, increasing independent responses, and reducing reinforcement to natural levels. In addition, teaching plans should be designed to promote the generalization of the skill to typical settings.

4. *Instructional decisions about the effectiveness of the teaching plan are driven by student performance data.* Embedded instruction needs to be tailored to the individual learning needs of the student. Consequently, data on student progress is collected regularly and reviewed to make instructional decisions.

For example, consider Hannah in the opening vignette. The IEP team worked closely together to identify vocabulary in language arts and science that could be used to teach Hannah to use a common dictionary on her iPad to look up words to obtain the pronunciation and definition of the word. Her special education teacher observed language arts and science lessons and identified a number of opportunities to provide embedded instructional trials into Hannah's adapted reading materials and to provide discrete, distributed instructional trials during transitions and independent seat work. Hannah's teacher also developed a written teaching plan to support the implementation of embedded instruction procedures by her general education teacher and several peers during language arts and science periods.

RESEARCH ON THE
EFFECTIVENESS OF EMBEDDED INSTRUCTION

Research on embedded instruction has focused on two primary areas including the effectiveness in teaching students new skills within ongoing activities in general education classes and the effectiveness of various instructional strategies within an embedded instruction teaching format. This research is important because general and special education teachers often express concerns about whether instruction provided in the general education classroom can meet the unique needs of students with disabilities (D'Alonzo, Giordano, & Vanleeuwen, 1997). Indeed, research in each of these areas suggests that embedded instruction produces promising outcomes for students with disabilities who participate in general education classes.

Effectiveness of Embedded Instruction

Embedded instruction is a consistent and reliable instructional strategy that can be used to promote learning in general education classrooms across different age groups (Collins, Evans, Creech-Galloway, Karl, & Miller, 2007; Jameson, McDonnell, Polychronis, & Riesen, 2008; Jimenez, Browder, Spooner, & DiBiase, 2012; Johnson & McDonnell, 2004; Johnson, McDonnell, Hozwarth, & Hunter, 2004; McDonnell, Johnson, Polychronis, & Riesen, 2002; Wolery, Anthony, & Werts, 1997). For example, Johnson and McDonnell (2004) used a multiple-probe design across participants to evaluate the effectiveness of embedded instruction in general education classrooms. Three elementary students with developmental disabilities and two general education teachers participated in the study. Each teacher selected instructional targets to teach students using an embedded instruction format during regularly scheduled activities. These targets included 1) teaching functional sight words, 2) teaching a student to independently request assistance by signing HELP, and 3) identifying the two-digit number that was greater than the other when presented with two numerals. The results of the study suggest that embedded instruction promoted acquisition of the targeted skill for two of the three students.

Participating teachers also reported that they believed embedded instruction was both effective and appropriate for each of their students.

In another example, McDonnell and colleagues (2002) used a multiple-baseline design across behaviors to examine the effectiveness of embedded instruction implemented in junior high school general education classrooms. Four junior high school students with moderate to severe disabilities were taught either to read or define 15 words selected from the general education content area, including food and nutrition, health, and computer classes. Each of the students acquired the target word skills in the existing structure of the general education classroom. The study supported that embedded instruction is an effective method to teach students with moderate to severe disabilities in the general education curriculum.

Research also has demonstrated that a variety of individuals can implement embedded instruction. For example, Collins and colleagues (2007) trained special education staff from elementary, middle, and secondary schools to implement embedded instruction in general education classrooms. In another study, Jameson and colleagues (2008) used a parallel multiple-probe design across participants to evaluate the efficacy of the training package developed to train peer tutors to implement embedded instruction in general education classrooms. They selected three middle school peer tutors to use an embedded constant time delay procedure to teach students with intellectual disability material that was aligned with the general education curriculum. Results showed that middle school peer tutors could be quickly trained to deliver embedded instruction with a high level of accuracy. Finally, McDonnell and colleagues (2002) trained three paraprofessionals to implement embedded instruction procedures in general education classes with middle school students with intellectual disability.

Several researchers also have compared embedded instruction to other instructional formats and found that embedded instruction is as effective as traditional approaches (Jameson et al., 2008; Jameson, Walker, Utley, & Maughan, 2012; McDonnell et al., 2006). McDonnell and colleagues (2006) used a single-subject alternating-treatment design to compare the effectiveness of embedded instruction in general education settings to small group instruction in a special education classroom. The embedded instruction procedure was implemented with four middle school students in their general education science class while small group instruction was implemented in the students' self-contained special education classroom. During the embedded instruction condition, a paraprofessional used constant time delay procedures during natural transitions and breaks to teach students to verbally define five vocabulary words obtained from the general education curriculum. During small group instruction, a paraprofessional used constant time delay to teach word groups and community-based site words. The study showed that embedded instruction and small group instruction were equally effective in promoting the acquisition of the target skill.

The utility of embedded instruction is strengthened by the fact that it can be used to teach a variety of skills to students with disabilities. For example, Collins and colleagues (2007) used embedded instruction in the general education classroom to teach four students with moderate to severe disabilities functional and core content words. Jameson and colleagues (2012) conducted a study that compared embedded total task instruction on academic behavior chains in general education settings with more one-to-one massed trials in special education settings. They successfully taught two students phonological and phonemic awareness and taught two students to use different resources (e.g., dictionaries, glossaries, thesauruses) to determine the meaning of unknown words. Jimenez and colleagues (2012) used peer-mediated embedded instruction to teach five students with moderate to severe disabilities science vocabulary words. Finally, McDonnell and colleagues (2002) used embedded instruction to teach four junior high school students with moderate intellectual disability to read and read or define vocabulary words.

Embedded instruction also is considered to be socially valid by students, peers, paraprofessionals, and teachers. For example, Jameson and colleagues (2008) reported that both teachers and peer tutors provided positive feedback about the utility of embedded instruction and its acceptability. Similarly, Johnson and colleagues (2004) asked teachers participating in a study on embedded instruction to complete a written questionnaire that assessed the utility and acceptability of embedded instruction. The results indicated that teachers believed embedded instruction to be both effective and appropriate and that it did not disrupt the flow of the classroom.

Instructional Approaches and Strategies Used in Embedded Instruction Formats

Embedded instruction is designed to incorporate validated instructional strategies with the ongoing structure of the general education classroom. Several studies have examined the instructional strategies that can be implemented within embedded instruction and have determined that a variety of these strategies may be used in the general education classroom (Collins et al., 2007; McDonnell et al., 2002; Riesen, McDonnell, Johnson, Polychronis, & Jameson, 2003). For example, Riesen and colleagues (2003) used an adapted alternating-treatment design to compare constant time delay and simultaneous prompting within an embedded instruction format. Four students with moderate to severe disabilities and the paraprofessionals who supported these students in the general education classroom participated in the study. Each paraprofessional used either simultaneous prompting or constant time delay to teach students to read or define words selected for the general education content classes. The results of the study indicated that both response-prompting strategies were effective. However, two of the students' acquisition of the target skill was better under the time delay condition, whereas two of the students' acquisition was better under the simultaneous prompting condition. Although both procedures were effective, the authors recommended that the instructional strategy to use in an embedded instruction format be based on several factors including the students' learning history, the experience of the staff implementing the instruction, and the overall structure of the general education classroom.

These studies suggest that embedded instruction can be easily adjusted to meet the unique learning needs of students. Furthermore, this flexibility increases the likelihood that embedded instruction can be adjusted to fit within the typical instructional and classroom management activities.

DESIGNING AND IMPLEMENTING EMBEDDED INSTRUCTION

Embedded instruction relies on empirically validated instructional strategies that have shown to be effective in teaching a wide range of routines, activities, and academic skills to students with severe disabilities (Browder & Spooner, 2011; Snell & Brown, 2011). The process for developing embedded instruction teaching plans includes the systematic selection of instructional examples, response prompting and fading, error correction, and reinforcement procedures that are tailored to the student's current level of performance and learning needs. Teachers also need to regularly gather data on the student's acquisition of the targeted skills in order to adapt instructional procedures to maximize the student's rate of learning. As discussed previously, the primary difference between many teaching formats and embedded instruction is that embedded instruction distributes instructional trials within and across the typical activities of the general education classroom rather than presenting instructional trials one after another in a single teaching session.

McDonnell and colleagues (2008) recommended that practitioners complete four general steps to develop an embedded instruction teaching plan: 1) identify appropriate instructional targets from the core curriculum and/or the student's IEP, 2) establish the student's baseline performance, 3) develop a teaching plan, and 4) implement the teaching plan.

Identify Appropriate Instructional Targets

Over the past few years, several authors have argued that the selection of academic content and skills from the core curriculum for instruction should be driven by a person-centered planning process that is designed to improve the student's immediate and future quality of life (Browder, Spooner, & Jimenez, 2011; Hunt, McDonnell, & Crockett, 2012; Kleinert & Kearns, 2010). Specifically, the reading/literacy, mathematics, and science standards chosen for instruction should directly contribute to improving the student's happiness, well-being, independence, productivity, and autonomy in home, school, and community settings. The linkage between quality-of-life outcomes and common core standards provides a rational framework for selecting academic knowledge and skills for instruction that are meaningful and relevant to students' specific needs. Once academic core standards have been selected within a person-centered framework, the IEP team should develop specific goals and objectives on the common core standards that reflect the student's communication skills and symbol use.

For example, Hannah's IEP team identified quality-of-life goals that would expand her knowledge of the community, nation, and world through increased access to literature and media, and increase her independence in participating and completing activities at school and at home. With these outcomes as a back drop, and taking into consideration her current reading and literacy skills, Hannah's IEP team selected a standard for instruction from the CCSS in "Vocabulary Acquisition and Use" that focused on the use of reference materials (i.e., dictionary, thesaurus) to find the pronunciation and definition of words. Based on this standard, the team developed an IEP goal for Hannah to help her learn to look up unknown words in her adapted books and other materials using an available dictionary and feature on her iPad that allowed her to hear the pronunciation and definition of the word.

Establish the Student's Baseline Performance

Practitioners should conduct a baseline assessment of the student's performance on a target skill prior to developing the embedded instruction teaching plan. This assessment has three general purposes. First, it allows the practitioner to determine how well the student can perform the skill before embedded instruction begins so that the practitioner can assess the student's progress toward meeting his or her goal. In Hannah's case the baseline assessment showed that she was not able to independently complete any of the steps in the task analysis on using her iPad to look up words in the dictionary. This information will allow her IEP team to gauge the amount of progress that she is making in achieving her goal once embedded instruction begins.

A second purpose of obtaining baseline data is to determine what types of examples the student can or cannot complete correctly. This information can be used to select instructional examples to be presented to the student during embedded instruction. For example, during her baseline assessment Hannah was able to enter unknown words with four or less letters into the dictionary search window independently and with high levels of accuracy. As the words got longer, the number of errors that she made in completing the task analysis increased significantly. This information helped the teacher select words from the reading and science curricula for instruction that built on her current skill levels and then develop an instructional sequence that would allow Hannah to improve her proficiency in using the dictionary across time.

Finally, baseline data provides an opportunity to determine the level of assistance that the student will need to successfully complete the target skill. This can be accomplished by using a system of most prompts. For example, Hannah did not initiate the step of highlighting the word when she was presented with the word *sign*. When Hannah did not initiate this step, her teacher presented her with the verbal prompt, "Highlight the word *sign*." When Hannah did not initiate the response, the teacher repeated the verbal prompt and pointed to the word *sign* on the display. Following the presentation of these prompts Hannah was able to correctly highlight the word. The teacher coded the level of prompts that Hannah needed to complete the response correctly on a baseline data form.

Figure 2.1 presents the baseline data form Hannah's teacher used to assess Hannah's ability to use the dictionary on her iPad. The form includes the steps that Hannah should complete in looking up a word and the list of words (i.e., examples) that were presented to her during the baseline sessions. The teacher entered a code for the level of assistance (i.e., *V* – direct verbal prompt, *M* – model) that Hannah required to complete the step of the task analysis correctly. The teacher used this information to select and sequence the word examples presented to Hannah during instruction and to design a response prompting and fading procedure to increase her independent performance across instructional trials.

Develop a Teaching Plan

Embedded instruction teaching plans include the procedures for distributing instructional trials within or across activities and the specific procedures to be used to teach the skill to the student. The purpose of the plan is to ensure that the procedures are implemented accurately and consistently. The teaching plan should be organized in an easy-to-use format that allows the instructor to quickly review the teaching procedures at each stage of instruction. Figure 2.2 presents an example teaching plan.

Date: 1/6

Student: Hannah

Baseline Data Form

Prompt code
I – Indirect verbal   M – Model   + – Independent
V – Verbal   P – Physical prime   correct
G – Gestural   F – Full physical

Word	Sign	Wade	Index	Route	Signal	Energy	Illegal	Capital	National	Underground
Open dictionary application	V	V	V	V	V	V	V	V	V	V
Type word in search window	+	+	V + G	V + G	V + G	V + G	V + G	V + G	V + G	V + G
Push search button	V	V	V	V	V	V	V	V	V	V
Highlight word	V + G	V + G	V + G	V + G	V + G	V + G	V + G	V + G	V + G	V
Pronounce word	V	V	V	V	V	V	V	V	V	V
Highlight definition	V + G	V + G	V + G	V + G	V + G	V + G	V + G	V + G	V + G	V + G
Repeat definition	V	V	V	V	V	V	V	V	V	V

Figure 2.1. Example of a baseline data form.

Embedded Instruction Teaching Plan

Student: Hannah_____   Instructors: John, Matt, Tim, and Shamby_____

Goal: When presented with an unknown word, Hannah will use the dictionary on her iPad to
       look up the word, say the word, and repeat the definition with 100% accuracy on two
       consecutive instructional days.

Trial distribution schedule: At least five trials per period.
  1. Two words embedded daily in assigned reading materials.
  2. One instructional trial during transition from teacher demonstration to individual or group
     activities.
  3. Two instructional trials during independent seat work.

Instructional sequence:
  1. Break, enjoy, image, messy, route
  2. Classic, energy, nation, signal, retain
  3. Random presentation of words in Sets 1 and 2
  4. Absence, capital, illegal, honesty, section
  5. Random presentation of words in Sets 1–3
  6. National, solitary, thunderstorm, thermometer, underground

Strategy step	Prompts
Open dictionary application	a. 0-second delay — "Open the app." b. 3-second delay — "Open the app."
Type word in search window	a. 0-second delay — "Enter the word." (And teacher points to letters.) b. 3-second delay — "Enter the word." (And teacher points to letters.)
Push search button	a. 0-second delay — "Press search." b. 3-second delay — "Press search."
Highlight word	a. 0-second delay — "Highlight word." (And teacher points to word.) b. 3-second delay — "Highlight word." (And teacher points to word.)
Pronounce word	a. 0-second delay — "Say the word." b. 3-second delay — "Say the word."
Highlight definition	a. 0-second delay — "Highlight the definition." (And teacher points to definition.) b. 3-second delay — "Highlight the definition." (And teacher points to definition.)
Repeat definition	a. 0-second delay – "Repeat the definition." b. 3-second delay – "Repeat the definition."

Error correction: 1. Say, "No."
                  2. Provide the "a" level prompt.
                  3. Provide instructive feedback.

Reinforcement: Provide verbal praise to Hannah after completing the strategy without assistance.
                "Wow, you did that all by yourself." "That's right that is what the word ___ means."

Figure 2.2.   Example of a teaching plan.

Develop a Trial Distribution Schedule   The function of the trial distribution
schedule is twofold. First, it ensures that the student receives a sufficient number
of instructional trials to support adequate rates of learning. Students with disabilities often require significant amounts of practice in order to master a skill. The trial

distribution schedule helps the instructor provide an adequate number of instructional trials to the student each day.

The number of instructional trials scheduled must reflect the student's individual learning needs. Consequently, the number of trials provided to a student will be based on a number of factors including 1) the student's functioning level, 2) the complexity of the skill being taught, 3) the student's previous learning history, and 4) the structure of the routines and activities of the general education class. Based on previous experience, Hannah's teacher decided that she needed to design the teaching plan to provide Hannah at least five instructional trials during both the reading and science period.

The second purpose of the schedule is to determine how instructional trials are presented within the typical routines and activities of the general education class. Although opportunities to teach a skill often occur as part of the typical flow of classroom instruction, it may be difficult to ensure that instructors will have a sufficient number of these unplanned teaching opportunities to promote efficient student learning. Consequently, McDonnell and colleagues (2008) suggested that, in additional to these unplanned opportunities, teachers should use two different types of planned embedded instructional trials to teach the targeted skill. The first and most important type are naturalistic trials that are built into the typical learning activities that students are completing as part of the lesson being provided by the classroom teacher. Typically this can be accomplished by arranging the student's interactions with the teacher, their peers, or instructional materials to create an opportunity for the student to use the skill. For example, in order to help Hannah learn the process of using the dictionary on her iPad, her teacher made sure to insert at least two words that she did not know from the reading or science vocabulary lists into her adapted stories and other work materials each day (see Figure 2.2). By doing this Hannah was provided opportunities to use the dictionary in a way that was similar to how she would need to use it when reading books or other materials for interest or pleasure. These naturalistic trials can help promote the development of generalized skills that are likely to be maintained across time because they closely simulate the stimulus and response demands of typical performance conditions (Drasgow, Wolery, Halle, & Hajiaghamohseni, 2011; Horner, McDonnell, & Bellamy, 1986; Rosenthal-Malek & Bloom, 1998).

Supplemental instructional trials are another way of providing embedded instruction to students within typical routines and activities. These are planned teaching opportunities that are embedded within the transitions between instruction activities, such as moving from teacher demonstration of a learning activity to small groups; natural breaks in activities, such as when students complete learning activities early; or when students are working independently. In Hannah's case, her teacher designed the embedded instruction teaching plan to provide at least five supplemental trials during transitions between instructional activities and during independent seat work periods (see Figure 2.2). In these supplemental trials, Hannah was presented with an unknown word on a flashcard and was asked to look the word up in her dictionary, listen to the pronunciation and definition, and then say the word and restate the definition. Teachers can use supplemental instructional trials to ensure that students are receiving an adequate amount of practice each day on the skill.

Develop the Teaching Procedures Embedded instruction can be designed
to incorporate a wide range of empirically validated teaching procedures for students with severe disabilities (Snell & Brown, 2011; Spooner, Browder, & Mims, 2011;
Westling & Fox, 2008). Although a full discussion of these procedures is beyond the
scope of this chapter, McDonnell and colleagues (2008) suggested that embedded
instruction teaching plans should be designed using several key principles:

- *Select teaching examples to promote generalization of the target skill.* Specifically, the teaching examples selected for instruction should present the range
  of variation that a student will encounter across common materials, typical
  activities, and actual performance settings (Horner et al., 1986). For Hannah
  this meant identifying or creating opportunities for her to use her dictionary
  across different books and reading materials at home and school. It also meant
  developing teaching examples for supplemental instructional trials that varied
  the relevant and irrelevant dimensions of the word examples presented (i.e.,
  types of font styles and sizes, type color) to Hannah.

- *Develop a presentation sequence for instructional examples that controls difficulty and promotes regular review.* The sequence should be structured to minimize the number of errors that a student makes within and across instructional
  sessions. This can be controlled through the relative difficulty of the examples
  presented to the student. For example, Hannah's accuracy in entering words into
  the search window in her dictionary went down as the number of letters in the
  word increased. To address this issue, her teacher developed a sequence that
  gradually increased the length of the words that were presented to her. Another
  way to control difficulty is through the number of examples that are presented to
  a student within a teaching session. In Hannah's case, her teacher decided that
  presenting words one at time would be too easy and that presenting 10 words at
  a time would be too difficult. Based on Hannah's previous learning history, her
  teacher settled on presenting one set of five words (one word per trial) to her
  until she was able to look up all of the words in the set independently. Finally,
  Hannah's teacher built regular review steps into the sequence so that she would
  have to read and define previously introduced words (see Figure 2.2).

- *Select response prompting and fading procedures that minimize errors for
  students during instruction.* These procedures include the system of most-
  to-least prompts, time delay, and simultaneous prompting. The specific procedure selected for instruction must take into account the nature of the skill being
  taught and the student's learning history. Hannah's teacher selected a constant
  time-delay procedure because Hannah had previously responded positively to
  it and because researchers had reported that this procedure was easy to implement in chained tasks such as looking up words in a dictionary (Schuster et
  al., 1998). On the teaching plan form (Figure 2.2), Hannah's teacher created a
  constant-time delay procedure that included 0-second and 3-second delay conditions. For example, in the "a" condition on Step 1 of the task analysis, the
  instructor gave the verbal prompt "Open the app" immediately after the iPad
  was given to Hannah. The verbal prompt "Open the app" had been identified
  during the baseline probe as the level of prompt that she needed to complete
  the response correctly. In the "b" condition, the instructor delayed the prompt 3
  seconds after the iPad was given to Hannah. Although this example shows the

use of this format for a constant time-delay procedure, it can be easily adapted to a progressive time delay by assigning a letter to each delay interval (i.e., a – 0-second delay, b – 1-second delay, c – 2-second delay, d – 3-second delay) or to a system of most prompts by assigning a letter to each type of prompt (i.e., a – model, b – gestural, c – verbal).

- *Develop reinforcement procedures that are socially valid and compatible with the typical routines and activities of the general education class.* Although the decision about the type and intensity of reinforcement needs to be based on the students' needs and learning history, teachers are encouraged to use stimuli that are similar to those available to peers without disabilities and that are acceptable to the general education teacher and other staff. Because Hannah responds extremely well to positive praise from teachers and peers, her teacher included several examples of reinforcing statements in the teaching plan that could be used to praise her when she accurately looked up the word, pronounced it, and defined the word.

- *Develop systematic procedures to correct student errors.* In spite of all efforts to minimize errors, students are likely to make some mistakes during instruction. Research suggests that the effectiveness of a teaching plan can be improved if student errors are systematically corrected each time they occur (Barbetta, Heron, & Heward, 1993; Barbetta, Heward, Bradley, & Miller, 1994). The recommended procedure includes stopping the instructional trial immediately and providing the student with feedback, representing the example and instructional cue, providing the assistance necessary to ensure that the student makes the correct response, and providing feedback to the student confirming that he or she made the correct response. Hannah's teacher used this basic structure in developing the error correct procedure for the teaching plan.

Implement the Teaching Plan

Successful implementation of the teaching plan requires that the teacher complete three procedural steps to ensure the ongoing quality and consistency of instruction. These steps are especially important when multiple individuals are implementing the teaching plan with the student.

Train Peers and Staff   Research has shown that when provided systematic training and support, general and special education teachers, paraprofessionals, and peers can successfully implement embedded instruction with a high degree of fidelity (Jameson, McDonnell, Johnson, Riesen, & Polychronis, 2007; Johnson et al., 2004; McDonnell et al., 2002; Wolery et al., 1997). Our experience suggests that training that is directly linked to the written teaching plan is the most efficient approach to obtain the necessary quality and consistency of instruction with the student. Training should begin with a review of the teaching plan to explain how the procedures are implemented during each training trial. In addition, the instructor should be provided explicit guidelines for when trials should be presented to the student. We have found that modeling the procedures with the student in the general education class and then having the instructor implement the procedures with the student while receiving feedback is the most efficient strategy to establish reliable implementation of the procedures. It also is important to give the instructor an opportunity to implement the procedures on both naturalistic and supplemental instructional trials. Modeling and feedback should continue until the individual can implement the procedures in the written teaching plan accurately and consistently. Following training, the teacher should regularly observe the instructor to ensure that his or her accurate implementation of the procedures is maintained across time.

Gather and Analyze Student Performance Data   It is well established that the efficacy of instruction is improved if teachers gather regular data on a student's performance and then use that information to adjust instructional procedures to the needs of the student (Farlow & Snell, 1994). It is common for teachers working with students with severe disabilities to collect trial-by-trial data on a student's performance during the acquisition phase. Figure 2.3 presents the data collection form that Hannah's teacher had instructors use each time they presented an instructional trial to her. The instructor would enter + if Hannah completed a step of the task analysis independently. If the instructor presented the prompt with a 0-second delay on a task analysis, then he or she would enter an *a* in the appropriate example column. If the instructor presented the prompt with a 3-second delay, then he or she would enter a *b* in the column. Finally, if Hannah incorrectly completed the response, the instructor would enter a *0* in the column. This format allows the teacher to identify specific steps of the task analysis or specific words that are difficult for Hannah.

Although trial-by-trial data is a very effective approach to tracking student progress toward achieving a goal, it can also be difficult to gather data consistently in embedded instruction because instructional trials are being distributed across activities during the day. One alternative to trial-by-trial data collection is to conduct regular probes of the student's performance. Probes can be thought of as tests of the student's performance when provided no assistance or feedback (Farlow & Snell, 1994). During probes, the instructor simply presents the examples to the student and records his or her response as either correct or incorrect. The instructor provides no prompts, reinforcement, or error corrections to the student. The probes should be conducted on a fixed schedule and done during a time that does not interfere with the student's participation in class activities. The decision about how often probes should be conducted should be based on the student's previous learning history, the complexity of the task, and the organization of the general education class.

As with all instructional programs, teachers need to regularly review the student performance data and adjust instructional procedures in order to accommodate the student's learning needs and to maximize learning rates (Farlow & Snell, 1994; McDonnell et al., 2008). This requires teachers to analyze the data to identify potential patterns in the student's day-to-day performance and consistent response errors. Typically this analysis is focused on several key questions:

- Are the instructional procedures being implemented across instructional trials, and if not why?

- Are the instructional examples being presented to the student too easy or too difficult?

Data Collection Form

+ — Independent correct
a/b — Prompt level
0 — Incorrect

Date: 1/10

Word	break	enjoy	image	messy	route
1. Open dictionary application	b	b	+	+	b
2. Type word in search window	a	0	a	a	0
3. Push search button	b	b	b	b	b
4. Highlight word	a	a	a	a	a
5. Pronounce word	b	b	+	+	+
6. Highlight definition	0	0	a	0	a
7. Repeat definition	b	b	b	b	b

Date:

Word					
1. Open dictionary application					
2. Type word in search window					
3. Push search button					
4. Highlight word					
5. Pronounce word					
6. Highlight definition					
7. Repeat definition					

Date:

Word					
1. Open dictionary application					
2. Type word in search window					
3. Push search button					
4. Highlight word					
5. Pronounce word					
6. Highlight definition					
7. Repeat definition					

Date:

Word					
1. Open dictionary application					
2. Type word in search window					
3. Push search button					
4. Highlight word					
5. Pronounce word					
6. Highlight definition					
7. Repeat definition					

Date:

Word					
1. Open dictionary application					
2. Type word in search window					
3. Push search button					
4. Highlight word					
5. Pronounce word					
6. Highlight definition					
7. Repeat definition					

Figure 2.3. Example of a trial-by-trial data collection form.

- Is the student being provided enough assistance to correctly complete the responses?

- Do the type and intensity of reinforcement sufficiently match the difficulty and complexity of the task being completed by the student?

An examination of these issues can help the teacher develop a logical hypothesis for why the student may be experiencing difficulty and then adjust the instructional procedures in the teaching plan to address these specific concerns.

Track the Distribution of Instructional Trials Embedded instruction is structured to avoid the numerous unintended negative effects that have been documented from the overuse of parallel professional support for students in general education classes (Giangreco, 2010). The objective of embedded instruction is to create a teaching arrangement that allows teachers, paraprofessionals, and peers to provide systematic instruction to the student in a way that does not set him or her apart from the other members of the class. Consequently, one of the challenges of successfully implementing embedded instruction is ensuring that the instructional trials that a student receives each day are in fact being distributed across activities rather than being presented one after another in a massed trial teaching format. The teacher must closely monitor the distribution of instructional trials and provide teachers and peers with strategies for determining when instructional trials should be conducted. This could include strategies such as linking the presentation of trials to specific activities or transitions during the day, or using a time-based self-monitoring system that allows the instructor to track the number of trials presented to the student during specific time blocks.

Other Considerations

Embedded instruction has been shown to be an effective strategy for promoting the acquisition of academic skills and the generalization of these skills to other stimulus materials, tasks, and settings in the general education class and school (McDonnell et al., 2008). However, few studies have systematically examined whether embedded instruction promotes the generalization of complex academic skills to functional routines and activities completed by students each day. Although much more research is needed on embedded instruction as well as other instructional approaches to address this issue, we believe that teachers can enhance the effectiveness of embedded instruction in producing generalized skill use if they follow several additional guidelines (Hunt et al., 2012).

Combine Embedded Instruction with Other Instructional Formats to Teach Target Skills Based on the available research, we believe that embedded instruction is most effective in producing generalized responding when it is used as part of a larger package of instructional strategies to teach academic skills (Albin & Horner, 1988; Drasgow et al., 2011; McDonnell & Brown, 2010). Other approaches and strategies that have shown to be effective in teaching academic skills in general education classes include cooperative learning (Cushing, Kennedy, Shukla, Davis, & Meyer, 1997; Hunt et al., 1994), peer-mediated instruction (Kamps, Barbetta, Leonard, & Delquardri, 1994; McDonnell et al., 2000), and heterogeneous small group instruction (Rankin et al., 1999; Schoen & Ogden, 1995). By combining embedded instruction with these other approaches the teacher can create additional opportunities to use the skill across settings, tasks, and materials. For example, Hannah's teacher provided an opportunity for her to practice the use of her dictionary by creating adapted materials for her to use during cooperative learning groups in other subject areas and in shared reading activities with peers during language arts.

Use Multiple Instructors to Provide Embedded Instruction   Another way of promoting the generalization of academic skills to typical activities and settings is to use multiple individuals including general educators and peers to deliver embedded instruction to students (Carter & Kennedy, 2006; Drasgow et al., 2011; McDonnell, 2011). One of the advantages of using multiple instructors is that it creates the capacity in the general education class to provide embedded instruction to the student when unplanned opportunities arise for the student to practice the skill within the flow of typical class activities. Embedding instruction in authentic tasks not only provides more opportunities for students to apply the skill in day-to-day activities but also has the potential to increase the motivation of students to learn difficult concepts and operations because the application of the skill has immediate meaning and utility. A second advantage of using multiple instructors is that it reduces the unintended negative effects of all instruction being provided exclusively by special education staff (Giangreco, 2010). Taking these issues into account, Hannah's teacher trained the general educator and several of her peers that sat next to her to implement the embedded instruction teaching plan. This approach increased the likelihood that Hannah would get more practice using the skills when unplanned opportunities presented themselves during the course of the school day.

Promote the Application of Concepts, Operations, and Skills in Home and Community Settings   It has been well established that the likelihood of generalization is improved if students are encouraged and supported to use skills in activities outside of school (Albin & Horner, 1988; Horner et al., 1986). Teachers will need to work with parents and families to identify specific activities in home and community settings in which students can use the skill. These activities should be identified during the IEP meeting so that the team can identify ways that these opportunities can be provided regularly to the student. For example, Hannah's IEP team thought she would have many potential opportunities to use her dictionary when she went to the library, attended church classes and events, and prepared for and went to Girl Scout meetings. These were activities that she did routinely, and there were peers and adults who were willing to provide her with the support necessary to practice this skill.

SUMMARY

The emphasis on teaching academic content to students with severe disabilities in inclusive classes has increased the need for empirically validated strategies that can promote student learning and are compatible with the ongoing activities of the general education class. One approach that has been shown to be effective in meeting these challenges is embedded instruction. The available evidence suggests that embedded instruction is effective in teaching a wide range of academic skills; can be implemented by teachers, paraprofessionals, and peers; can be designed to use an array of teaching strategies and procedures; and is perceived by professionals as being an appropriate approach to meeting the instructional needs of students with severe disabilities in general education classes.

The utility of embedded instruction is enhanced when teachers analyze the activities of the class to identify opportunities to provide instructional trials within typical assignments and tasks or in contexts when embedded instruction will not interrupt the instruction being provided by the classroom teacher. Teachers should identify naturalistic teaching trials that are embedded within the typical interactions with teachers, peers, and instructional materials. Additional supplemental instructional trials that are presented during transitions, breaks in activities, or independent seat work can be used to ensure that the student is receiving a sufficient number of opportunities to practice the skill.

The effectiveness of embedded instruction can be enhanced through the development of a written teaching plan that incorporates instructional procedures that are tailored to a student's unique learning needs. Teaching plans provide guidance to the individuals who are implementing the procedures about when instructional trials should be presented to a student and to ensure that procedures are implemented consistently across instructors. Regular student performance data must be collected and reviewed by the teacher in order to evaluate the effectiveness of the teaching plan. This information must be used to adjust the instructional procedures as necessary to promote continuous learning.

One of the key challenges in embedded instruction is promoting the student's application of the skills he or she is learning in typical home and community settings. Although much more research is needed in this area, the generalization and maintenance of academic skills may be enhanced by combining embedded instruction with other teaching approaches in a comprehensive instructional package that teaches the skill in different ways, using multiple instructors to implement embedded instruction, and identifying specific activities and settings in which the application of the skill can be supported by parents and peers.

REFERENCES

Albin, R.W., & Horner, R.H. (1988). Generalization with precision. In R.H. Horner, G. Dunlap, & R.L. Koegel (Eds.), *Generalization and maintenance: Life-style changes in applied settings* (pp. 99–120). Baltimore, MD: Paul H. Brookes Publishing Co.

Barbetta, P.M., Heron, T.E., & Heward, W.L. (1993). Effects of active student response during error correction on the acquisition, maintenance, and generalization of sight words by students with developmental disabilities. *Journal of Applied Behavior Analysis, 26,* 111–119.

Barbetta, P.M., Heward, W.L., Bradley, D.M., & Miller, A.D. (1994). Effects of immediate and delayed error correction on the acquisition and maintenance of sight words by students with developmental disabilities. *Journal of Applied Behavior Analysis, 27,* 177–178.

Browder, D.M., & Spooner, F. (2011). *Teaching students with moderate and severe disabilities.* New York, NY: The Guilford Press.

Browder, D.M., Spooner, F., & Jimenez, B. (2011). Standards-based individualized education plans and progress monitoring. In D.M. Browder & F. Spooner (Eds.), *Teaching students with moderate and severe disabilities* (pp. 42–91). New York, NY: The Guilford Press.

Carter, E.W., Cushing, L.S., Clark, N.M., & Kennedy, C.H. (2005). Effects of peer support interventions on students' access to the general curriculum and social interactions. *Research and Practice for Persons with Severe Disabilities, 30,* 15–25.

Carter, E.W., & Hughes, C. (2007). Social interaction interventions: Promoting socially supported environments and teaching new skills. In S.L. Odom, R.H. Horner, M.E. Snell, & J. Blacher (Eds.), *Handbook of developmental disabilities* (pp. 310–329). New York, NY: The Gilford Press.

Carter, E.W., & Kennedy, C.H. (2006). Promoting access to the general curriculum using peer support strategies. *Research and Practice for Persons with Severe Disabilities, 31,* 284–292.

Collins, B.C., Evans, A., Creech-Galloway, C., Karl, J., & Miller, A. (2007). Comparison of the acquisition and maintenance of teaching functional and core content sight words in special education and general education settings. *Focus on Autism and Other Developmental Disabilities, 22,* 220–233.

Common Core State Standards Initiative (2012). *English Language Arts Standard >>4>>c.* Retrieved from http://www.corestandards.org/ELA-Literacy/L/5/4/c

Conroy, M.A., Sutherland, K.S., Snyder, A.L., & Marsh, S. (2008). Classwide interventions: Effective instruction makes a difference. *TEACHING Exceptional Children, 40*(6), 24–30.

Cushing, L.S., Kennedy, C.H., Shukla, S., Davis, J., & Meyer, K.A. (1997). Disentagling the effects of curricular revision and social grouping within cooperative learning arrangements. *Focus on Autism and Other Developmental Disabilities, 12,* 231–240.

D'Alonzo, B.J., Giordano, G., & Vanleeuwen, D.M. (1997). Perceptions by teachers about the benefits and liabilities of inclusion. *Preventing School Failure, 42,* 4–11.

Drasgow, E., Wolery, M., Halle, J., & Hajiaghamohseni, Z. (2011). Systematic instruction of students with severe disabilities. In J.M. Kauffman & D.P. Hallahan (Eds.), *Handbook of special education* (pp. 516–531). New York, NY: Routledge.

Dymond, S.K., Renzaglia, A., Rosenstein, A., Chun, E.J., Banks, R.A., Niswander, V., & Gilson, C.L. (2006). Using participatory action research approach to create a universally designed inclusive high school science course: A case study. *Research and Practice for Persons with Severe Disabilities, 31,* 293–308.

Farlow, L.J., & Snell, M.E. (1994). *Making the most of student performance data.* Washington, DC: American Association on Mental Retardation.

Fisher, D., & Frey, N. (2001). Access to the core curriculum: Critical ingredients for student success. *Remedial and Special Education, 22,* 148–157.

Giangreco, M.F. (2010). One-to-one paraprofessionals for students with disabilities in inclusive classrooms: Is conventional wisdom wrong? *Intellectual and Developmental Disabilities, 48,* 1–13.

Giangreco, M.F., Dennis, R., Cloninger, C., Edelman, S., & Schattman, R. (1993). "I've counted Jon": Transformational experiences of teachers in the education of students with disabilities. *Exceptional Children, 59,* 359–371.

Hemmeter, M. (2000). Classroom-based interventions: Evaluating the past and looking toward the future. *Topics in Early Childhood Special Education, 20*(1), 56–61.

Horner, R.H., McDonnell, J., & Bellamy, G.T. (1986). Efficient instruction of generalized behaviors: General case programming in simulation and community settings. In R.H. Horner, L.H. Meyer, & H.D. Fredericks (Eds.), *Education of Learners with Severe Handicaps* (pp. 289–314). Baltimore, MD: Paul H. Brookes Publishing Co.

Hunt, P., & McDonnell, J. (2007). Inclusive education. In S.L. Odom, R.H. Horner, M. Snell, & J. Blacher (Eds.), *Handbook on developmental disabilities* (pp. 269–291). New York, NY: Guilford Press.

Hunt, P., McDonnell, J., & Crockett, M.A. (2012). Reconciling an ecological curriculum framework focusing on quality of life outcomes with the development and instruction of standards-based academic goals. *Research and Practice for Persons with Severe Disabilities, 37,* 139–152.

Hunt, P., Soto, G., Maier, J., & Doering, K. (2003). Collaborative teaming to support students at risk and students with severe disabilities in general education classrooms. *Exceptional Children, 69,* 315–332.

Hunt, P., Staub, D., Alwell, M., & Goetz, L. (1994). Achievement by all students within the context of cooperative learning groups. *Journal of the Association for Persons with Severe Handicaps, 19,* 290–301.

Individuals with Disabilities Education Improvement Act (IDEA) of 2004, PL 108-446, 20 U.S.C. §§ 1400 *et seq.*

Jameson, J.M., McDonnell, J., Johnson, J.W., Riesen, T., & Polychronis, S. (2007). A comparison of one-to-one embedded instruction in the general education classroom and one-to-one massed practice instruction in the special education classroom. *Education and Treatment of Children, 30,* 23–44.

Jameson, J.M., McDonnell, J., Polychronis, S., & Riesen, T. (2008). Training middle school peer tutors to embed constant time delay instruction for students with significant cognitive disabilities in inclusive middle school settings. *Intellectual and Developmental Disabilities, 46,* 346–365.

Jameson, J.M., Walker, R., Utley, K., & Maughan, R. (2012). A comparison of embedded total task instruction in teaching behavioral chains to massed-on-one instruction for students with intellectual disabilities: Accessing general education settings and core academic content. *Behavior Modification, 36,* 320–340.

Jimenez, B.A., Browder, D.M., Spooner, F., & DiBiase, W. (2012). Inclusive inquiry science using peer-mediated embedded instruction for students with moderate intellectual disabilities. *Exceptional Children, 78,* 301–317.

Johnson, J.W., & McDonnell, J. (2004). An exploratory study of the implementation of embedded instruction by general educators with students with developmental disabilities. *Education & Treatment of Children, 27,* 46–63.

Johnson, J.W., McDonnell, J., Hozwarth, V., & Hunter, K. (2004). The efficacy of embedded instruction for students with developmental disabilities enrolled in general education classes. *Journal of Positive Behavioral Interventions, 6,* 214–227.

Kamps, D.M., Barbetta, P.M., Leonard, B.R., & Delquardri, J. (1994). Classwide peer tutoring: An integration strategy to improve reading skills and promote peer interactions among students with autism and general education peers. *Journal of Applied Behavior Analysis, 27,* 49–62.

Kleinert, H.L., & Kearns, J.F. (2010). *Alternate assessment for students with significant cognitive disabilities.* Baltimore, MD: Paul H. Brooks Publishing Co.

Knight, V., Browder, D., Agnello, B., & Lee, A. (2010). Academic instruction for students with severe disabilities. *Focus on Exceptional Children, 42,* 1–14.

Lipsky, D.K., & Gartner, A. (1997). *Inclusion and school reform: Transforming America's classrooms.* Baltimore, MD: Paul H. Brookes Publishing Co.

McDonnell, J. (2011). Instructional contexts. In J.M. Kauffman & D.P. Hallahan (Eds.), *Handbook of special education* (pp. 532–543). New York, NY: Routledge/Taylor & Francis Group.

McDonnell, J., & Brown, B.E. (2010). Inclusion in general education classes. In J. McDonnell, & M.L. Hardman (Eds.), *Successful transition programs: Pathways for students with intellectual and developmental disabilities* (pp. 140–172). Los Angeles, CA: Sage.

McDonnell, J., Johnson, J.W., & McQuivey, C. (2008). *Embedded instruction for students with developmental disabilities in general education classes.* Alexandria, VA: Division of Developmental Disabilities, Council for Exceptional Children.

McDonnell, J., Johnson, J.W., Polychronis, S., & Riesen, T. (2002). The effects of embedded instruction on students with moderate disabilities enrolled in general education classes. *Education and Training in Mental Retardation and Developmental Disabilities, 37,* 363–377.

McDonnell, J., Johnson, J.W., Polychronis, S., Riesen, T., Jameson, J.M., & Kercher, K. (2006). A comparison of one-to-one embedded instruction in general education classes with small group instruction in special education classes. *Education and Training in Developmental Disabilities, 41,* 125–138.

McDonnell, J., Thorson, N., Allen, C., & Mathot-Buckner, C. (2000). The effects of partner learning during spelling for students with severe disabilities and their peers. *Journal of Behavioral Education, 10,* 107–122.

National Governors Association Center for Best Practices, Council of Chief State School Officers. (2010). *Common Core State Standards (English language arts).* Washington, DC: Authors. Retrieved from http://www.corestandards.org/

No Child Left Behind Act of 2001, PL 107-110, 115 Stat. 1425, 20 U.S.C. §§ 6301 *et seq.*

Rankin, D.H., Logan, K.R., Adcock, J., Angelica, J., Pittman, C., Sexton, A., & Straight, S. (1999). Small group learning: Effects of including a student with intellectual disabilities. *Journal of Developmental and Physical Disabilities, 11*(2), 159–177.

Riesen, T., McDonnell, J., Johnson, J.W., Polychronis, S., & Jameson, M. (2003). A comparison of time delay and simultaneous prompting within embedded instruction in general education classes with students with moderate to severe disabilities. *Journal of Behavioral Education, 12*, 241–260.

Rosenthal-Malek, A., & Bloom, A. (1998). Beyond acquisition: Teaching generalization for students with developmental disabilities. In A. Hilton & R. Ringlaben (Eds.), *Best and promising practices in developmental disabilities* (pp. 139–155). Austin, TX: Pro-Ed.

Saunders, A., Bethune, K., Spooner, F., & Browder, D. (2013). Solving the common core equation. *TEACHING Exceptional Children, 45*(3), 24–33.

Schoen, S.F., & Ogden, S. (1995). Impact of time delay, observational learning, and attentional cueing upon word recognition during integrated small-group instruction. *Journal of Autism and Developmental Disorders, 25*, 503–519.

Schuster, J.W., Morse, T.E., Ault, M.J., Doyle, P.M., Crawford, M.R., & Wolery, M. (1998). Constant time delay with chained tasks: A review of the literature. *Education & Treatment of Children, 21*, 74–106.

Snell, M.E., & Brown, F. (2011). *Instruction of students with severe disabilities.* Boston, MA: Pearson.

Spooner, F., Browder, D.M., & Mims, P.J. (2011). Evidenced-based practices. In D.M. Browder & F. Spooner (Eds.), *Teaching students with moderate and severe disabilities* (pp. 92–124). New York, NY: The Gilford Press.

U.S. Department of Education (2012). *Thirty-first annual report to congress on the implementation of the Individuals with Disabilities Education Act, 2009.* Washington, D.C.: Office of Special Education and Rehabilitative Services, Office of Special Education Programs.

Wehmeyer, M.L., Yeager, D., Bolding, N., Agran, M., & Hughes, C. (2003). The effects of self-regulation strategies on goal attainment for students with developmental disabilities in general education classes. *Journal of Developmental and Physical Disabilities, 15*, 79–91.

Westling, D.L., & Fox, L. (2008). *Teaching students with severe disabilities* (4th ed.). Upper Saddle River, NJ: Merrill.

Wolery, M., Anthony, L., & Werts, M.G. (1997). Training elementary teachers to embed instruction during classroom activities. *Education & Treatment of Children, 20*, 40–58.

Yell, M.L., Shriner, J.G., & Katsiyannis, A. (2006). Individuals with Disabilities Education Improvement Act of 2004 and IDEA Regulations of 2006: Implications for educators, administrators, and teacher trainers. *Focus on Exceptional Children, 39*, 1–24.

FOR FURTHER INFORMATION

Monograph

McDonnell, J., Johnson, J.W., & McQuivey, C. (2008). *Embedded instruction for students with developmental disabilities in general education classes.* Alexandria, VA: Division of Developmental Disabilities, Council for Exceptional Children. Retrieved from http://daddcec.org/Publications/BooksVideos/DADDPrismSeries.aspx

Research Articles

Jameson, J.M., Walker, R., Utley, K., & Maughan, R. (2012). A comparison of embedded total task instruction in teaching behavioral chains to massed one-on-one instruction for students with intellectual disabilities: Accessing general education settings and core academic content. *Behavior Modification, 36*, 320–340.

Jimenez, B.A., Browder, D.M., Spooner, F., & Dibiase, W. (2012). Inclusive inquiry science using peer-mediated embedded instruction for students with moderate intellectual disability. *Exceptional Children, 78*, 301–317.

Smith, B.R., Spooner, F., & Wood, C.L. (2013). Using embedded computer-assisted explicit instruction to teach science to students with autism spectrum disorder. *Research in Autism Spectrum Disorders, 7*, 433–443.

Web Sites

CAST

http://www.cast.org

CAST is an educational research and development organization that works to expand learning opportunities for all individuals through universal design for learning.

Embedded Instruction for Early Learning

http://embeddedinstruction.net/research-project

This is the web site for The Impact of Professional Development on Preschool Teachers' Use of Embedded Instruction Practices project.

Leadscape

http://www.niusileadscape.org

This web site provides online tools and resources for principals, school leaders, and educators in inclusive schools.

Maryland Coalition for Inclusive Education (MCIE)

http://www.mcie.org

MCIE is a nonprofit organization dedicated to the inclusion of students with disabilities in their neighborhood schools.

CHAPTER 3

Common Core State Standards Primer for Special Educators

Shawnee Y. Wakeman and Angel Lee

Sara has been provided the links to the Common Core State Standards (CCSS; National Governors Association Center for Best Practices, Council of Chief State School Officers, 2010) by her administrator. She has listened to her general education counterparts discuss the changes from the existing state standards to the CCSS, and she has participated in the fourth-grade team's discussion of how to address the new content within the scope of the curriculum. She hasn't yet felt comfortable participating in the discussions as she is simply unsure of how to address this content with her students with moderate and severe disabilities. Because there are so many standards to review for her students that are in third, fourth, and fifth grade, she is overwhelmed. Previously her state provided teachers of students in alternate assessments based on alternate achievement standards (AA-AAS) a prioritized subset of the state standards to use for instruction and the assessment. Sara also is unsure how to navigate the CCSS because math looks completely different than English language arts (ELA). As one of two special education teachers at her school, Sara feels somewhat isolated and embarrassed that she has basic questions when the general education teachers are becoming more fluent with the standards at every meeting. Sara also finds some of the content within the standards to be unfamiliar. Although the fourth-grade teachers have been sharing the lessons they have designed, Sara is not confident she would have the math concept correct if she were to contribute lesson ideas. In addition, as a special education teacher, she has not yet been invited to participate in CCSS professional development training provided by her school district. With the previous state standards, teachers met in a professional learning community (PLC) for 2 years to develop curriculum resources and supports for all teachers in the district to use. Because the PLC has not yet developed new information about the CCSS, Sara is not confident she can accurately line up the previously developed material with the new standards. To date, Sara's only strategy is to teach standards that are familiar from previous years' of instruction without much consideration for how those standards build student understanding across time or how they align with the assessment. Sara is eager to find resources to build her knowledge and subsequent use of the CCSS in designing lessons for her students.

Sara is likely not alone in her feelings of being overwhelmed by the CCSS. Many teachers of students with significant cognitive disabilities are still searching for resources that will help them adapt instruction that aligns with the CCSS. Although the CCSS are relatively new, having to use state content standards to plan instruction is not new for most teachers of students with moderate and severe disabilities. Over the past decade, most teachers have revised their instructional approach to address state standards to prepare students for the newly emerging alternate assessments. In a five-state survey, Karvonen, Wakeman, Browder, Rogers, and Flowers (2011) found that curriculum for students with significant cognitive disabilities has shifted to include academics in the instructional targets for this population. In contrast, although students are being taught a wide range of academic content, the most intensive instruction is still grounded in functional academic areas that may or may not link to state standards. This supports other research that shows teachers may lack resources or buy-in to teach state standards. Ryndak, Moore, Orlando, and Delano (2009) found that the extent to which students have access to academic content instruction differs greatly by state and across students.

A number of research studies have used academic content standards to design and implement instruction with students with moderate and severe intellectual disability. Research literature reviews of academic content instruction with students within this population (Browder, Spooner, Ahlgrim-Delzell, Harris, & Wakeman, 2008; Browder, Wakeman, Spooner, Ahlgrim-Delzell, & Algozzine, 2006) identified that prior to 2004, the content focus within the research represented a very narrow range of academics (i.e., sight words, money, time). In the past couple of years, a number of studies have extended beyond functional academic skills to content more typical of general education state standards. For example, Browder and colleagues (2012) implemented four math and four science units addressing national content standards and found increases in student test scores after instruction for students. In addition, Browder, Trela, and Jimenez (2007) examined the effect of a read-aloud using an adapted middle school novel with students with moderate to severe disabilities and autism. After the intervention, students were able to complete five skills successfully related to vocabulary and literacy development (i.e., identify vocabulary in text, read repeated story lines, participate in reading routines [e.g., turn the page], read new words, answer questions by referencing text). The emerging evidence supports the least dangerous assumption of teaching academic content standards to students within this population.

STATE CONTENT STANDARDS

Prior to the development of the CCSS, every state in the nation had either required or suggested standards for teachers to use to design instruction. Because these standards were state-specific, students in one state may or may not have had instruction on the same content in the same sequence as their neighbors in the next state. One of the No Child Left Behind Act of 2001 (PL 107-110) requirements for AA-AAS is that the assessment content must be aligned to the grade-level content. As Towles-Reeves, Kleinert, and Muhomba (2009) described, states have had the significant challenge to ensure that their alternate assessments and the other components within the system (e.g., extended content standards) were aligned to grade-level content standards. Many states developed several iterations of alternate or extended content standards that were designed specifically for students who participated in AA-AAS. Researchers found mixed outcomes for how well these early attempts of extending content aligned with the original standards (Flowers, Browder, & Ahlgrim-Delzell, 2006; Johnson & Arnold, 2004; Kohl, McLaughlin, & Nagle, 2006). Altman and colleagues (2010) surveyed state directors of special education, including eight unique states such as Guam. Twenty-seven responders indicated that they used extended or expanded academic content standards. Cameto and colleagues (2009) used data from the 2006–2007 school year to identify a number of features about the alternate assessment systems within each state and also found that many used extended content standards. (See the report for information about each state.) Some states now are in the process of creating extensions for the CCSS, for example Kansas (http://www.ksde.org/Default.aspx?tabid=2384), North Carolina (http://www.ncpublicschools.org/acre/standards/extended), and Colorado (http://www.cde.state.co.us/CoExtendedEO/StateStandards.asp).

CONCEPTUAL CONTENT ARRANGEMENTS

Although the CCSS will serve as the content base for the next generation of AA-AAS, states are seeking alternatives to simply extending the standards. One reason may be the mixed results for the degree of alignment between the extended standards and the general education standards (Flowers et al., 2006; Roach, Elliott, & Webb, 2005). Other conceptual arrangements of the content are being developed to inform instruction and assessment for students with significant cognitive disabilities. Two national consortia—Dynamic Learning Maps (http://dynamiclearningmaps.org) and the National Center and State Collaborative (NCSC; http://www.ncscpartners.org)—funded by the Office of Special Education Programs and consisting of state partners and psychometric and special education experts, have been charged to design new AA-AAS for use in the 2014–2015 school year. Both of these consortia are using new conceptual arrangements of how students learn the content to significantly guide the development of the AA-AAS. These include learning progressions and learning maps.

Learning Progressions

Although content standards illustrate what should be taught to students at each grade level or span, conceptual hypotheses about how students learn the content have begun to emerge. One trending topic is the development of learning progressions. Popham defined a learning progression as "a carefully sequenced set of building blocks that students must master en route to mastering a more distant curricular aim. These building blocks consist of subskills and bodies of enabling knowledge" (2007; p. 83). Learning progressions have been hypothesized, and at times tested, in several content areas, particularly science, for how typically developing students would learn the content (e.g., New Zealand Ministry of Education, 2007; Smith, Wiser, Anderson, & Krajcik, 2006; Steedle & Shavelson, 2009). One such learning progression that is being used by NCSC was developed by math and reading experts using existing research from each content area and was based on four guiding principles articulated by Hess (2008; http://www.naacpartners.org/

publications/ELA_LPF_12.2011_final.pdf [Hess, 2011]; http://www.naacpartners
.org/publications/IntroForMath_LPF.pdf [Hess, 2010]). Learning progressions are
not content standards; instead, they articulate the content knowledge or skills
needed for students to build understanding toward a larger curriculum or content
area goal.

Learning Maps

A second conceptual arrangement for content is a concept or learning map. Concept maps are common in education and can be used to graphically organize and
show relationships among concepts. McAleese (1998) provided substantial information about the definition, background, and models of concept maps. There is
some literature about students with and without learning disabilities regarding the
effectiveness of using concept maps to improve student learning (e.g., Guastello,
Beasely, & Sinatra, 2000; Strum & Rankin-Erickson, 2002), but there is little about
students with moderate and severe disabilities. Using the foundational underpin-
nings for conceptual maps, Dynamic Learning Maps created learning maps specifically designed for students who participate in an alternate assessment in which
related skills are linked to other skills. The maps are intended to illustrate how
skills work together across multiple pathways to reach curricular goals.

PURPOSE AND DEVELOPMENT OF
THE COMMON CORE STATE STANDARDS

The CCSS were written to represent the knowledge and skills necessary for all students, including those with intellectual disability, to be college and career ready.
Wakeman (2012) explained that the array of skills needed for college and career
readiness for students with moderate and severe disabilities not only includes academic content but also those skills identified within each student's individualized
education program (IEP). These may include daily living, self-help, communication,
social, and transition skills. Much of the focus within transitional efforts for students with significant disabilities in the past has been employment (Wagner, Newman, Cameto, Levine, & Garza, 2006). In the past few years, however, an increase
in college and postsecondary education opportunities for students with moderate
and severe intellectual disability has emerged (Hart & Grigal, 2010). Kearns and
colleagues (2010) identified five goals for helping students with significant cognitive disabilities become college and career ready, including 1) developing communicative competence by kindergarten; 2) cultivating fluency in math and ELA
for learning, leisure, or vocational purposes; 3) using age-appropriate social skills
and working in small groups; 4) demonstrating independent work and assistance-
seeking behaviors; and 5) accessing support systems. Given the purpose of the
CCSS, it is imperative that teachers of all students, including those with intellectual
disability, are able to use the CCSS as a primary resource to design instruction.

The authors of the standards provided several purposeful intentions that include
driving effective practice, aligning with college and work guidelines, targeting higher
order skills and rigorous content, promoting global competiveness, and following a
research and evidence base (see http://www.corestandards.org/assets/Criteria.pdf).
The authors intended to help frame a set of standards that allow students across the
country (in the states that choose to adopt the CCSS) to receive instruction based

on the same set of content and learning targets and, therefore, become globally com- *[Not how to teach but What]*
petitive. The CCSS focus on results rather than means. That is, the standards do not
provide instruction for *how* to teach, but instead represent *what* to teach in ELA
and mathematics. Each state has the ability to decide 1) whether or not to adopt the
CCSS, and 2) if they do adopt any portion of the CCSS (states can choose to adopt
only one content area), to enhance the CCSS with additional standards determined
to be essential for learning by students within their state.

Development of the CCSS was led by states (in collaboration with teachers,
administrators, and education experts) and coordinated by the National Governors Association Center for Best Practices (NGA) and the Council of Chief State
School Officers (CCSSO). Several items were used to help frame the content of the
CCSS, including research, stakeholder surveys, assessment data, and current state
standards, as well as the standards from other nations, the National Assessment of
Educational Progress ELA frameworks, and results of student performance studies. Criteria used to frame the development of the standards included

Alignment with expectations for college and career success

Clarity

Consistency across all states

Inclusion of content and the application of knowledge through higher-order skills

Improvement upon current state standards and standards of top-performing nations

Reality-based, for effective use in the classroom

Evidence and research-based (Council of Chief State School Officers, n.d.).

[Criteria]

As of this writing, 45 states, Washington D.C., and 4 U.S. territories have
adopted the CCSS. (See http://www.corestandards.org/in-the-states for the full
list.) In addition, individual states can decide to write alternate standards that are
linked to the CCSS and represent the state's judgment of the highest expectations
possible for students with moderate and severe disabilities. Wisconsin (http://dpi
.wi.gov/sped/assmt-ccee.html) and North Carolina (http://www.ncpublicschools
.org/acre/standards/extended) are just two states that have undertaken this type
of work. *[How many states now?]*

STRUCTURE OF THE COMMON CORE STATE STANDARDS

The following sections describe the structure of the content within the CCSS for
mathematics and English language arts.

Mathematics

The mathematics section in the CCSS is composed of two components: practice and
content. There are eight mathematical practices outlined as critical for instruction:

1. Make sense of problems and persevere in solving them.
2. Reason abstractly and quantitatively.
3. Construct viable arguments and critique the reasoning of others.

[8 Criteria for Math]

4. Model with mathematics.

5. Use appropriate tools strategically.

6. Attend to precision.

7. Look for and make use of structure.

8. Look for and express regularity in repeated reasoning. (National Governors Association Center for Best Practices, Council of Chief State School Officers, 2010)

These practices are composed of processes defined by the National Council of Teachers of Mathematics and by proficiencies defined by the National Research Council. The eight standards are written for all grades, as they represent processes all students should engage in within the context of mathematical content. (For a full description of each mathematical practice, please visit http://www.corestandards.org/Math/Practice.)

The content standards are written by grade level using domains, clusters, and individual standards for Grades K–8. In high school, the standards are no longer written by grade level but are instead written by conceptual categories that may align with courses (i.e., Number and Quantity, Algebra, Functions, Modeling, Geometry, Statistics and Probability). Figures 3.1–3.3 provide examples taken from the introductory section of the CCSS for Mathematics and views of the differing structures of the standards for mathematics in Grades K–8 and high school. Each domain represents the group of related standards. For example, in third grade there are five domains: Operations and Algebraic Thinking, Number and Operations in Base Ten, Numbers and Operations-Fractions, Measurement and Data, and Geometry (http://www.corestandards.org/Math/Content/3/introduction). Within each domain there is a cluster of standards. The individual standards taken as a group represent the cluster under each domain. For example, in the third-grade Measurement and Data

Standards define what students should understand and be able to do.

Clusters summarize groups of related standards. Note that standards from different clusters may sometimes be closely related, because mathematics is a connected subject.

Domains are larger groups of related standards. Standards from different domains may sometimes be closely related.

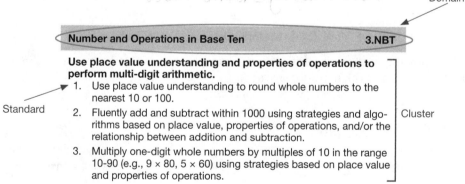

Figure 3.1. Illustration of how to read the math Common Core State Standards. (From National Governors Association Center for Best Practices, Council of Chief State School Officers. [2010]. *Common Core State Standards.* Washington, DC: Authors; reprinted by permission. Retrieved from http://www.corestandards.org/Math/Content/introduction/how-to-read-the-grade-level-standards)

Statistics and Probability	7.SP

Use random sampling to draw inferences about a population.

1. Understand that statistics can be used to gain information about a population by examining a sample of the population; generalizations about a population from a sample are valid only if the sample is representative of that population. Understand that random sampling tends to produce representative samples and support valid inferences.

2. Use data from a random sample to draw inferences about a population with an unknown characteristic of interest. Generate multiple samples (or simulated samples) of the same size to gauge the variation in estimates or predictions. *For example, estimate the mean word length in a book by randomly sampling words from the book; predict the winner of a school election based on randomly sampled survey data. Gauge how far off the estimate or prediction might be.*

Draw informal comparative inferences about two populations.

3. Informally assess the degree of visual overlap of two numerical data distributions with similar variabilities, measuring the difference between the centers by expressing it as a multiple of a measure of variability. *For example, the mean height of players on the basketball team is 10 cm greater than the mean height of players on the soccer team, about twice the variability (mean absolute deviation) on either team; on a dot plot, the separation between the two distributions of heights is noticeable.*

4. Use measures of center and measures of variability for numerical data from random samples to draw informal comparative inferences about two populations. *For example, decide whether the words in a chapter of a seventh-grade science book are generally longer than the words in a chapter of a fourth-grade science book.*

Investigate chance processes and develop, use, and evaluate probability models.

5. Understand that the probability of a chance event is a number between 0 and 1 that expresses the likelihood of the event occurring. Larger numbers indicate greater likelihood. A probability near 0 indicates an unlikely event, a probability around 1/2 indicates an event that is neither unlikely nor likely, and a probability near 1 indicates a likely event.

Figure 3.2. An example of the structure of the Common Core State Standards in K–8 mathematics. (From National Governors Association Center for Best Practices, Council of Chief State School Officers. [2010]. *Common Core State Standards.* Washington, DC: Authors; reprinted by permission. Retrieved from http://www.corestandards.org/assets/CCSSI_Math%20Standards.pdf)

domain there are four clusters of standards: 1) solve problems involving measurement and estimation of intervals of time, liquid volumes, and masses of objects; 2) represent and interpret data; 3) geometric measurement: understand concepts of area and relate area to multiplication and to addition; and 4) geometric measurement: recognize perimeter as an attribute of plane figures and distinguish between linear and area measures (http://www.corestandards.org/Math/Content/3/MD). And, within each cluster there are individual standards. Following the same example, the Represent and Interpret Data cluster includes two standards:

1. 3.MD.B3 Draw a scaled picture graph and a scaled bar graph to represent a data set with several categories. Solve one- and two-step "how many more" and "how many less" problems using information presented in scaled bar graphs. For example, draw a bar graph in which each square in the bar might represent 5 pets.

2. 3.MD.B4 Generate measurement data by measuring lengths using rulers marked with halves and fourths of an inch. Show the data by making a line plot, where the horizontal scale is marked off in appropriate units- whole numbers, halves, or quarters. (National Governors Association Center for Best Practices, Council of Chief State School Officers, 2010; http://www.corestandards.org/Math/Content/3/MD)

Seeing Structure in Expressions

- Interpret the structure of expressions.

    1. Interpret expressions that represent a quantity in terms of its context.
        a. Interpret parts of an expression, such as terms, factors, and coefficients.
        b. Interpret complicated expressions by viewing one or more of their parts as a single entity. *For example, interpret $P(1 + r)^n$ as the product of P and a factor not depending on P.*

    2. Use the structure of an expression to identify ways to rewrite it. *For example, see $x^4 - y^4$ as $(x^2)^2 - (y^2)^2$, thus recognizing it as a difference of squares that can be factored as $(x^2 - y^2)(x^2 + y^2)$.*

- Write expressions in equivalent forms to solve problems.

    3. Choose and produce an equivalent form of an expression to reveal and explain properties of the quantity represented by the expression.
        a. Factor a quadratic expression to reveal the zeros of the function it defines.
        b. Complete the square in a quadratic expression to reveal the maximum or minimum value of the function it defines.
        c. Use the properties of exponents to transform expressions for exponential functions. *For example, the expression 1.15^t can be rewritten as $(1.15^{1/12})^{12t} \approx 1.012^{12t}$ to reveal the approximate equivalent monthly interest rate if the annual rate is 15%.*

    4. Derive the formula for the sum of a finite geometric series (when the common ratio is not 1), and use the formula to solve problems. *For example, calculate mortgage payments.*

Figure 3.3.   An example of the structure of Common Core State Standards for high school mathematics. (From National Governors Association Center for Best Practices, Council of Chief State School Officers. [2010]. *Common Core State Standards*. Washington, DC: Authors; reprinted by permission. Retrieved from http://www.corestandards.org/assets/CCSSI_Math%20Standards.pdf)

English Language Arts

College and career readiness anchor standards in Reading, Writing, Speaking and Listening, and Language serve as the framework or structure for ELA in the CCSS. These anchor standards are identical for every grade but vary in number depending on the domain (i.e., there are 10 in Reading and Writing but only 6 in Speaking and Listening and 6 in Language; see Figure 3.4 for an example). Table 3.1 lists the categories for anchor standards for each domain within ELA. Each set of standards are written in K–5 and 6–12 spans, with individual standards at each grade level, except in high school, in which the standards are grouped into grade bands (i.e., 9–10 and 11–12). See Figures 3.5 and 3.6 for examples of how the K–5 and 6–12 strands are structured for ELA. Grades 6–12 include additional grade-level standards for Literacy in History/Social Studies/Science and Technical Subjects. Through these standards, the CCSS emphasize the need for students to learn to read, write, speak, listen, and use language in content areas other than the traditional English class. The CCSS in ELA also include three appendices of resource material. These will be discussed in detail later in this chapter.

There are a number of important factors to consider within the CCSS for ELA. First, though the standards are divided into Reading, Writing, Speaking and Listening, and Language strands, there are intentional connections across the strands. For example, Writing Standard 5 reads, "With guidance and support from peers and

College and Career Readiness Anchor Standards for Reading

The K–5 standards on the following pages define what students should understand and be able to do by the end of each grade. They correspond to the College and Career Readiness (CCR) anchor standards below by number. The CCR and grade-specific standards are necessary complements—the former providing broad standards, the latter providing additional specificity—that together define the skills and understandings that all students must demonstrate.

Key Ideas and Details

1. Read closely to determine what the text says explicitly and to make logical inferences from it; cite specific textual evidence when writing or speaking to support conclusions drawn from the text.
2. Determine central ideas or themes of a text and analyze their development; summarize the key supporting details and ideas.
3. Analyze how and why individuals, events, and ideas develop and interact over the course of a text.

Craft and Structure

4. Interpret words and phrases as they are used in a text, including determining technical, connotative, and figurative meanings, and analyze how specific word choices shape meaning or tone.
5. Analyze the structure of texts, including how specific sentences, paragraphs, and larger portions of the text (e.g., a section, chapter, scene, or stanza) relate to each other and the whole.
6. Assess how point of view or purpose shapes the content and style of a text.

Integration of Knowledge and Ideas

7. Integrate and evaluate content presented in diverse media and formats, including visually and quantitatively, as well as in words.*
8. Delineate and evaluate the argument and specific claims in a text, including the validity of the reasoning as well as the relevance and sufficiency of the evidence.
9. Analyze how two or more texts address similar themes or topics in order to build knowledge or to compare the approaches the authors take.

Range of Reading and Level of Text Complexity

10. Read and comprehend complex literary and informational texts independently and proficiently.

*Please see "Research to Build and Present Knowledge" in Writing and "Comprehension and Collaboration" in Speaking and Listening for additional standards relevant to gathering, assessing, and applying information from print and digital sources.

Note on range and content of student reading

To build a foundation for college and career readiness, students must read widely and deeply from among a broad range of high-quality, increasingly challenging literary and informational texts. Through extensive reading of stories, dramas, poems, and myths from diverse cultures and different time periods, students gain literary and cultural knowledge as well as familiarity with various text structures and elements. By reading texts in history/social studies, science, and other disciplines, students build a foundation of knowledge in these fields that will also give them the background to be better readers in all content areas. Students can only gain this foundation when the curriculum is intentionally and coherently structured to develop rich content knowledge within and across grades. Students also acquire the habits of reading independently and closely, which are essential to their future success.

Figure 3.4. College and career anchor standards for reading. (From National Governors Association Center for Best Practices, Council of Chief State School Officers. [2010]. *Common Core State Standards.* Washington, DC: Authors. Retrieved from http://www.corestandards.org/assets/CCSSI_ELA%20Standards.pdf)

Table 3.1.   English language arts anchor standards

Reading
- Key Ideas and Details
- Craft and Structure
- Integration of Knowledge and Ideas
- Range of Reading and Level of Text Complexity

Writing
- Text Types and Purposes
- Production and Distribution of Writing
- Research to Build and Present Knowledge
- Range of Writing

Listening and Speaking
- Comprehension and Collaboration
- Presentation of Knowledge and Ideas

Language
- Conventions of Standard English
- Knowledge of Language
- Vocabulary Acquisition and Use

Source: National Governors Association Center for Best Practices, Council of Chief State School Officers (2010).

① Conventions of English

② Research skills and media

③ Shared responsibility pertaining to students' literacy

adults, develop and strengthen writing as needed by planning, revising, and editing" (http://www.corestandards.org/ELA-Literacy/CCRA/W). In order to meet this standard a student must also meet Language Standards 1–3 that focus on conventions of standard English (http://www.corestandards.org/ELA-Literacy/CCRA/L).

Another point of interest in the CCSS is the emphasis on research skills and media, which are embedded throughout the standards. The 21st century skills demand that students be able to function in a technological society. Students must be able to gather, comprehend, and synthesize information in order to solve problems.

Last, is the idea of the shared responsibility pertaining to students' literacy development. The standards support the notion that students' literacy development will need to occur across content areas. This is made clear through the addition of grade-level standards for History, Social Studies, Science, and Technical Subjects that are seen through the lens of ELA (e.g., RH.6-8.8: "Distinguish among fact, opinion and reasoned judgment in a text" [http://www.corestandards.org/ELA-Literacy/RH/6-8]; RST.9-10.3: "Follow precisely a complex multistep procedure when carrying out experiments, taking measurements, or performing technical tasks, attending to special cases or exceptions defined in the text" [http://www.corestandards.org/ELA-Literacy/RST/9-10]).

THE NEED FOR ADDITIONAL SUPPORT

It is clear that Sara from the opening vignette needs resources to help her teach the CCSS. She is not alone. Some evidence (Browder, Karvonen, Davis, Fallin, & Courtade-Little, 2005; Jimenez, Mims, & Browder, 2012) suggests that the capacity of a teacher to plan instruction based on academic content can be positively influenced by effective professional development. The need for professional development for all teachers regarding the CCSS is monumental, but such development may not always occur or may not occur in a timely fashion. Teachers of students within this population have indicated that they lack training regarding academic content and are not receiving professional development about how to teach it (e.g., Cameto

→ Need more professional development for teachers in Spec. Ed.

The following standards for K–5 offer a focus for instruction each year to help ensure that students gain adequate mastery of a range of skills and applications. *Students advancing through the grades are expected to meet each year's grade-specific standards and retain or further develop skills and understandings mastered in preceding grades.*

Kindergartners:	Grade 1 students:	Grade 2 students:
Comprehension and Collaboration		

1. Participate in collaborative conversations with diverse partners about *kindergarten topics and texts* with peers and adults in small and larger groups.
  a. Follow agreed-upon rules for discussions (e.g., listening to others and taking turns speaking about the topics and texts under discussion).
  b. Continue a conversation through multiple exchanges.
	1. Participate in collaborative conversations with diverse partners about *grade 1 topics and texts* with peers and adults in small and larger groups.
	  a. Follow agreed-upon rules for discussions (e.g., listening to others with care, speaking one at a time about the topics and texts under discussion).
	  b. Build on others' talk in conversations by responding to the comments of others through multiple exchanges.
	  c. Ask questions to clear up any confusion about the topics and texts under discussion.
		1. Participate in collaborative conversations with diverse partners about *grade 2 topics and texts* with peers and adults in small and larger groups.
		  a. Follow agreed-upon rules for discussions (e.g., gaining the floor in respectful ways, listening to others with care, speaking one at a time about the topics and texts under discussion).
		  b. Build on others' talk in conversations by linking their comments to the remarks of others.
		  c. Ask for clarification and further explanation as needed about the topics and texts under discussion.

2. Confirm understanding of a text read aloud or information presented orally or through other media by asking and answering questions about key details and requesting clarification if something is not understood.	2. Ask and answer questions about key details in a text read aloud or information presented orally or through other media.	2. Recount or describe key ideas or details from a text read aloud or information presented orally or through other media.
3. Ask and answer questions in order to seek help, get information, or clarify something that is not understood.	3. Ask and answer questions about what a speaker says in order to gather additional information or clarify something that is not understood.	3. Ask and answer questions about what a speaker says in order to clarify comprehension, gather additional information, or deepen understanding of a topic or issue.
Presentation of Knowledge and Ideas		
4. Describe familiar people, places, things, and events and, with prompting and support, provide additional detail.	4. Describe people, places, things, and events with relevant details, expressing ideas and feelings clearly.	4. Tell a story or recount an experience with appropriate facts and relevant, descriptive details, speaking audibly in coherent sentences.
5. Add drawings or other visual displays to descriptions as desired to provide additional detail.	5. Add drawings or other visual displays to descriptions when appropriate to clarify ideas, thoughts, and feelings.	5. Create audio recordings of stories or poems; add drawings or other visual displays to stories or recounts of experiences when appropriate to clarify ideas, thoughts, and feelings.
6. Speak audibly and express thoughts, feelings, and ideas clearly.	6. Produce complete sentences when appropriate to task and situation. (See grade 1 Language standards 1 and 3 on page 26 for specific expectations.)	6. Produce complete sentences when appropriate to task and situation in order to provide requested detail or clarification. (See grade 2 Language standards 1 and 3 on page 26 for specific expectations.)

Figure 3.5. An example of the structure of the Common Core State Standards for K–8 English language arts. (From National Governors Association Center for Best Practices, Council of Chief State School Officers. [2010]. *Common Core State Standards.* Washington, DC: Authors; reprinted by permission. Retrieved from http://www.corestandards .org/assets/CCSSI_ELA%20Standards.pdf)

The CCR anchor standards and high school grade-specific standards work in tandem to define college and career readiness expectations—the former providing broad standards, the latter providing additional specificity.

Grades 9–10 students:	Grades 11–12 students:
Key Ideas and Details	
1. Cite strong and thorough textual evidence to support analysis of what the text says explicitly as well as inferences drawn from the text.	1. Cite strong and thorough textual evidence to support analysis of what the text says explicitly as well as inferences drawn from the text, including determining where the text leaves matters uncertain.
2. Determine a theme or central idea of a text and analyze in detail its development over the course of the text, including how it emerges and is shaped and refined by specific details; provide an objective summary of the text.	2. Determine two or more themes or central ideas of a text and analyze their development over the course of the text, including how they interact and build on one another to produce a complex account; provide an objective summary of the text.
3. Analyze how complex characters (e.g., those with multiple or conflicting motivations) develop over the course of a text, interact with other characters, and advance the plot or develop the theme.	3. Analyze the impact of the author's choices regarding how to develop and relate elements of a story or drama (e.g., where a story is set, how the action is ordered, how the characters are introduced and developed).
Craft and Structure	
4. Determine the meaning of words and phrases as they are used in the text, including figurative and connotative meanings; analyze the cumulative impact of specific word choices on meaning and tone (e.g., how the language evokes a sense of time and place; how it sets a formal or informal tone).	4. Determine the meaning of words and phrases as they are used in the text, including figurative and connotative meanings; analyze the impact of specific word choices on meaning and tone, including words with multiple meanings or language that is particularly fresh, engaging, or beautiful. (Include Shakespeare as well as other authors.)
5. Analyze how an author's choices concerning how to structure a text, order events within it (e.g., parallel plots), and manipulate time (e.g., pacing, flashbacks) create such effects as mystery, tension, or surprise.	5. Analyze how an author's choices concerning how to structure specific parts of a text (e.g., the choice of where to begin or end a story, the choice to provide a comedic or tragic resolution) contribute to its overall structure and meaning as well as its aesthetic impact.
6. Analyze a particular point of view or cultural experience reflected in a work of literature from outside the United States, drawing on a wide reading of world literature.	6. Analyze a case in which grasping point of view requires distinguishing what is directly stated in a text from what is really meant (e.g., satire, sarcasm, irony, or understatement).
Integration of Knowledge and Ideas	
7. Analyze the representation of a subject or a key scene in two different artistic mediums, including what is emphasized or absent in each treatment (e.g., Auden's "Musée des Beaux Arts" and Breughel's *Landscape with the Fall of Icarus*).	7. Analyze multiple interpretations of a story, drama, or poem (e.g., recorded or live production of a play or recorded novel or poetry), evaluating how each version interprets the source text. (Include at least one play by Shakespeare and one play by an American dramatist.)
8. (Not applicable to literature)	8. (Not applicable to literature)
9. Analyze how an author draws on and transforms source material in a specific work (e.g., how Shakespeare treats a theme or topic from Ovid or the Bible or how a later author draws on a play by Shakespeare).	9. Demonstrate knowledge of eighteenth-, nineteenth- and early-twentieth-century foundational works of American literature, including how two or more texts from the same period treat similar themes or topics.
Range of Reading and Level of Text Complexity	
10. By the end of grade 9, read and comprehend literature, including stories, dramas, and poems, in the grades 9–10 text complexity band proficiently, with scaffolding as needed at the high end of the range. By the end of grade 10, read and comprehend literature, including stories, dramas, and poems, at the high end of the grades 9–10 text complexity band independently and proficiently.	10. By the end of grade 11, read and comprehend literature, including stories, dramas, and poems, in the grades 11–CCR text complexity band proficiently, with scaffolding as needed at the high end of the range. By the end of grade 12, read and comprehend literature, including stories, dramas, and poems, at the high end of the grades 11–CCR text complexity band independently and proficiently.

Figure 3.6. An example of the structure of the Common Core State Standards for high school English language arts. (From National Governors Association Center for Best Practices, Council of Chief State School Officers. [2010]. *Common Core State Standards.* Washington, DC: Authors; reprinted by permission. Retrieved from http://www.core standards.org/assets/CCSSI_ELA%20Standards.pdf)

et al., 2010; Karvonen et al., 2011). This section provides information regarding resources and support material both within the CCSS and from external sources.

Support from Within the Common Core State Standards

User-friendly resources for the CCSS are quickly being developed. Some of the primary resources can be found within the CCSS. The CCSS web site includes a page dedicated to parent, teacher, and administrator resources (http://www.core standards.org/resources). One noteworthy resource located on this web site is titled "Understanding the Standards." This document links viewers to a YouTube site (http://www.youtube.com/user/TheHuntInstitute#g/u) that displays a library of CCSS-related videos. These videos range from general information (e.g., Common Core State Standards: A New Foundation for Student Success; also available in Spanish) to content-specific information (e.g., Literary Non-Fiction in the Classroom: Opening New Worlds for Students) to information on special populations (e.g., Tri-State Summit: Meeting the Needs of Disadvantaged Youths in Afterschool Hours).

The standards themselves include resources that provide additional information to support understanding and implementation of the standards. For example, in mathematics, a glossary is provided to define key terms used throughout Grades K–12. The mathematics section also provides tables showing common addition, subtraction, multiplication, and division situations; properties of operations; equality; and inequality.

glossary provided in Math.

Both the ELA and the mathematics standards have supporting appendices. The mathematics section includes one appendix: Designing High School Mathematics Courses Based on the Common Core State Standards (http://www.core standards.org/assets/CCSSI_Mathematics_Appendix_A.pdf). The ELA section includes three appendices, all of which have been highly publicized as crucial resources for successful implementation of the standards and are described in the following sections.

Supported appendix for ELA & Math.

Appendix A: Research Supporting Key Elements of the Standards, Glossary of Terms ELA Appendix A contains a wealth of research-based information related to language arts. To supplement the Reading Standards: Foundations Skills, figures are included that illustrate phoneme–grapheme correspondences and provide consonant and vowel graphemes with definitions and examples. Additional information in Appendix A includes a progression of phonological awareness skills and phoneme awareness skills; a summary of writing, speaking, and listening and its role in literacy; and finally the conventions of language. The appendix also includes a glossary of key terms. User-friendly tables are provided to show how certain skills progress across grades (e.g., language, phoneme awareness) as well as figures providing word examples for each consonant and vowel sound (e.g., /n/ = *nice, knight, gnat*).

A large portion of Appendix A is dedicated to text complexity. Text complexity is emphasized throughout the reading standards as well as in other CCSS documents in which there is a belief that students need to be able to read and comprehend more complex texts (Calkins, Ehrenworth, & Lehman, 2012). Appendix A notes research that shows a gap between the level of reading required for students after high school, entering college or the work force, and the level of reading that is currently required for high school students (http://www.corestandards.org/assets/ E0813_Appendix_A_New_Research_on_Text_Complexity.pdf). Because the CCSS are not a curriculum and therefore do not provide the specific text that students will read, Appendix A provides a three-part model for measuring text complexity. This model consists of qualitative measures, quantitative measures, and reader and task considerations. In addition to Appendix A, David Coleman and Susan Pimentel, contributing authors of the CCSS, also developed the Revised Publishers' Criteria for the Common Core State Standards in English Language Arts and Literacy, Grades 3–12 (http://www.corestandards.org/assets/Publishers_Criteria_for_3-12. pdf). This document provides criteria for text selection, questions and tasks, academic vocabulary, and writing to sources and research.

Appendix B: Text Exemplars and Sample Performance Tasks   Appendix B consists of text exemplars illustrating the complexity, quality, and range of reading appropriate for various grade levels with accompanying sample performance tasks. This appendix is provided in order to assist districts and teachers when selecting texts. Included in this appendix is a list of text by grade band. Each grade band is divided into the text types that are required in the standards. These text exemplars represent a range of text complexity even within grade bands (Calkins et al., 2012). For example, within the Grade 2–3 band, two books listed are *Poppleton in Winter* (Rylant, 2001) and *Sarah, Plain and Tall* (MacLachlan, 1985). *Poppleton in Winter* is generally considered on target for the end of first grade, whereas *Sarah, Plain and Tall* is considered on target for the end of third grade. With books listed in the same grade band differing in their difficulty levels teachers will need to pay close attention to the overall complexity of text (Calkins et al., 2012).

Appendix C: Samples of Student Writing   Appendix C includes annotated samples of student writing. These writing samples demonstrate the level of performance required to meet the standards. Samples are provided for each grade level, K–12. In addition, because the CCSS requires that students meet standards for narrative, informational, and persuasive writing, this appendix provides examples of student writing for different purposes at each grade level.

Additional Support for the Common Core State Standards

Expected implementation of the CCSS will begin with the 2014–2015 school year; however, professional development and the development of teacher resources have been underway for some time. For now, many resources can be found online with a number of these resources being created by the CCSS authors themselves (see For Further Information at the end of this chapter for a list of online resources that can be accessed at no cost). Race to the Top funds have been used within a number of states to develop tools and resources including video libraries, sample lesson plans, and unpacking documents. A first step for teachers to promote understanding and use of the CCSS should be a review of state and locally developed resources. One state that has been deeply involved in pilot implementation of the CCSS and has a host of resources is New York. New York has established an extensive video library that was completed in collaboration with David Coleman, a contributing author on the CCSS (http://www.engageny.org). Several teachers from Queens have participated in videos illustrating how they have implemented the CCSS.

Although not a traditional resource, these videos are useful in that they show real teachers and students engaging in lessons that align with the CCSS. There also are videos for all grade spans on YouTube (e.g., to view the high school pilot program, visit http://www.youtube.com/watch?v=jiNLkgfniZM).

In addition, a number of states have developed unpacking documents that are designed to support teacher understanding. The unpacking documents describe in detail what students are expected to do in relation to that standard and provide an instructional example for the standard. One benefit of the unpacking documents is the boost they provide for teacher understanding of content. Many teachers, especially elementary teachers, will struggle with the math content in the CCSS (Sawchuk, 2012) and will find the unpacking document a great tool for developing their own understanding of what the standards entail. In one example, North Carolina has unpacked the content for all grades in mathematics and ELA. Figure 3.7 shows a sample of North Carolina's math unpacking document (the complete document can be found at http://www.ncpublicschools.org/acre/standards/common-core-tools/).

THE COMMON CORE STATE STANDARDS IN PRACTICE

Other chapters in this book provide information about designing lessons that target specific CCSS. This section provides examples of how to translate the content within specific CCSS. In math, we will focus on fifth grade. The first standard, 5.OA.3, is "Generate two numerical patterns using two given rules." This standard could be completed using word problems with tables of data and rules, tables with data to determine the rules, or tables without data and rules provided. This information contributes to students' knowledge of the coordinate plane and builds toward the foundation for ratios and proportions in later grades. In Number and Operations Base Ten, 5.NBT.7 ("Add, subtract, multiply, and divide decimals to hundredths, using concrete models or drawings and strategies based on place value, properties of operations, and/or the relationship between addition and subtraction") builds on previously learned place value concepts of composing and decomposing whole numbers into decimals. Students can use base ten blocks that represent decimals, fraction strips to the tenth place that can be converted to decimals, pictorial models, number lines and other graphic organizers, written numerals, and expanded notation to complete operations. In addition, rounding and estimations strategies can be used to check answers. In Number and Operations Fractions, 5.NF.1 ("Add and subtract fractions with unlike denominators") is a common learning target for fifth-grade students that builds on adding fractions with common denominators from previous grades. The use of visual diagrams and models significantly aid students to understand the problem and the proportions. Students can also use previously learned skills of finding equivalent fractions or multiplication to find a common denominator. In Measurement and Data, volume is an important concept within fifth grade and is found in three standards. In 5.MD.4 ("Measure volumes by counting unit cubes, using cubic cm, cubic in, cubic ft, and improvised units") students can use a variety of models to fill space in both solid and liquid forms. Once students have the concept, different representations—in either pictorial or numeric forms—can be used. Finally, Geometry, 5.G.4 ("Classify two-dimensional figures in a hierarchy based on properties") represents content spiraling from previous grades. Figures from fourth grade are revisited and evaluated based on their

How does this happen with "my" students?

Ratios and Proportional Relationships
6.RP

Common Core Cluster

Understand ratio concepts and use ratio reasoning to solve problems.

Mathematically proficient students communicate precisely by engaging in discussion about their reasoning using appropriate mathematical language. The terms students should learn to use with increasing precision with this cluster are: **ratio, equivalent ratios, tape diagram, unit rate, part-to-part, part-to-whole, percent**

A detailed progression of the Ratios and Proportional Relationships domain with examples can be found at http://commoncoretools.wordpress.com/

Common Core Standard	Unpacking What does this standard mean that a student will know and be able to do?
6.RP.1 Understand the concept of a ratio and use ratio language to describe a ratio relationship between two quantities. *For example, "The ratio of wings to beaks in the bird house at the zoo was 2:1, because for every 2 wings there was 1 beak." "For every vote candidate A received, candidate C received nearly three votes."*	**6.RP.1** A ratio is the comparison of two quantities or measures. The comparison can be part-to-whole (ratio of guppies to all fish in an aquarium) or part-to-part (ratio of guppies to goldfish). Example 1: A comparison of 6 guppies and 9 goldfish could be expressed in any of the following forms: $\frac{6}{9}$, 6 to 9 or 6:9. If the number of guppies is represented by black circles and the number of goldfish is represented by white circles, this ratio could be modeled as ●● ●● ●● OOO OOO OOO These values can be regrouped into 2 black circles (goldfish) to 3 white circles (guppies), which would reduce the ratio to, $\frac{2}{3}$, 2 to 3 or 2:3. ●● ●● ●● OOO OOO OOO Students should be able to identify and describe any ratio using "For every _____, there are _____." In the example above, the ratio could be expressed saying, "For every 2 goldfish, there are 3 guppies".
6.RP.2 Understand the concept of a unit rate a/b associated with a ratio a:b with b ≠ 0, and use rate language in the context of a ratio relationship.	**6.RP.2** A unit rate expresses a ratio as part-to-one, comparing a quantity in terms of one unit of another quantity. Common unit rates are cost per item or distance per time.

6th Grade Mathematics • Unpacked Content

February, 2012

Figure 3.7. Sample unpacked standard from North Carolina. (From North Carolina Department of Public Instruction. [n.d.]. *NC common core instructional support tools.* Retrieved from http://www.ncpublicschools.org/acre/standards/common-core-tools)

common properties and relationship to one another. Visuals with and without high-lights and graphic organizers can contribute to students building hierarchies.

In ELA, we will focus on sixth grade. It should be noted that in ELA it is common for skills to be taught across text types. For example, 6.RL.1 and 6.RI.1 both read, "Cite textual evidence to support analysis of what the text says explicitly as well as inferences drawn from the text." Not only is it appropriate to teach this skill using various types of literary genres (e.g., narrative, poetry, myths), it should also be taught using a variety of informational texts. Although students have already become accustomed to making inferences, citing textual evidence is first taught in the sixth grade and continues through high school. This foundational skill can be taught through teacher modeling and guided practice. Group activities such as think/pair/share can also be used. When making inferences, students may use graphic organizers to combine textual content as well as their own prior knowledge to arrive at new information in the form of inferences. Two standards focus on the skill of comparing and contrasting information: 6.RL.7 ("Compare and contrast the experience of reading a story, drama, or poem to listening to or viewing an audio, video, or live version of the text") and 6.RL.9 ("Compare and contrast texts in different forms or genres [e.g., stories and poems; historical novels and fantasy stories]"). Although both skills can be taught using a Venn diagram, 6.RL.7 allows teachers to choose audio and/or video materials based on student interest. Standard 6.RL.9 may allow teachers to make connections between literary text and informational text. As is often the case in ELA, multiple standards are accessed within each lesson. When teaching any of the previously discussed standards, Speaking and Listening standards such as 6.SL.1 ("Engage effectively in a range of collaborative discussions [one-to-one, in groups, and teacher led]") can also be a focus of instruction. In addition, instruction can be extended to include writing standards. Standard 6.W.3 ("Write narratives to develop real or imagined experiences or events using effective technique, relevant descriptive details, and well-structured event sequence") can be taught using narrative text as source material. Students use graphic organizers (e.g., story maps) not only to map the events in a text but also to organize their own writing. Other graphic organizers (e.g., character analyses) can be used to help students choose relevant details and sensory language.

SUMMARY

Sara's experiences and feelings are not uncommon for teachers of students with disabilities. Although she has some promising practices and opportunities (i.e., part of the fourth-grade planning team, a PLC with other teachers of students with disabilities), the need to develop first an understanding of how to read the CCSS, to then understand the content within the CCSS, and to then finally design effective instruction based on the CCSS is critical.

#1: Learn to Read CCSS
#2: Understand content. of CCSS
#3: design effective instruction

REFERENCES

Altman, J.R., Lazarus, S.S., Quenemoen, R.F., Kearns, J., Quenemoen, M., & Thurlow, M.L. (2010). *2009 survey of states: Accomplishments and new issues at the end of a decade of change.* Minneapolis: University of Minnesota, National Center on Educational Outcomes.

Browder, D.M., Karvonen, M., Davis, S., Fallin, K., & Courtade-Little, G. (2005). The impact of teacher training on state alternate assessment scores. *Exceptional Children, 71,* 267–282.

Browder, D.M., Spooner, F., Ahlgrim-Delzell, L., Harris, A., & Wakeman, S.Y. (2008). A meta-analysis on teaching mathematics to students with significant cognitive disabilities. *Exceptional Children, 74,* 407–432.

Browder, D.M., Trela, K., Courtade, G.R., Jimenez, B.A., Knight, V., & Flowers, C. (2012). Teaching mathematics and science standards to students with moderate and severe developmental disabilities. *The Journal of Special Education, 46,* 26–35.

Browder, D., Trela, K., & Jimenez, B. (2007). Training teachers to follow a task analysis to engage middle school students with moderate and severe developmental disabilities in grade appropriate literature. *Focus on Autism & Other Developmental Disabilities, 22,* 206–219.

Browder, D.M., Wakeman, S.Y., Spooner, F., Ahlgrim-Delzell, L., & Algozzine, B. (2006). Research on reading instruction for individuals with significant cognitive disabilities. *Exceptional Children, 72,* 392–408.

Calkins, L., Ehrenworth, M., & Lehman, C. (2012). *Pathways to the common core: Accelerating achievement.* Portsmouth, NH: Heineman.

Cameto, R., Bergland, F., Knokey, A.-M., Nagle, K. M., Sanford, C., Kalb, S.C., ... & Ortega, M. (2010). *Teacher perspectives of school-level implementation of alternate assessments for students with significant cognitive disabilities. A report from the National Study on Alternate Assessments* (NCSER 2010-3007). Menlo Park, CA: SRI International.

Cameto, R., Knokey, A.-M., Nagle, K., Sanford, C., Blackorby, J., Sinclair, B., & Riley, D. (2009). *State profiles on alternate assessments based on alternate achievement standards: A report from the National Study on Alternate Assessments* (NCSER 2009-3013). Menlo Park, CA: SRI International.

Council of Chief State School Officers (n.d.). *Frequently asked questions.* Retrieved from http://www.corestandards.org/resources/frequently-asked-questions

Flowers, C., Browder, D.M., & Ahlgrim-Delzell, L. (2006). An analysis of three states' alignment between language arts and mathematics standards and alternate assessments. *Exceptional Children, 72,* 201–215.

Guastello, E.F., Beasely, T.M., & Sinatra, R.C. (2000). Concept mapping effects on science content comprehension of low-achieving inner-city seventh grader. *Remedial & Special Education, 21,* 356–365.

Hart, D., & Grigal, M. (2010). The spectrum of options—Current practices. In M. Grigal & D. Hart (Eds.), *Think college! Postsecondary education options for students with intellectual disabilities* (pp. 49–86). Baltimore, MD: Paul H. Brookes Publishing Co.

Hess, K. (2008). *Developing and using learning progressions as a schema for measuring progress.* Retrieved from http://www.nciea.org/publications/CCSSO2_KH08.pdf

Hess, K. (2010). *Learning progressions frameworks designed for use with the Common Core State Standards in mathematics K-12 (v.2).* Dover, NH: National Alternate Assessment Center at the University of Kentucky and the National Center for the Improvement of Educational Assessment. Retrieved from http://www.naacpartners.org/publications/IntroForMath_LPF.pdf

Hess, K. (2011). *Learning progressions frameworks designed for use with the Common Core State Standards in English language arts & literacy K-12.* Retrieved from http://www.naacpartners.org/publications/ELA_LPF_12.2011_final.pdf

Jimenez, B.A., Mims, P.J., & Browder, D.M. (2012). Data-based decisions guidelines for teachers of students with severe intellectual and developmental disabilities. *Education and Training in Autism & Developmental Disabilities, 47,* 407–413.

Johnson, E., & Arnold, N. (2004). Validating an alternate assessment. *Remedial & Special Education, 25,* 266–275.

Karvonen, M., Wakeman, S.Y., Browder, D.M., Rogers, M.A.S., & Flowers, C. (2011). *Academic curriculum for students with significant cognitive disabilities: Special education teacher perspectives a decade after IDEA 1997.* Retrieved from ERIC database. (ED521407)

Kearns, J., Kleinert, H., Harrison, B., Sheppard-Jones, K., Hall, M., & Jones, M. (2010). *What does 'college and career ready' mean for students with significant cognitive disabilities?* Lexington: University of Kentucky.

Kohl, F.L., McLaughlin, M.J., & Nagle, K. (2006). Alternate achievement standards and assessments: A descriptive investigation of 16 states. *Exceptional Children, 73,* 107–123.

MacLachlan, P. (1985). *Sarah, plain and tall.* New York, NY: HarperCollins.

McAleese, R. (1998). The knowledge arena as an extension to the concept map: Reflection action. *Interactive Learning Environments, 6,* 251–272.

National Governors Association Center for Best Practices, Council of Chief State School Officers. (2010). *Common Core State Standards.* Washington, DC: Authors. Retrieved from http://www.corestandards.org/

New Zealand Ministry of Education. (2007). *Literacy learning progressions: Meeting the reading and writing demands of the curriculum.* Wellington, New Zealand: Learning Media Limited.

No Child Left Behind Act of 2001, PL 107-110, 115 Stat. 1425, 20 U.S.C. §§ 6301 *et seq.*

North Carolina Department of Public Instruction. (n.d.). *NC common core instructional support tools.* Retrieved from http://www.ncpublicschools.org/acre/standards/common-core-tools

Popham, J. (2007). The lowdown on learning progressions. *The Prepared Graduate, 64*(7), 83–84.

Roach, A.T., Elliott, S.N., & Webb, N.L. (2005). Alignment of an alternate assessment with state academic standards: Evidence for the content validity of the Wisconsin alternate assessment. *The Journal of Special Education, 38,* 218–231.

Rylant, C. (2001). *Poppleton in winter.* New York, NY: Scholastic Inc./Blue Sky Press.

Ryndak, D.L., Moore, M.A., Orlando, A., & Delano, M. (2009–2010). Access to the general curriculum: The mandate and role of context in research-based practice for students with extensive support needs. *Research & Practice for Persons with Severe Disabilities, 34,* 199–213.

Sawchuk, S. (2012). Many teachers not ready for the Common Core. *Education Digest, 78*(2), 16–22.

Smith, C.L., Wiser, M., Anderson, C.W., & Krajcik, J. (2006). Implications of research on children's learning for standards and assessment: A proposed learning progression for matter and the atomic-molecular theory. *Measurement, 4,* 1–98.

Steedle, J.T., & Shavelson, R.J. (2009) Supporting valid interpretations of learning progression level diagnoses. *Journal of Research in Science Teaching, 46,* 699–715.

Strum, J.M., & Rankin-Erickson, J.L. (2002). Effects of hand-drawn and computer-generated concept mapping on the expository writing of middle school students with learning disabilities. *Learning Disabilities Research & Practice, 17,* 124–140.

Towles-Reeves, E., Kleinert, H.L., & Muhomba, M. (2009). Alternate assessment: Have we learned anything new? *Exceptional Children, 75,* 233–252.

Wagner, M., Newman, L., Cameto, R., Levine, P., & Garza, N. (2006). *An overview of findings from wave 2 of the National Longitudinal Transition Study-2 (NLTS2).* (NCSER 2006-3004). Menlo Park, CA: SRI International.

Wakeman, S. (2012, Fall). Why are the Common Core State Standards important for students with severe disabilities? *TASH Connections, 38*(3). Retrieved from http://tash.org/accessing-tash-connections/

FOR FURTHER INFORMATION

Alternate Assessment

Dynamic Learning Maps

http://dynamiclearningmaps.org

This web site provides information regarding an alternate assessment being developed by Dynamic Learning Maps, one of two national consortia creating an AA-AAS for students with significant cognitive disabilities. Dynamic Learning Maps is developing an online, computer-based, large-scale state assessment for this population of students.

National Center and State Collaborative (NCSC)

http://www.ncscpartners.org

This web site provides information regarding an alternate assessment being developed by NCSC, the second of two national consortia creating an AA-AAS for students with significant cognitive disabilities. The web site outlines the project's development of a comprehensive model of curriculum, instruction, assessment, and professional development.

Partnership for Assessment of Readiness for College and Careers (PARCC)

http://www.parcconline.org

This web site provides information regarding the general education assessment being developed by PARCC as well as links to resources. Information included on the site addresses the development of the K–12 assessment system designed to measure the full range of the CCSS.

Smarter Balanced Assessment Consortium

http://www.smarterbalanced.org

This web site provides information regarding the general assessment being developed as well as links to resources.

Common Core State Standards

Dunkle, C.A. (2012). *Leading the Common Core State Standards: From common sense to common practice.* Thousand Oaks, CA: Sage Publications.

Achieve the Core

http://www.achievethecore.org/

This web site provides resources that will help with the transition in math and ELA. There are also tools for teachers such as a checklist for determining text complexity. This web site will be used as a repository, so it will continue to grow.

ASCD

http://www.ascd.org/

This web site provides links to ASCD resources as well as external resources.

Common Core State Standards (CCSS) Initiative

http://www.corestandards.org

This is the official web site of the CCSS Initiative.

Common Core State Standards:
Printable Resources from Booklist Publications

*http://booklistonline.com/GeneralInfo.aspx?id=68&AspxAutoDetectCookie
Support=1*

This web site provides CCSS-related materials such as booklists, newsletters, and blogs.

Common Core State Standards: Resources

http://www.corestandards.org/resources

This web site provides resources to support the implementation of the CCSS.

Council of Chief State School Officers (CCSSO)

http://www.ccsso.org/Resources.html

This web site provides a list of tools and resources to support the implementation of the CCSS.

EduCore

http://educore.ascd.org

This web site provides a range of recourses for teachers in both ELA and mathematics. Created through the Bill and Melinda Gates Foundation, it features videos such as "From Common Core Standards to Curriculum: Five Big Ideas" and lesson plans such as a seventh-grade lesson on ancient civilizations.

EngageNY

http://www.engageny.org

This web site provides CCSS-related resources for teachers, parents, and administrators.

Mid-Illini Educational Cooperative

http://mid-illini.org/Common_Core_Resources.html

This web site is the home of Mid-Illini Educational Cooperative. Links are provided to general web sites related to the CCSS and also to states such as Hawaii, Indiana, and Kentucky that have developed tools and resources.

North Carolina Department of Public Instruction

http://www.ncpublicschools.org/acre/standards/common-core-tools/

This web site provides ELA and mathematics unpacking documents.

YouTube: TheHuntInstitute

http://www.youtube.com/user/TheHuntInstitute#g/u

This web site provides a library of CCSS-related videos.

Common Core State Standards: English Language Arts

Shanahan, T. (2012). The common core ate my baby and other urban legends. *Educational Leadership*, 70(4), 42–46.

Silver, H.F., Dewing, R.T., & Perini, M.J. (2012). *The core six: Essential strategies for achieving excellence with the Common Core.* Alexandria, VA: Association for Supervision and Curriculum Development. Retrieved from http://www.ascd.org/Publications/Books/Overview/The-Core-Six.aspx

Common Core

http://www.commoncore.org

This web site includes a link to curriculum maps for ELA. The maps are provided for a fee, but sample maps and lesson plans are provided at no cost.

The Common Core State Standards for English Language Arts

http://www.corestandards.org/ELA-Literacy

This is the homepage for the ELA standards within the CCSS.

International Reading Association

http://www.reading.org/resources/ResourcesByTopic/CommonCore-resource type/CommonCore-rt-resources.aspx

This web site provides online articles and blogs that are free to access.

The National Council of Teachers of English

http://www.ncte.org/standards/common-core

This web site offers books, online learning, articles, lesson plans, and more.

Revised Publishers' Criteria for the Common Core State Standards in English Language Arts and Literacy, Grades 3–12

http://www.corestandards.org/assets/Publishers_Criteria_for_3-12.pdf

The Revised Publishers' Criteria is designed to guide publishers by providing criteria that will ensure alignment with the standards in ELA.

Common Core State Standards: Mathematics

Burns, M. (2012). Go figure: Math and the common core. *Educational Leadership*, 70(4), 42–46.

The Common Core State Standards for Mathematics

http://www.corestandards.org/Math

This is the homepage for the mathematics standards within the CCSS.

Math Reasoning Inventory

https://mathreasoninginventory.com

This web site provides the Math Reasoning Inventory (MRI). The MRI is an online tool for assessing students' numeracy proficiency. The inventory focuses on skills required by the CCSS at the middle-school level.

The Mathematics Common Core Coalition

http://www.nctm.org/standards/mathcommoncore/

The Mathematics Common Core Coalition works to provide expertise and advice on issues related to the effective implementation of the Common Core State Standards for School Mathematics (CCSSM).

The National Council of Teachers of Mathematics

http://www.nctm.org

The National Council of Teachers of Mathematics (NCTM) is an organization designed to support teachers of mathematics through numerous resources, professional development opportunities, and research. The web site includes information about math content and pedagogy.

Teaching Common Core Language Arts

CHAPTER 4

Passage Comprehension and Read-Alouds

Leah Wood, Diane M. Browder, and Maryann Mraz

When Justin began middle school, he had a mix of literacy skills. He could identify numerous sight words after years of intensive instruction. Unfortunately, however, he was much better at identifying these words than comprehending them. He primarily used a picture response system to communicate and had begun to use sight words paired with pictures or symbols to answer questions in his academic classes. His fifth-grade teacher was the first to try to teach Justin to read, and he learned to recognize initial consonant sounds but was unable to decode words. Justin's sixth-grade teacher, Ms. Griffith, realized that he lacked a critical set of skills needed to engage with the text of his grade level. Without skills to comprehend passages of text, he would be severely limited in not only language arts but also in social studies and science, and even in working with word problems in mathematics. Any participation in general education at the middle school level would be severely restricted if Justin could not work with text. He also would be lacking skills needed for adult living, such as being able to glean information from a job ad, manual, web site, or magazine. Ms. Griffith also had seen how much her students enjoyed the novels of their age group. Having meaningful access to literature would potentially give Justin a lifelong leisure skill. This chapter provides the information teachers such as Ms. Griffith can use to promote access to grade-level text and teach comprehension skills for students at any age or grade level.

ACCESSING TEXT

The way in which students typically access text can differ based on their age or ability. The following section describes access to text from both a general education and a special education perspective.

General Education Perspective

Traditionally, in general education instruction, students begin to access text through read-alouds. In early literacy environments, reading aloud to students helps to foster enjoyment of books and to build an understanding of concepts of print. Through read-alouds, students develop a schema for stories as they are provided with engaging models of story structure elements, such as plots, characters, settings, and themes. Read-alouds also provide models of writing by introducing students to authors and illustrators, as well as enrich vocabulary development and provide opportunities to improve comprehension (Vacca et al., 2012).

Although especially popular with younger children, general educators use read-alouds at all grade levels as a way to engage students with the text. When new stories or poems are introduced, students are encouraged to talk about these new texts, to make predications, and to make connections to their own background knowledge. Both during and after read-alouds, students share their interpretations; then the teacher helps to clarify text meaning to support comprehension. These opportunities for social interactions help to develop language and literacy skills as well as an interest in reading (Galda, Ash, & Cullinan, 2000). Teachers often reread favorite stories to their students and encourage students' independent reading of favorite read-alouds.

As technological advances have become infused with instructional practices, opportunities to access texts through multiliteracies are increasingly apparent in general education settings. The term *multiliteracies* refers to the variety of ways in which literacy can be defined and implemented, given the wide array of new communications technologies available. As concepts of *literacy* expand with changing technologies, so does the concept of *text* (Neilsen, 2006). Literacy is no longer limited to words on a printed page; becoming literate more frequently requires students to learn how to interact with texts that include multimodal elements. Traditional printed texts, for example, require students to read linearly, from top to bottom, left to right, and front to back. By contrast, electronic texts often offer the option of clicking on hyperlinks that will take one reader on a path that may differ from the path selected by another reader (Reinking, 1997; Vacca, Vacca, & Mraz, in press). A hypertext format allows a reader to connect to other illustrations, documents, or resources related to the main text. When sounds, graphics, photos, and videos are included in hypertext, the format is often referred to as *hypermedia*. A multiliteracies approach focuses on preparing students to read, produce, and interpret texts in both traditional and multimedia modalities.

Multiliteracies offer a variety of formats through which students can interact with one another as they comprehend text: *Threaded discussions* involve students in exploring, reflecting, and problem-solving texts and text topics. *Blogs* allow students to keep an interactive electronic journal of their experiences and reflections. *Wikis* invite readers to increase their knowledge and comprehension of a topic by contributing facts and insights to the construction of a collaborative text to which other readers also contribute. *Internet inquiries* allow students to identify and synthesize information from a variety of resources, and to generate their own questions about a topic. In *Internet workshops* educators model skills and strategies needed for the effective use of multiliteracies (Vacca et al., in press). Although students must continue to learn how to comprehend print-based texts, it is increasingly important that they also learn how to interact with screen-based texts that include images, motion, and sound in order to comprehend texts and topics (Kress, 2003).

Special Education Perspective

Educators of students with severe disabilities must make decisions about *what* texts to use and *how* to make the texts accessible to all learners. Historically, access to text was equated with being able to read the text independently. Because students with severe disabilities might not be able to read, few books were used for literacy once students were too old for preschool picture books. Over the past several years, however, researchers have applied read-aloud strategies for older students with disabilities using the literature typically accessed by their same-age peers (i.e., grade-level text; Browder, Trela, & Jimenez, 2007; Mims, Hudson, & Browder, 2012).

For example, Browder and colleagues (2007) used a read-aloud format to teach comprehension of grade-appropriate middle school novels to students with intellectual disability and autism. In this study, three middle school educators were trained in the read-aloud procedures using a task-analyzed literacy template. Students learned to identify vocabulary in text, read repeated story lines, participate in reading routines, read new words, and reference the text to answer comprehension questions. Similarly, Mims and colleagues (2012) examined the effects of systematic instruction on text-dependent listening comprehension for four students in middle school with intellectual disability and autism. In this study, grade-level biographies were adapted and read aloud. All participants improved in listening comprehension measures of the grade-appropriate texts.

All students should have the opportunity to learn to read independently. Educators are finding more ways to teach students with moderate and severe intellectual disability to decode text (Allor, Mathes, Roberts, Jones, & Champlin, 2010; Browder, Ahlgrim-Delzell, Courtade, Gibbs, & Flowers, 2008; Browder, Ahlgrim-Delzell, Flowers, & Baker, 2012). In contrast, many students with moderate and severe disabilities also will need alternate strategies to access passages of text because their reading skills may lag far behind the demands of their assigned grade level (e.g., a seventh grader who has learned to read at a first-grade level). Learning to access text through an interactive read-aloud with a teacher or peer opens the door for the student to engage with grade-appropriate text. Technology also opens the door for students with severe disabilities to access text. Students may learn to navigate web sites and other text online (e.g., Zisimopoulos, Sigafoos, & Koutromanos, 2011). Text-to-speech features make it possible to hear text read aloud while using a computer. Students with severe disabilities now need skills for accessing multiliteracies to take full advantage of new resources in print.

TEXT SELECTION AND ACCESS

The following section describes important considerations for selecting text and promoting access to text for students with severe disabilities.

Text Selection

Students with severe disabilities need opportunities to access text for academic learning, leisure pursuits, and adult living. Although picture books are grade-appropriate for young students in early grades (e.g., kindergarten through second grade), students in Grades 3 or higher need chapter books or novels. Providing access to grade-level texts allows students of all abilities the opportunity to learn from a broad scope of narrative and informational content. Texts with greater complexity (e.g., chapter books) contain the story elements and rich content aligned with the Common Core State Standards (CCSS). Also, the themes and topics of chapter books provide students with severe disabilities access to the literature enjoyed by their peers. Through collaboration, general and special educators can identify text that is appropriate for the student's age and grade, typically used by the student's peer group, and amenable to teaching CCSS. Consideration of the student's interests, preferences, and future adult goals can suggest additional text to target for instruction (e.g., favorite web site or social media). Figure 4.1 shows the kinds of texts that may be important for students to comprehend. As educators plan for each student's individualized education, consideration can be given to the relative importance of each type of text for that student.

Text Access

Students with severe disabilities may access texts in a variety of ways depending on their decoding and comprehension skills and their physical and motor capabilities. Some students benefit from adapted texts in which the material is rewritten as summaries at a reduced reading level. Lexile text measures provide information about a text's semantic elements and syntax. The teacher may rewrite the text to match a lower Lexile text measure of comprehension and readability (MetaMetrics, 2011). Some students will need to have adapted texts presented in a read-aloud format, whereas other students may be able read the text at the reduced reading level. (See Figure 4.2 for an example of an adapted chapter and related comprehension questions.) Students may be able to access some text without adaptations using text-to-speech technology. An additional option is to abbreviate the original

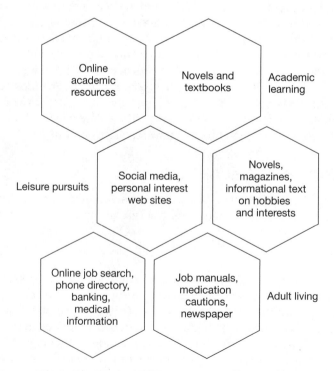

Figure 4.1. Examples of texts students may need to comprehend.

Adapted text	Comprehension questions
Bud, Not Buddy by Christopher Paul Curtis Chapter 5 Bud wants to find his dad. His dad's town is far away. Bud will have to walk a long time. He starts his walk. He walks past three towns. It is late at night. A car stops. A man gets out. The man wants to take Bud back home. Bud does not want to go back. He tricks the man. Bud locks the man out of the car. Bud drives the car away.	What does Bud take?
	Why does the man stop his car?
	How does Bud trick the man?
	Who does Bud want to find?
	Where does Bud walk?
	When does the man in the car stop?

Figure 4.2.   Sample of one chapter of adapted text from the book *Bud, Not Buddy* (Curtis, 1999). Six literal comprehension questions were developed for each chapter. This book was adapted to be 10 chapters long and match the readability level of a student reading at a first-grade reading level (decoding and comprehension). The Lexile Measure of this adapted text is 190L. The Lexile Measure of the original text is 950L.

or adapted text by focusing on selected passages. A general rule of thumb is to use text as close to the original as possible and only to simplify the text to the extent the student requires for comprehension. Even when using simplified text summaries, the teacher may read aloud selected passages from the original text to expose the student to its tone, style, and other features.

In addition to simplifying, abbreviating, and summarizing the original text, teachers may provide additional supports to promote comprehension. Literature for young children often promotes understanding through the use of repetition, including exact repetitions of a story line. This same strategy can be made age appropriate by repeating the main idea of an adapted chapter summary at the end of each page (e.g., for *Call of the Wild* [London, 1963], a repeated line for Chapter 1 might be "Buck loved his home."). Pictures also can be used to promote comprehension of the text. Although caution needs to be exercised when using pictures in teaching decoding, pairing them with text has the potential to promote understanding in read-alouds. Students with visual impairments or those who have the most severe disabilities may benefit from having actual objects affixed to the page of the book. As the teacher reads about an object (e.g., wind in the grass), the student finds the object on the page (e.g., tuft of artificial grass). Later these same objects may be used to answer comprehension questions. The teacher also may want to preteach key vocabulary in the passage prior to the read-aloud. The student may be taught to identify each key word and demonstrate understanding by using it to complete a sentence or by matching it to a picture. With all of these support strategies, however, it is important not to overly support comprehension. If the student can access the text without repeated story lines or picture supports, these should be omitted.

In addition to comprehension supports, students may need physical supports to work with a print version of text. Pages can be laminated or printed on heavy cardstock for durability. Materials can be affixed to the edges of each page to help students grab and turn pages independently (e.g., popsicle sticks, cardstock tabs, small sponge page "fluffers"). The pages of an existing book can be cut apart and placed in a binder with clear page protectors. For some students, the best option is to access all text through technology (e.g., computer or tablet) because of the many options for locating and managing text using a mouse or switch.

The final form of support the student may need to access the text is either a human or technological reader. In her dissertation study (Hudson & Browder, 2013), Hudson trained peers to provide read-alouds in a general education elementary class using summaries of the novel all the students were using. The students with moderate intellectual disability increased their comprehension skills with the support of peer readers. Peers may serve in a variety of roles to help students with disabilities, including helping with vocabulary reviews, reading aloud the text or text summary, offering prompts to focus on the general educator's instruction, and helping engagement with a cooperative learning group or center-based activity. Teachers also can serve as the human reader. Often a read-aloud can be conducted as a small-group or whole-class activity with students taking turns providing answers.

Although students with disabilities will likely need experiences with human readers, it also is important to promote independence in accessing text with technology. Similar to the independence a reader without a disability asserts when picking up a book to read alone, students with disabilities who can use text-to-speech software are able to access text without assistance. Students may require systematic instruction to learn to use text-to-speech features and also may need human reader support to grow accustomed to the new voice technology provides. For example, the human reader may sit with the student who is first learning to access online text to offer prompts such as, "Listen again to what this passage says."

TEACHING COMPREHENSION

The following section describes both the *what* and the *how* of teaching comprehension. Many of the CCSS in English language arts (ELA) include comprehension of various types of texts. Teaching comprehension across standards requires an understanding of levels of comprehension and awareness of text structure. Recent research has finally examined the effectiveness of applying strategies to increase text comprehension for students with severe disabilities.

Teaching Common Core State Standards: English Language Arts

In 2010, the National Governors Association and the Council of Chief State School Officers released the CCSS for literacy and mathematics. The CCSS Mission Statement (2010) explains the purpose of these new standards:

> The Common Core State Standards provide a consistent, clear understanding of what students are expected to learn, so teachers and parents know what they need to do to help them. The standards are designed to be robust and relevant to the real world, reflecting the knowledge that our young people need for success in college and careers. With American students fully prepared for the future, our communities will be best positioned to compete successfully in the global economy. (p. 11)

The ELA Common Core standards focus on the following domains: reading literature, reading informational texts, foundational skills, writing, speaking and listening, and language. Compared with previous standards, the CCSS place a greater emphasis on comprehension, writing, and reading across the content areas. The standards call for increased emphasis on nonfiction texts, the integration of global awareness, and professional development for educators in order to support the implementation of rigorous standards.

The CCSS do not impose rigid guidelines in terms of implementation, but rather provide schools with the flexibility to decide how to effectively implement standards at different grade levels (Phillips & Wong, 2010). A major goal of the CCSS is to support all learners in developing a strong knowledge base by integrating thinking and learning processes across the curriculum. In doing so, students have the potential to develop independent learning skills and to be active in their application of these skills as they comprehend a wide variety of texts.

Comprehension is embedded in many of the ELA anchor standards in the CCSS. Particularly, the 10 anchor standards in reading all include various levels of comprehension. Effectively teaching comprehension through these standards to students with severe disabilities requires consideration and planning. Table 4.1

Table 4.1. Examples of teaching comprehension skills derived from the English language arts Common Core State Standards

Key ideas and details
- *Reading anchor standard:* Literacy.CCRA.R.1: Read closely to determine what the text says explicitly and to make logical inferences from it; cite specific textual evidence when writing or speaking to support conclusions drawn from the text.
    - ○ *Teaching example:* Use a graphic organizer and time delay to teach the meaning of wh- words. Use a system of least prompts to teach students to identify if an answer is "in the book" or "not in the book."
- *Reading anchor standard:* CCSS.ELA-Literacy.CCRA.R.2: Determine central ideas or themes of a text and analyze their development; summarize the key supporting details and ideas.
    - ○ *Teaching example:* Use a task analysis for finding details and generating a central idea or theme. First, identify details (say, point, highlight) and add them to a graphic organizer. When the graphic organizer is full, use the details to generate a central idea statement.
- *Reading anchor standard:* CCSS.ELA-Literacy.CCRA.R.3: Analyze how and why individuals, events, or ideas develop and interact over the course of a text.
    - ○ *Teaching example:* Teach definitions of *how* and *why* (e.g., *How* tells about *ways, Why* tells about *reasons*). Use multiple exemplars and interject many personal examples related to the students' lives (e.g., Why do you feel sad sometimes? How did you get to school today?).

Craft and structure
- *Reading anchor standard:* CCSS.ELA-Literacy.CCRA.R.4: Interpret words and phrases as they are used in a text, including determining technical, connotative, and figurative meanings, and analyze how specific word choices shape meaning or tone.
    - ○ *Teaching example:* Teach a "toolbox" of literary words and phrases using examples and non-examples or time delay. Incorporate feelings into instruction, and make graphic organizers of words that students associate with different feelings.
- *Reading anchor standard:* CCSS.ELA-Literacy.CCRA.R.5: Analyze the structure of texts, including how specific sentences, paragraphs, and larger portions of the text (e.g., a section, chapter, scene, or stanza) relate to each other and the whole.
    - ○ *Teaching example:* Use a graphic organizer with sections for beginning, middle, and end (for literary texts) or major themes (for expository texts). Identify important details as a group and add these to the sections of the graphic organizer. Highlight any details that are the same across sections.
- *Reading anchor standard:* CCSS.ELA-Literacy.CCRA.R.6: Assess how point of view or purpose shapes the content and style of a text.
    - ○ *Teaching example:* Teach the concepts of *teach* and *entertain* as two major purposes for writing. Provide examples of how authors who teach give us "facts," and authors who entertain give us "feelings." Provide multiple examples of facts and feelings. Use response cards for students to identify *teach* examples versus *entertain* examples. Collect a tally after each page of the adapted text of students' responses—was this to teach or entertain?

(continued)

Table 4.1. *(continued)*

Integration of knowledge and ideas

- *Reading anchor standard:* CCSS.ELA-Literacy.CCRA.R.7: Integrate and evaluate content presented in diverse media and formats, including visually and quantitatively, as well as in words.
  - ° *Teaching example:* Incorporate multiliteracies (e.g., eBooks, Internet searches). Use a system of least prompts to teach students steps to a task analysis for developing a PowerPoint presentation about a topic they have studied. Incorporate elements of a KWHL (Know, What, How, Learn) chart into the presentation so that the students can express what they already knew, what questions they generated, how they answered their questions, and what they learned.
- *Reading anchor standard:* CCSS.ELA-Literacy.CCRA.R.8: Delineate and evaluate the argument and specific claims in a text, including the validity of the reasoning as well as the relevance and sufficiency of the evidence.
  - ° *Teaching example:* Use a graphic organizer to teach and illustrate examples and nonexamples of *validity*. Incorporate a step into a KWHL process in which students must evaluate if their sources were "valid" or "not valid." Use a system of least prompts to teach components of the KWHL process.
- *Reading anchor standard:* CCSS.ELA-Literacy.CCRA.R.9: Analyze how two or more texts address similar themes or topics in order to build knowledge or to compare the approaches the authors take.
  - ° *Teaching example:* First, use examples and nonexamples to teach the concept of *same*. Use the graphic organizers used to teach details and central themes from two related texts. Ask students to evaluate if two details or concepts are the same (yes or no).

Range of reading and level of text complexity

- *Reading anchor standard:* CCSS.ELA-Literacy.CCRA.R.10: Read and comprehend complex literary and informational texts independently and proficiently.
  - ° *Teaching example:* Use a system of least prompts to teach the steps of a task analysis for accessing eBooks or other multiliteracies with text-to-speech or read-aloud capabilities. Use a system of least prompts to teach students to generate and answer their own questions about a text.

Source: National Governors Association Center for Best Practices, Council of Chief State School Officers (2010).

provides examples of strategies for teaching comprehension across these anchor standards in reading. Depending on the range of grade levels, the first decision when planning for instruction is to identify the student's assigned grade level (based on chronological age). Educators of students with severe disabilities often teach students from different grade levels, so a read-aloud may need to have comprehension questions that vary for different students in the reading group. One benefit of the CCSS in ELA is the vertical alignment of many of the standards across grade levels. Core concepts such as the author's purpose or central theme/main idea repeat across grades, making planning for multigrade reading groups more manageable. The challenge becomes which text to select for the multigrade group. If an educator is delivering instruction to a group with third-, fourth-, and fifth-grade students, the educator may alternate among novels from these various grades. Ideas for which novels to select can be generated through collaboration with general education teachers and by reviewing the CCSS, which includes recommended titles of texts by grade level (see Appendix B of the CCSS in ELA).

In planning for instruction, educators will need to become familiar with both the standards and the grade-level pacing guide, which can occur by attending CCSS workshops, collaborating with general educators, and using online resources such as the CCSS (http://www.corestandards.org), the Partnership for Assessment of Readiness for College and Careers (PARCC; http://www.parcconline.org), and the Smarter Balanced Assessment Consortium (http://www.smarterbalanced.org) web sites. Collaborating with general educators can help special educators decide what to teach and the sequence in which to teach standards. General educators typically have a longer history of experience incorporating specific standards into instruction. In addition, many states and school districts have produced resources for the CCSS. In North Carolina, the Department of Public Instruction has developed Unpacking Standards (NC Department of Public Instruction, 2012), as part of its Instructor Toolkit, which provides online documents explaining each standard in detail, including specific explanations of what the student must know, understand, and demonstrate.

By design, the CCSS are intended to promote college and career readiness. As a result, the CCSS in ELA intentionally include an increase in informational texts (70% of texts are informational by the 12th grade). Comprehending both types of texts (literary and informational) has value to all learners, but the increased emphasis on informational texts aligns closely with the charge of special educators to promote positive postschool outcomes. Comprehension of informational texts does not need to occur exclusively in the upper grades. Educators can begin promoting the comprehension of informational texts at the elementary level. Selecting texts related to science or social studies units is a way to connect literacy comprehension to content across other academic domains. For instance, a special educator may plan a science unit on food chains. During literacy, the teacher may use a read-aloud of an informational text about food chains. Target vocabulary can be selected and taught during the literacy lesson. These same vocabulary terms can be practiced, used, and assessed during a subsequent science lesson. For instance, if the book discusses terms such as *herbivore*, *omnivore*, and *carnivore*, these terms can be taught during a literacy lesson. Later, during science, educators can review the target vocabulary, use the terms while teaching the lesson, and then use the terms in a word bank when testing for comprehension of the science concepts (e.g., "Here is a lion. Is a lion an herbivore, an omnivore, or a carnivore?"). Science and social studies content also lends itself to lessons related to functional or life skills. Cooking and nutrition are scientific by nature. Students can learn about health and self-care by listening to adapted texts related to the human body. Similarly, social studies content extends to topics of community, civics, and the economy. Another way to teach comprehension of informational texts is to supplement a literary chapter book with related informational texts. For instance, if the class is reading *Charlotte's Web* (White, 1952), educators can supplement lessons with informational texts about the life cycles of animals, farming, or community events (e.g., county fair).

Once an educator decides what standards to address, he or she needs to develop measureable objectives. As objectives are written, the teacher targets the alternate achievement expected for the grade-level CCSS. For instance, an objective may be for the student to use a graphic organizer to sequence the events in the text as occurring first, next, and last. Table 4.1 offers examples of CCSS and learning targets for students with moderate and severe disabilities.

Levels of Comprehension

In general education settings, reading comprehension has been defined as, "the construction of meaning of a written or spoken communication through a reciprocal, holistic interchange of ideas between the interpreter and the message" (Harris

& Hodges, 1995, p. 39). This description emphasizes that comprehension requires the reader to do more than simply recall or restate information encountered in a text. Comprehension requires the reader to be actively involved in interpreting text, and in connecting his or her own prior knowledge to a new text. Comprehension involves the knowledge and experience already possessed by the reader, as well as the information stated in the text by the author. As Rasinski and Padak (2008) explain, "Readers filter the text through their own background knowledge, biases, and other predispositions that affect how they interpret text" (p. 2).

In teaching comprehension, teachers may consider Pearson and Gallagher's (1983) Gradual Release of Responsibility Model. The model identifies three phases of comprehension learning. In Phase 1, the educator assumes more direct responsibility for the lesson by describing processes or strategies and modeling those strategies. By Phase 2, educators and students share responsibility, with students actively involved in implementing previously presented strategies. In this phase, the educator may observe, provide feedback, or offer support as it is needed. By Phase 3, students are able to assume more responsibility for comprehension strategy implementation. They are able to work independently and require limited support from the educator.

To promote the release of responsibility as described by Pearson and Gallagher (1983), it is helpful to ask students questions that will enable them to understand what they have read or heard. Questions should consider the three categories, or levels, of comprehension: *literal, inferential,* and *applied* (Vacca et al., 2012). Each level requires the reader to know the different information sources that can be used to answer different types of questions.

At the literal level of comprehension, students are asked to answer questions by using information that is explicitly stated in the text. Questions that address this level of comprehension are referred to as "right there" questions (Raphael, 1986) because students can find the answers right there in the text. The literal level of comprehension requires students to "read the lines." For example, in a story that states, "Mary ate dinner at an Italian restaurant," a literal question might ask, "Where did Mary eat dinner?" An appropriate response would be, "Mary ate dinner at an Italian restaurant."

At the inferential level of comprehension, also called the interpretative level, students must answer questions by using their background knowledge in combination with information from the text. Questions that address this level of comprehension are referred to as "think and search" or "author and you" questions (Raphael, 1986) because students need to combine information stated in the text with their prior knowledge in order to make inferences. The inferential level requires students to "read between the lines." Continuing with the Italian restaurant example, an inferential question might ask, "What might Mary have ordered at the Italian restaurant?" An appropriate response would include, "Mary might have ordered lasagna," or other types of entrees that would be served at an Italian restaurant.

At the applied level of comprehension, sometimes called the evaluative level, students are asked to evaluate or to make judgments about what they have read. Questions that address this level of comprehension are referred to as "on my own" questions (Raphael, 1986) because the applied level requires students to "read beyond the lines." In the Italian restaurant example, an applied question might ask, "Why do you think Mary went to a restaurant to eat?" Examples of appropriate responses would include, "Because she liked Italian food," or "Because she was celebrating a happy occasion."

Teaching students to ask and to generate questions across all three levels of comprehension helps them to remain actively engaged in the reading process. Although literal questions are often the first type of questions that come to one's mind, asking higher level questions, such as inferential and applied questions, will support students in making important connections as they seek to comprehend the text.

In addition to asking questions across different levels of comprehension, teaching comprehension also involves activating students' prior knowledge, teaching them to visualize as they are reading, and teaching them to make connections as they read. Harvey and Goudvis (2000) suggested that comprehension is enhanced when students are encouraged to make different types of connections. They suggest the following:

- *Text-to-self connections:* These connections ask the reader to reflect on how the text or reading experiences relate to events in his or her own life. For example, in an early elementary unit study on transportation, students might be encouraged to share their experiences with traveling in different types of vehicles.

- *Text-to-text connections:* These connections encourage students to recognize when a new text reminds them of a character, setting, event, or problem that they may have encountered in a previously read text. For example, in the unit study on transportation example, students might recall stories or poems about the theme of transportation that they have previously read or heard.

- *Text-to-world connections:* These connections tend to be more advanced and require broader background knowledge or personal experiences than the previous types of connections. For example, using the transportation example, after reading a newspaper article or hearing a news broadcast, students might be aware of a community transportation issue, such as establishing a local train system. That experience or knowledge could then be discussed as part of the theme study of transportation.

Making connections helps students to recognize the relevance of varied text to their own lives and to their communities. These connections support comprehension.

Awareness of Text Structure

Text structure helps to organize ideas presented in a text. When readers perceive that structure, learning and comprehension can be improved. *External text structure* refers to the overall format features of a text and the organizational aids that are included in the text to support reading and understanding. Such features include the table of contents, appendixes, indexes, headings, graphs, charts, and illustrations.

Internal text structure refers to the interrelationships among ideas in the text as well as to the relationships among text elements. In narrative texts, text structure is characterized by elements such as the plot, characters, settings, problems, solutions, and themes. Story elements typically include a beginning or initiating event, a problem to be solved, attempts to solve the problem, one or more outcomes, a resolution, and a reaction that expresses a character's response to success or failure in solving the problem. In informational texts, the following five text structures are common (Vacca et al., in press):

1. *Description:* This text structure provides information about a topic, concept, event, or person. The text explains facts and characteristics related to its main topic. Key phrases or signal words such as *to begin with, most important, also,* and *for example* give the reader clues to help identify and comprehend this text structure.

2. *Sequence:* In a sequence text structure, the author explains steps in a process or traces the development of a topic or event. Signal words such as *on, now, before, after, first, second, then,* and *finally* help the reader to identify and comprehend this text structure.

3. *Comparison and contrast:* A comparison and contrast text structure explains the similarities and/or differences among facts, people, events, and topics. Signal words such as *however, on the other hand, either/or, while,* and *similarly* help the reader to identify and comprehend this text structure.

4. *Cause and effect:* A cause and effect text structure shows how events or concepts occur because of other events or concepts. Signal words such as *because, since, therefore, as a result, if/then,* and *thus* help the reader to identify and comprehend this text structure.

5. *Problem and solution:* A problem and solution text structure shows the development of a problem and one or more solutions to the problem. Signal words for the problem and solution text structure are similar to those that signal the cause and effect text structure.

Readers can learn to recognize text structures and text patterns that an author uses. Understanding how the text is organized can help the reader to better comprehend and retain the information read.

Teaching Comprehension to Students with Moderate and Severe Disabilities

Comprehending text is a complex and critical skill (Mastropieri & Scruggs, 1997; Wahlberg & Magliano, 2004). Browder, Wakeman, Spooner, Ahlgrim-Delzell, and Algozzine (2006) identified and analyzed 128 literacy-based studies for students with severe disabilities and determined the majority of the interventions focused on sight words, and only a few of these measured comprehension. In a similar comprehensive review of literature, Chiang and Lin (2007) found only two studies in which text comprehension was taught to students with autism. Given that comprehension is fundamental to literacy, it is surprising how few researchers have focused on this important outcome.

In the past few years researchers have identified new guidance for teaching comprehension to students with developmental disabilities. Williamson, Carnahan, and Jacobs (2012) identified characteristics specific to students with autism who were the most skilled in answering comprehension questions. Students who were successful in comprehending text regardless of the text features (e.g., use of pictures, length of passages, type of text) demonstrated both academic interests and a general interest in reading. These students also could identify personal connections with the texts, ask questions about the text, and create visual images. Even these stronger readers, however, had difficulty responding to prediction questions and determining the emotional state of others.

One of the ways to teach students to make connections with text and create visual images is to use an interactive read-aloud. When applied to literature, these may be called "story-based lessons." Browder and colleagues (2007) developed a task analysis of steps teachers could apply for a story-based lesson using adapted novels with middle school students. In a review of this and several other studies using interactive-read alouds, Hudson and Test (2011) found story-based lessons to be an evidence-based practice for teaching literacy skills to students with moderate and severe developmental disabilities.

Students often need instruction in new vocabulary that will be introduced in the text. This vocabulary can be taught using time delay. Multiple studies have indicated that time delay is an evidence-based practice for teaching sight word or picture recognition to students with severe disabilities (Browder, Ahlgrim-Delzell, Spooner, Mims, & Baker, 2009). In time delay, the prompt is paired with the target stimulus at no delay. For example, the teacher displays an array of four vocabulary words and asks the student to point to the word *suddenly* while simultaneously pointing to the correct answer. If the student can imitate a model, he or she will likely locate the correct answer without making an error. This is repeated with the entire list of vocabulary words with the array shuffled between trials. After some predetermined number of trials (e.g., one round of presenting the sight words or across two days), the teacher delays the introduction of the prompt. Now the array is displayed and the teacher gives the command to point to *suddenly* but waits before showing the answer. After some increment of delay (e.g., 4 seconds), the teacher points to the correct answer if the student has not anticipated the correct response. Time delay is effective when the student begins to anticipate the correct response prior to the teacher's model. The teaching trials also should include some comprehension response. For example, the student might use the word *suddenly* in a sentence or be given sentence strips and select the best words to complete each one. Or, the student may match the word to a picture (if the words are easily depicted words). Time delay can be used across content area vocabulary. For example, Jameson, McDonnell, Johnson, Riesen, and Polychronis (2007) embedded constant time delay instruction in a general education class to teach definitions for states of matter (i.e., boil, melt, and freeze) and teen living themes (e.g., best friend's wedding, preparing for marriage) on a symbol chart. Jameson, McDonnell, Polychronis, and Riesen (2008) used embedded constant time delay instruction to teach three students with moderate intellectual disability key word definitions for health (e.g., lungs: get air, can get cancer) and art (e.g., firing: heating clay in a special oven) classes. Jimenez, Browder, Spooner, and DiBiase (2012) used time delay to teach science vocabulary definitions and concepts to students in middle school.

Besides word-level comprehension, students also will need to learn to answer comprehension questions about a passage of text. One model to teach this comprehension is to use a system of least intrusive prompting. Least intrusive prompting was first developed for teaching daily living skills and included a hierarchy of verbal, model, gestural, and physical prompts (Wolery, Ault, & Doyle, 1992). When applied to reading comprehension, the hierarchy will include some level of rereading of the text passage. Mims (2009) modified a least intrusive prompt hierarchy by making the first prompt a reread of the sentence that contained the answer. Students then received a model and, as needed, physical guidance to select the comprehension response from an array of pictures. Mims and colleagues (2012) further developed the system of least intrusive prompting to include a rule for answering *wh-* question rules as the first verbal prompt in the instructional hierarchy. For example, if a student did not respond to the question, after a designated wait time, the instructor might say, "When you hear *what,* listen for a *thing.*"

Hudson, Browder, and Jimenez (in press) further developed this system of least intrusive prompting to teach passage comprehension by using progressive levels of rereading the text with students with moderate intellectual disability. In the first level, the peer tutor reread the paragraph containing the answer. In the second level, the tutor reread the sentence containing the answer. In the third level, the tutor reread the word or phrase that told the answer and pointed to the correct answer on the response board. If needed, the tutor then guided the student's hand to point to the answer. The student with disabilities could direct the peer to give the next prompt by using a symbol to signify *more help.* After reading the chapter, the peer would ask the comprehension question. If the student with disabilities did not give the correct answer or used the *more help* symbol, the peer used the first prompt (reread the key paragraph). If the answer was still not given or the student asked for help, the peer used the next level prompt (reread the key sentence). After waiting again for the answer, the peer used the next prompt if needed (reread key word and show the answer). All of the participating students improved their comprehension. Figure 4.3 shows this method of prompting.

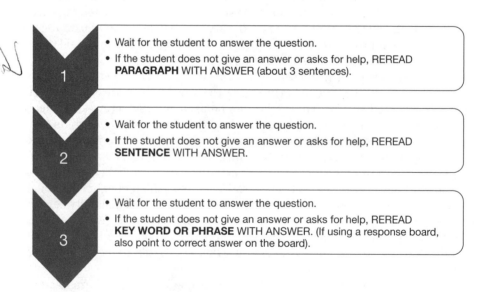

Figure 4.3. A system of least intrusive prompting for teaching passage comprehension during a read-aloud with students with moderate and severe disabilities.

Prompts also can be varied to represent the type of question asked. Literal questions can be taught through prompts that direct students to the particular text in which the answer is located. Inferential questions might require a think-aloud prompt, in which the instructor provides a verbal prompt telling the student to make a personal connection. The model prompt might include the instructor modeling how to make a personal connection or access background knowledge in order to construct or identify an answer to the question.

APPLYING RESEARCH-BASED STRATEGIES TO TEACH COMPREHENSION

Promoting text comprehension for students with severe disabilities requires the consideration of several components, including planning read-alouds, selecting and adapting text, writing comprehension questions, planning how students will respond, using instructional methods to teach comprehension, and considering peer readers.

Planning Read-Alouds

One of the best ways to promote comprehension is to use interactive read-alouds across a variety of texts (e.g., stories, informational text). This interactive-read aloud can be implemented with task analytic instruction as a series of steps. The first step may be to engage the student with the topic of the text. This may include using a variety of activities or attention getters to build background knowledge. For example, prior to reading about oyster fishing, the students may be shown real oyster shells and a video clip of deep sea fishing. The next step might be to do a brief vocabulary review using the time delay strategies described previously. For example, the student might learn words such as *oyster, fishing,* and *livelihood.* Then the teacher can let the student open the text (e.g., pull up the web site or open the book) and make a prediction about the topic or ask some question about the text (e.g., "Where do they fish?"). For some students, it may be beneficial to have them locate text features such as the title, author, and title page. During the read-aloud itself, steps of the task analysis may include responses such as turning pages, locating vocabulary words on the page, reading a repeated story line using assistive technology, or listening for specific information on each page. Students also may make predictions during the reading about what will happen next. Either during the reading or when it is completed, the teacher asks a series of comprehension questions.

Selecting and Adapting Text

As described previously, the text may be summarized, excerpted, or adapted. There are no research-based guidelines for specifically how to simplify or summarize the text. Browder and colleagues (2007) summarized text at a third-grade reading level for the read-aloud and augmented it with pictures and repeated story lines for the main ideas of chapters. The adaptation may condense chapters of the original into multiple chapter summaries or have one adapted chapter for each original chapter. Teachers may need to try different formats of text to find what works best for individual students. In research studies such as those by Hudson and colleagues (in press) and Browder and colleagues (2007), one adapted book was created and then used for all students. This also makes it possible to use a small-group format for the read-aloud. Once chapter books are introduced, students typically each have their own copy of the book for reference. Adapted books can be copied, collated or bound as small books, and given to each student in the reading group. The number of days the teacher spends on each chapter of the book will depend both on the complexity of the chapter and the students' entry skills. Teachers may read a new chapter each lesson or repeat the same chapter across days for a week. Some caution is needed not to overteach each chapter of the book, as students may begin to memorize answers to comprehension questions. For expository text, a summary might be created for either the entire chapter or for each key section of the chapter.

When planning text selection, it is important also to use multiple related texts as some CCSS require students to compare texts. During a unit on a novel, the teacher might select poems and informational passages on the same topic or themes. For example, when teaching a novel that takes place in Brazil, the teacher might include a poem by an author from this region and informational text about the country. In a science unit on ecosystems, the teacher could read several expository texts on animals and their habitats. Many web sites contain ready-made eBooks on a variety of topics. For instance, the Discovery Education web site (http://discoveryeducation .com) offers eBooks leveled by grade on varying academic content.

Writing Comprehension Questions

A good framework for writing comprehension questions is Bloom's taxonomy of knowledge (Bloom, Engelhart, Furst, Hill, & Krathwohl, 1956). According to this taxonomy, levels of learning include *knowledge, comprehension, application, analysis, synthesis,* and *evaluation.* Comprehension questions can be written at each level of this taxonomy and targeted to a student's current level of performance. For example, a question at the *analysis* level of the taxonomy requires students to break information into smaller parts. A simplified analysis question could be, "Here are animals from our story. Which animals are mammals? Which animals are reptiles?" A harder version of this same analysis question could be, "We read about mammals and reptiles. How are mammals and reptiles the same? How are mammals and reptiles different?" Finally, a difficult question could be, "Are you a mammal or a reptile? Why?" Adhering to the CCSS in ELA, comprehension questions also will include a variety of skills such as sequencing, identifying the central theme or main idea, or identifying the author's purpose for writing the text. As described previously in this chapter, questions can also be literal or inferential.

Planning How Students Will Respond

The most difficult way for students to answer comprehension questions is to construct the response. That is, the teacher asks the question and the student generates the answer using speech or a communication device. Many students will need some type of multiple choice response options to answer comprehension questions. For example, the teacher might use a four-choice picture array. In this array, some of the distractor items should be plausible (e.g., other characters in the story), but at least one may be implausible (e.g., "tree") to check if the student understands the *wh-* question. As students increase in comprehension, response options may be introduced with larger arrays. Hudson and Browder (2013) used a book of response options with each page dedicated to a type of *wh-* question. After asking a "who" question, the student found the "who" page and then selected from the pictures of characters. Communication applications for personal tablets (e.g., GoTalk Now, Proloquo2Go) can be used to create portable and changeable response boards for comprehension questions.

Rather than answering questions, students may use other activities to demonstrate comprehension such as completing a graphic organizer. Students can use the graphic organizer to search for words in the text that will help them identify the point of view. Students also can use graphic organizers to record story elements such as the author, setting, time, and events. Zakas, Browder, Ahlgrim-Delzell, and Heafner (2013) used a graphic organizer for students with autism to identify key information from social studies passages such as who, where, and what of key events.

Teaching Comprehension

As shown in Table 4.1, comprehension questions and activities can be created to address the CCSS for the student's assigned grade level. During the read-aloud, comprehension questions should be interjected after short passages (i.e., after every paragraph or two) for younger students. Older students may be able to answer questions at the end of the read-aloud if they have begun to build comprehension skills. Sometimes students may need to listen for target information and stop the reading to answer the question at that point. This can help students listen actively for the answer. For example, the teacher may have the students raise their hands or use response cards when they hear where the fishing took place. Teachers also can insert definitions of key vocabulary words while reading the text (e.g., "The English settlers formed a colony, *or a place where people lived.*"). To teach students to answer specific questions, teachers can also use the least intrusive prompt strategy described previously and illustrated in Figure 4.3. The goal will be for students to learn to answer the question with few to no rereads. Being able to answer the question after the first reading may be an unrealistic goal for more complex text, as many listeners require some rereading to locate information. If students learn to create their own highlighting text for technology to read aloud or request human assistance, they will have the strategies needed throughout their life to find the answer.

Students also may benefit from being taught the rules for *wh-* questions. For example, Browder, Hudson, and Wood (in press) taught students the rules for *wh-* questions using definitions and a visual referent. To follow their strategy, the teacher would place the following words on the table in front of a student: *people, things, places, times, reasons, ways.* Then, using a 0-second delay, the teacher shows a *wh-* word card (e.g., *who*), reads it, and immediately points to the corresponding definition ("a person or animal"). In subsequent rounds, the teacher would wait 4 seconds before providing the model prompt to select the definition.

Think-aloud procedures are useful for inferential questions. For instance, if asked, "Why were the girls scared?" the first prompt, if needed, might be, "Think of a time when you felt scared. Why did you feel scared? Why do you think the girls were scared?" The next prompt might be, "I can think of a time when I felt scared. I felt scared because I was alone. The girls were alone in the story. Why do you think the girls were scared?" In this instance, the prompts help the student make the personal connection necessary to understand what is happening to the characters in the story.

Finally, students may generate their own questions when listening to any type of text. The teacher can model how to construct a question. For example, first the student chooses a *wh-* word. Then the student chooses a topic word (e.g., treasure). Then the student uses helper words to make a whole sentence (e.g., "What treasure did they find?"). The use of graphic organizers, question answering, and question generating are all strategies recommended by the National Reading Panel (2000) for supporting text comprehension.

Considering Peer Readers

Although teachers will likely use read-alouds on an ongoing basis to teach academic content, peers also can be effective in promoting comprehension (Hudson et al., in press). Carter, Cushing, and Kennedy (2009) recommend four primary components for using peer supports: 1) peer tutor selection, 2) peer tutor training, 3) peer-delivered instruction, and 4) adult monitoring. Peer tutors should be selected based on being in the grade aligned with the students with disabilities, wanting to participate, and being able to read the text fluently. When training peer tutors to deliver read-aloud instruction, the teacher should explain the expectation and responsibilities of peer tutors. Next, peers need specific guidance for how to provide help to students with fine or gross motor, auditory, or visual needs. Peer tutors will need to learn a specific method to deliver instruction. For example, they may be given the steps to follow in a task analysis or a visual referent for using a system of least intrusive prompts (e.g., Figure 4.3). Finally, peer tutors need some ongoing monitoring to be sure they are delivering instruction as intended.

SUMMARY

Accessing text has little purpose if the student does not learn to comprehend its meaning. Although comprehension has been overlooked in the majority of research on teaching literacy to students with moderate and severe disabilities (Browder et al., 2006), new strategies are emerging. Read-aloud formats provide an important option for engaging students with age-appropriate text that is beyond their reading level. As students learn to interact with text with the support of human readers and technology, they gain skills to access text for lifelong learning. Comprehension strategies such as using text rereads and teaching definitions of *wh-* words can give students the tools they need to glean meaning from a wide variety of literature and informational text.

REFERENCES

Allor, J.H., Mathes, P.G., Roberts, J.K., Jones, F.G., & Champlin, T.M. (2010). Teaching students with moderate intellectual disabilities to read: An experimental examination of a comprehensive reading intervention. *Education and Training in Autism and Developmental Disabilities, 45,* 3–22.

Bloom, B.S., Engelhart, M.D., Furst, E.J., Hill, W.H., & Krathwohl, D.R. (1956). *Taxonomy of educational objectives: The classification of educational goals; Handbook I: Cognitive Domain.* New York, NY: Longman.

Browder, D.M., Ahlgrim-Delzell, L., Courtade, G., Gibbs, S.L., & Flowers, C. (2008). Evaluation of the effectiveness of an early literacy program for students with significant developmental disabilities. *Exceptional Children, 75*, 33–52.

Browder, D.M., Ahlgrim-Delzell, L., Flowers, C., & Baker, J.N. (2012). An evaluation of a multicomponent early literacy program for students with severe developmental disabilities.
Remedial and Special Education, 33, 237–246.

Browder, D.M., Ahlgrim-Delzell, L., Spooner, F., Mims, P., & Baker, J. (2009). Using time
delay to teach literacy to students with severe developmental disabilities. *Exceptionality
Children, 75*, 343–364.

Browder, D.M., Hudson, M.E., & Wood, L. (in press). Teaching students with moderate intellectual disability who are emergent readers to comprehend text. *Exceptionality.*

Browder, D.M., Trela, K., & Jimenez, B. (2007). Training teachers to follow a task analysis
to engage middle school students with moderate and severe developmental disabilities in
grade-appropriate literature. *Focus on Autism and Other Developmental Disabilities,
22*, 206–219.

Browder, D.M., Wakeman, S.Y., Spooner, F., Ahlgrim-Delzell, L., & Algozzine, B. (2006).
Research on reading instruction for individuals with significant cognitive disabilities.
Exceptional Children, 72, 392–408.

Carter, E.W., Cushing, L.S., & Kennedy, C.H. (2009). *Peer support strategies for improving
all students' social lives and learning.* Baltimore, MD: Paul H. Brookes Publishing Co.

Chiang, H.M., & Lin, Y.H. (2007). Reading comprehension instruction for students with
autism spectrum disorders. *Focus on Autism and Other Developmental Disabilities,
22*, 259–267. doi:10.1177/1088357607220040801

Curtis, C.P. (1999). *Bud, not Buddy.* New York, NY: Delacorte Press.

Galda, L., Ash, G.E., & Cullinan, B.E. (2000). Children's literature. In M.L. Kamil, P.B. Mosen-
thal, P.D. Pearson, & R. Barr (Eds.), *Handbook of reading research* (pp. 361–379). Mahwah, NJ: Lawrence Erlbaum Associates.

Harris, T.L., & Hodges, R.E. (Eds.). (1995). *The literacy dictionary: The vocabulary of
reading and writing.* Newark, DE: International Reading Association.

Harvey, S., & Goudvis, A. (2000). *Strategies that work: Teaching comprehension to
enhance understanding.* York, ME: Stenhouse.

Hudson, M.E., & Browder, D.M. (2013). *Using peers and grade-level read-alouds to teach
listening comprehension to students with moderate intellectual disability.* Manuscript
in preparation.

Hudson, M.E., Browder, D.M., & Jimenez, B. (in press). Effects of a peer-delivered system
of least prompts intervention and adapted science read-alouds on listening comprehension for participants with moderate intellectual disability. *Education and Training in
Autism and Developmental Disabilities.*

Hudson, M.E., & Test, D.W. (2011). Evaluating the evidence base for using shared story reading to promote literacy for students with extensive support needs. *Research and Practice
for Persons with Severe Disabilities, 36*, 34–45.

Jameson, J.M., McDonnell, J., Johnson, J.W., Riesen, T., & Polychronis, S. (2007). A comparison of one-to-one embedded instruction in the general education classroom and one-to-
one massed practice instruction in the special education classroom. *Education & Treatment of Children, 30*, 23–44.

Jameson, J.M., McDonnell, J., Polychronis, S., & Riesen, T. (2008). Embedded, constant time
delay instruction by peers without disabilities in general education classrooms. *Intellectual and Developmental Disabilities, 46*, 346–363.

Jimenez, B.A., Browder, D.M., Spooner, F., & DiBiase, W. (2012). Inclusive inquiry science
using peer-mediated embedded instruction for students with a moderate intellectual disability. *Exceptional Children, 78*, 301–317.

Kress, G. (2003). *Literacy in the new media age.* London, England: Routledge.

London, J. (1963). *The call of the wild.* New York, NY: Macmillan.

Mastropieri, M.A., & Scruggs, T.E. (1997). Best practices in promoting reading comprehension in students with learning disabilities. *Remedial and Special Education, 18*, 197–213.

MetaMetrics. (2011). *Lexile analyzer* [Internet software]. Retrieved from http://lexile.com.

Mims, P.J. (2009). *The effects of the system of least prompts on teaching comprehension skills during a shared story to students with significant intellectual disabilities*
(Unpublished doctoral dissertation). University of North Carolina at Charlotte, NC.

Mims, P.J., Hudson, M., & Browder, D.M. (2012). The effects of systematic instruction on teaching comprehension skills during a biography to students with significant intellectual disabilities. *Focus on Autism and Other Developmental Disabilities, 27*, 67–80.

National Governors Association Center for Best Practices, Council of Chief State School Officers. (2010). *Common Core State Standards (English language arts)*. Washington, DC: Authors. Retrieved from http://www.corestandards.org/

National Reading Panel. (2000). *Teaching children to read: An evidence-based assessment of the scientific research literature on reading and its implications for reading instruction*. (NIH Publication No. 00-4754). Washington, DC: US Department of Health and Human Services.

Neilsen, L. (2006). Playing for real: Performantive texts and adolescent identities. In D. Alvermann, K. Hinchman, S. Phelps, & S. Waff (Eds.), *Reconceptualizing the literacies in adolescents' lives* (pp. 5–28). Mahwah, NJ: Lawrence Erlbaum Associates.

North Carolina Department of Public Instruction. (2012). English language arts and math unpacking standards. Retrieved from http://www.ncpublicschools.org/acre/standards/common-core-tools/#unpacking

Pearson, P.D., & Gallagher, M.C. (1983). The instruction of reading comprehension. *Contemporary Educational Psychology, 8*, 317–344.

Phillips, V., & Wong, C. (2010). Tying together the common core of standards, instruction, and assessments. *Phi Delta Kappan, 91*, 37–42.

Raphael, T.E. (1986). Teaching question-answer relationships, revisited. *The Reading Teacher, 39*, 516–522.

Rasinski, T.V., & Padak, N.D. (2008). *Evidence-based instruction in reading: A professional development guide to comprehension*. Boston, MA: Pearson.

Reinking, D. (1997). Me and my hypertext: A multiple digression analysis of technology and literacy. *The Reading Teacher, 50*, 626–643.

Vacca, J.L., Vacca, R.T., Gove, M.K., Burkey, L.C., Lenhart, L.A., & McKeon, C.A. (2012). *Reading and learning to read* (8th ed.). Boston, MA: Pearson.

Vacca, R.T., Vacca, J.L., & Mraz, M. (in press). *Content area reading: Literacy and learning across the curriculum* (11th ed.). Boston, MA: Pearson.

Wahlberg, T., & Magliano, J.P. (2004). The ability of high function individuals with autism to comprehend written discourse. *Discourse Processes, 38*, 119–144. doi:10.1207/s15326 950dp3801_5

White, E.B. (1952). *Charlotte's web*. New York, NY: Harper Brothers.

Williamson, P., Carnahan, C.R., & Jacobs, J.A. (2012). Reading comprehension profiles of high-functioning students on the autism spectrum: A grounded theory. *Exceptional Children, 78*, 449–469.

Wolery, M., Ault, M.J., & Doyle, P.M. (1992). *Teaching students with moderate to severe disabilities: Use of response prompting strategies*. New York, NY: Longman.

Zakas, T., Browder, D., Ahlgrim-Delzell, L., & Heafner, T. (2013). *Teaching social studies content to students with autism using a graphic organizer intervention*. Manuscript in preparation.

Zisimopoulos, D., Sigafoos, J., & Koutromanos, G. (2011). Using video prompting and constant time delay to teach an internet search basic skill to students with intellectual disabilities. *Education and Training in Autism and Developmental Disabilities, 46*, 238–250.

FOR FURTHER INFORMATION

Research Articles

Browder, D.M., Hudson, M.E., & Wood, L. (in press). Teaching students with moderate intellectual disability who are emergent readers to comprehend text. *Exceptionality*.

Browder, D.M., Lee, A., & Mims, P.J. (2011). Using shared stories and individual response modes to promote comprehension and engagement in literacy for students with multiple, severe disabilities. *Education and Training in Autism and Developmental Disabilities, 46*, 339–351.

Browder, D.M., Trela, K., & Jimenez, B. (2007). Training teachers to follow a task analysis to engage middle school students with moderate and severe developmental disabilities in grade-appropriate literature. *Focus on Autism and Other Developmental Disabilities, 22*, 206–219.

Hudson, M.E., & Browder, D.M. (2013). *Using peers and grade-level read-alouds to teach listening comprehension to students with moderate intellectual disability.* Manuscript under review.

Hudson, M.E., Browder, D.M., & Jimenez, B. (in press). Effects of a peer-delivered system of least prompts intervention and adapted science read-alouds on listening comprehension for participants with moderate intellectual disability. *Education and Training in Autism and Developmental Disabilities.*

Mims, P., Browder, D.M., Baker, J., Lee, A., & Spooner, F. (2009). Increasing comprehension of students with significant intellectual disabilities and visual impairments during shared stories. *Education and Treatment in Developmental Disabilities, 44*, 409–420.

Mims, P.J., Hudson, M., & Browder, D.M. (2012). The effects of systematic instruction on teaching comprehension skills during a biography to students with significant intellectual disabilities. *Focus on Autism and Other Developmental Disabilities, 27*, 67–80.

Saunders, A., Spooner, F., Browder, D.M., Wakeman, S., & Lee, A. (in press). Building the meaning of texts: Teaching the common core in English language arts to students with severe disabilities. *TEACHING Exceptional Children.*

Resources for Adapted Texts

Lee, A., Mims, P., & Browder, D. (2009). *Pathways to literacy.* Verona, WI: Attainment Co.
Zakas, T., & Schrieber, L. (2010). *Building with stories.* Verona, WI: Attainment Co.

CAST UDL Book Builder

http://bookbuilder.cast.org

This web site provides a free service for creating and sharing adapted digital texts.

Discovery Education

http://discoveryeducation.com

This web site serves as a resource for grade-aligned science e-texts.

Lexile Analyzer

http://www.lexile.com/analyzer

This web site provides a free service for analyzing text complexity for uploaded files.

Web Sites Related to the Common Core State Standards

Common Core State Standards Initiative

http://www.corestandards.org

This web site contains the English Language Arts and Mathematics standards across grade levels, including supporting documents.

Common Core State Standards for English Language Arts: Appendix B: Text Exemplars and Sample Performance Tasks

http://www.corestandards.org/assets/Appendix_B.pdf

This web site contains examples of standards-based, grade-aligned texts.

North Carolina Department of Public Instruction

http://www.ncpublicschools.org/acre/standards/common-core-tools

This web site provides links to Unpacking Standards, English Language Arts progression documents, text examples, and graphic organizers.

**Partnership for Assessment of
Readiness for College and Careers (PARCC)**

http://www.parcconline.org

This web site provides assessment and implementation information for teaching English Language Arts standards.

Smarter Balanced Assessment Consortium

http://www.smarterbalanced.org

This web site provides sample assessments aligned to the Common Core State Standards as well as information about teacher collaboration and professional development.

CHAPTER 5

Reading for Students Who Are Nonverbal

Lynn Ahlgrim-Delzell, Pamela J. Mims, and Jean Vintinner

Isa is 12 years old and in seventh grade. He has severe intellectual disability and is nonverbal. He has some gross motor limitations such that his movements are slow, but deliberate. He consistently uses gestures, objects, and vocalizations to communicate and gain social attention. He attempts to communicate his daily wants and needs. He is learning to communicate with pictures and currently uses about 10 pictures consistently to follow his daily schedule. New pictures are being paired with objects to increase his picture vocabulary throughout the day. He participates in reading shared stories and can answer literal comprehension questions using a picture/object paired response system with up to two distractors while using the system of least prompts.

Ophelia is 6 years old and in first grade. She has moderate intellectual disability and Down syndrome. She consistently attempts to vocalize her wants and needs, but her articulation makes it difficult for others to understand her, so she uses pictures and some words to supplement her communications. She has a vocabulary of about 50 pictures and five sight words that she can consistently use throughout her school day. She receives literacy instruction using a published literacy curriculum. She is making good progress in learning to text point, completing a repeated story line, identifying letter sounds, increasing her sight word vocabulary, and clapping out the syllables in words. Ophelia enjoys listening to books on tape and can often be found looking at books during her free time.

Godfrey is 9 years old and in fourth grade. He has severe autism. Godfrey is often heard repeating several phrases to himself, and he responds to verbal communication by repeating what has been said to him. Although he is verbal, he cannot participate in a spontaneous verbal conversation. He communicates his wants and needs with gestures and an augmentative and alternative communication (AAC) device with pictures and words in the cells. He completed a published early literacy curriculum and is beginning to learn phonics. He can identify more than 100 sight words and most letter–sound correspondences in isolation and as a beginning sound in words using his AAC device.

This chapter begins by reviewing the expectations of the foundations for learning to read from the Common Core State Standards (CCSS) in English language arts (ELA). A quick review of these skills and how they are defined will help maintain adherence to the general concept for teaching these skills to students who do not communicate verbally. Research on teaching reading to this specific population is then reviewed, which leads to a discussion of how this research translates into practice.

COMMON CORE EXPECTATIONS OF EARLY LITERACY FOUNDATIONAL SKILLS

The CCSS in ELA attempt to create a "staircase of increasing complexity" (p. 8) that supports students as they build on the framework of reading skills they develop in early years (National Governors Association Center for Best Practices, Council of Chief State School Officers, 2010). Formally beginning in kindergarten, the CCSS prescribe instruction in foundational skills necessary to foster reading skills, such as concepts about print, which build a basic understanding of how to interact with text, and phonemic awareness, phonics, word recognition, and fluency, all of which allow students to decode and identify words with increasing accuracy and automaticity allowing for comprehension. In addition to these essential skills, the CCSS also recognize the abilities of emerging readers and planning instruction to lay the groundwork for ways of understanding and reflecting on literary and informational texts. Students begin exploring ideas that ask them to make connections to and between texts much earlier than previous state and local curriculums previously required, making learning to read a meaningful and engaging task.

Print Concepts

As students learn to read, they first learn to interact with text. The concepts about print (Clay, 2000) outlined in the CCSS for kindergarten and first grade include behaviors that are precursors to decoding and have been correlationally linked to future performance in reading (National Institute of Child Health and Human Development [NICHD], 2010). These behaviors include an understanding of directionality—that text should be read from left to right and from top to bottom—and an understanding that words are separated by spaces, which allow a reader to meaningfully group letters to convey a message. Students also learn to recognize letters, a skill that has been linked to future abilities in both reading and writing (NICHD, 2010). And as a precursor to phonological and phonemic awareness, children begin to understand that spoken words can be represented in text. For students to become successful readers, they need to master an understanding of these basic concepts about print.

Phonological Awareness

The next stage of development in reading—phonological awareness—is also a reliable predictor of future reading and writing ability (NICHD, 2000, 2010) and has been incorporated into the CCSS for primary grades. During this stage, emergent readers learn to manipulate letter sounds and recognize rhymes, often practicing this ability by deleting, adding, or replacing individual sounds in words to form new words. They learn to break words apart into segments and bring them back together in blends. Practice in manipulating sounds in words is a necessary preliminary ability to the systematic study of phonics, which takes the next step to connect these sounds to letters and words in print.

Phonics and Word Recognition

Phonics instruction develops the understanding of the relationship between letters and sounds (NICHD, 2000, 2010). As readers develop automaticity in their word recognition, the influence of phonics begins to wane but remains a necessary skill for decoding new and unfamiliar words.

According to the National Reading Panel (NRP; NICHD, 2000), there are five types of phonics instruction:

1. *Analogy:* Readers are taught to connect new knowledge to letter–sound or word correlations with which they are already familiar, capitalizing on students' existing schema.

2. *Analytical phonics:* Instruction supports students as they analyze new words by making connections to those words previously learned.

3. *Embedded phonics:* A less explicit method in which students engage in shared reading and decode words in text. This process aims to support students understanding of the relevance of decoding through the practical application of the skill during reading texts. Practices such as this are beneficial to helping students recognize decoding as a means to an end, placing focus on blending and whole word recognition.

4. *Spelling lessons:* Students are taught to segment words into phonemes and learn both sound and spelling patterns in the process.

5. *Synthetic phonics instruction:* Requires readers to convert letters into sounds then blend together the sounds to recreate words.

A more mature aspect of phonics implemented by the CCSS includes morphology: the study of meaningful word parts such as prefixes, suffixes, and root words. Morphology requires readers to have basic decoding and word recognition skills. More than half of words in the English language include Greek and Latin roots. Knowledge of common affixes can help students decode more than 60% of unknown words encountered in text (Bromley, 2007; Nagy & Anderson, 1984).

Fluency

Fluency is the ability to read with the appropriate rate, accuracy, and expression to support comprehension. The assumption is that students who read too slowly or too quickly, with too many errors, or without a true understanding of the voice of the author will not fully understand the content (NICHD, 2000).

In order to build fluency, guided and repeated oral reading is the most effective method of instruction and assessment, allowing students and teachers to hear reading performance. Although silent reading is a more authentic way of reading (NICHD, 2000), reading out loud offers students an opportunity to hear themselves as they read orally with the purpose of practicing word identification and self-correction through the use of strategies such as self-corrections during rereading and use of context to determine accuracy. This type of shared reading experience has been recognized as the most valuable tool in supporting literacy development in the areas of print knowledge and oral language (NICHD, 2010).

REVIEW OF LITERACY RESEARCH WITH STUDENTS WITH MODERATE TO SEVERE INTELLECTUAL DISABILITY

There is a body of research that suggests students with moderate to severe intellectual disability can learn to read as a result of instruction of the literacy skills identified by the NRP (NICHD, 2000) using systematic instructional techniques common with this population of students. Although a majority of this early research concentrated on sight word acquisition (Browder, Wakeman, Spooner, Ahlgrim-Delzell, & Algozzine, 2006), investigations of the other four essential components identified by the NRP—phonemic awareness, phonics, comprehension, and fluency—(NICHD, 2000) is emerging, but mostly with students with the ability to respond with the verbal facility necessary to participate in choral responding, produce reasonable productions of the individual phonemes, and manipulate the phoneme sounds in blending and segmenting activities during instruction or through the selection of tests used in measuring the dependent variables (e.g., Allor, Mathes, Roberts, Jones, & Champlin, 2010; Bradford, Shippen, Alberto, Houchins, & Flores, 2006; Conners, Rosenquist, Sligh, Atwell, & Kiser, 2006; Coyne, Pisha, Dalton, Zeph, & Smith, 2010; Flores & Ganz, 2009). In this section the reading research involving students who do not communicate verbally is reviewed.

As described previously, print concepts are those early prereading skills needed to interact with text, such as reading from left to right and top to bottom and turning pages, in order to establish the understanding that spoken words can be represented in text. There is a series of studies on the use of read-alouds (shared stories) with a task analysis of 10–16 steps for students to engage in age-appropriate text and systematic instruction to teach print concepts to students who require alternatives to verbal responding. Two studies (Browder, Lee, & Mims, 2011; Browder, Mims, Spooner, Ahlgrim-Delzell, & Lee, 2008) used shared story experiences with individualized response adaptions to the task analysis to improve the engagement and responding of students with profound multiple disabilities. Students responded through touching or gazing at pictures, vocalizations such as laughing, or selecting from pictures/words on voice output devices. Mims, Browder, Baker, Lee, and Spooner (2009) embedded objects during the reading of a shared story that were then used along with distractor objects as the response options to comprehension questions about the story. Although the students in this study had visual impairments, the process of using objects can be applied to students with speech impairments as well. These studies were conducted with elementary-age students, but this process can also be used for older students by adapting grade-level text with software such as Writing with Symbols (Mayer-Johnson, 2000), pairing words with pictures or picture symbols, and use of voice output devices preprogrammed with voiced options by which students can select an answer (Browder, Trela, & Jimenez, 2007).

There also is research to support the instruction of phonological awareness and phonics skills for students with speech impairments. Although phonological awareness is the ability to manipulate letter sounds, phonics pairs these sounds to the printed letter and word. Wolff-Heller and colleagues (Heller, Fredrick, & Diggs, 1999; Heller, Fredrick, Tumlin, & Brineman, 2002) have developed a strategy called the Nonverbal Reading Approach that is designed to be used in conjunction with other reading programs to teach students to use internal speech to promote the acquisition of phonetic reading skills. This approach has been successful in teaching students to use internal speech to sound out words in their head then select a written word to represent it. Although these two studies and one more study (Swinehart-Jones & Heller, 2009) were successful in increasing the number of words read with students with mild intellectual disability, one study also demonstrated success with students with moderate intellectual disability (Cohen, Heller, Alberto, & Fredrick, 2008). By using diagnostic distractor arrays, in which the response choices offered to the student are carefully planned to support error analysis, instruction can be planned to include additional practice on the specific errors a student makes. A more detailed discussion about planning response options for students is provided later in this chapter.

Systematic instruction such as most-to-least prompting and time delay has also proved to be effective in teaching early literacy skills including phonological awareness skills and beginning phonics instruction with students with moderate to severe intellectual disability who do not communicate verbally (Browder, Ahlgrim-Delzell, Courtade, Gibbs, & Flowers, 2008). They used teacher script and systematic instruction practices along with nonverbal student response materials using letters, pictures, and words. A longitudinal study of students with moderate to severe disability demonstrated that such students could learn these skills using pointing and eye gazing as a nonverbal responding format (Browder, Ahlgrim-Delzell, Flowers, & Baker, 2010).

Many children with speech difficulties rely on the use of AAC devices. These devices use pictures and word referents on individual cells where the word or phrase is voiced for the child when he or she presses the cell. Fallon, Light, McNaughton, and colleagues have documented the successful instruction of phonological awareness and decoding skills of children who use these devices using direct instruction techniques and response foils on cards by which the students pointed or gazed to the correct response (Fallon, Light, McNaughton, Drager, & Hammer, 2004) or by incorporating the use of an AAC device for the student to respond (Light, McNaughton, Weyer, & Karg, 2008). Although it is clear by the student descriptions in the research studies that some students had intellectual disability, the severity of intellectual disability is not clear because the speech difficulty and use of an AAC device were the primary factors in the participant selection criteria.

BUILDING ON RESEARCH FOR PRACTICE

When planning for literacy instruction for students with intellectual disability who do not communicate verbally, is important to use what is known from research. The research described in the previous section supports systematic instruction, use of shared stories, and scripted curricula.

Systematic Instruction

Response and stimulus prompting strategies essential in systematic instruction come in a variety of forms (e.g., verbal, pictorial, partial physical) and are often used in combination with error correction and reinforcement strategies. There are two prompt fading approaches that include response prompting and stimulus prompting strategies. Response prompting strategies include progressive time delay, constant time delay, simultaneous prompting, system of least prompts, most-to-least prompts, and graduated guidance. Stimulus prompting strategies include superimposition, stimulus shaping, and stimulus fading. All of these strategies can be used in teaching components of reading to students who are nonverbal, although some are easier to use than others.

Research has shown that several response prompting strategies have been successful in teaching components of reading to students with significant disabilities who do not communicate verbally. For example, both progressive and constant time delay have been identified as an evidence-based practice for teaching picture and word recognition (Browder, Ahlgrim-Delzell, Spooner, Mims, & Baker, 2009). System of least prompts has been used to teach comprehension in several studies (Mims et al., 2009; Mims, Hudson, & Browder, 2012). Simultaneous prompting has been used to teach words (Singleton, Schuster, Morse, & Collins, 1999; Smith, Schuster, Collins, & Kleinert, 2011), sounds, and blending skills to students with significant disabilities (Waugh, Fredrick, & Alberto, 2009). Most-to-least prompts and graduated guidance have been used to teach picture symbols (Massey & Wheeler, 2000). Stimulus shaping and stimulus fading have been used to teach sight words for students with significant disabilities (Lalli & Browder, 1993). Finally, superimposition and stimulus fading have been shown to be effective in teaching sight words to students with autism (Birkan, McClannahan, & Krantz, 2007).

Shared Stories

Shared stories are an approach to systematically teaching emergent literacy skills such as concepts about print. A shared story can also embed other reading skills, vocabulary, word recognition, and phonics using text from the story. This section describes 1) how books may need to be adapted, 2) how to incorporate an AAC device, 3) how to embed other reading skills, and 4) how to apply a task analysis when using a shared story with students with speech impairments.

Adapting Books   Adapting books is very important for students with disabilities, as it provides a means for this group of students to access age- and grade-appropriate books. For students who do not communicate verbally, there are several adaptations that need to be considered. First, it is important to preserve the integrity of the overall message/subject of the book, but it may also be important to reduce the amount of text on the page, as often too much text can be unappealing and overwhelming. One way to do this without compromising the integrity of the text is to preread, summarize, and rewrite the book using language and supports that are appropriate for the students. There are several resources educators can use to check for the readability of an adapted version. One resource is The Lexile Framework for Reading (http://www.lexile.com). Another resource is to use the readability scale found in Microsoft Word. This can be found under Proofing within the Options menu (check "Show readability statistics"). The scale is known as the Flesch-Kincaide Grade Level test and provides a rate for the text based on U.S.

school grade levels. A score of 2.0 using this method means that a second grader can understand the text. Finally, the Simple Measure of Gobbledygook (SMOG), created by Harry McLaughlin, is another tool that estimates the readability of a text (http://www.harrymclaughlin.com/SMOG.htm). When rewriting the text it is important to consider adding in definitions, explanations, and targeted vocabulary. All of these additions can help promote comprehension of the text.

Another book adaptation that may need to occur, especially in chapter books in which pictures are few and far between, is to add photo, picture, and/or object support. Some popular software to consider in adding picture support include Writing with Symbols (Mayer-Johnson, 2000), SymWriter (Mayer-Johnson, n.d.), Boardmaker (Mayer-Jonhson, n.d.), and Picture It! (SunCastle Technology, n.d.), all of which come with a library of pictures that can accompany the text. Adding in salient objects can be especially helpful for students who do not yet use pictures or words to communicate or who are not yet demonstrating intentional responding (Browder, Lee, et al., 2011). In a study by Mims and colleagues (2009), salient objects were added to adapted grade-appropriate books as a means for students to "read" with the instructor. These same objects were then paired with distractor objects and used as response options to answer comprehension questions.

Teachers also need to consider how physically accessible the book is for students with motor disabilities. One option to help with the physical accessibility of the book is to take it apart, laminate and hole punch each page, and rebind the book by putting it in a three-ring binder. This provides durability to the book, which is often needed when working with students with significant disabilities. To add further support for students with motor disabilities, page turners such as popsicle sticks, page fluffers, or spacers can be placed on each page to allow the reader to participate in turning the pages on his or her own.

Incorporating an Augmentative and Alternative Communication Device

In addition to adapting books, students who do not communicate verbally often need to use an AAC device to have the best success at learning to read and participate in story-based lessons. AAC devices are powerful tools that can help promote access to a variety of activities. For example, students can use a prerecorded voice output device, such as a BIGmack communicator (Mayer-Johnson, n.d.) when participating in anticipating the repeated storyline during a story-based lesson. So while participating in a shared story based on *Alexander and the Terrible, Horrible, No Good, Very Bad Day* by Judith Viorst, for example, the teacher would read aloud to the class and when coming to the repeated story line of "Alexander was having a terrible, horrible, no good, very bad day," the teacher would stop reading before saying "bad day" and wait for the student to fill in the repeated storyline. For students with speech impairments, they could easily activate the section on the AAC device that is prerecorded to say BAD DAY in order to participate in reading the repeated story line. AAC devices can also be used to answer comprehension questions by using a picture communication board with the target answer and distractors. This was used in a study by Mims and colleagues (2012) in which students with autism answered *wh-* questions during a shared reading from adapted grade-aligned biographies using picture symbol response options for the presentation of each comprehension question.

Embedding Other Reading Skills   During a shared story it is important to think about embedding the five areas of reading as identified by the NRP (NICHD, 2000). The five components of reading identified by the NRP included vocabulary, comprehension, phonological awareness, phonics, and fluency. Vocabulary can be addressed when adapting a book to make sure that the targeted vocabulary is incorporated into the text. Before conducting the lesson the teacher can preteach the vocabulary using constant time delay, and then during the shared story, the teacher can stop on the page containing the target word and ask for students to identify the key vocabulary word on the page. A student who has speech impairments can participate by activating the appropriate vocabulary word on his or her AAC device.

To address phonemic awareness and phonics during a story-based lesson, the teacher can easily embed quick teaching trials. For example, to embed phonemic awareness in the shared story, the teacher could easily work on blending by saying "I want you to find the vocabulary word I say the slow way. Point to the word I say. Get ready, sssssiiit." The student should point to the picture that represents *sit*. When addressing phonics, the teacher could have students point to the word(s) on the page that begin with the /s/ sound.

Comprehension is easily added during a shared story. It is important that the teacher ask a variety of comprehension questions that vary in the depth of understanding (e.g., Bloom's Taxonomy; Anderson & Krathwohl, 2001). Questions can range from recall (e.g., "What did Alexander have in his mouth when he went to bed?") to evaluation (e.g., "Alexander decided to move to Australia because he was having a very bad day. What else could Alexander have done to make his day better?"). The teacher should preread the text/chapter to identify different types of questions to ask and have preset response options and distractors ready to present in a symbol form appropriate for students (e.g., photo, picture, word).

Fluency can be addressed through repeated readings of the same text. Progressive time delay for word or phoneme recognition may be useful to decrease the response time and increase the number of words/phonemes identified in a set period of time. The speed element may be more difficult for students that have motor difficulties that are associated with speech impairments (e.g., cerebral palsy) when pointing and gazing at responses.

Applying a Task Analysis   Another common feature in systematic instruction is the use of task analysis instruction in which a chained skill (one that is made up of multiple components) is broken down into smaller discrete skills. This has recently been used as an approach to implementing a shared story, also known as a story-based lesson or a read-aloud (Browder, Trela, & Jimenez, 2007). A shared story is made up of different components all designed to develop early emergent literacy skills such as the concepts of print, words, and letters (Browder, Courtade-Little, Wakeman, & Rickelman, 2006). Browder and colleagues (2006) recommended 10 steps for participating in a shared story. These steps include: 1) finding an anticipatory set, 2) orienting the book, 3) finding the author, 4) finding the title, 5) asking a prediction question, 6) opening the book, 7) turning the page, 8) pointing to text, 9) understanding vocabulary, and 10) asking a comprehension question. A good way to teach these steps is through total task chaining. Total task chaining is an approach to teaching a chained skill that allows the learner to learn each step of the task analysis each time it is presented, as opposed to forward or backward chaining in which only one step is taught at a time until mastery before adding on a new step (Spooner, Browder, & Mims, 2011). When using total task chaining to teach a shared story, the instructor needs to present each of the steps of the shared story each time.

Scripted Curricula

Commercially available, scripted curricula designed for classroom instruction has long been available in general education classrooms. These resources provide premade materials with scripted lessons that teachers can use in individualized, small-group or classroomwide instruction. This has not been true, however, for special education classrooms with students with severe disabilities such as autism or developmental disabilities. Perhaps it is the philosophy of individualized instruction, but historically teachers of such students not only create the academic curricula through individualized education programs but also frequently make or modify the materials needed. Use of scripted curricula is controversial. Advocates say that scripted curricula provide teachers with effective, research-based models that can be followed with fidelity (Beatty, 2011). Opponents say that scripted curricula limits teacher autonomy and restricts the teacher's ability to respond to individual student needs (Beatty). Having access to such curricula in special education classrooms can be one more option.

Direct Instruction

Direct instruction has long been used as a successful teaching approach for all students, including those with disabilities (Watkins & Slocum, 2004). Some of the essential components of direct instruction include careful program design that focuses on the big ideas, organization of instruction, and student–teacher interactions. An important feature that falls under student–teacher interactions is known as active student responding (ASR; Heward, 1994). ASR strategies are those that promote students' active participation during instruction, thus reducing off-task behaviors and ultimately increasing student learning. One common ASR procedure, known as model-lead-test (MLT), provides teachers with a format that includes the teacher modeling, the teacher leading the whole class in unison responding, and the whole class providing a unison response without the teacher model. This method can be modified for students who do not communicate verbally by providing students with an AAC device or response cards, which allows them to actively participate in the unison response.

GETTING STARTED

This section provides examples of how the information from the first part of this chapter can be implemented by discussing how to plan for student responding and how adapting for alternatives for verbal responding may change the nature of the skill as defined in the CCSS. Next, examples of how to use the evidence-based practice described previously are used to develop Systematic Instruction Plans, task analysis for a shared story, commercially available curricula, and MLT scripts.

Planning for Student Responding

Providing students who do not communicate verbally a viable option to express wants and needs is of paramount importance. Planning how a student will demonstrate knowledge should first consider the typical manner in which the student communicates. In this section, we review some considerations for creating response options that use pointing, eye gazing, and AAC devices.

Requiring students to point to pictures, words, and letters printed on paper is a common form of student response. How the response options are created and displayed (e.g., font, size, color) can be varied to the needs of individual students. Different fonts form different variations of letters. While Times New Roman is often the default in word processing programs, notice how it represents the letters a and g. In many early grades, an *a* is typically formed as a, and a *g* is typically formed as g. Comic Sans MS, a font type available in Microsoft Office, forms letters such as those used in early reading text that can be used in creating response options to avoid confusion between different letter formations. Increasing the size of the font may be useful for not only students with visual impairments but also students with physical impairments that need a bigger space in order to point accurately. Color can be used as a stimulus prompt by using a different font color or by placing a colored border to designate the correct answer.

The number of response options from which the student is to select a response can also be varied. As the number of distractor (incorrect) cards increase, so does the difficulty of the task. For example, if two options are placed before a student whereby one is the correct answer, the odds of a student guessing the correct answer is 1 out of 2 (i.e., 50/50 or 50%). The odds of a student guessing the correct answer with four options in which one is the correct answer is 1 out of 4 (i.e., 25%). The two-option model may be useful when teaching a new vocabulary word or phoneme, but the number of distractors should be increased over time to at least four.

It also is a good idea to print response options so that each option is on an individual piece of paper or index card rather than all of the options on a single sheet. With individual cards, the position of the options can be varied at each trial. For example, with four options in a 2x2 array, the correct answer might be in the upper left corner on the first trial and then switched to the lower right corner on the second trial. Varying the location prevents memorization and will teach the student to look at all of the options before making a selection.

The difficulty of the task can also be varied by level of discrimination needed to select the correct answer in the response options. Distractor items that are clearly different from the correct answer are easier than distractor items that are increasingly more similar to the correct answer. Discriminations can be made by content, letter/word formation, or phoneme pronunciation. For example, when using an array of response options to answer a comprehension question about a story, an easy discrimination will be distractor words that do not appear in the story and do not make conceptual sense. A more difficult array will include other vocabulary words in the story as distractor options, but may not make sense in answering the specific comprehension question. An even more difficult array will be one in which the distractor words make logical sense but are not the correct answer in context of the specific story. Figure 5.1 provides an illustration of how distractor options may vary based on content.

An easy distractor array to a comprehension question: What was in Alexander's hair when he woke up in the morning?

| gum | yellow | fast | stop |

The distractor words do not appear in the story and do not make logical sense to answer the question.

A slightly more difficult distractor array to a comprehension question: What was in Alexander's hair when he woke up in the morning?

| gum | bad | day | car |

The distractor words appear in the story, but they do not make logical sense to answer the question.

A difficult distractor array to a comprehension question: What was in Alexander's hair when he woke up in the morning?

| gum | brush | candy | cereal |

The distractor words appear in the story and are reasonable substitutes to answer the question.

Figure 5.1. Varying the difficulty of distractor options based on content.

Response options that vary on letter/word formation and phoneme pronunciation are those words that contain beginning or ending letters/letter sounds that are similar or distinctly different from the correct answer. Using variations of beginning and ending letters of words is especially useful for demonstrating knowledge of recognizing irregular words. Irregular words are those with one or more letters that do not use the most common phoneme sound, such as *the* or *was*. For example, demonstrating knowledge of the word *the*, distinctly different options in the easy distractor may include *yellow, fast, stop*. A more difficult array may include *top, she*, and *tea*. An even more difficult array may include *that, there*, and *them*. Phoneme-based arrays are most useful for regular words in which the phoneme sounds are a common sound such as CVC (consonant-vowel-consonant) words (e.g., *bad, gum*). An example of an easy phoneme-based array for blending the word /b/ /a/ /d/ could be *gum, cot*, and *men*. A more difficult array might use *peg, bug*, and *pup*. An even more difficult array might use *bed, bag*, and *bat*.

Heller and colleagues (2002) described how distractor options can also be used for error analysis in identifying difficulty with specific phonemes. By systematically varying the phonemes in the response options, repeated student errors can be used for reteaching specific phonemes. In the example for sounding out *bad*, if the student repeatedly picks an option with a different vowel sound, such as *bed*, then the student may need additional practice with distinguishing between the /a/ and /e/ sounds. If the student repeatedly picks words with a different ending sound such as *bag*, then the student may need additional practice with ending sounds.

AAC devices can also be used for student responding. The advantage for using an AAC device is the ability to hear the phoneme being pronounced as a result of the student selection. The student can hear the sound of the letter selected and then he or she can confirm that this was the sound he or she intended to select. The distractor suggestions for color, font, number, and variations can also be used with AAC devices by varying the content of the cells and the number of cells that are preprogrammed with the responses. There are some possible limitations depending on the specific device, however. Sound quality may be a particular issue, especially in the ability to distinguish between similar phonemes such as /f/ and /s/ or /b/ and /p/. A second issue to consider before using an AAC device is the spacing between sounds when teaching blending or segmenting skills. The silent space between the phonemes when using a device needs to be limited so that the word being blended can be distinguished. Too much space can distort the blending in order to hear the word being formed. A third issue to consider when using an AAC device when the phonemes are preprogrammed manually in the cells is the correct pronunciation of each phoneme. Some phonemes are held longer than others and are categorized as either continuous or stop sounds. Continuous sounds hold the sound for 2–3 seconds, such as *sssss* for /s/. Stop sounds such as *d* for /d/ are a single abrupt sound. Stop sounds such as /c/ are particularly easy to mispronounce in isolation as needed to be programmed into a single cell for a blending activity. Be careful not to add a vowel sound at the end of a stop sound such as recording *pa* for /p/. Requesting the assistance of a speech-language professional to produce or review the sounds for an AAC device is a good practice.

Contemporary technology is available to assist with overcoming some of the potential issues with specific AAC devices. Use of text-to-speech software can eliminate the need for teachers to preprogram words and phonemes. There are a variety of male and female voices and accents available. There is still a need to review the words formed by blending individual phonemes, though, as the text-to-speech software may not understand the specific word to be formed using only phonemes. For example, to correctly blend the phonemes for the word *toss* use /t/ /o/ /s/; however, the text-to-speech software may think the word is meant to be pronounced as *toes*. In such cases, after the student correctly presses /t/ /o/ /s/, you can simply press the cell and add an extra /s/ and say, "Yes, you are correct, and this is how we spell *toss* in order to hear the correct word." Another option that can be useful is auditory cuing. Auditory cuing requires the user to press each cell twice before it is displayed as the student response. This allows the user to press a cell once to hear the letter sound/word selected to confirm that this is what he or she intended or to self-correct if it was not. After hearing the letter sound/word, the cell is then pressed a second time to display it as the student response. After hearing the selection, if it was not the intended answer, a different cell can be selected to self-correct, then pressed again to be displayed as the response.

While some of these newer technologies may not be available on all AAC devices, they are available through the GoTalk NOW (Attainment Company) application specifically developed for use on an iPad. Teachers can make specific response templates with words and letters or use a picture from the gallery. The GoTalk NOW app is being used to develop a phonics curriculum called *Early Reading Skills Builder* (Ahlgrim-Delzell, Browder, & Wood, in development), which uses text-to-speech software to produce the phoneme sounds and blend individual phonemes selected by the student to form words without the quality and silent space issue that an AAC device might have. *Early Reading Skills Builder* has many functions such as auditory cuing, scanning for a student who uses an eye gaze, and a quiz feature that randomly rotates the response options programmed in the response cells.

When using response cards or an AAC device with letters, words, or pictures to enable a student to demonstrate knowledge nonverbally, we need to be careful about maintaining integrity of the skill as described in the CCSS. This is a particular problem with the distinction between phonemic awareness and phonics. Phonemic awareness is the knowledge of letter sounds in the absence of the written referent. Pairing the sound to the written referent is phonics. One way to teach and allow students who do not communicate verbally the opportunity to demonstrate knowledge of phonemic awareness is to use pictures on the response cards. Pictures of common nouns or verbs can be used to teach the first sound of the word such as /f/ for *fish*. Once the letter is visible on the response card, the skill becomes a phonics skill.

Systematic Instruction Plans

One strategy that teachers can employ to ensure consistent instruction, which in turn leads to faster skill acquisition, is through the use of systematic instruction plans (SIPs; Spooner et al, 2011). A SIP provides a detailed description of how to teach a skill. A SIP typically includes the learning objective, schedule for instruction, prompting system to be used, description for fading out prompts, description of feedback to be used during instruction, and a plan for generalization and maintenance of the skill.

SIPs can be used when teaching a variety of skills as described in the preceding section. Figure 5.2 displays an example of a SIP to teach phonemic awareness skills, and Figure 5.3 illustrates the accompanying data sheet. Notice the link to the CCSS use of an adapted age/grade-level book, and the detailed instructional procedures with fading, feedback, error correction, and a plan for generalizing the learned skill in all the SIPs. A SIP for teaching participation in a shared story

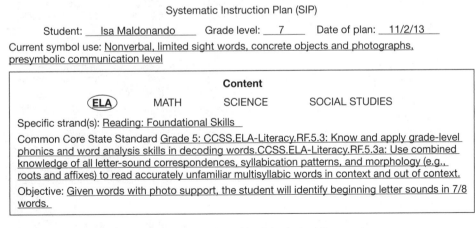

Systematic Instruction Plan (SIP)

Student: ___Isa Maldonando___   Grade level: ___7___   Date of plan: ___11/2/13___

Current symbol use: Nonverbal, limited sight words, concrete objects and photographs, presymbolic communication level

Content
(ELA)   MATH   SCIENCE   SOCIAL STUDIES

Specific strand(s): Reading: Foundational Skills

Common Core State Standard Grade 5: CCSS.ELA-Literacy.RF.5.3: Know and apply grade-level phonics and word analysis skills in decoding words.CCSS.ELA-Literacy.RF.5.3a: Use combined knowledge of all letter-sound correspondences, syllabication patterns, and morphology (e.g., roots and affixes) to read accurately unfamiliar multisyllabic words in context and out of context.

Objective: Given words with photo support, the student will identify beginning letter sounds in 7/8 words.

Figure 5.2.   Example of a systematic instruction plan to identify beginning letter sounds.

(continued)

Figure 5.2. *(continued)*

FORMAT

Unit description (what, from where): <u>Unit on values and decision making (*The Outsiders*)</u>

Materials: <u>Vocab words from *The Outsiders*, adapted book: Greasers, Heroes, Mad, Sick, Brothers, Friend, Police, and Die</u>

Adaptations needed (if any) <u>Laminated photo symbols with printed word of all vocabulary, adapted chapter book</u>

Alternate materials (if any): <u>Magnet board with magnet pieces for vocab words</u>

Setting/when: <u>Three trials right before the lesson within the general education classroom for entire unit of instruction</u>

Who will teach this target behavior: <u>Special education teacher and peer mentor</u>

INSTRUCTIONAL PROCEDURES

Attention Cue: <u>"Isa, look here" while pointing to the stimulus materials</u>

Task analysis (TA):   Yes   ☐ Backward chaining   Ⓝⓞ (If yes, include TA steps)
                                      ☐ Forward chaining
                                      ☐ Total task chaining

Prompting

Specific prompt(s) to be used: <u>Controlling prompt: Model prompt</u>

  Fading (check one):

       ☐ *None (simultaneous prompting)*

       ☐ *Least-to-most intrusive prompts*

       ☑ *Time delay: Progressive _____ or Constant __x__*

       ☐ *Most-to-least intrusive prompts*

       ☐ *Graduated guidance*

       ☐ *Stimulus fading and shaping*

       ☐ *Other (describe)* _____

Define planned fading schedule: <u>Display four words at a time (with different first letter sounds). First three instructional sessions provide a zero-delay round for each target beginning sound/ word while shuffling words between trials (i.e., gives the prompt with the target stimulus; no delay). Label all pictures then say, "Point to the word that starts with the (target first letter sound)" while modeling pointing to the correct answer. If the student consistently responds to the zero delay round, then on the fourth session provide the delay round (3-second delay) by labeling all pictures then presenting the target stimulus, "Find the word that begins with (target first letter sound)" and wait 3 seconds for the student to respond before providing the prompt. Repeat delay round for all targeted first letter sounds. Shuffle words between trials. Only collect data on the delay round.</u>

  Feedback

Praise: <u>Correct answers following prompt, "Nice job, (target word) begins with the (target sound)"; independent correct answer: Provide an enthusiastic high five and say "YES! (Target word) begins with the (target sounds); Incorrect answers: Block and redirect to target word (no praise).</u>

Fading schedule for praise: <u>After three consecutive independent correct answers, start to praise every other correct response.</u>

Error correction: <u>If student starts to answer wrong, block and redirect to correct answer and label correct answer, "This is the word that begins with the (target sound)."</u>

  Generalization procedures

Define plans for student to generalized learned target behavior: <u>Different grade-appropriate text with same target sounds, different photos representing same word, with teacher and peers.</u>

  Promotion of self-directed learning

Define plans: <u>Isa can choose which text to work on and select peer groups to work with in the general education classroom.</u>

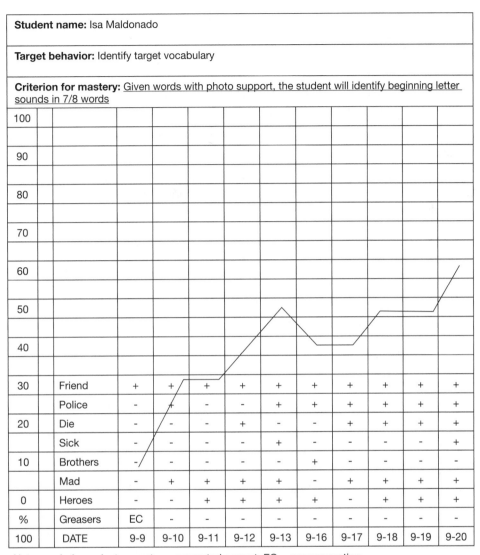

Student name: Isa Maldonado

Target behavior: Identify target vocabulary

Criterion for mastery: <u>Given words with photo support, the student will identify beginning letter sounds in 7/8 words</u>

		9-9	9-10	9-11	9-12	9-13	9-16	9-17	9-18	9-19	9-20
30	Friend	+	+	+	+	+	+	+	+	+	+
	Police	-	+	-	-	+	+	+	+	+	+
20	Die	-	-	-	+	-	-	+	+	+	+
	Sick	-	-	-	-	+	-	-	-	-	+
10	Brothers	-	-	-	-	-	+	-	-	-	-
	Mad	-	+	+	+	+	-	+	+	+	+
0	Heroes	-	-	+	+	+	+	-	+	+	+
%	Greasers	EC	-	-	-	-	-	-	-	-	-
100	DATE	9-9	9-10	9-11	9-12	9-13	9-16	9-17	9-18	9-19	9-20

Note: + = independent correct; − = prompted correct; EC = error correction.

Figure 5.3. Example of a data sheet for the systematic instruction plans to teach beginning letter sounds.

would include the 10-step task analysis outlined previously. Teaching identification of phonemes, blending, or segmenting skills could also include a time-delay technique.

In the data sheet example, the teacher used + to indicate independent correct responses, − to indicate prompted responses, and *EC* to indicate a student error that was corrected. The dates of instruction appear along the bottom, and the specific words are listed. The codes are entered into the boxes above the date across from each word. The percent correct can be graphed and used to evaluate student progress.

Task Analysis

In the previous section we described task analysis and its use in participation in a shared story. Table 5.1 describes how a teacher can modify the task analysis so that a student may respond nonverbally to each of the steps. Some steps, however, do not need to be adapted for nonverbal responding (e.g., pointing to the title and author of the book) because the response is already in a nonverbal format.

Published Curricula

There are several commercially available scripted literacy curricula that have been used to teach literacy skills with students with moderate to severe intellectual disability who do not communicate verbally. In the *Early Literacy Skills Builder* (ELSB; Browder, Gibbs, Courtade-Little, Ahlgrim-Delzell, & Lee, 2007) curriculum, teachers are provided with instructional scripts and materials to teach concepts of print, phonemic awareness, and beginning phonics. The student materials are also provided on a CD so that teachers can adapt them as needed for individual students. Response boards for students who use GoTalk communication devices also are available. The upper level of the ELSB was designed to overlap the phonics sequence of traditional remedial reading curricula such as *Reading Mastery* (McGraw-Hill, 2002). The *Early Reading Skills Builder* (Ahlgrim-Delzell et al., in development) curriculum is a follow-up to the ELSB for those students who will not be able to participate in traditional remedial reading curricula because they cannot respond verbally.

Pathways to Literacy (Lee, Mims, & Browder, 2011) provides a scripted curriculum and materials for students who require objects in order to participate in shared stories, and *Building with Stories* (Zakas & Schreiber, 2010) provides teacher scripts, adapted books, and materials for students who communicate nonverbally so that they can participate in a shared story following the task analysis described earlier in this chapter. Both of these curricula were created using ideas from the authors' research. While the ELSB is designed for students with severe to moderate intellectual disability, *The Explicit Phonemic Alphabetic Connections Curriculum* (Oudeans, 2003) is designed for students with mild to moderate intellectual disability. It also uses scripted lessons and provides materials for students to respond nonverbally to instruction of phonemic awareness, alphabetic understanding, and fluency. *MEville to WEville* (Erickson, 2004) is a literacy program that addresses beginning literacy and communication that integrates AAC. It is not a scripted curriculum but does provide materials to build vocabulary using word walls and writing in the context of character development.

The *Accessible Literacy Learning Reading Program* (ALL; Light & McNaughton, 2008) is also based from NRP recommendations using a direct instruction approach with scripted curriculum for a broad range of students with language delays, speech impairments, or other disabilities. Some of the skills— such as sight words, blending, and segmenting—are similar to those found in the other curricula. It is compatible with Boardmaker (Mayer-Johnson, n.d.) and the DynaVox voice output device (Mayer-Johnson, n.d.). A print version is also available.

Table 5.1.   How a shared story can be adapted for a student to respond nonverbally

Teacher action	Nonverbal adaption	Student action	How a student may respond
Anticipatory set	No adaption needed; same presentation of item associated with story	Responds to attention getter	Vocalization, touch, facial expression, signing, augmentative and alternative communication (AAC) device comment
Ask student to point to the title	No adaption needed; same presentation of book cover	Points to title	No adaption needed; touches title on book cover
Ask student to point to author	No adaption needed; same presentation of book cover	Points to author	No adaption needed; touches author on book cover
Ask student prediction question	Presents response options on cards (or AAC device) from which the student can select an answer	Student makes a prediction (does not have to be accurate)	Student selects from the set provided by pointing, eye gazing, or activating AAC button
Ask student to open the book	No adaption needed; same presentation of book	Opens the book	No adaption needed; opens book
Read story/ask student to finish a repeated story line	Presents options on cards (or AAC device) from which the student can select an answer; The cards or AAC device need to be present at the start of reading the book in a place accessible for the student so that presentation of options or device is not the cue to read the repeated story line	Anticipates repeated story line using their voice or assistive technology to read it	Completes the repeated line by pressing preprogrammed AAC device or selecting word card
Ask student to point to each word as read	No adaption needed; same presentation of text in book	Points to words as teacher points	No adaption needed; points to text as teacher reads
Ask student to identify key vocabulary	Teacher can voice the word or present options on cards (or AAC device) from which the student can select an answer	Correctly finds the key vocabulary word in text	Student points to word in the text itself or selects from the set provided by pointing, eye gazing, or activating AAC button
Ask student to turn pages as read story	No adaption needed; same presentation of book	Turns one or more pages	No adaption needed; student turns pages
Ask student comprehension questions	Presents options on cards (or AAC device) from which the student can select an answer	Answers comprehension questions correctly	Student selects from the set provided by pointing, eye gazing, or activating AAC button

Source: Browder, Spooner, and Ahlgrim-Delzell (2011).

Direct Instruction Script

Earlier in the chapter we described direct instruction using the MLT format. In this format, teachers model the correct response, they lead the group in unison responding, and then the group responds in unison without the teacher model. MLT is a great way to actively engage students who do not communicate verbally in phonemic awareness and phonics skill instruction. By using a preprogrammed AAC device or response card options, students who do not communicate verbally can easily participate in a small group and demonstrate what they know. Figure 5.4 is an example of an MLT script for teaching blending skills with AAC devices.

SUMMARY

Providing opportunities for students who do not communicate verbally to demonstrate what they know requires come creativity. In this chapter, the CCSS for ELA, research identifying evidence-based practices for teaching literacy skills for stu-

---

Blending consonant-vowel-consonant words

Teacher: We are going to use our letter sounds to make some words.

Teacher: What sound does this letter make? *Point to the* m.

Student: (Prerecorded voice output device) /mmmmm/

Teacher: That's right. This letter makes the /mmmmm/ sound.

Teacher: What sound does this letter make? *Point to the* a.

Student: (Prerecorded voice output device) /aaaaaaa/

Teacher: That's right. This letter makes the /aaaaaaa/ sound.

Teacher: What sound does this letter make? *Point the* n.

Student: (Prerecorded voice output device) /nnnnnn/

Teacher: That's right. This letter makes the /nnnnnn/ sound.

Teacher: Let's blend those sounds together. When I point to the letters you say the sounds. My turn first.

Teacher: *Point to the letters, sweeping finger in a fluid motion.* /mmmmm aaaaa nnnnn/

Teacher: Listen as I say it again. *Point to the letters.* /mmmmm aaaaa nnnnn/

Teacher: Now, let's do it together. *Point to the letters.*

Teacher and student: (Prerecorded voice output device) /mmmmm aaaaa nnnnn/

Teacher: Now you do it. I will touch the letters, and you say the sounds. *Point to the letters with a sweeping motion.*

Student: (Prerecorded voice output device) /mmmmm aaaaa nnnnn/

Teacher: That is right. Now say that word the fast way. *Give a signal.*

Student: (Prerecorded voice output device) Man

Teacher: Yes. Those letters say *man.*

Figure 5.4. Example of using a model-lead-test script with an augmentative and alternative communication device.

dents who do not communicate verbally, and guidelines for using these practices were reviewed and some examples of how these practices can be implemented were provided. Systematic instruction, task analysis, and direct instruction can be used to create SIPs to teach concepts of print, phonemic awareness, and phonics skills. The use of response cards or AAC devices can be used to allow students to demonstrate their knowledge and the special considerations needed to vary the difficulty of the response selections. Currently published curricula may be useful for this population of students. When adapting for nonverbal performance it is essential to refer to the key definition of the skill and consider how supplying the picture, letter, or word as response options may alter the integrity of the skill being taught.

REFERENCES

Ahlgrim-Delzell, L., Browder, D., & Wood, L. (in development). *GoTalk Phonics*. Verona, WI: Attainment Company.

Allor, J.H., Mathes, P.G., Roberts, J.K., Jones, F.G., & Champlin, T.M. (2010). Teaching students with moderate intellectual disabilities to read: An experimental examination of a comprehensive reading program. *Education and Training in Autism and Developmental Disabilities, 45*, 3–22.

Anderson, L.W., & Krathwohl, D.R. (Eds.) (2001). *A taxonomy for learning, teaching, and assessing: A revision of Bloom's taxonomy of educational objectives*. New York, NY: Longman.

Beatty, B. (2011). The dilemma of scripted curriculum: Comparing teacher autonomy, fidelity, and resistance in the Frobelian kindergarten, Montessori, direct instruction, and Success for All. *Teachers College Record, 113*, 395–430.

Birkan, B., McClannahan, L.E., & Krantz, P.J. (2007). Effects of superimposition and background fading on the sight-word reading of a boy with autism. *Research in Autism Spectrum Disorders, 1*, 117–125.

Bradford, S., Shippen, M.E., Alberto, P., Houchins, D.E., & Flores, M. (2006). Using systematic instruction to teach decoding skills to middle school students with moderate intellectual disabilities. *Education and Training in Developmental Disabilities, 41*, 333–343.

Bromley, K. (2007). Nine things every teacher should know about words and vocabulary instruction. *Journal of Adolescent and Adult Literacy, 50*, 528–537. doi:10.1598/JAAL.50.7.2

Browder, D.M., Ahlgrim-Delzell, L., Courtade, G., Gibbs, S.L., & Flowers, C. (2008). Evaluation of the effectiveness of an early literacy program for students with significant developmental disabilities using group randomized trial research. *Exceptional Children, 75*, 33–52.

Browder, D.M., Ahlgrim-Delzell, L., Flowers, C., & Baker, J.N. (2010). An evaluation of a multicomponent early literacy program for students with severe developmental disabilities. *Remedial and Special Education, 43*, 237–246. doi:10.1177/0741932510387305

Browder, D., Ahlgrim-Delzell, L., Spooner, F., Mims, P., & Baker, J. (2009). Using time delay to teach picture and word recognition to identify evidence-based practice for students with severe developmental disabilities. *Exceptional Children, 75*, 343–364.

Browder, D.M., Courtade-Little, G., Wakeman, S., & Rickelman, R.J. (2006). From sight words to emerging literacy. In D.M. Browder & F. Spooner (Eds.), *Teaching language arts, math, and science to students with significant cognitive disabilities* (pp. 63–91). Baltimore, MD: Paul H. Brookes Publishing Co.

Browder, D., Gibbs, S., Courtade-Little, G., Ahlgrim-Delzell, L., & Lee, A. (2007). *Early literacy skills builder*. Verona, WI: Attainment Company.

Browder, D.M., Lee, A., & Mims, P.J. (2011). Literacy for students with multiple disabilities: Using systematic instruction, individualized responses, and assistive technology. *Education and Training in Developmental Disabilities, 46*, 339–351.

Browder, D.M., Mims, P.J., Spooner, F., Ahlgrim-Delzell, L., & Lee, A. (2008). Teaching elementary students with multiple disabilities to participate in shared stories. *Research and Practice for Persons with Severe Disabilities, 33,* 1–10.

Browder, D.M., Spooner, F., & Ahlgrim-Delzell, L. (2011). Literacy. In D.M. Browder & F. Spooner (Eds.), *Teaching students with moderate and severe disabilities* (pp. 125–140). New York, NY: Guilford Press.

Browder, D.M., Trela, K., & Jimenez, B. (2007). Training teachers to follow a task analysis to engage middle school students with moderate and severe developmental disabilities in grade-appropriate literature. *Journal of Special Education, 46,* 26–35.

Browder, D.M., Wakeman, S., Spooner, F., Ahlgrim-Delzell, L., & Algozzine, R. (2006). Research on reading instruction for individuals with significant cognitive disabilities. *Exceptional Children, 72,* 392–408.

Clay, M.M. (2000). *Concepts about print: What have children learned about printed language?* Portsmouth, NH: Heinemann.

Cohen, E.T., Heller, K.W., Alberto, P., & Fredrick, L.D. (2008). Using a three-step decoding strategy with constant time delay to teach word reading to students with mild and moderate mental retardation. *Focus on Autism and Other Developmental Disabilities, 23,* 67–78. doi:10.1177/1088357608314899

Conners, F.A., Rosenquist, C.J., Sligh, A.C., Atwell, J.A., & Kiser, T. (2006). Phonological reading skills acquisition by children with mental retardation. *Research in Developmental Disabilities, 27,* 121–137.

Coyne, P., Pisha, B., Dalton, B., Zeph, L., & Smith, N.C. (2010). Literacy by design: A Universal Design for Learning approach for students with significant intellectual disabilities. *Remedial and Special Education, 33,* 162–172.

Erickson, K.A. (2004). *MEville to WEville.* Roseville, MN: AbleNet, Inc.

Fallon, K.A., Light, J., McNaughton, D., Drager, K., & Hammer, C. (2004). The effects of Direct Instruction on the single-word reading skills of children who require augmentative and alternative communication. *Journal of Speech, Language, and Hearing Research, 47,* 1424–1439.

Flores, M.M., & Ganz, J.B. (2009). Effects of Direct Instruction on the reading comprehension of students with autism and developmental disabilities. *Education and Training in Developmental Disabilities, 44,* 39–53.

Heller, K.W., Fredrick, L.D., & Diggs, C.A. (1999). Teaching reading to students with severe speech and physical impairments using the Nonverbal Reading Approach. *Physical Disabilities: Education and Related Services, 18,* 3–34

Heller, K.W., Fredrick, L.D., Tumlin, J., & Brineman, D.G. (2002). Teaching decoding for generalization using the Nonverbal Reading Approach. *Journal of Physical and Developmental Disabilities, 14,* 19–35.

Heward, W.L. (1994). Three "low-tech" strategies for increasing the frequency of active student response during group instruction. In R. Gardner, D.M. Sainato, J.O. Cooper, T.E. Heron, W.L. Heward, J. Eshleman, & T.A. Grossi (Eds.), *Behavior analysis in education: Focus on measurably superior instruction* (pp. 283–320). Monterey, CA: Brooks/Cole.

Lalli, J.S., & Browder, D.M. (1993). Comparison of sight word training procedures with validation of the most practical procedure in teaching reading for daily living. *Research in Developmental Disabilities, 14,* 107–127.

Lee, A., Mims, P., & Browder, D. (2011). *Pathways to literacy.* Verona, WI: Attainment Company.

Light, J., & McNaughton, D. (2008). *Accessible Literacy Learning Reading Program.* Pittsburgh, PA: Mayer-Johnson.

Light, J., McNaughton, D., Weyer, M., & Karg, K. (2008). Evidence-based literacy instruction for individuals who require augmentative and alternative communication: A case study of a student with multiple disabilities. *Seminars in Speech and Language, 29,* 120–132.

Massey, G.N., & Wheeler, J.J. (2000). Acquisition and generalization of activity schedules and their effects on task engagement in a young child with autism in an inclusive preschool classroom. *Education and Training in Mental Retardation and Developmental Disabilities, 35,* 326–335.

Mayer-Johnson. (2000). *Writing with symbols.* Pittsburgh, PA: Author.

Mayer-Johnson. (n.d.). *BIGmack communicator.* Retrieved from http://www.mayer-johnson.com/bigmack-communicator.

Mayer-Johnson. (n.d.). *Boardmaker*. Pittsburgh, PA: Author.

Mayer-Johnson. (n.d.). *DynaVox*. Retrieved from http://www.dynavoxtech.com/default.aspx.

Mayer-Johnson. (n.d.). *Sym Writer*. Pittsburgh, PA: Author.

McGraw-Hill Education. (2002). *Reading Mastery*. Columbus, OH: Author.

Mims, P.J., Browder, D., Baker, J., Lee, A., & Spooner, F. (2009). Increasing participation and comprehension of students with significant cognitive disabilities and visual impairments during shared stories. *Education and Training in Developmental Disabilities, 44*, 409–420.

Mims, P.J., Hudson, M., & Browder, D.M. (2012). The effects of systematic instruction on teaching comprehension skills during a biography to students with significant intellectual disabilities. *Focus on Autism and Other Developmental Disabilities, 27*, 67–80.

Nagy, W.E., & Anderson, R.C. (1984). How many words are there in printed school English? *Reading Research Quarterly, 19*, 304–330.

National Governors Association Center for Best Practices, Council of Chief State School Officers. (2010). *Common Core State Standards (English language arts)*. Washington DC: Authors. Retrieved from http://www.corestandards.org/

National Institute of Child Health and Human Development. (2000). *Report of the National Reading Panel. Teaching children to read: An evidence-based assessment of the scientific research literature on reading and its implications for reading instruction: Reports of the subgroups* (NIH Publication No. 00-4754). Washington, DC: U.S. Government Printing Office.

National Institute of Child Health and Human Development. (2010). *Developing early literacy: Report of the National Early Literacy Panel*. Washington, DC: U.S. Government Printing Office.

Oudens, M.K. (2003). *The explicit phonemic alphabetic connections curriculum*. Verona, WI: Attainment Company.

Singleton, D.K., Schuster, J.W., Morse, T.E., & Collins, B.C. (1999). A comparison of antecedent prompt and test and simultaneous prompting procedures in teaching grocery words to adolescents with mental retardation. *Education and Training in Mental Retardation and Developmental Disabilities, 34*, 182–199.

Smith, B.R., Schuster, J.W., Collins, B., & Kleinert, H. (2011). Using simultaneous prompting to teach restaurant words and classification as non-target information to secondary students with moderate to severe disabilities. *Education and Training in Autism and Developmental Disabilities, 46*, 251–266.

Spooner, F., Browder, D., & Mims, P. (2011). Using evidence-based instructional strategies. In D. Browder & F. Spooner (Eds.). *Curriculum and instruction for students with moderate and severe disabilities*. New York, NY: Guilford Press.

SunCastle Technology. (n.d.). *Picture It*. Suffolk, VA: Author.

Swinehart-Jones, D., & Heller, K.W. (2009). Teaching students with severe speech and physical impairments a decoding strategy using internal speech and motoric indicators. *Journal of Special Education, 43*, 131–144.

Viorst, J. (1987). *Alexander and the terrible, horrible, no good, very bad day*. Chicago, IL: Aladdin Books.

Watkins, C., & Slocum, T. (2004). The components of Direct Instruction. In N.E. Marchand-Martella, T.A. Slocum, & R.C. Martella (Eds.), *Introduction to Direct Instruction* (pp. 28–45). Boston, MA: Allyn & Bacon.

Waugh, R., Fredrick, L.D., & Alberto, P.A. (2009). Using simultaneous prompting to teach sounds and blending skills to students with moderate intellectual disabilities. *Research in Developmental Disabilities: A Multidisciplinary Journal, 30*, 1435–1147.

Zakas, T., & Schreiber, L. (2010). *Building with stories*. Verona, WI: Attainment Company.

FOR FURTHER INFORMATION

Web Sites for Adapted Books

Note: When adapting a copyrighted book or printing a copy of an adapted book from one of these web sites, you must also buy the book.

Baltimore City Public Schools

http://www.baltimorecityschools.org/site/Default.aspx?PageID=1445

Provides books adapted using Boardmaker.

New York City Department of Education

http://schools.nyc.gov/Offices/District75/Departments/Literacy/AdaptedBooks/
  default.htm

Provides books adapted to different reading levels using Boardmaker, Writing with Symbols, PowerPoint, and Adobe.

Paul V. Sherlock Center on Disabilities

http://www.ric.edu/sherlockcenter/wwslist.html

Provides books adapted for PowerPoint and Adobe.

University of North Carolina at Charlotte General Curriculum Access Projects

http://coedpages.uncc.edu/access/adaptedbooks.htm

Provides adapted books using Boardmaker or Writing with Symbols.

Common Core State Standards

Common Core State Standards Initiatives

http://www.corestandards.org/

This is the official Common Core State Standards web site, which is sponsored by the Chief Council of State School Officers and the National Governors Association.

Establishing the Reading Level of Adapted Text

ATOS for Text by Renaissance Learning

http://www.renlearn.com/atos/analyze.aspx?type=3

Text can be submitted to this web site to establish a readability level that is linked to Common Core State Standards grade bands.

The Lexile Framework for Reading

http://www.lexile.com

Lexile is a measure of reading difficulty of a passage of text. The Lexile Analyzer can be used to estimate the reading difficulty when adapting a book.

Simple Measure of Gobbledygook (SMOG)

http://www.harrymclaughlin.com/SMOG.htm

SMOG estimates the years of education necessary to understand a piece of submitted text.

Identifiying Skills Important in Developing Literacy Skills

National Early Literacy Panel. (2008). *Developing early literacy: Report of the National Early Literacy Panel.* Washington, DC: Author. Retrieved from http://lincs.ed.gov/publications/pdf/NELPSummary.pdf
Reviews research on the skills associated with developing literacy skills.

National Institute for Literacy. (2008). *Put reading first: Kindergarten through grade 3: The research building blocks for teaching children to read* (3rd ed.). Jessup, MD: Author. Retrieved from http://lincs.ed.gov/publications/pdf/PRF booklet.pdf
Defines terms associated with the reading literature and describes the five components of reading with examples of how to teach them.

National Reading Panel. (2000). *Teaching children to read: An evidence-based assessment of the scientific research literature on reading and its implications for reading instruction.* Washington, DC: U. S. Department of Health and Human Services [NIH Pub. No. 00-4754].
Reviews research on the skills associated with learning to read later defined as the five components of reading (vocabulary, phonemic awareness, phonics, comprehension and fluency).

Literacy and Reading Curricula for Students with Disabilities

Ahlgrim-Delzell, L., Browder, D.M., & Wood, L. (in progress). *Early Reading Skills Builder.* Verona, WI: Attainment company.
To be available through Attainment company. Phonics curriculum via an iPad app for students who do not communicate verbally.

Browder, D., Gibbs, S., Courtade-Little, G., Ahlgrim-Delzell, L., & Lee, A. (2007). *Early literacy skills builder.* Verona, WI: Attainment Company.
http://www.attainmentcompany.com/elsb
Curriculum for early literacy skills such as text pointing, sight words, and phonemic awareness needed to learn to read.

Erickson, K.A. (2004). *MEville to WEville.* Roseville, MN: AbleNet, Inc.
http://www.ablenetinc.com/Curriculum/MEville-to-WEville-Literacy
Curriculum for fundamental reading skills such as concept of print and vocabulary.

Lee, A., Mims, P., & Browder, D. (2011). *Pathways to literacy.* Verona, WI: Attainment Company.
http://www.attainmentcompany.com/pathways-literacy
Curriculum for teaching engagement during reading for students who do not yet use symbolic communication.

Light, J., & McNaughton, D. (2008). *Accessible Literacy Learning Reading Program.* Pittsburgh, PA: Mayer-Johnson.
http://www.mayer-johnson.com/all-reading-curriculum
Curriculum for phonological awareness, decoding, and reading comprehension of text.

Oudens, M.K. (2003). The explicit phonemic alphabetic connections curriculum. Verona, WI: Attainment Company.
http://www.attainmentcompany.com/epacc
Concentrates on instruction of phonemic awareness skills needed to learn to read.

Zakas, T., & Schreiber, L. (2010). *Building with stories.* Verona, WI: Attainment Company.
http://www.attainmentcompany.com/building-stories
For ages 5–10, contains 5 adapted books and instructional materials.

Software with Picture Support for Text

Boardmaker by Mayer-Johnson

http://www.mayer-johnson.com/boardmaker-software

Software to adapt text and create communication boards with picture symbol support. Free trial available.

Picture It! by Slater Software

http://www.slatersoftware.com/pit.html

Software to adapt text and create communication boards with picture symbol support.

Writing with Symbols/SymWriter by Mayer-Johnson

http://www.mayer-johnson.com/writing-with-symbols-bundle

Software to adapt text and create communication boards with picture symbol support. Writing with Symbols is now bundled with SymWriter, a talking word processor with speech support in addition to writing support.

CHAPTER 6

Comprehensive Beginning Reading

Jill Allor, Stephanie Al Otaiba, Miriam Ortiz, and Jessica Folsom

Tom is 7 years old and is in second grade. During his preschool years he was identified as having a developmental delay and began receiving intensive special education services, including evidence-based early literacy instruction. In addition, his parents received training to engage Tom in shared book reading activities to foster an interest in books and develop oral language. With an IQ of 48, he will likely be classified as having an intellectual disability in the near future. The cause of his disability is unknown. As is typical of many students with intellectual disability, his attention span, working memory, and both expressive and receptive language skills are very weak for his age. He also exhibits some mild behavior problems, though these have decreased over time and now tend to occur only when he is having extreme difficulty with a task. Although he has participated in literacy instruction in a general education classroom since he was in preschool, this instruction is heavily modified, and his primary literacy instruction has been provided by a special education teacher either individually or in a small group of no more than two or three students.

When he entered first grade, Tom was able to attend to short stories read to him orally, attend to pictures, and turn pages in books appropriately. He could identify the names of only a few common letters and their sounds (e.g., he could name the letter *T* and say its sound, /t/). He had not demonstrated any progress on phonological awareness skills. Specifically, he was unable to isolate the first sound in a spoken word or blend onsets and rimes.

Now in the middle of second grade, Tom has made meaningful progress, but he is still performing well below grade-level expectations. He can say the names and sounds of most common letters and is scoring between 10 and 15 letter–sounds per minute on the nonsense word fluency measure of *Dynamic Indicators of Basic Early Literacy Skills* (DIBELS; Good & Kaminski, 2002). His phonological awareness skills are progressing, as he can usually say the first sound in a spoken word, and he consistently blends onsets and rimes. On DIBELS phoneme segmentation fluency, he is scoring between 15 and 20 segments per minute. He can also identify a few sight words (i.e., *the, a, he, she*)

The work presented in this chapter was supported by Grant No. H324K040011-05 from the Institute of Education Sciences. This article does not necessarily reflect the positions or policies of this funding agency, and no official endorsement should be inferred.

and is beginning to sound out a few simple short-vowel words (e.g., *sat, fan, man*) and read short sentences made up of these words.

I n this chapter the latest research on beginning reading instruction for students with intellectual disability and the practical techniques for putting this research into practice for students such as Tom is described. After reading this chapter it will be clear that converging research supports that what works instructionally for struggling readers, also works for students with intellectual disability; however, it is not enough. Considerable modifications in pacing are needed to ensure instruction is at "just the right" level for individual children, and that texts are also at "just the right" level to support fluent practice of words students can recognize. References to some texts that may be helpful (Carnine, Silbert, Kame'enui, & Tarver, 2004; Honig, Diamond, & Gutlohn, 2013; Hougan & Smartt, 2012; O'Connor, 2007) are provided. Special education teachers and literacy experts need to pool their efforts to provide effective instruction for students with intellectual disability.

BEGINNING READING INSTRUCTION

According to the National Reading Panel (NRP), there are five major components of beginning reading instruction (National Institute of Child Health and Human Development [NICHD], 2000): vocabulary (and oral language), comprehension, phonological awareness, phonics, and fluency. These five components have become prominent in beginning reading core curriculum programs and in the Common Core State Standards (CCSS; National Governors Association Center for Best Practices, Council of Chief State School Officers, 2010) for kindergarten through third grade. The Individuals with Disabilities Education Improvement Act (IDEA) of 2004 (PL 108-446) reemphasizes the importance of access to the general education curriculum. And furthermore, all students are required to participate in reading assessments related to state standards, including students who participate in alternative assessments (which may be limited to prerequisite skills or "access points" [Florida Department of Education, 2007]). There is considerable evidence that students with intellectual disability need explicit and intensive instruction in all of these components and that they can learn a wider range of literacy skills than just sight words (Allor, Mathes, Roberts, Cheatham, & Al Otaiba, in press; Browder, Ahlgrim-Delzell, Courtade, Gibbs, & Flowers, 2008; Browder, Trela, & Jimenez, 2007).

Gough and Tunmer (1986) described one theoretical model, *The Simple View of Reading*, suggesting that reading is the product of listening comprehension and decoding skills. Therefore, it is helpful for teachers to conceptualize the components of vocabulary (oral language) and comprehension as meaning-focused skills and the components of phonological awareness and phonics as code-focused skills. However, these skills interact and should be linked, when feasible. Furthermore, fluency is a bridging skill that emerges as students develop accurate word reading and activate their background knowledge, enabling them to read for meaning and with expression. In other words, all of the strands integrate over time to facilitate the complex act of reading for meaning.

Oral Language, Vocabulary, and Comprehension (Meaning-Focused Skills)

Oral language includes semantics (vocabulary), syntax (grammar), morphology (meaning units), and pragmatics (language use). Of these, vocabulary is one of the first strands introduced in foundational reading instruction. Oral vocabulary is knowledge of word meanings—both receptive and expressive—and this knowledge of words is a reliable predictor of future reading success in beginning readers (National Early Literacy Panel, 2008). Comprehension then involves building meaning from texts while reading or while listening to texts. (Note that listening comprehension is described in greater detail in Chapter 4 of this book.) The new CCSS address the oral language, vocabulary, and comprehension skills of beginning readers starting with the foundational skills of speaking and listening. The CCSS expect students to confirm their understanding of information given orally by asking and answering questions and/or requesting an explanation when they are confused. Furthermore, students should ask for clarification about unfamiliar words in a text, along with being able to demonstrate that they understand the conventions of standard English grammar when speaking.

Phonological Awareness and Phonics (Code-Focused Skills)

In order to gain access to the meaning of text, students must be able to recognize words (i.e., they must understand the alphabetic code). Students must connect the phonological aspects of spoken language to print. These strands include phonological awareness as well as phonics and word recognition.

Phonological Awareness   The NRP defined phonological awareness as the understanding and awareness of sounds in oral language (i.e., words, syllables, and onsets and rimes along with the smaller parts such as phonemes; NICHD, 2000). The NRP reported that explicit phonological awareness instruction leads to stronger reading outcomes, particularly for struggling beginning readers. The CCSS also emphasize phonological awareness, stating that students should demonstrate understanding of spoken words, syllables, and sounds. In addition, the CCSS require students to count, pronounce, blend, and segment syllables in spoken words.

Phonics and Word Recognition   In addition to explicitly teaching phonological awareness, phonics and word recognition are critical code-focused skills. Teachers should focus systematically on helping students master letter–sound correspondences. This is the first step within the strand encompassing phonics and word recognition. Phonics is defined as the instruction of organized associations between letters and combinations of letters in written and spoken language, and how to use these associations to read and spell words (Honig et al., 2013; NICHD, 2000). Word recognition also includes reading irregularly spelled words that are more difficult or not possible to sound out. Many high-frequency words are irregular and, therefore, children should be taught to recognize them by sight; that is why they are known as *sight words.*

The CCSS address both phonics and word recognition, and there are several standards that address these skills specifically. From kindergarten to third grade, students should be able to

1. Decode words by applying grade-level word analysis and phonics skills

2. Understand one-to-one letter–sound correspondence and produce the most common sound for each consonant

3. Recognize that vowels have a long and short sound and associate those sounds with their most common spellings

4. Read high-frequency words by sight

5. Differentiate words spelled similarly by recognizing the sounds of the letters that are different

6. Identify words with irregular but common spelling-sound correspondence

7. Recognize the common vowel pair conventions that produce vowel sounds

Fluency

The final strand we discuss in beginning reading instruction is fluency. Fluency is the correct reading of connected text at a conversational rate with appropriate expression (Honig et al., 2013). Fluency instruction is crucial because of its relationship to reading comprehension. Students struggling to decode a text will find it difficult to read with expression and subsequently to understand what has just been read; thus, comprehension involves the integration of accurate and fluent decoding, along with accessing the meaning of words and sentences. The CCSS call for students to be able to read grade-level texts with purpose and understanding and with enough fluency to support comprehension. Students should also be able to read these grade-level texts with precision, appropriate rate, and expression. The CCSS require students to use context in order to confirm or self-correct word recognition and understanding.

EARLY READING RESEARCH-BASED PRACTICE

There have been two major trends over the past several years in special education that are particularly visible among students with moderate to severe disabilities: an increased emphasis on achievement and a broadening of instructional practices (Kauffman & Hung, 2009). These have been made clear through literature reviews on instruction for this population. Early reviews (Browder & Xin, 1998; Conners, 1992) focused primarily on sight word instruction to promote functional, daily living skills. Historically, there has been very little research on phonics-based instruction (Joseph & Seery, 2004). In one review (Browder, Wakeman, Spooner, Ahlgrim-Delzell, & Algozzine, 2006), research was categorized according to the NRP's five components of evidence-based reading instruction. The researchers found that, although the majority of research was still related to sight word instruction, preliminary evidence supported instruction in phonics, phonemic awareness, and comprehension as effective instructional practices.

At the time of this writing, the instructional focus, as well as the measures used to document progress, has continued to shift from functional reading to reading that is more closely aligned with that of evidence-based reading instruction in the general education curriculum (Folsom, 2012). Students with intellectual disability are now being taught to process the internal structure of words through phonemic awareness and phonics, and to integrate skills to accomplish the complex act of reading with comprehension (Allor et al., in press; Allor, Mathes, Roberts, Cheatham, & Champlin, 2010; Allor, Mathes, Roberts, Jones, & Champlin, 2010).

Researchers have implemented preexisting reading curriculum, created new comprehensive curricula, or created targeted interventions for a specific skill impairment. For example, Flores, Shippen, Alberto, and Crowe (2004) reported the effects of *Corrective Reading* (Engelmann et al., 2002); Lemons and Fuchs (2010) reported the effects of *Kindergarten Peer-Assisted Learning Strategies* (Fuchs, Fuchs, Thompson, et al., 2013), *Peer-Assisted Learning Strategies* (Fuchs, Fuchs, Svenson, et al., 2013), and the *Phonological Awareness Kit* (Robertson & Salter, 1995); and Riepl, Marchand-Martella, and Martella (2008) reported the effects of *Reading Mastery Plus* (Engelmann & Bruner, 2002) and *Spelling Mastery Plus* (Dixon & Engelman, 1999). All researchers implementing preexisting curricula did so with modifications to meet the needs of the students. For example, one team extended an existing curriculum, *Early Interventions in Reading* (Mathes & Torgesen, 2005), by developing a new prerequisite level (Allor et al., in press; Allor & Mathes, 2012). Another team developed a new comprehensive reading curriculum, the *Early Literacy Skills Builder* (Browder et al., 2008; Browder, Gibbs, Ahlgrim-Delzell, Courtade, & Lee, 2007). Other researchers focused on targeted skill instruction such as decoding strategies (Cohen, Heller, Alberto, & Fredrick, 2008) and letter-sound correspondence and blending (Waugh, Fredrick, & Alberto, 2009). Across various studies, instructional practices incorporated explicit, systematic instruction, with modeling and frequent opportunities to respond. Incorporating direct instruction techniques to teach the skills aligned with the general education reading curriculum provided a strong foundation for evidence-based reading instruction for students with intellectual disability. Despite positive results, intensive practice over long periods of time was needed to make meaningful gains (Allor et al., in press).

Researchers frequently have modified instruction to meet individual student needs and have provided instruction in small groups or to individual students. Modifications to preexisting curricula ranged from changing the instructional sequence (Flores et al., 2004); to selecting only specific activities, expanding on directions, extending practice, and adding additional skills (Lemons & Fuchs, 2010); to adding additional introductory levels or lessons to teach foundational skills required in the preexisting curriculum (Allor et al., in press). Additional instructional methods included constant time delay (Cohen et al., 2008), simultaneous prompting (Waugh et al., 2009), or delayed prompting with picture integration and errorless discrimination (Conners, Rosenquist, Sligh, Atwell, & Kiser, 2006). Other instructional supports included expanding directions by providing task analysis (Browder et al., 2008) and providing extra opportunities to respond (Burns, 2007).

Despite the positive results of current research, researchers consistently point out that the interventions are not sufficient and that students need extensive practice and support to meet their full potential. In addition, in the research, the individuals providing instruction were highly trained on the specific instructional techniques used. One of the most cited needs of students with intellectual disability is extended instructional time in instructional periods that accommodate the student's attention span. The notion that what research says is good but is not enough is particularly true when maintaining the strategies and skills over time and generalizing strategies and skills learned to new situations. That is, the most progress is seen with measures that directly assess the skills taught, or in some cases, the specific letters, sounds, or words taught. Furthermore, research has shown that progress on more distal and general reading measures requires extended periods of time (Allor et al., in press), particularly on comprehension measures. Therefore, it is important for teachers to incorporate instruction for maintenance and generalization of skills.

BUILDING ON RESEARCH FOR PRACTICE: GUIDELINES FOR BEGINNING READING INSTRUCTION

Teachers of students with severe disabilities must not only provide evidence-based reading instruction, but they must also consider the specific challenges faced by their students. The challenges facing Tom, the second grader in the opening vignette, are common to students with intellectual disability and include problems transferring and integrating skills, behavior problems, low motivation, a need for intense and targeted practice and cumulative review, low expressive and receptive language skills, difficulty with abstract concepts, and short- and long-term memory weakness. Typical school-based curricular challenges, particularly in Tier 1 settings (i.e., general education instruction), include inadequate levels of practice, insufficient focus on key skills, pacing that is too fast, programs and procedures that lack alignment, and limited opportunities to conduct team planning. Students such as Tom will benefit from participating in Tier 1 instruction only with careful planning and adaptation. Throughout this chapter recommendations from the authors' research for addressing these challenges are provided. In this section guidance related to the teaching of core skills is provided. In the next section, guidance about how to get started in developing and implementing effective evidence-based and individualized literacy instruction is provided.

Oral Language, Vocabulary, and Comprehension (Meaning-Focused Skills)

Guidance for teaching students with intellectual disability to master beginning meaning-focused literacy skills is limited. In our research with students with intellectual disability, we applied and expanded on the research available for struggling readers. General strategies included explicit modeling, guided practice, and independent practice of basic comprehension strategies, including making and checking predictions, sequencing, making inferences, content webbing, and writing brief summaries. Initially, oral language, vocabulary, and comprehension skills were presented simultaneously and primarily taught through listening comprehension (Allor, Mathes, Champlin, & Cheatham, 2009). Teachers used storybooks and read-alouds to discuss basic story grammar, such as setting and characters. Early sequencing (i.e., beginning, middle, and ending events) was taught through the use of simple graphic organizers. Vocabulary instruction was infused throughout this process by using simple definitions, as well as pictures, videos, and gestures to teach new words. Later, when students independently decoded words and read simple sentences, comprehension instruction became more complex and shifted to supporting the ability to understand the texts read by students. For Tom, this shift will occur toward the end of his second-grade year as he is expected to begin to read simple decodable books at that time.

Phonological Awareness and Phonics (Code-Focused Skills)

Similar to other students with reading difficulties, students with intellectual disability require specific, explicit, and individualized instruction in code-focused skills including, phonological awareness, phonics, and sight word instruction.

Phonological Awareness The most important phonological awareness skills are blending and segmenting at the phoneme level; therefore, for students such as Tom these should be targeted. In our research, we gradually increased the difficulty of these tasks, beginning with onset and rime and then moving on to single phoneme blending and segmenting. Initially, students practiced blending the onset and rime of short words beginning with continuous sounds (e.g., /sss/ -un; "What word?" *sun*) and segmenting by saying the first sound of these words (e.g., "What is the first sound in *sun*?" /sss/). We observed that students were more easily able to blend and segment words when they were presented as stretched and connected (i.e., we stretched continuous sounds such as /sss/ and connected the onset and rime by not stopping between the onset and rime). We also applied this principle later as students practiced blending and segmenting all of the sounds in single-syllable words (e.g., /sss/ /uuu/ /nnn/; "What word?" *sun* and "Say the sounds in *sun*." /sss/ /uuu/ /nnn/). Stretching and connecting was an important scaffold for the students in our research. We also connected phonological awareness skills with meaning in order to build links between the sound of language and the meaning of language. For example, when practicing the items just discussed we would use a picture of the sun. We were also mindful not to add sounds at the end of phonemes during phonological awareness activities, as students often have difficulty blending sounds when /uh/ is added to the end of phonemes (i.e., should say /b/ /a/ /t/ instead of /buh/ /a/ /tuh/).

Phonics and Word Recognition Similar to phonological awareness instruction, direct instruction in phonics should systematically move from teaching basic letter sound correspondences to decoding patterns of words, while integrating phonological awareness skills. Once a few letter sounds were learned, students were taught to read simple consonant-vowel-consonant (CVC) words sound by sound and eventually to unitize, or read the word as a whole unit. Patterns gradually became more complex (e.g., CVCC, CCVCC, CVC-e). Students were also taught to read irregular sight words. As with all skills, intense practice of new skills was always followed by cumulative review. Other instructional strategies included teaching mnemonic clues such as *snake* for the sound /sss/ (as /sss/ is the sound made by a snake and can be shaped like an *s*), using picture prompts, and using consistent hand gestures when students were sounding out words (e.g., tapping when pointing to a stop sound, /t/, or holding for two seconds when pointing to a continuous sound, /sss/).

Fluency

To help students with intellectual disability learn to transfer skills taught during lessons to the fluent act of reading, students read and reread decodable texts that included taught word patterns and sight words. We found that some decodable texts were challenging because they included words that were not in the students' oral language. For example, a word such as "*hat*" was more familiar (and, therefore, easier to decode) than the word "*cap*" or, even worse, "*tam.*" These unfamiliar words frustrated the students. During a storybook reading students were prompted to gradually increase reading fluency with individual words. As fluency goals were reached, text difficulty (more complex phonics patterns and more challenging irregular words) was gradually increased. Because some students took so long to master word patterns and unitize words, we also created additional texts (see Allor, Gifford, Al Otaiba, Miller, & Cheatham, 2013). For additional practice, we recommend writing sentences made up of the words students are learning or using images for content words that are not made up of taught sounds but rather words the students use in their oral language (e.g., may use a picture of a slide if the i-e pattern has not been taught).

GETTING STARTED

Integrating all of these strands into an effective individualized program involves careful planning. First, teachers should select target skills and goals. Second, teachers should select curriculum and materials that are most likely to be effective in teaching those skills to their students. Third, teachers should develop specific lessons for individuals or small homogeneous groups. Finally, teachers should plan accommodations and modifications for Tier 1 instruction.

Selecting Target Skills and Goals

When targeting reading skills for instruction, teachers should consider not only the relevant CCSS for a grade level and alternative standards but also the student's individualized education program (IEP) goals. As discussed in the previous section, teachers should focus on critical skills across all content strands, explicitly teaching students to transfer skills from one strand to another (e.g., applying the letter-sounds learned in isolation to blending words from a word list to reading those words in a sentence or story).

As we mentioned previously, all students now participate in some type of reading assessment, including students who participate in an alternate assessment that may focus more on prerequisite skills. With the implementation of the response to intervention (RTI) approach, most schools also use curriculum-based measures to assess students' reading (e.g., letter naming fluency, word identification fluency, oral reading fluency) and their progress toward a benchmark or criteria for grade-level performance. These measures are designed to be general outcome measures that sample an array of reading skills from the annual curriculum (for typically developing children). One challenge for teachers and researchers is setting reasonable goals and benchmarks for students with intellectual disability, as they tend to make progress much more slowly than students without disabilities. In our research, some students with intellectual disability took two or more years to achieve clear progress on these types of measures, depending on the severity of the disability and the particular skill being assessed. Therefore, these curriculum-based measures are useful for long-term progress monitoring but will not be sensitive to weekly growth, as they may not align closely enough to instruction on a more limited range of reading skills that are growing slowly (see Allor et al., in press, Lemons et al., 2013). For example, we found that it took as long as 4 years for some students with intellectual disability to successfully achieve the benchmark of reading 40 words correct per minute on first-grade passages, which is the minimum score for ending first-grade level. Some children, particularly among children with IQs in the range of 40–55 never achieved this benchmark, and overall, there was marked variability in RTI. The lesson we learned in our research was to give all students opportunities to learn key skills and monitor progress carefully on these skills to determine pacing.

Teachers, therefore, will need to create curriculum-based assessments that formatively track student progress and can inform instructional decisions. Teacher-created curriculum-based assessments that are very closely aligned to instructional targets will be needed to determine if instruction is effective or if further adaptations need to be made. For example, a student may be working on a limited number of phonics patterns and sight words; therefore, an oral reading fluency first-grade passage may be less sensitive to growth than a teacher-made curriculum-based word list type of assessment of the exact skills being taught (e.g., CVC words with short *a* and short *e*). In addition, information about a student's current level of performance should guide placement and pacing within a curriculum. Thus, hand in hand with considering what skills to teach, it is important to consider how to formatively gauge the success of the instructional approach so that adaptations can be made and evaluated along the way.

Selecting Curriculum and Materials

Although research has demonstrated that students with intellectual disability respond favorably to evidence-based reading instruction that is typically part of Tier 1 curricular programs, there are a number of reasons why Tier 1 instruction will not be sufficient in meeting their unique needs:

1. They have limited skills and need intensive practice, including repetition of groups of lessons.

2. They need careful instruction moving from accurate reading of discrete skills to transfer to untaught words and to texts.

3. They have a limited oral vocabulary, so it is particularly important to read texts with familiar and meaningful words.

4. They have limited background knowledge and need texts with familiar topics.

5. They have limited grammar and working memory and may struggle with complex sentences.

6. Among their early skills, letter sounds and sight word acquisition is a faster process than their phonetic decoding, which may not match the curriculum.

In addition, examples of beginning reading interventions that supplement (but do not substitute for) core curriculum include *Peer Assisted Learning Strategies*

(Fuchs, Fuchs, Svenson, et al., 2013; Fuchs, Fuchs, Thompson, et al., 2013; Mathes, Torgesen, Allen, & Allor, 2001) and *Sound Partners* (Vadasy et al., 2005). In addition, Browder, Gibbs, and colleagues (2007) developed the *Early Literacy Skills Builder*, an assessment-guided multiyear curriculum as a stand-alone for students with moderate to severe intellectual disability. Another program used effectively with students with intellectual disability is *Early Interventions in Reading* (Allor & Mathes, 2012; Mathes & Torgesen, 2005), which can be used as a stand-alone or supplemental program. For further details regarding implementation and methods for increasing intensity see Allor, Champlin, Gifford, and Mathes (2010) and Allor and colleagues (2009).

Planning Small-Group Instruction

Teachers should heed research guidance to provide homogeneous small-group or individual instruction for students with intellectual disability and supplement that instruction with practice in multiple settings, including Tier 1 instruction, as well as additional practice with peers, volunteers, and family members. Figure 6.1 provides examples of lesson plans for prereaders (a lesson appropriate for Tom near the beginning of his first-grade year) and for early readers who are just beginning to sound out words and recognize a few sight words (a lesson appropriate for Tom in the middle of his second-grade year). These lessons include review, careful scaffolding for new skills, explicit instruction in transferring skills across tasks, listening to meaningful text, and, in the early reader lesson, reading comprehension at the sentence level. Later lessons would incorporate more decodable text and gradually shift from listening comprehension to more reading comprehension. Although initially students may have difficulty attending to entire lessons, in our research we found we could lengthen sessions by establishing routines and providing positive reinforcement.

The lesson plan also mentions the use of supplemental student materials. This is to ensure adequate practice and to motivate students to stay on task and engaged. Supplemental game-like materials can be helpful. Examples include Elkonin sound boxes (i.e., an activity in which students can push an object or letter as they say each sound), puzzles, flashcards, card games such as Go-Fish, and bingo, all of which can support letter–sound correspondence, phonological awareness, decoding, and sight word practice. (For some helpful downloadable examples, visit http://www.fcrr.org/for-educators/sca.asp and see Allor, Champlin, et al., 2010.)

As we mentioned earlier, it is important to monitor progress on both curriculum-based benchmarks and on mastery of subsets of skills being taught. Thus it is important for teachers to track progress of all students in the classroom, use this data to adjust small-group assignments, individualize pacing and practice, and keep track of students' RTI.

Planning for Inclusion in Tier 1 Instruction

It is not likely that students with intellectual disability will keep up with the pace of their typically developing peers, so it is vital for teachers to consider how best to link their individual student's target skills to Tier 1 instructional objectives for the larger classroom and to implement accommodations and modifications. As dis-

Strand/skill	Prereading lesson	Early reading lesson
Phonological awareness: Blending and segmenting	*Blend onset/rime.* Teacher says onset/rime (/sss/ -un), and students find picture card. *Say first sound.* Students draw picture cards and say first sound of objects.	*Blend phonemes into words.* Teacher says phonemes (/sss/ /uuu/ /nnn/), and students say word and find picture card. *Say the sounds.* Students draw picture cards and say all the phonemes.
Word recognition: Phonics	*Recognize shapes of letters.* Students match magnetic letters to letters on cards. *Recognize letter sounds.* Teacher uses flashcards or magnetic letters to present the sound of a new letter and practice taught letter sounds. Teacher says sound and students point to letter.	*Say sounds of letters.* Teacher uses flashcards to present new letter sounds and practice taught letter sounds. *Sound out words.* Teacher uses flashcards to model sounding out and provides guided practice. Students use magnetic letters to build words.
Word recognition: Sight words	*Preskill: Point to words in spoken sentences.* Teacher reads short sentence, pointing to each word as it is read. Students repeat sentence while pointing to each word.	*Recognize irregularly spelled words.* Teacher uses flashcards to present a new sight word and practice review words.
Fluency		*Read simple sentences with expression.* Students practice reading sentences made up of taught words.
	(Fluency with underlying skills addressed in other strands.)	
Vocabulary/ comprehension	*Retell the beginning, middle, and end of a story.* Teacher uses a graphic organizer to model and provide guided practice.	*Retell the beginning, middle, and end of a story.* Teacher uses a graphic organizer to model and provide guided practice.
Cumulative review	Students participate in various review games and activities.	Students participate in various review games and activities.

Figure 6.1. Sample lesson activities.

cussed throughout this chapter, the goal is for students with intellectual disability to access the general curriculum in a manner that is functional and meaningful. In addition to their state standards, many states provide access points that give teachers a way to modify instruction and demonstrate that their students with intellectual disability have mastered each skill (e.g., Florida Department of Education, 2007). Browder and colleagues (2003) conducted a content analysis of states' alternate assessment performance indicators for students with intellectual disability. They found that states that had clear links between academic content and assessment provided students with intellectual disability with more academic contexts than states with mixed or weak links. In addition, Browder and colleagues describe several accommodations and modifications to instruction for students with intellectual disability. For instruction in phonics and word recognition, students were asked to recognize survival words and logos, read a predetermined number of words, and match pictures to words. These skills can be infused in the general education context through the inclusion of sentences, stories, or materials that use the specific sight words being practiced. Instruction in vocabulary called for students to associate cues, symbols, objects, and pictures with their meanings. Instruction to develop comprehension required students to anticipate patterns in unfamiliar stories, relate personal experience to stories, and answer questions related to a sequence of events. General educators can facilitate instruction of these skills through the use of Social Stories, text written for specific students (e.g., recipes, reminders), cooperative learning, peer tutoring, and positive behavior supports.

Teachers need to use evidence-based methods for Tier 1 instruction that benefit both students with intellectual disability and their typically developing peers. Table 6.1 provides examples of good and poor methods to use during reading instruction. Teachers should also use additional evidence-based strategies to help students with intellectual disability access the general curriculum. Specifically, Browder and Cooper-Duffy (2003) suggested 1) team planning, 2) target responses, 3) instructional support, and 4) assistive technology. Using these strategies can help educators facilitate access to the general curriculum and promote positive academic outcomes for students with intellectual disability.

Table 6.1.   Examples of good and poor instructional techniques

Phonemic awareness (e.g., initial sound segmentation)
- *Good example:* Teaching the first sound in *cat* is /c/ and the first sound in *dog* is /d/ because these are stop sounds that are easily distinguished from one another in familiar words.
- *Poor example:* Teaching the first sound in *pat* is /p/ and the first sound in *bat* is /b/ because these are voiced and voiceless pairs that are not easily distinguished.

Decoding
- *Good example:* Teaching decoding with familiar words such as *hat*.
- *Poor example:* Teaching to decode with unfamiliar words such as *tam* or *cap*.

Sight words
- *Good example:* Teaching high-frequency irregular words that are likely to appear in future readings.
- *Poor example:* Teaching rare irregular words that are not meaningful to the student, or teaching sight words that are visually similar, such as *of* and *off*.

Vocabulary
- *Good example:* Introducing familiar words that are imageable or easy to represent with a picture. Teaching the word using everyday language.
- *Poor example:* Overemphasizing words that are not within the students' oral vocabulary, for example function words such as *with*.

Comprehension
- *Good example:* Using visuals such as graphic organizers to show text structure (e.g., sequence chart with pictures from the story to support a retell); Priming background knowledge (e.g., You have a cat. A cat is an animal that could be a good pet, but a lion would not be a good pet because lions can be dangerous).
- *Poor example:* Introducing too many topics or introducing too many unrelated stories without priming background knowledge and reviewing prior themes.

Fluency
- *Good example:* Using partners or peer-assisted reading to promote fluency; Using texts that are at the readers' level of difficulty.
- *Poor example:* Using a text in which the student exhibits more than 10 errors per 100 words.

Team Planning   Team planning is a vital part of facilitating access to the general curriculum for students with intellectual disability. Team planning provides a time for general educators, special educators, parents, and administrators to discuss classroom strategies and potential challenges during the inclusion process (Salisbury, Evans, & Palombaro, 1997). This allows parents to be involved in the educational process of their children. An additional benefit to team planning is the development of positive behavior supports. Positive behavior supports set the student up for success and make the classroom a safe and enjoyable learning environment.

Instructional Support   Teachers should also consider instructional supports in the classroom context as another important factor for facilitating access to the general curriculum for students with intellectual disability. For example, teachers may choose to use peer tutors or cooperative learning groups during instruction to facilitate students learning from each other by increasing language and opportunities to respond. Teachers may also choose to implement observational learning where the student learns from watching the task being modeled by someone else.

Assistive Technology   Teachers will also want to use technology in multiple ways. Tables 6.2 and 6.3 provide additional technology resources and applications that can be used by or with students with intellectual disability. Some students may require the use of an augmentative and alternative communication device; this device can help decrease problem behaviors and can be used to increase peer interaction. Technology may also be used as a reward for participation or reaching a particular goal. Specific technologies may include applications for smart phones or tablets that provide literacy activities at the students' skill level. Apple provides applications such as "Autism Apps" in which individuals can access a list of applications being used by people with special needs. "Same Meaning Magic" helps students understand synonyms, and "Story Wheel" allows students to choose pictures and record their voice to create their own story. Social networking sites such as ebuddies.org and specialfriendsonline.com allow students to communicate with peers with and without disabilities.

Table 6.2.   Useful mobile applications

Bluster: A vocabulary app with more than 800 words.

Kids Word Match HD: An app in which kids can match common words with their corresponding pictures and their pronunciation.

LAZ Leveled Readers: Decodable digital stories for beginning readers that also review concepts such as main idea, cause and effect, and sequencing events.

ABC Magic Phonics: An app in which students learn the most common sound of each letter in the alphabet through matching pictures with letters.

Beginning Sounds Interactive Game: An app in which students can match words that have the same beginning sounds.

Build a Word Express: An app in which the student is prompted to write a word by dragging the appropriate letters onto the board.

Spelling Bus: An app in which students learn to read, pronounce, and spell sight words using pictures.

Table 6.3. Useful web sites

The Family Center on Technology and Disability: A reference and review of numerous assistive and instructional technology resources (http://www.fctd.info/resources)

The Rocky Mountain Down Syndrome Association Technology Resource Guide: A list of resources that can be used by or for students with various needs (http://www.rmdsa.org/resources/techresourceguide.html).

Apps for Children with Special Needs: A web site created by a parent of two students with special needs that reviews apps that have been created for various special need populations (http://a4cwsn.com).

Bridging Apps: A site that is maintained by the Easter Seals that was co-founded by a parent of a child with Down syndrome (http://www.bridgingapps.org).

iAutism: A site that features categories of apps such as art or music for iPads, iPhones, and Androids (http://wwwiAutism.info).

SUMMARY

Expectations for literacy outcomes for students with intellectual disability such as Tom are higher than in the past because we now know much more about how to provide effective early literacy instruction. Fortunately, students with intellectual disability are now able to benefit from the decades of research on struggling readers in general. Students such as Tom need to be given the opportunity to learn basic literacy skills with multiple opportunities for extensive practice of new skills and sensitive attention to transferring these skills to reading for meaning in connected text. Our understanding of how to teach students with intellectual disability, particularly those with severe disabilities, is growing; however, it is imperative that we apply what we do know now as we continue our search for more effective ways to adapt instruction to the unique needs of students such as Tom.

REFERENCES

Allor, J.H., Champlin, T.M., Gifford, D.B., & Mathes, P.G. (2010). Methods for increasing the intensity of reading instruction for students with intellectual disabilities. *Education and Training in Autism and Developmental Disabilities, 45*, 500–511.

Allor, J.H., Gifford, D.B., Al Otaiba, S., Miller, S.J., & Cheatham, J.P. (2013). Teaching students with intellectual disabilities to unitize words and transfer early reading skills to connected text. *Remedial and Special Education, 34*, 346–356. doi: 10.1177/0741932513494020.

Allor, J.H., & Mathes, P. (2012). *Early interventions in reading: Level K.* Columbus, OH: SRA/McGraw-Hill.

Allor, J.H., Mathes, P.G., Champlin, T., & Cheatham, J.P. (2009). Research-based techniques for teaching early reading skills to students with intellectual disabilities. *Education and Training in Developmental Disabilities, 44*, 356–366.

Allor, J.H., Mathes, P., Roberts, K., Cheatham, J.P., & Al Otaiba, S. (in press). Is scientifically-based reading instruction effective for students with below-average IQs? *Exceptional Children.*

Allor, J.H., Mathes, P.G., Roberts, J.K., Cheatham, J.P., & Champlin, T.M. (2010). Comprehensive reading instruction for students with intellectual disabilities: Findings from the first three years of a longitudinal study. *Psychology in the Schools, 47*, 445–466. doi:10.1002/pits.20482

Allor, J.H., Mathes, P.G., Roberts, J.K., Jones, F.G., & Champlin, T.M. (2010). Teaching students with moderate intellectual disabilities to read: An experimental examination of a comprehensive reading intervention. *Education and Training in Autism and Developmental Disabilities, 45*, 3–22.

Browder, D.M., Ahlgrim-Delzell, L., Courtade, G.R., Gibbs, S.L., & Flowers, C. (2008). Evaluation of the effectiveness of an early literacy program for students with significant developmental disabilities. *Exceptional Children, 75*, 33–52.

Browder, D., & Cooper-Duffy, K. (2003). Evidence-based practices for students with severe disabilities and the requirement for accountability in "No Child Left Behind." *The Journal of Special Education, 37*, 157–163. doi:10.1177/00224669030370030501

Browder, D., Gibbs, S., Ahlgrim-Delzell, L., Courtade, G., & Lee, A. (2007). *Early literacy skills builder.* Verona, WI: Attainment Company.

Browder, D., Spooner, F., Ahlgrim-Delzell, L., Flowers, C., Algozzine, B., & Karvonen, M. (2003). A content analysis of the curriculuar philosophies reflected in states' alternate assessment performance indicators. *Research and Practice for Persons with Severe Disabilities, 28*, 165–181. doi:10.2511/rpsd.28.4.165

Browder, D.M., Trela, K., & Jimenez, B. (2007). Training teachers to follow a task analysis to engage middle school students with moderate and severe developmental disabilities in grade-appropriate literature. *Focus on Autism and Other Developmental Disabilities, 22*, 206–219. doi:10.1177/10883576070220040301

Browder, D.M., Wakeman, S.Y., Spooner, F., Ahlgrim-Delzell, L., & Algozzine, B. (2006). Research on reading instruction for individuals with significant cognitive disabilities. *Exceptional Children, 72*, 392–408.

Browder, D.M., & Xin, Y.P. (1998). A meta-analysis and review of sight word research and its implications for teaching functional reading to individuals with moderate and severe disabilities. *The Journal of Special Education, 32*, 130–153. doi:10.1177/002246699803200301

Burns, M.K. (2007). Comparison of opportunities to respond within a drill model when rehearsing sight words with a child with mental retardation. *School Psychology Quarterly, 22*, 250–263. doi:10.1037/1045-3830.22.2.250

Carnine, D., Silbert, J., Kame'enui, E.J., & Tarver, S.G. (2004). *Direct instruction reading* (4th ed.). Columbus, OH: Merrill.

Cohen, E.T., Heller, K.W., Alberto, P., & Fredrick, L.D. (2008). Using a three-step decoding strategy with constant time delay to teach word reading to students with mild and moderate mental retardation. *Focus on Autism and Other Developmental Disabilities, 23*(2), 67–78. doi:10.1177/1088357608314899

Conners, F.A. (1992). Reading instruction for students with moderate mental retardation: Review and analysis of research. *American Journal on Mental Retardation, 96*, 577–597.

Conners, F.A., Rosenquist, C.J., Sligh, A.C., Atwell, J.A., & Kiser, T. (2006). Phonological reading skills acquisition by children with mental retardation. *Research in Developmental Disabilities, 27*(2), 121–137. doi:2004.11.015

Dixon, R.C., & Engelmann, S. (1999). *Spelling mastery series guide.* Columbus, OH: SRA/McGraw-Hill.

Engelmann, S., & Bruner, E.C. (2002). *Reading mastery plus.* Columbus, OH: SRA/McGraw-Hill.

Engelmann, S., Meyer, L., Carnine, L., Becker, W., Eisele, J., & Johnson, G. (2002). *Corrective reading.* Columbus, OH: SRA-McGraw Hill.

Flores, M.M., Shippen, M.E., Alberto, P., & Crowe, L. (2004). Teaching letter-sound correspondence to students with moderate intellectual disabilities. *Journal of Direct Instruction, 4*, 173–188.

Florida Department of Education. (2007). *Next generation sunshine state standards.* Retrieved from http://www.cpalms.org/page24.aspx

Folsom, J.S. (2012). *A comparison of reading growth and outcomes of kindergarten students with cognitive impairments to their typical peers: The impact of instruction* (Doctoratal dissertation). Retrieved from ProQuest Dissertations and Theses database. (UMI No. 3519316)

Fuchs, D., Fuchs, L.S., Svenson, E., Yen, L., Thompson, A., McMaster, K.L., Al Otaiba, S., & Kearns, D. M. (2013). *Peer-assisted learning strategies: First grade reading.* Nashville, TN: Vanderbilt University.

Fuchs, D., Fuchs, L.S., Thompson, A., Al Otaiba, S., Yen, L., McMaster, K. L., Yang, N. J., Svenson, E., & Braun, M. (2013). *Peer-assisted learning strategies: Kindergarten reading.* Nashville, TN: Vanderbilt University.

Good, R.H., & Kaminski, R.A. (2002). *Dynamic indicators of basic early literacy skills* (6th ed.). Retrieved from http://dibels.uoregon.edu

Gough, P.B., & Tunmer, W.E. (1986). Decoding, reading, and reading disability. *Remedial and Special Education, 7*(1), 6–10. doi:10.1177/074193258600700104

Honig, B., Diamond, L., & Gutlohn, L. (2013). *CORE teaching reading sourcebook* (2nd ed.). Novato, CA: Arena Press.

Hougan, M.C., & Smartt, S.M. (2012). *The fundamentals of literacy instruction and assessment, pre-K–6*. Baltimore, MD: Paul H. Brookes Publishing Co.

Individuals with Disabilities Education Improvement Act (IDEA) in of 2004, PL 108-446, 20 U.S.C. §§ 1400 et seq.

Joseph, L.M., & Seery, M.E. (2004). Where is the phonics? A review of the literature on the use of phonetic analysis with students with mental retardation. *Remedial and Special Education, 25*(2), 88–94. doi:10.1177/07419325040250020301

Kauffman, J.M., & Hung, L.Y. (2009). Special education for intellectual disability: Current trends and perspectives. *Current Opinion in Psychiatry, 22,* 452–456. doi:10.1097/YCO.0b013e32832eb5c3

Lemons, C.J., & Fuchs, D. (2010). Modeling response to reading intervention in children with Down syndrome: An examination of predictors of differential growth. *Reading Research Quarterly, 45,* 134–169. doi:10.1598/RRQ.45.2.1

Lemons, C.J., Zigmond, N., Kloo, A., Hill, D.R., Mrachko, A.A., Paterra, M.F.,... Davis, S.M. (2013). Performance of students with significant cognitive disabilities on early grade curriculum-based measures of word and passage reading fluency. *Exceptional Children, 79,* 408–426.

Mathes, P.G., & Torgesen, J. (2005). *Early interventions in reading.* Columbus, OH: SRA/McGraw-Hill.

Mathes, P.G., Torgesen, J.K., Allen, S.H., & Allor, J.H. (2001). *First-grade PALS: Peer-assisted literacy strategies.* Longmont, CO: Sopris West.

National Early Literacy Panel. (2008). *Developing early literacy: Report of the National Early Literacy Panel.* Washington, DC: National Institute for Literacy.

National Governors Association Center for Best Practices, Council of Chief State School Officers. (2010). *Common Core State Standards.* Washington, DC: Authors. Retrieved from http://www.corestandards.org/

National Institute of Child Health and Human Development. (2000). *Report of the National Reading Panel. Teaching children to read: An evidence-based assessment of the scientific research literature on reading and its implications for reading instruction* (NIH Publication No. 00-4769). Washington, DC: U.S. Government Printing Office.

O'Connor, R.E. (2007). *Teaching word recognition: Effective strategies for students with learning difficulties.* New York, NY: Guilford Press.

Riepl, J.H., Marchand-Martella, N.E., & Martella, R.C. (2008). The effects of "Reading Mastery Plus" on the beginning reading skills of students with intellectual and developmental disabilities. *Journal of Direct Instruction, 8,* 29–39.

Robertson, C., & Salter, W. (1995). *The phonological awareness kit: Primary.* East Moline, IL: Linguisystems.

Salisbury, C.L., Evans, I.M., & Palombaro, M.M. (1997). Collaborative problem solving to promote the inclusion of young children with significant disabilities in the primary grades. *Exceptional Children, 63,* 195–209.

Vadasy, P.F., Wayne, S.K., O'Connor, R.E., Jenkins, J.R., Pool, K., Firebaugh, M., & Peyton, J. (2005). *Sound partners: A tutoring program in phonics-based early reading.* Longmont, CO: Sopris West.

Waugh, R.E., Fredrick, L.D., & Alberto, P.A. (2009). Using simultaneous prompting to teach sounds and blending skills to students with moderate intellectual disabilities. *Research in Developmental Disabilities, 30,* 1435–1447. doi:10.1016/j.ridd.2009.07.004

FOR FURTHER INFORMATION

Curricular Materials

Early Interventions in Reading

https://www.mheonline.com/program/view/4/1/2542/SRAEIRLV11

This site includes a phonemic awareness/early phonics game, *Stop and Go*, which can be purchased separately.

Allor, J.H., & Mathes, P.G. (2012). *Early interventions in reading: Level K*. Columbus, OH: SRA/McGraw-Hill.

Mathes, P.G., & Torgesen, J.K. (2012). *Early interventions in reading, Level 1*. Columbus, OH: SRA/McGraw-Hill.

Mathes, P.G., & Torgesen, J.K. (2012). *Early interventions in reading, Level 2*. Columbus, OH: SRA/McGraw-Hill.

Mondo Bookshop Phonics

Allor, J.H., & Minden-Cupp, C. (2009). *Bookshop phonics intervention*. New York, NY: Mondo.

Allor, J.H., & Minden-Cupp, C. (2007). *Bookshop phonics for kindergarten*. New York, NY: Mondo.

Allor, J.H., & Minden-Cupp, C. (2007). *Bookshop phonics for first grade*. New York, NY: Mondo.

Responsive Reading Instruction

http://www.soprislearning.com/literacy/responsive-reading-instruction

Reading Instruction

Common Core State Standards for English Language Arts

http://www.corestandards.org/ELA-Literacy

This web site provides a detailed explanation of the standards for each component of reading by grade level.

The IRIS Center

http://iris.peabody.vanderbilt.edu

This web site provides multiple resources for practitioners regarding reading behavior and disabilities.

National Center on Response to Intervention

http://www.rti4success.org/

This web site provides a definition of *response to intervention* as well as resources for implementing instruction and measuring student progress.

National Dissemination Center for Children with Disabilities

http://nichcy.org

This is a federally funded center that provides information on programs and services for infants, children, and youth with disabilities.

Research Articles

Allor, J.H., Champlin, T.M., Gifford, D.B., & Mathes, P.G. (2010). Methods for increasing the intensity of reading instruction for students with intellectual disabilities. *Education and Training in Autism and Developmental Disabilities, 45*, 500–511.

Allor, J.H., & Chard, D.J. (2011). A comprehensive approach to improving reading fluency for students with disabilities. *Focus on Exceptional Children, 43*, 1–12.

Allor, J.H., Mathes, P.G., Champlin, T.M., & Cheatham, J.P. (2009). Research-based techniques for teaching early reading skills to students with intellectual disabilities. *Education and Training in Developmental Disabilities, 44*, 356–366.

Allor, J.H., Mathes, P.G., Jones, F.G., Champlin, T.M., & Cheatham, J.P. (2010). Individualized research-based reading instruction for students with intellectual disabilities. *TEACHING Exceptional Children, 42*, 6–12.

Allor, J.H., Mathes, P.G., Roberts, J.K., Cheatham, J.P., & Al Otaiba, S. (in press). Is scientifically based reading instruction effective for students with below-average IQs? *Exceptional Children.*

Tutoring Programs

Peer Assisted Learning Strategies (PALS)

www.kc.vanderbilt.edu/pals

Mathes, P.G., & Allor, J.H. (2001). *Teacher-directed PALS: Paths to achieving literacy success.* Longmont, CO: Sopris West.

Mathes, P.G., Torgesen, J.K., Allen, S.H., & Allor, J.H. (2001). *First-grade PALS: Peer-assisted literacy strategies.* Longmont, CO: Sopris West.

Sound Partners

http://www.soprislearning.com/literacy/sound-partners

Together We Can!

http://www.soprislearning.com/professional-development/together-we-can!

CHAPTER 7

Teaching Written Expression to Students with Moderate to Severe Disabilities

Robert Pennington and Monica Delano

The feverish chatter of her peers about Facebook and other social media fascinates Tamika. She observes the rich and animated discussion around Facebook and wants to participate along with her classmates. She seeks assistance from her 10th-grade teacher, Mrs. Collins, in developing her online presence. Mrs. Collins is happy to oblige and sets forth designing a program to teach Tamika to be a competent Facebook user. Mrs. Collins is confident she can use response-prompting strategies (e.g., time delay) to teach Tamika to navigate the software but is perplexed as to how Tamika will actually add content to her page. Tamika has not acquired several critical writing skills, including basic spelling conventions.

Mrs. Collins frequently uses touch screen technology (e.g., SMART Boards, iPads) with her students and sees this as a potential avenue for helping Tamika. She works with Tamika and her peers to program responses into augmentative and alternative communication (AAC) software that has been loaded onto a web-enabled tablet. They select a wide array of responses including general statements about Tamika's day (e.g., "rough day today," "today was awesome") and specific statements designed to evoke peer feedback (e.g., "I am watching *Grey's Anatomy* tonight, what about you?"). Tamika has a limited sight word vocabulary, so Mrs. Collins pairs pictures with each text statement. In addition, she enables the software's auditory feedback feature so that Tamika can hear the selected response and make corrections when necessary. A peer suggests that she, Mrs. Collins, and Tamika meet every couple of days to update Tamika's device. Mrs. Collins teaches Tamika how to use shortcuts to copy her selected text into a Facebook post. In addition, she teaches her how to use the built-in camera on the tablet so that she can directly post images taken throughout the day on to her personal page.

After several weeks of instruction, Mrs. Collins' data indicate that Tamika has learned the skills necessary to be a Facebook regular. Tamika has become the talk of her peers and family members, as her picture and text posts reflect her unique perspectives. Mrs. Collins smiles as she observes Tamika increasingly engage in literacy activities that are naturally reinforced by those most important to her.

The importance of developing the ability to compose text cannot be overstated. Writing is a topography that serves multiple communicative functions. In educational environments, written expression is often the primary means of demonstrating content knowledge. In addition, writing tasks provide excellent contexts for supporting the development of reading and language skills. Writing also serves many functions outside of the school setting. For example, writing is a necessary skill to succeed in most work environments. The use of self-management tools (e.g., calendars, schedules, checklists) requires the use of written language. In contemporary society, written language plays a critical role in social interaction and friendships. Adequate writing skills are necessary to engage in sending emails, texting, participating in chat rooms, and using social media. Perhaps most importantly, writing provides a way for individuals to express their thoughts, opinions, and feelings, and may serve as a tool to enhance self-determination.

Historically, educators have not expected students with moderate or severe disabilities to develop skills in written expression. Consequently, students with these types of disabilities have not had access to the many benefits of being skilled writers. Instead, educators and researchers have focused solely on developing effective intervention strategies for teaching functional communication skills. Researchers have established several effective practices, most of which are rooted in applied behavior analysis, for teaching vocal, sign, and picture-based communication. Now, however, all students, including students with moderate and severe disabilities, are required to meet the Common Core State Standards for English language arts and literacy (National Governors Association Center for Best Practices, Council of Chief State School Officers, 2010). In addition to requiring achievement in English language arts, these standards include an emphasis on literacy in content areas such as social studies and science, as well as college and career readiness. Thus students are required to develop skills in speaking, reading, listening, and writing. In essence, the teaching of writing must now play a significant part in developing the communication skills of students with moderate and severe disabilities. Given the limited research in this area and the challenges some students face in developing functional communication skills, teachers face a seemingly daunting task.

The purpose of this chapter is to provide educators with an understanding of the current knowledge base in teaching writing and provide a framework for designing effective writing instructional programs for students with moderate and severe disabilities. This framework is grounded in writing research and will enable teachers to apply the same behavioral principles they use in teaching other forms of communication to the teaching of writing. The chapter begins with a discussion of the complexity of writing and a brief overview of the research base in teaching writing. This is followed by a description of specific approaches to developing writing skills for students with moderate and severe disabilities.

COMPLEXITY OF WRITTEN EXPRESSION

Though writing is a critical skill, the complexity of the writing process makes the acquisition of writing skills challenging for many students. Writing development occurs over many years as students gradually develop the necessary skills to compose sophisticated stories and essays. Bruner (1991) suggested that stories have four basic characteristics: 1) sequentiality, 2) particularity, 3) intentional states, and 4) canonicity and breach. Typically, preschoolers begin telling stories orally that may initially center on their daily experiences (McKeough, Palmer, Jarvey, & Bird, 2007). These stories may include a specific sequence of events and focus on a particular event, but they lack characters' emotional states and intentions. As students enter school and begin writing stories, the complexity of their stories gradually increases. Throughout elementary school students learn to create characters with specific intentions and emotions. Story plots become more complex, and the focus extends beyond immediate and actual events. During middle and high school, students not only continue to develop story writing skills but also learn to write across the curriculum, composing essays and using writing to explore content. Little is known about how children with moderate and severe disabilities develop complex writing skills. As with typically developing children, it is likely that the development of writing skills will need to parallel development of oral language and/or AAC.

In addition to considering children's overall development in oral and written language, it is important to understand that in all writing activities students must engage in a variety of tasks (e.g., recalling information, word retrieval, planning, transcribing language to text, motor planning) simultaneously. They need to demonstrate knowledge of a topic, awareness of an audience, motivation to compose text, and a means to put text to paper (e.g., typing, writing, using an adapted writing instrument; McCutchen, 2006). Managing these tasks and the cognitive demands of composing text may make writing especially difficult for individuals with moderate and severe disabilities. Weaknesses in executive functioning skills and oral language may impede the development of writing skills. In addition, students with disabilities bring a variety of abilities and skill sets to writing tasks. For example, students with autism spectrum disorders may display relative strengths in spelling, but have few skills in composing text (Koppenhaver & Erickson, 2009). Students may have limited vocabularies and be unfamiliar with grammar and syntax. Students also will represent various stages of acquiring verbal language or using AAC. Finally, students' working memory and long-term memory may be impaired, interfering with the recall of information about a topic or planning and composing text.

As educators attend to children's writing development, they must remember that, like all students, students with moderate and severe disabilities bring a variety of experiences and learning histories to writing tasks. Some students come from environments that include literacy-rich homes and repeated exposure to text through reading with caregivers and participating in activities of daily living (e.g., creating grocery lists, maintaining calendars). Unfortunately, there is some research that suggests that parents of children with moderate and severe disabilities engage in reading to their children less frequently than other parents and place a lower priority on literacy activities (Fitzgerald, Roberts, Pierce, & Schuele, 1995; Marvin, 1994; Marvin & Miranda, 1993). However, research over the past few years paints a different picture and suggests that these students have had a variety of instructional experiences (Al Otaiba, Lewis, Whalon, Dyrlund, & McKenzie, 2009). Due to low academic expectations, there may be students who have had few opportunities to engage in writing tasks and who have received little or no previous instruction in writing. Other students may be more advanced in their knowledge of writing conventions.

Given the limited knowledge of writing development in students with moderate and severe disabilities, educators must attend to students' language and communication development, understanding of a story structure, prior experiences, and unique learning profiles. The task for educators is to target children's current skills and link instruction to core content standards. This requires educators to identify individual support needs and the demands of various writing tasks. Knowledge of current writing research and a framework for teaching writing to students with moderate and severe disabilities will assist teachers in this task.

USING RESEARCH TO DEVELOP
EFFECTIVE INSTRUCTIONAL PROGRAMS

Because the research literature does not yet provide a set of evidence-based practices to teach written expression to students with moderate and severe disabilities, a four-step process can assist educators in developing instructional programs to teach writing to students with intellectual disabilities.

Reviewing the literature on writing instruction for students without disabilities and students with mild disabilities is a useful first step. Graham and Perrin (2007) identified several highly effective strategies for teaching writing to other populations of students, including the following:

1. Teaching students strategies for planning, editing and revising

2. Teaching procedures for summarizing reading materials

3. Using instructional arrangements in which students collaborate in planning, drafting, revising, and editing compositions

4. Setting clear goals for what students will accomplish with their writing

5. Providing opportunities to use word processing

6. Teaching students how to combine sentences to make them more complex

7. Using writing activities to enhance inquiry skills

8. Providing activities to assist students in gathering and organizing information before writing

9. Providing models of good writing

10. Providing professional development on implementing the writing process.

Writing instructional programs for students with moderate and severe disabilities may include these practices or adapted versions of these practices, again with an emphasis on individualization. Researchers also have identified several effective general classroom procedures such as daily writing across content areas, teacher–student conferencing, predictable writing routines, teacher modeling, the use of reading to support writing development, and frequent assessment (Graham, Harris, & Larsen, 2001; Mason & Graham, 2008). These procedures can easily be included in writing programs for students with moderate and severe disabilities.

In addition to incorporating evidence-based practices for teaching writing to other populations of students, teachers may consider the limited body of research on writing instruction for students with moderate and severe disabilities (including autism spectrum disorders). Unfortunately, this literature does not yet identify evidence-based practices. However, the literature does demonstrate that students with autism or moderate to severe disabilities can acquire skills in spelling (Kinney, Vedora, & Stromer, 2003; Schlosser & Blischak, 2004; Schlosser, Blischak, Belfiore, Bartley, & Barnett, 1998; Stromer, Mackay, Howell, & McVay, 1996), sentence construction in response to pictures (Basil & Reyes, 2003; Yamamoto & Miya, 1999), using adjectives and adverbs (Delano, 2007; Rousseau, Krantz, Poulson, Kitson, & McClannahan, 1994), and story writing (Bedrosian, Lasker, Speidel, & Politsch, 2003; Delano, 2007; Pennington, Ault, Schuster, & Sanders, 2011; Pennington, Collins, Stenhoff, Turner, & Gunselman, in press; Pennington, Stenhoff, Gibson, & Ballou, 2012). The literature also suggests the potential benefits of several intervention components, including computer-assisted instruction, response prompting, modeling, selection-based responding, picture exchange, and video modeling. Though future research will identify evidence-based practices, the current literature may provide educators with a starting point for developing writing programs.

A third step in developing a writing program for students is to apply evidence-based practices for teaching students with moderate and severe disabilities to the teaching of writing. Systematic instruction, task analysis, and response prompting are critical components of any intensive instructional program for learners in this population. Peer-mediated instruction, student-directed learning, and universal design for learning are likely to be applicable to writing instruction. Thus, writing instruction does not require a totally new set of instructional strategies. Educators can apply familiar evidence-based practices to the teaching of writing.

Finally, progress monitoring and making data-based instructional decisions are integral parts of effective instructional programs. Given the lack of research in teaching writing to students with moderate and severe disabilities, it is critical that educators collect continuous data, conduct data analysis, and modify ineffective programs. This will prevent students from losing precious instructional time and help educators begin to identify effective means of providing high-quality writing instruction.

AN ADAPTED PROCESS APPROACH FOR STUDENTS WITH MODERATE TO SEVERE DISABILITY

Though the available research literature on teaching written expression to students with moderate and severe disabilities is limited, there are several areas of related research from which practitioners can draw to design potentially effective programs. First, the most current literature at the time of this writing on teaching writing to students without disabilities reflects an emphasis on meaning (Mercer, Mercer, & Pullen, 2011). This meaning-based or process approach to writing directs teachers to address traditional writing conventions within the context of purposeful activities. For example, instead of teaching sentence structure by requiring students to write multiple simple sentences out of context, teachers might shape multiple writing conventions as students develop drafts around preferred content. In these meaningful contexts, students are motivated to engage in writing activities, which ultimately may result in more rapid acquisition of targeted writing skills.

Second, though often relegated to the world of academic skills, written expression is considered a form/topography of communication and, therefore, may be subject to many of the same principles of instruction. For example, handing a card depicting a picture symbol to a communicative partner is analogous to handing a written note to a communicative partner. Both messages may be under control of the same relevant antecedent stimuli (e.g., a request to describe an event, motivation to access a preferred activity), and both may result in the same consequence (e.g., peer attention, access to an activity). The literature is replete with methods for teaching a variety of communicative responses to students with moderate and severe disabilities, and many of these methods can be adapted to teach written expression. More importantly, the available data suggest a curriculum and sequence for teaching communication that might be helpful in designing programs for teaching written expression. For example, typically developing children first learn to make requests for items in their environment prior to learning to describe them. Yet, teachers of students with moderate and severe disabilities may attempt unsuccessfully to teach students to write about things in their environment before students have learned that words are used to affect the behavior of a reader.

Assessing Students' Current Repertoire

Prior to selecting instructional targets, practitioners should determine students' current writing and general communication repertoires. Several formal and standardized assessments are available in both areas (e.g., Test of Early Written Language–3 [Hresko, Herron, Peak, & Hicks, 2012], Comprehensive Assessment of Spoken Language [Carrow-Woolfolk, 1999], Peabody Picture Vocabulary Test–4 [Dunn & Dunn, 2007]), but it is important to note that most of these measures are not standardized on students with moderate or severe disabilities, thus limiting their validity for use with this population. Assessments of communicative functioning should target both speaker and listener skills. Speaker skills, often referred to as expressive skills, involve those communication skills that affect the behaviors of others, whereas listener skills or receptive skills involve responding to the words of others. Prior to designing a writing program, teachers must first understand which communicative responses the student already uses to have an impact on his or her environment and in the presence of which words or combination of words the student can respond. These data are critical in designing meaningful programs. For example, without understanding the extent of a child's listener/receptive vocabulary, a child's writing in response to the auditory presentation of a story may not accurately reflect his or her understanding.

Teachers also may benefit from the availability of curriculum-based assessment tools that address a broad array of skills relevant to the instruction of writing (e.g., fine motor, communication, visual discrimination, imitation). An advantage to using these assessments is that teachers can conduct them with minimal training within natural settings. In addition, these assessments often provide a scope and sequence of skills that will help educators easily determine instruction targets and objectives. One assessment, the Verbal Behavior Milestones Assessment and Placement Program (VB-MAPP; Sundberg, 2008), provides prescriptive guidance on the selection of instructional objectives. Once a teacher scores a child's performance, he or she can refer to the scoring guide for recommendations for the selection of targets. For example, after acquiring basic communication and tracing skills, teachers are directed to target beginning copying skills (e.g., letters, numbers).

Making Writing Meaningful

When teachers reflect on their own experiences in learning to write, they may recall tracing countless lines of horizontal letters or carefully drafting narratives in response to a prompt written on the chalkboard. In both cases, students turned in their work, waited for teacher feedback, and likely hoped that they would not be directed to address multiple errors and resubmit. This approach leaves students without an understanding of the critical communicative functions of writing. In addition, it requires students to perform difficult tasks with limited and delayed feedback or reinforcement, which may result at best in decreased performance and at worst problem behavior. It is also important that the mechanics of writing (e.g., handwriting, grammar, spelling) do not prevent a student from accomplishing the purpose of writing. The mechanics of writing for some students with moderate and severe disabilities may involve word/picture selection or typing. This mode of writing will enable students to write for a variety of purposes including requesting, explaining, persuading, and entertaining. Strategies to address the mechanics of writing may be individualized so that all students can write with a purpose.

The first step in creating meaningful writing experiences is to determine what is important and potentially reinforcing to students. Once identified, these reinforcing stimuli can be used to directly reinforce responses or as engaging topics for written narratives. A variety of procedures are available for identifying potential reinforcers. In some cases, it may be appropriate to ask parents or students to identify preferred stimuli. Unfortunately, many students with moderate and severe disabilities may not have the language skills to accurately identify powerful reinforcers. In this case, there are a variety of procedures, called stimulus preference assessments (SPAs) that can assist teachers in finding reinforcers. These procedures differ from survey methods in that they are conducted immediately prior to instructional tasks and have been demonstrated to more accurately identify stimuli that serve as reinforcers. Pennington and colleagues (2012) used an SPA (i.e., multiple stimulus without replacement) to determine main characters for use during story instruction tasks. Pictures of potentially reinforcing characters were presented to each participant along with the directive, "Whom would you like to write about?" Once the student selected a picture, the researchers presented the remaining pictures and repeated the directive. They continued until the student had selected all of the pictures. After conducting the procedure three times, they selected the three most preferred characters for use during instruction.

For some students without prior writing experience, teachers may consider pairing prewriting behaviors with reinforcing stimuli. This procedure has been applied to the vocal responses of children with autism and has resulted in increased frequency of vocal responses (Caroll & Klatt, 2008). When using this procedure, teachers immediately deliver reinforcement following students' performance of writing-related behaviors (e.g., holding a crayon, scribbling, pressing keys on a computer, drawing on a SMART Board). The intent is to increase the frequency of writing behavior and to condition reinforcing properties of writing tools. Engaging in these prewriting behaviors may serve to increase students' strength in the muscles required to perform fine motors tasks necessary for handwriting or keyboarding. Once students frequently engage in these early writing responses, teachers may find it easier to shape more conventional writing responses.

In the early stages of communication, intervention should start with teaching students to request preferred items. These requesting responses, referred to as mands, are powerful in that they give individuals direct control over their environment and are the only responses that directly benefit the speaker (Skinner, 1957). Mands are responses that specifically name a desired reinforcer (e.g., child signs COOKIE and receives a cookie). In teaching the communicative function of writing, teachers might first consider teaching students to exchange written words for preferred items. Lavigna (1977) demonstrated that students with severe intellectual disability could be trained to exchange written words for preferred items. This beginning writing strategy has several advantages. First, it clearly demonstrates a relationship between the written word and reader behavior. This relationship may be less salient to students while engaging in other more arbitrary writing activities. Second, it requires little response effort in that students are not required to spell or perform fine motor tasks required for writing. Again, students learn a functional use of words without having to first acquire more complex fine motor and cognitive skills. Finally, the written word may be less ambiguous than other symbols to a reader and, therefore, more easily understood by the communicative partner, resulting in more immediate reinforcement.

Early instruction should include basic mand training procedures that involve capturing or contriving student motivation, presenting the preferred stimulus, using response-prompting procedures (e.g., most-to-least prompting, time delay) to ensure the student responds correctly, and then providing access to the named reinforcing item. Once students acquire these basic responses, teachers may increase the complexity of these responses by requiring students to mand for increasingly specific items. For example, a teacher may first train a student to access a cookie by handing the word *cookie* to a partner. Subsequently, the student may combine the words *big* and *cookie* to indicate a preference for a larger cookie. Teachers might consider using a format similar to that used in the latter stages of the Picture Exchange Communication System (PECS; Frost & Bondy, 2002), whereas the student selects symbols from an array and affixes them to a sentence strip. The student then hands the strip to a communicative partner. When training students to exchange words for reinforcers, it will be important to consider students' current communicative repertoire to ensure that teaching a new response form will not have an inhibitive effect on acquiring targeted communication responses. Students in the early stages of acquiring mands may be confused when presented a requirement to emit competing responses (e.g., saying *cookie* versus writing *cookie*) to access a preferred item. In general, students should first acquire a strong mand repertoire using the response form that the educational team has targeted to be the individual's primary mode of communication prior to starting writing instruction.

Imitation

In early communication training programs, students are taught to imitate the responses of others. Skinner (1957) used the term *copying to text* to describe individuals' imitation of written responses. Initially, copying to text is an important skill for students to acquire because teachers then can use the written word to prompt student responses instead of relying on hand-over-hand prompting. Once students acquire the ability to copy words, they can use print within the environment as models to support spelling. Consider, for example, the student that cannot remember how to spell the word *milk* when writing her grocery list. If she has acquired the skill to copy text, then she can walk to the old milk carton and use the label as a model. Once students can copy from a model, teachers can enhance written expression skills by requiring students to write words to make requests. Teachers also may provide lists of words from which students can copy to construct of variety of messages. For example, teachers could train students to enter words from a list into a search engine to locate academic content (e.g., videos on the solar system) or to engage in leisure activities (e.g., games, music videos).

Once students acquire this *see–write* relationship, they may use the print readily available in their educational environment to practice new copying skills and to potentially develop a spelling repertoire. Typically developing children often incorporate environmental text into early written products. Teachers may need to facilitate this attention to environmental print by incorporating words in various locations as models during copying-to-text instruction. For some students, teachers may need to gradually shape students' copying of environmental print by incrementally increasing the distance between the writer and the written model.

When learning to copy words, some students may require the use of assistive technology to circumvent weaknesses in fine motor skills. Teachers can use a variety of response-prompting strategies to teach keyboarding skills but also may need to use adapted keyboards or AAC selection displays. There are several adapted keyboards available that address a range of students' needs (e.g., alphabetical, one-handed, large print). In addition, some students also may require the use of scanning technology due to physical disabilities that have an impact on gross and fine motor functioning.

Spelling

Once students learn to copy other words, they can progress to spelling words after hearing them spoken. This skill, called transcription (Skinner, 1957), is valuable as teachers can shape students' spelling responses under the control of specific spoken targets. Consider the child that writes the word *cook* on a piece of paper. Without knowing the controlling antecedent variable, it would be difficult to assess spelling accuracy. The child's response could reflect an attempt at spelling *cookie*, *cook*, or *Corkie*. Teachers can use a variety of strategies for establishing transcription responses. Teachers may consider using a constant time delay strategy, in which the word written on an index card serves as the controlling prompt. Teachers also may use a backward chaining strategy in which the teacher presents the spoken word and then provides a written model for the student to trace. On subsequent trials, the teacher fades the written model by incrementally removing the letters in the word from the last letter to the first.

Teachers also must instruct students to spell words in the presence of pictured stimuli. This critical skill will help students write about things in their environment and serve as a valuable tool in accessing general education curriculum. The limited body of research indicates that computer-assisted instruction may be effective in teaching spelling to picture skills (Stromer et al., 1996). During instruction, a student is presented with a word/picture combination then is initially required to select letters from a computer-based array to construct the word shown. On subsequent trials, the word is faded and correct responses are reinforced.

For most students with moderate and severe disabilities, developing early spelling skills will require intensive one-to-one or small-group instruction. Fortunately, once students acquire basic spelling skills, teachers can use other strategies to help expand their repertoire without intensive teacher interaction. For example, researchers have demonstrated the effectiveness of cover, copy, compare (CCC) techniques for learners with intellectual disability (Cordes, McLaughlin, Derby, & Higgins, 2012; Membrey, McLaughlin, Derby, & Antcliff, 2011). In this technique, students are presented with a piece of paper divided into four columns. The first column contains the targeted spelling word. Students are taught to copy the word and write it in the second column. Then the student folds the first column on the left toward the center, covering the second column. The student writes the word from memory in the third column and unfolds their paper and compares. If the student makes an error, he or she copies the word three times in the final column. Teachers also can use the CCC technique for students with motor impairments by incorporating assistive technology. For example, Schlosser and Blischak (2004) adapted the CCC procedure for use with a voice output communication aid. Instead of copying words presented on a CCC worksheet, students typed words as they were presented on index cards.

Some teachers may consider using video models during instruction. Kinney and colleagues (2003) demonstrated that a student with autism learned new spelling skills after watching a model of her teacher writing words on a chalkboard. This method provides a unique advantage in that the videos can be stored and used for multiple students. Video models may be easily displayed on a computer desktop while children type or write the words. Teachers can use editing software (e.g., iMovie) to embed instructional procedures. For example, a video may depict a teacher writing the word, followed by a pause to allow the child time to copy the word. Then the teacher can insert a blank screen, during which the child writes the word from memory, followed by the presentation of the original model. Although procedures such as CCC and video modeling require time in teacher preparation, they provide students with the opportunity to practice skills independently. Furthermore, teachers can share training videos with families or teach them to use CCC methods to provide student opportunities to practice skills outside of the classroom.

Some students may benefit from spelling tools built into word processing software. In a recent investigation, researchers demonstrated the effectiveness of strategies for teaching students with moderate and severe disabilities to use spell check to assist in writing activities (Kagohara, Sigafoos, Achmadi, O'Reilly, & Lancioni, 2012). Like Kinney and colleagues, the researchers used video models to teach the targeted skills. During instruction, students observed videos played on an iPad and received praise for correct responses. It is likely that a variety of instructional strategies could be effective in teaching students to use spell check. Teachers should consider selecting spell check usage as an important curricular item for some students, as it can lead to greater independence and quality during writing.

Sentence Construction

Prior to instruction on sentence writing, teachers must consider whether students have acquired the spelling skills necessary to compose more complex writing responses. If students have not acquired sufficient spelling skills, then they will require the use of selection-based writing software (e.g., Pixwriter [Slater & Slater, 1994], Clicker 6 [Crick Software, 2005]) in which words or combinations of words are presented within arrays on a computer screen (Figure 7.1). These versatile tools offer several advantages, including 1) eliminating the need for spelling skills, 2) the ability to embed and fade picture or positional prompts within arrays, 3) digitized auditory feedback, and 4) the ability to save electronic files for editing and assessment.

When teaching complex written responses, it is important for teachers to remember that although complexity certainly refers to variation in the topography of a response, it also involves using the same words to express multiple meanings. Many students with moderate and severe disabilities may develop complex written requesting skills (e.g., "I want milk") but will not show the same progress when asked to write about a picture or to construct a story. Teachers must assess each function separately at the word level before moving to more complex skills. Again, teachers can use basic communication training techniques to teach students to use words to make requests, and then expand those requests using mand frames (e.g., "I want," "Can I have?"). Data suggest that mand frames may facilitate the emergence of new responses (Hernandez, Hanley, Ingvarsson, & Tiger, 2007). Once students are taught to complete the frames to make sentences, some students may write new sentences without direct instruction. Finally, teachers can increase the complexity of the mands by teaching the student to use attributes to ask for increasingly specific items (e.g., "Can I have the big red truck?").

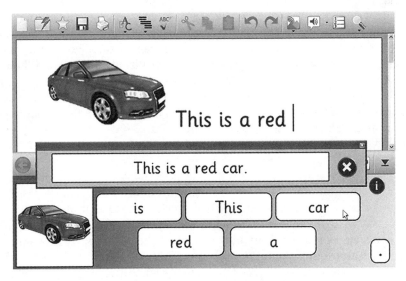

Figure 7.1.   Clicker 6 screenshot. (Used by permission of Crick Software, Inc.)

Teachers may find it more difficult to teach other functions of writing (e.g., describing, conversational), as they do not directly benefit the writer. During instruction, teachers again must deliver powerful reinforcers, but those reinforcers will not be named by the written response. Teachers should begin instruction by teaching students to write, type, or select words when presented with a picture or object. Once students have acquired a small word-to-picture repertoire (e.g., 50 words), teachers can use sentence starters or autoclitic frames (e.g., "I see a _____," "The boy is _____") to expand the length of these responses. Using backward chaining techniques, teachers can then fade the sentence starters so that students are independently constructing sentences. During this phase of training, students also may benefit from activities that involve matching words or simple sentences to pictures. Again, data reflect the importance of concurrent writing and reading programming (Graham et al., 2001).

Some students with moderate and severe disabilities may benefit from opportunities to evaluate their own writing products. For example, Kameenui and Simmons (1990) described a simple sentence as "naming somebody or something and tells more about that person or thing" (p. 438). Teachers may consider teaching students to self-monitor their use of these two components during editing and revision activities. In addition, teachers should introduce basic punctuation conventions as students learn to construct simple sentences, but again maintain focus on the students' ability to communicate a clear message.

Once students can write a single sentence about a picture, teachers can encourage students to write multiple sentences about a picture (Kameenui & Simmons, 1990). Teachers should present pictures containing a variety of stimuli and at first may highlight features of the picture to help students identify content in which to describe or label. These prompts can then be faded to ensure students can choose to write about the stimuli that they deem important. Teachers must then provide opportunities for students to write about multiple pictures as they may serve as prompts for future writing activities.

Finally, it will be important that teachers fade pictures so that students can eventually write about things they have learned. Initially, instruction may involve showing the student a stimulus and then removing it from sight by turning the picture over or placing the object out of view. The teacher then may slowly increase the amount of time between the observation of the visual stimulus and the writing response. Teachers also may insert other tasks (e.g., reading a sight word, motor imitation task) between the presentation of the visual stimulus and the request to write. This step of fading the visual stimulus is important, as few tasks in typical academic settings require students to write about things immediately present in their environment.

Writing Narratives

The acquisition of complex writing skills is critical in that it allows students to elaborate on what they know and share their perspective on the world around them. Data suggest that students may acquire these complex writing skills when presented with carefully planned instructional activities (Collins, Branson, Hall, & Rankin, 2001; Pennington et al., 2011, 2012, in press). Furthermore, student gains in the complexity of their writing responses may translate to improvements in vocal responding (Pennington et al., in press).

For many students with moderate and severe disabilities, instruction will begin with teaching students to write simple paragraphs. Teachers can train students to use the rule that a paragraph names a topic and tells more about the topic (Kameenui & Simmons, 1990). Students are then taught to apply the rule when writing a paragraph about a picture. Teachers might begin by helping the student to identify the content of a topic sentence by highlighting a key element within the picture. The teacher can then present a visual organizer and teach the student to use it during planning and while writing his or her paragraphs. Once students can write or construct a paragraph about a picture, teachers again must fade the use of visual supports. This will likely be difficult for many students, so teachers should initially use stimuli in which students have had a great deal of practice.

Students also must learn to write simple stories about themselves and others. Teachers can use a series of pictured events or may consider using video recordings of real-life events (e.g., child plays ball, child falls down, child cries). During training, teachers should present a variety of picture series or videos to facilitate generalization. The goal is not to teach students to write about a set of particular events but to acquire the skills to write about the multitudes of events they will experience in their lifetime.

Some students may learn to write simple stories in the absence of pictured stimuli (Pennington et al., 2012). Using selection-based software, teachers can prompt students to create stories about preferred items or events. Teachers must first design an array that students can use to construct stories. The complexity and arrangement of the array will depend on each student's discrimination skills. For example, students may use words arranged randomly on a 5×5 grid, whereas some students may require positional cues (e.g., subject, verb, object) or pictured stimuli paired with words. Teachers initially should use known words or pictures within each array, but some data suggest that students can learn to read new words when they are included within the word sets (Pennington et al.). During each session, teachers should present a probe or an opportunity to write independently. These probes will provide assessment (e.g., number of words, sentences, story elements) data to determine student progress. Subsequently, teachers should prompt students through several stories. To promote generalization, teachers should present students with different stories that follow the same general format. For example, during the first trial the teacher might prompt the simple story, "There was a monkey. The monkey lived in the zoo. The monkey jumped in the tree. The monkey was silly." On a subsequent trial, the teacher might prompt, "There was a lion. The lion lived in the zoo. The lion roared. The lion was angry." Upon completion of each story, teachers should read the story to the student and reinforce the prompted response. When appropriate, teachers should probe students' vocal and handwritten responses to assess the emergence of storytelling skills across these other important topographies (Figure 7.2).

Teachers may also improve student performance by providing visual supports during planning and drafting activities. For example, teachers might provide students pictures to sequence prior to writing a fictional story or discuss a picture taken during a family vacation prior to writing a personal narrative. These

Student	*John Hancock*	Program	*Story Elements*
Behavioral objective	When presented with the computer-based word bank and the directive "write a story," the student will use a mouse or keyboard to construct a story containing at minimum a character, locale, action (plot), and response to that action (resolution) with 100% accuracy across three consecutive and different written products.		
Start date	September 23		
Standards	CCSS.ELA-Literacy.W.2.3		
Setting	Language arts class	Time	9:00–9:15
Instructor	Mrs. Ault	Arrangement	1:1
Materials	Pixwriter/Clicker 6 software installed on a computer Note cards with 10 stories for each character written on them		
#Stimuli/Session	1 story topic	Trials per stimulus	3
Instructional procedure	Simultaneous prompting		
Antecedent target stimulus (discriminative stimulus)	Presentation of the word bank and the request to write a story	Prompt hierarchy	NA
Response interval	60 seconds to start, 30 seconds between words	Controlling prompt	Point to the correct word on the computer screen.

Don't forget to deliver expectations for student behavior during instruction.

Instructional steps
1. Conduct a preference assessment to determine interesting topics for writing.

2. Conduct daily probes. Present the word bank and the request to write a story. Wait 60 seconds for John to start writing. If he doesn't start writing then ask if he has more to write. If yes, wait 60 seconds more for him to respond; if he says no then discontinue the probe. Finally, if he does not start after 20 seconds then discontinue the probe.

3. Present a template and say, "Let's write a story." Prompt John through the construction of the story. Upon completion, use playback to listen to the story and deliver reinforcement for the completed story. Repeat two more times but construct different versions of the story each time. Attach a task analysis if teaching a chained task.

Feedback	Generalization and maintenance
Probes Deliver general verbal praise after each probe (e.g., "nice try," "good sitting"). Upon completion of the probes, review with John (using a checklist) the components he included in his narrative. *During training* Prompted correct: Deliver verbal praises.	Present multiple versions of the story across a variety of characters. Assess emergence of vocal responses and handwritten responses. Assess performance across instructors.

Figure 7.2. Sample lesson plan for story writing.

activities are suited for cooperative arrangements in which students with and without disabilities could work collectively on a single or individual written product. Bedrosian and colleagues (2003) demonstrated an effective use of peer supports during a story-writing activity. Two students worked together through four phases of writing: 1) joint planning, 2) writing, 3) revising, and 4) publishing. Students used storyboards to plan their narrative and then used software during writing and revision stages. Most interestingly, the researchers programmed an AAC device with messages geared toward joint planning. This example reflects the potential benefits students can enjoy when careful planning is used to facilitate meaningful peer interactions during writing activities.

Editing and Revision

Teaching students to improve the clarity of their written responses ensures that students' messages are accurately received and ultimately reinforced. Teachers can improve the quality of students' writing by training students to identify the presence of specific elements within their written responses. Though a wide range of elements have an impact on the quality of written responses, teachers should present only one element at a time for instruction. For example, after teaching a student to write simple sentences, a teacher might instruct the student to identify whether he or she has included both a person or a thing and something more about the subject. Subsequently, the teacher can direct the student to look for ending punctuation. Generally, when teaching students to identify missing elements, teachers should first present a variety of examples and require the student to record the presence or absence of the elements. Then teachers should provide opportunities for students to evaluate their own written products and provide feedback accordingly.

Teachers also may consider teaching students to use checklists to increase the inclusion of critical elements during writing activities. For example, during instruction on how to write resume cover letters, Pennington, Delano, and Scott (in press) trained students to evaluate their letters using a checklist containing six letter elements (i.e., salutation, statement of the job in which the applicant is interested, statement of applicant's skill related to the job, statement of thanks for considering the application, a cover letter closing, a signature). In addition, students can be directed to graph their use of writing elements and monitor their own progress. As students learn to evaluate their own writing, it is likely that they will become more independent and effective writers.

SUMMARY

Despite a limited body of research evidence, a range of instructional activities and considerations can be used for teaching written expression to students with moderate or severe disabilities. Writing practices for students with moderate and severe disabilities can be aligned with the most current research on communication instruction and writing instruction for other populations. In general, writing instruction must be carefully planned, involve deliberate and systematic procedures, and should occur in the context of meaningful communicative exchanges. Most importantly, in the absence of a definitive set of evidence-based practices, a teacher must carefully assess students' progress and make moment-by-moment decisions to ensure students are not exposed to ineffective instruction. Students with moderate and severe disabilities deserve instruction in the area of written expression, as it is integral to daily life for people without disabilities. Learning to write, type, and/or select communicative responses will provide richer opportunities for students to demonstrate what they know and interact with the people around them.

REFERENCES

Al Otaiba, S., Lewis, S., Whalon, K., Dyrlund, A., & McKenzie, A. (2009). Home literacy environments of young children with Down syndrome: Findings from a web-based survey. *Remedial and Special Education, 30*, 96–107.

Basil, C., & Reyes, S. (2003). Acquisition of literacy skills by children with severe disability. *Child Language Teaching and Therapy, 19*, 27–49.

Bedrosian, J., Lasker, J., Speidel, K., & Politsch, A. (2003). Enhancing the written narrative skills of AAC students with autism: Evidence-based research issues. *Topics in Language Disorders, 23*, 305–324.

Bruner, J.S. (1991). The narrative construction of reality. *Critical Inquiry, 18*, 1–21.

Caroll, R.A., & Klatt, K.P., (2008). Using stimulus-stimulus pairing and direct reinforcement to teach vocal verbal behavior to young children with autism. *Analysis of Verbal Behavior, 24*, 135–146.

Carrow-Woolfolk, E. (1999). *Comprehensive assessment of spoken language.* Circle Pines, MN: American Guidance Service.

Collins, B.C., Branson, T.A., Hall, M., & Rankin, S.W. (2001). Teaching secondary students with moderate disabilities in an inclusive academic classroom setting. *Journal of Developmental and Physical Disabilities, 13*, 41–59.

Cordes, C., McLaughlin, T.F., Derby, M., & Higgins, S. (2012). Implementing and evaluating cover, copy, and compare spelling for a primary student with autism. A case report. *Academic Research Journal, 2*, 271–276.

Crick Software. (2005). Clicker 6 [Computer software]. Westport, CT: Crick Software.

Delano, M. (2007). Use of strategy instruction to improve the story writing skills of a student with Asperger syndrome. *Focus on Autism and Other Developmental Disabilities, 22*, 252–258.

Dunn, L.M., & Dunn, D.M. (2007). *Peabody picture vocabulary test–4.* Circle Pines, MN: American Guidance Service.

Fitzgerald, J., Roberts, J., Pierce, P., & Schuele, M. (1995). Evaluation of home literacy environment: An illustration with preschool children with Down syndrome. *Reading and Writing Quarterly, 11*, 311–334.

Frost, L., & Bondy, A. (2002). *Picture Exchange Communication System training manual* (2nd ed.). Newark, DE: Pyramid Educational Products.

Graham, S., Harris, K.R., & Larsen, L. (2001). Prevention and intervention of writing difficulties for students with learning disabilities. *Learning Disabilities Research & Practice, 16*, 74–84.

Graham, S., & Perrin, D. (2007). A meta-analysis of writing instruction for adolescent students. *Journal of Educational Psychology, 99*, 445–476.

Hernandez, E., Hanley, G.P., Ingvarsson, E.T., & Tiger, J.H. (2007). A preliminary evaluation of the emergence of novel forms. *Journal of Applied Behavior Analysis, 40*, 137–156.

Hresko, W.P., Herron, S.R., Peak, P.R., & Hicks, D.L. (2012). *Test of early written language* (Version 3). Austin, TX: Pro-Ed.

Kagohara, D.M., Sigafoos, J., Achmadi, D., O'Reilly, M., & Lancioni, G. (2012). Teaching children with ASD to check the spelling of words. *Research in Autism Spectrum Disorders, 6*, 304–310.

Kammenui, E.J., & Simmons, D.C. (1990). *Designing instructional strategies.* Englewood Cliffs, NJ: Merrill Publishing Company.

Kinney, E.M., Vedora, J., & Stromer, R. (2003). Computer-presented video models to teach generative spelling to a child with an autism spectrum disorder. *Journal of Positive Behavior Interventions, 5*, 22–29.

Koppenhaver, D.A., & Erickson, K.A. (2009). Literacy in individuals with autism spectrum disorders who use AAC. In P. Mirenda & T. Iacono (Eds.), *Autism spectrum disorders in AAC* (pp. 385–412). Baltimore, MD: Paul H. Brookes Publishing Co.

Lavigna, G. (1977). Communication training in mute autism adolescents using the written word. *Journal of Autism and Childhood Schizophrenia, 7,* 135–149.

Marvin, C. (1994). Home literacy experiences of preschool children with single and multiple disabilities. *Topics in Early Childhood Special Education, 14,* 436–454.

Marvin, C., & Miranda, P. (1993). Home literacy experiences of preschoolers enrolled in Head Start and special education programs. *Journal of Early Intervention, 17,* 351–367.

Mason, L.H., & Graham, S. (2008). Writing instruction for adolescents with learning disabilities: Programs of intervention research. *Learning Disabilities Research and Practice, 23,* 103–112.

McCutchen, D. (2006). Cognitive factors in the development of children's writing. In C. MacArthur, S. Graham, & J. Fitzgerald (Eds.), *Handbook of writing research* (pp. 115–130). New York, NY: The Guilford Press.

McKeough, A., Palmer, J., Jarvey, M., & Bird, S. (2007). Best narrative writing practices when teaching from a developmental framework. In S. Graham, C. MacArthur, & J. Fitzgerald (Eds.), *Best practices in writing instruction* (pp. 50–73). New York, NY: The Guilford Press.

Membrey, A.D., McLaughlin, T.F., Derby, K.M., & Antcliff, C. (2011). Use and modification of cover, copy, and compare in spelling for three middle school students with multiple disabilities. *International Journal of Social Sciences and Education, 1,* 491–505.

Mercer, C.D., Mercer, A.R., & Pullen, P.C. (2011). *Teaching students with learning problems.* Upper Saddle River, NJ: Prentice-Hall.

National Governors Association Center for Best Practices, Council of Chief State School Officers. (2010). *Common Core State Standards (English language arts).* Washington, DC: Authors. Retrieved from http://www.corestandards.org/

Pennington, R., Ault, M.J., Schuster, J.W., & Sanders, A. (2011). Using response prompting and assistive technology to teach story-writing to students with autism. *Assistive Technology Outcomes and Benefits, 7,* 24–38.

Pennington, R., Collins, B.C., Stenhoff, D.M., Turner, K., & Gunselman, K. (in press). Using simultaneous prompting to teach generative writing to students with autism. *Education and Training in Developmental Disabilities.*

Pennington, R., Delano, M.D., & Scott, R. (in press). An intervention for improving resume writing skills of students with intellectual disabilities. *Journal of Applied Behavior Analysis.*

Pennington, R., Stenhoff, D.M., Gibson, J., & Ballou, K. (2012). Using simultaneous prompting to teach story writing to a student with autism. *Education & Treatment of Children, 35,* 389–406.

Rousseau, M.K., Krantz, P.J., Poulson, C.L., Kitson, M.E., & McClannahan, L.E. (1994). Sentence combining as a technique for increasing adjective use in writing by students with autism. *Research in Developmental Disabilities, 15,* 19–37.

Schlosser, R.W., & Blischak, D.M. (2004). Effects of speech and print feedback on spelling by children with autism. *Journal of Speech, Language, and Hearing Research, 47,* 848–862.

Schlosser, R.W., Blischak, D.M., Belfiore, P.J., Bartley, C., & Barnett, N. (1998). Effects of synthetic speech output and orthographic feedback on spelling in a student with autism: A preliminary study. *Journal of Autism and Developmental Disorders, 28,* 309–319.

Skinner, B.F. (1957). *Verbal behavior.* Acton, MA: Copley Publishing Group.

Slater, J., & Slater, J. (1994). Pixwriter [Computer software]. Guffy, CO: Slater Software.

Stromer, R., Mackay, H.A., Howell, S.R., & McVay, A.A. (1996). Teaching computer-based spelling to individuals with developmental and hearing disabilities: Transfer of stimulus control to writing tasks. *Journal of Applied Behavior Analysis, 29,* 25–42.

Sundberg, M.L. (2008). Verbal behavior milestones assessment and placement program. Concord, CA: AVB Press.

Yamamoto, J., & Miya, T. (1999). Acquisition and transfer of sentence construction in autistic students: Analysis by computer-based teaching. *Research in Developmental Disabilities, 20,* 355–377.

FOR FURTHER INFORMATION

Augmentative and Alternative Communication

Johnston, S.S., Reichle, J., Feeley, K.M., & Jones, E.A. (2012). *AAC strategies for individuals with moderate to severe disabilities.* Baltimore, MD: Paul H. Brookes Publishing Co.

Software

Clicker 6 by Crick Software Inc.

http://www.cricksoft.com/us/home.aspx

My Story for iPad by HiDef Web Solutions

https://itunes.apple.com/us/app/my-story-book-maker-for-kids/id449232368?mt=8

PixWriter by Suncastle Technology

http://www.suncastletech.com/pixwriter.html

Proloquo2Go by Assistiveware

http://www.assistiveware.com/product/proloquo2go

StoryKit for iPhone by ICDL Foundation

https://itunes.apple.com/us/app/storykit/id329374595?mt=8

Writing with Symbols by Mayer-Johnson

http://www.mayer-johnson.com/writing-with-symbols-bundle/

Teaching Writing

Graham, S., & Harris, K.R. (2005). *Writing better: Effective strategies for teaching students with learning difficulties.* Baltimore, MD: Paul H. Brookes Publishing Co.

Graham, S., MacArthur, C.A., & Fitzgerald, J. (2013). *Best practices in writing instruction.* New York, NY: Guilford Press.

Harris, K.R., Graham, S., Mason, L.H., & Friedlander, B. (2008). *Powerful writing strategies for all students.* Baltimore, MD: Paul H. Brookes Publishing Co.

Kameenui, E.J., & Simmons, D.C. (1990). *Designing instructional strategies: The prevention of academic learning problems.* Upper Saddle River, NJ: Pearson.

Mason, L.H., Reid, R., & Hagaman, J.L. (2012). *Building comprehension in adolescents: Powerful strategies for improving reading and writing in content areas.* Baltimore, MD: Paul H. Brookes Publishing Co.

Teaching Writing to Students with Intellectual Disability/Autism Spectrum Disorder

Delano M.D., & Pennington R.C. (2012). Writing instruction for children with autism. In D. Perner & M. Delano. (Eds.), *A guide to teaching students with autism spectrum disorders.* Arlington, VA: Council On Exceptional Children.

Greer, D., & Ross, D. (2007). *Verbal behavior analysis: Inducing and expanding new verbal capabilities in children with language delays.* Upper Saddle River, NJ: Pearson.

Pennington, R. (2010). Exploring new waters: Writing instruction for students with autism. *Beyond Behavior, 19,* 17–25.

Wolfe, J.C., Williamson, P., & Carnahan, C. (2012). Writing instruction. In C. Carnahan & P. Williamson. (Eds.), *Quality literacy instruction for students with autism spectrum disorders.* Shawnee Mission, KS: AAPC Textbooks.

Teaching Common Core Mathematics and Teaching Science

CHAPTER 8

Beginning Numeracy Skills

Alicia F. Saunders, Ya-yu Lo, and Drew Polly

Janette, a fifth grader with moderate autism, attends a general education math class with her same-age peers. The general education teacher, Ms. Karon, designs lessons with activities using principles of universal design for learning so that Janette can participate successfully. In the inclusive class, Janette uses a calculator and a peer buddy as supports. Initially, Janette often needed the help of her peers to perform the most basic math skills, such as creating sets, counting with one-to-one correspondence, and adding with manipulatives. To improve Janette's basic math skills, Ms. Adams, Janette's special education teacher, has been working with Janette daily on early numeracy skills using evidence-based practices, such as constant time delay and least intrusive prompting. During one inclusive math class, Ms. Karon was teaching her students about division and many were having difficulty. She posed the problem "12 ÷ 3 = ?" Janette picked up the 12 counting chips in front of her and 3 set makers and quickly divided the 12 chips into 3 groups and then touched the number *4* response card. Her peer buddy shouted out to the teacher, "Ms. Karon, look! Janette solved the problem. The answer is 4!" Everyone was so proud of Janette. Later that day, Ms. Karon approached Ms. Adams and told her that if Janette had been exposed to the kind of intensive instruction she was receiving beginning in early grades, Janette would likely be able to perform grade-level math problems. Her early numeracy skill impairments were preventing Janette from accessing the general education math curriculum to the fullest extent possible.

The increasing emphasis on addressing student learning deficiencies in mathematics has been prevalent in both general education and special education (National Mathematics Advisory Panel, 2008; Sarama & Clements, 2009; Stigler & Heibert, 1999). Examination of the causes of mathematics deficiencies and potential ways to support struggling students, including students with severe disabilities, raises the question, "What foundational mathematical skills and understandings do these students lack?" In this chapter early numeracy (EN) skills and

Support for this chapter was provided in part by Grant No. R324A080014 from the U.S. Department of Education, Institute of Education Sciences, awarded to the University of North Carolina at Charlotte. The opinions expressed do not necessarily reflect the position or policy of the Department of Education, and no official endorsement should be inferred.

their importance as building blocks for children's mathematical understanding are described. EN skill descriptions are followed by research-based practices for teaching these critical skills and the specific steps educators can use to teach them.

IMPORTANCE OF EARLY NUMERACY SKILLS

Children's mathematical understanding in real life and in upper grades in school is empirically linked to their understanding of numbers, including what they are and how they relate to one another (Leinwand, 2012). Mathematics educators hold the term *number sense* as a broad phrase that includes multiple concepts and skills related to numbers. Teachers often describe students using phrases such as, "They have very little number sense," or "My students have a strong understanding of numbers." The National Council of Teachers of Mathematics (NCTM; 2000) defined number sense as an individual's ability to understand numbers and operations and use these concepts and strategies to make mathematical judgments and for more complex problem solving (McIntosh, Reys, & Reys, 1992).

Sample skills that fall under the umbrella of number sense and are discussed in this chapter include 1) rote counting; 2) number identification; 3) representation of numbers and counting with one-to-one correspondence; 4) creating sets; 5) composing and decomposing numbers; 6) early measurement concepts, such as identifying things as bigger/smaller and quantities as more/less; and 7) patterning. This list is not exhaustive of all skills that are encompassed under the term *number sense;* however, these skills are important for students with severe disabilities to master.

Regardless of whether EN skills are referred to by their individual skills or with the broad phrase *number sense,* research indicates that students' early mathematical understandings strongly influence later success in mathematics (Denton & West, 2002; National Mathematics Advisory Panel, 2008). Krajewski (2005) found that children's mathematical knowledge prior to first grade was a strong predictor of future quantitative understanding. Researchers who have studied gaps between populations of students found that students who struggle in mathematics lacked opportunities to develop EN skills, which are often provided prior to formal schooling and in the early years of school (Hiebert, 1986). It is critical for all students to develop EN skills so that they can function in the 21st century (Kilpatrick, Swafford, & Findell, 2001). Students who lack EN skills struggle to develop mathematical understandings far beyond their first years of school. Impairments in EN skills also prevent students such as Janette from fully accessing the general mathematics curriculum. Essentially, students who lack EN skills when entering formal schooling, including those with severe disabilities, need intensive, sound instruction in order to help develop the skills and bridge gaps (Gersten & Chard, 1999).

Mathematics educators (e.g., Fuson, 2004; Richardson, 2011; Sarama & Clements, 2009) have proposed empirically based trajectories and progressions of how children develop EN skills and number sense. In each of these trajectories and progressions, there are some skills that are foundational for success in students' understanding of mathematical concepts. For students with severe disabilities, these progressions provide a starting point that educators and curriculum developers can use to develop instructional materials (Browder et al., 2012; Jimenez,

Browder, & Saunders, 2013). By understanding foundational EN skills, and how to develop these skills in children through sound instructional pedagogies, teachers will be better prepared to develop the number sense of their students with severe disabilities.

RESEARCH-BASED PRACTICES FOR TEACHING EARLY NUMERACY SKILLS

Unlike most students without disabilities who often develop EN skills prior to any formal schooling, students with severe disabilities do not develop these skills without direct and intensive instruction (Judge & Watson, 2011; Morgan, Farkas, & Wu, 2009). Because EN skills are fundamental for mastering advanced knowledge in mathematics in later years of life (Denton & West, 2002; Jordan, Glutting, & Ramineni, 2010; Jordan, Kaplan, Ramineni, & Locuniak, 2009), it is especially important for students to receive effective, scientifically supported instruction in EN skills in very early grades (National Mathematics Advisory Panel, 2008). Even with this early EN skills instruction, students with severe disabilities may need additional focus on these skills during the elementary school years. Jimenez and colleagues (2013) found that EN skills for students with severe disabilities could still be developed between the ages of 5 and 11 with evidence-based practices.

Literature on mathematics instruction for students with severe disabilities traditionally has shown a primary focus on functional mathematics skills such as money computation, purchasing, budgeting, and banking (Browder & Grasso, 1999). With a shift to include students with severe disabilities in addressing academic content standards as a result of federal legislation (e.g., the No Child Left Behind Act of 2001 [PL 107-110]), slightly more research has become available on academic mathematics instruction for this student population. Browder, Spooner, Ahlgrim-Delzell, Harris, and Wakeman (2008) conducted a meta-analysis of 68 studies published between 1975 and 2005 that involved teaching academic mathematics skills to students with significant cognitive disabilities (i.e., developmental disabilities, autism, and moderate or severe intellectual disability) to identify evidence-based instructional practices. They found that systematic instruction with explicit prompting, prompt fading (e.g., least intrusive and constant time delay), and feedback is an evidence-based practice for teaching numbers, operations, and measurement skills to students with significant cognitive disabilities. In addition, in-vivo instruction, in which students applied their learning to real-world situations, was found to produce greater effects in students' learning than those studies without in-vivo instruction.

In the following sections, two types of instructional methods—systematic instruction and explicit instruction—that have produced positive learning in EN skills for students with severe disabilities are briefly discussed.

Systematic Instruction for Teaching Early Numeracy Skills

Systematic instruction refers to a well-designed plan of teaching that targets and evaluates a student's learning when given controlled and meaningful opportunities to practice the skills to reach mastery. It often involves specific procedures for systematically prompting and reinforcing operationalizing defined responses

(Collins, 2007; Snell & Brown, 2011). In systematic instruction for teaching mathematics skills to students with severe disabilities, defined response prompts and explicit prompt fading are essential (Browder et al., 2008). Response prompting instructional strategies, including time delay, system of least prompts, and simultaneous prompting, have received strong evidence of effectiveness in interventions for students with moderate to severe disabilities (Wolery, Ault, & Doyle, 1992). Although research on the use of these strategies in teaching specific EN skills is limited, the literature base provides support on how systematic instruction with response prompting and prompt fading can effectively improve the mathematics skills of students with severe disabilities.

Time Delay Time delay involves systematically delaying the amount of time a student has for making a correct response before being prompted. Time delay includes two variations: constant time delay and progressive time delay (Collins, 2007). In constant time delay, the delay interval starts with a 0-second delay between the task direction (e.g., "What number?") and the controlling prompt (i.e., a prompt that ensures a correct response from student), then increases to a fixed amount of time in subsequent sessions (e.g., 3-second delay interval). In progressive time delay, the delay interval is gradually increased over subsequent sessions (e.g., 0-second delay for session 1, 1-second delay for session 2, 2-second delay for session 3). Collins, Hager, and Galloway (2011) used 0-second and 3-second constant time delay procedures to teach language arts, science, and mathematics skills to three middle school students with moderate intellectual disability. The mathematics content involved teaching the order of operations while computing sales tax. One participant successfully met the mastery criterion of following all task analytic steps with 100% accuracy for three sessions, whereas the remaining two students had not met mastery due to time constraints in intervention implementation in mathematics.

System of Least Prompts System of least prompts involves providing increasing intrusive levels of prompts in a hierarchy following an incorrect response or no response until the student produces a correct answer (Wolery et al., 1992). Studies on teaching purchasing skills to students with moderate to severe disabilities showed that the hierarchy of prompts may involve verbal, model, and/or physical assistance prompts (e.g., Test, Howell, Burkhart, & Beroth, 1993), or it may consist of various levels of natural verbal and visual cues (e.g., Colyer & Collins, 1996). In one study, Skibo, Mims, and Spooner (2011) used a system of least prompts to teach three elementary students with severe disabilities to identify numerals 1–5 using preprinted response cards. A hierarchy of verbal (e.g., "Find the number that matches mine"), model (i.e., modeling and pointing to the correct number), and a full physical prompt was used with a 5-second response interval before the next intrusive prompt was delivered. All three participants increased their correct, independent responses in number identification using response cards.

Simultaneous Prompting Simultaneous prompting is a procedure during which a controlling prompt is provided along with the task direction to produce errorless learning, with probes conducted prior to the instruction to allow for assessment of skill acquisition (Waugh, Alberto, & Fredrick, 2011). Simultaneous prompting has been shown to be effective in teaching EN skills and other mathematics skills, including math symbol identification (Gursel, Tekin-Iftar, & Bozkurt, 2006), number identification (Akmanoglu & Batu, 2004), time telling (Birkan, 2005), multiplication facts recall (Rao & Mallow, 2009), basic addition (Fickel, Schuster, & Collins, 1998), and subtraction with decimals (Rao & Kane, 2009). For example, Akmanoglu and Batu (2004) taught three students with autism and developmental disabilities, ages 6–17, to identify numerals 1–9 using simultaneous prompting (e.g., "Which one is 5?" immediately followed by, "Look, this is 5" and "Now show me which one is 5") with verbal praise for correct responses. Results of this study showed that all three participants improved their number identification, maintained the skills, and generalized the skills to identify calendar pages.

Explicit Instruction for Teaching Early Numeracy Skills

The National Mathematics Advisory Panel (2008) defined explicit instruction as a practice involving 1) the teacher providing clear models of answering or solving problems with multiple examples, 2) students receiving ample opportunities to practice newly learned skills and to verbalize thought processes, and 3) students receiving extensive feedback with error correction and frequent reviews of skills. Explicit instruction has been found to improve the mathematics performance of students with mild disabilities or those with severe mathematical difficulties (Gersten et al., 2009; Kroesbergen & Van Luit, 2003); however, its application to include students with severe disabilities is still in its infancy.

Although explicit instruction alone has not been used widely to teach mathematics skills to students with severe disabilities, it can be combined with systematic instruction to teach students important concepts when learning specific mathematics skills (Browder et al., 2008). Cihak and Foust (2008) used a model-lead-test (MLT) procedure combined with the system of least prompts (i.e., verbal, gesture, gesture plus verbal explanation, modeling, and physical prompting) to teach three elementary students with moderate intellectual disability and autism how to use number lines and touch points to solve single-digit addition problems. Results of the study showed that the touch point instruction was an effective way for all three students to learn addition skills, and that the MLT procedure with systematic prompting and prompt fading contributed to the effects of the instruction. A replication study with three middle school students with moderate intellectual disability produced similar results (Fletcher, Boon, & Cihak, 2010). Using an explicit instructional approach of a concrete representation (e.g., manipulatives, number lines, equation charts) combined with systematic instruction of constant time delay with prompt fading and task analytic instruction, Jimenez, Browder, and Courtade (2008) taught three high school students with moderate intellectual disability to solve simple linear algebraic equations (e.g., $3 + X = 5$). All three participants successfully acquired the skills for solving simple equations after receiving the multicomponent mathematics instruction.

Providing explicit instruction when teaching EN skills to students with severe disabilities offers scaffolding as students learn the skills (Gersten et al., 2009) and supplements systematic instruction by providing conceptual demonstrations that go beyond simply guiding students in making specific responses (Browder et al., 2008).

STEPS FOR TEACHING SPECIFIC EARLY NUMERACY SKILLS

This section discusses the EN skills of rote counting, number identification, one-to-one correspondence, creating sets, composing and decomposing numbers, comparing quantities, and patterns. The skills are listed in a natural progression of learning. Students should have some understanding of rote counting, number identification, and one-to-one correspondence prior to introducing creating sets, composing and decomposing numbers, and comparing quantities. Patterns can be taught concurrently with any of the EN skills.

Rote Counting

Counting skills are the foundation for mathematics and a prerequisite for problem solving. Students begin by learning to rote count, or identify numbers in a sequence (Richardson, 2011). For students with severe disabilities, this can be broken down into small manageable increments (e.g., introduce numbers 1–5, 1–10, 1–15, 1–20, 1–30). Higher level rote counting skills include counting to 99 and 999. MLT is one method for teaching rote counting (see Figure 8.1 for a sample script).

Counting forward and backward from a given number are also important skills for students to learn, as they are precursor skills to composing and decomposing numbers (Van de Walle & Lovin, 2006). After students are proficient at counting from 1, students should engage in experiences in which they count on from a given number, such as "Start at 5 and count on until you get to 10." Rather than always starting at 1, it is beneficial to teach students to start from any number and count up or down.

Number Identification

Students also should recognize that numbers have numerical representations and verbal names. This skill can also be taught in small increments, as suggested in rote counting. It is important to consider both receptive and expressive number identification when teaching. For example, with receptive identification, the teacher states a directive such as "Show me 5," and the expected student response is to touch the numeral 5. For expressive number identification, the student may touch or hold up a numeral and verbally state its name, or the student may touch a button on a voice output device when the teacher asks, "What number?" Another consideration when teaching number identification is the placement of numbers. When first teaching, students may use a number line with the targeted numbers on it; however, to ensure the student has a true understanding of the numerical representation and verbal name, teachers can use an open number line in which some numbers are missing, scatter the numbers on a card, or use flashcards and have the student identify numbers out of sequential order. Constant time delay is an easy and effective method for teaching number identification.

One-to-One Correspondence

Counting with one-to-one correspondence is defined as coordinated counting with the touching or moving of objects to determine the quantity of a particular set (Van

Rote counting: Numbers 1–5		
	Teacher says/does	Student response
Model ("I do")	"Listen to me first. One, two, three, four, five."	Students listen.
Lead ("We do")	"Now, do it with me." Provide signal (e.g., point, clap) for students to respond in unison. "One, two, three, four, five."	Students state numbers with teacher.
Test ("You do")	"Your turn. Count to five."	Individual student states numbers in sequential order.
Rote counting: Numbers 1–10 (student has mastered 1–5)		
	Teacher says/does	Student response
Model ("I do")	"Today we are going to learn new numbers. Listen to me first. One, two, three, four, five, *six, seven, eight, nine, ten*" (emphasize 6–10). "Listen again. The new part is six, seven, eight, nine, ten."	Students listen.
Lead ("We do")	"Now, say the new part with me." Provide signal for students to respond in unison (e.g., point, clap). "Six, seven, eight, nine, ten." Students should repeat the sequence several times until they say it correctly. Once they say the new part correctly, put the entire sequence together. "Let's practice counting to ten." Provide signal (e.g., point, clap) for students to respond in unison. Count from 1 to 10.	Students state numbers with teacher.
Test ("You do")	"Your turn. Count to ten."	Individual student states numbers in sequential order.

Note: If a student makes an error, stop the student, model the sequence again, and then have the student repeat. This teaching sequence is appropriate for both group or individual instruction.

Figure 8.1. This is a sample instructional script for teaching rote counting numbers through 10 using the model-lead-test approach.

de Walle & Lovin, 2006). Commonly, teachers pour manipulatives on the table and have students count them. However, there is a recommended progression for teaching one-to-one correspondence to students with severe disabilities, beginning with a small number of objects (e.g., recommend 1–5 of the same object) and gradually building the quantity.

In order to teach students to visually organize, first teach students to count a small number of objects by moving them across a line, one by one from left to right. Next, introduce counting nonmoveable objects that are in a line, such as stickers placed on an index card. This fades the support of the line so that the students have to keep track of which object has been touched and counted, but the objects are still visually organized to aid in this development. Once students have grasped this concept, fade the visual organization and teach them to count scattered, moveable objects, such as a group of manipulatives on the table. Some students may have learned to keep track of what has been counted, whereas some students may push the objects into a line prior to counting. If the student is able to count the scattered manipulatives without lining them up, try having the student count scattered, nonmoveable objects, such as stickers on a page, or items on a worksheet. (For an illustration of this progression, see Figure 8.2.)

If a student is able to name the number of objects in a group without counting them out, the student is *subitizing*. This is a much higher skill than counting each item individually and is more efficient than counting (Clements, 1999). For example, if the teacher holds up three fingers or presents a domino with three dots and the student almost immediately responds, "three," then the student is subitizing. Typically, students develop subitizing skills by taking a quick look at an image

First, teach moving 1–5 objects across a line.

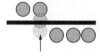

Next, teach scattered, nonmoveable objects in a line, such as an index card with stickers.

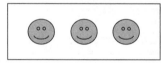

Then, teach scattered, moveable objects with no line, such as pouring counters out of a cup onto a mat.

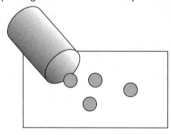

Finally, teach scattered, nonmoveable objects, such as stickers on a card or items on a worksheet.

Figure 8.2. Recommended progression for teaching one-to-one correspondence. Begin by using one to five objects. Once students have mastered up to five objects, increase the quantity to 10.

with dots, recreating the image with manipulatives or by drawing a pictorial representation, and then discussing the representation and quantity with the teacher and classmates.

When teaching students counting with one-to-one correspondence, it is important also to build cardinality, a prerequisite skill to creating sets, which is defined as understanding that the last count word stated is the amount in the set (Van de Walle & Lovin, 2006). For example, when the student finishes counting the number of objects, ask "How many?" to see if the student can recall the last number stated. If the student has to recount the number of items, the student does not understand cardinality. Teaching students to remember the last number stated when counting will help build other EN skills. The use of explicit instruction with simultaneous prompting (e.g., "How many?" immediately followed by "Listen, 1, 2, 3. There are *3* [emphasized] blocks. Now tell me, how many blocks?") can be useful in teaching cardinality.

Creating Sets

Once a student shows some understanding of the principle of cardinality, teachers can begin teaching creating sets. To build this skill, give the student a set of manipulatives, such as six counting chips, and tell the student, "Create a set of four." To respond to this task direction correctly, the student has to understand the principle of cardinality when counting with one-to-one correspondence in order to stop counting when she or he has created a set of four counters. For many students with severe disabilities, cardinality is a difficult skill to master. Students often continue to count out all of the counters until the counters are all gone. If the student is making this mistake, it may be helpful to use a visual and verbal prompt prior to having the student count. For example, after giving the student the counters and stating "Give me four," deliver a prompt, such as "Remember, four and stop," while simultaneously pointing to the number *4* and then pointing to a stop sign visual. Graphic organizers, such as a circle drawn on an index card, or even five- and ten-frames may help students create sets by teaching spatial organization.

Composing and Decomposing Numbers

After successfully creating sets, students should be ready to begin exploring ways to compose numbers from two different parts. The process of composing numbers can occur in two different instances, based on a part-part-whole model, in which the two parts are smaller quantities than the whole. This occurs in two basic types of tasks in which students need to find either one part or both parts that compose or make up the whole (Van de Walle & Lovin, 2006).

In the first type of task, students are given the whole and one of the parts and must find the missing part, as shown in the following word problem: *There are 2 birds in the tree. Some more birds fly onto the tree. If there are now 5 birds on the tree, how many birds flew onto the tree?*

Using manipulatives or pictorial representations students are able to find how many birds flew onto the tree. Students may do this by putting out two counters as shown in Figure 8.3, and then adding more counters until they have reached

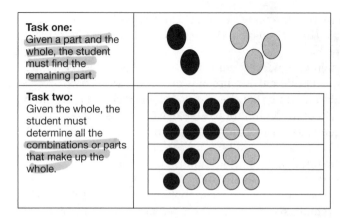

Figure 8.3. Teaching composing and decomposing numbers using part-part-whole relationships.

their total. Mentally, students may start with the number two in their head and then count forward saying, "three, four, five," and then see how many numbers they counted forward in order to reach the number five.

In the second type of task, students are given the whole and have to identify both parts. This type of task is more open-ended as there are multiple correct answers. An example directive would be the following: "There are five crayons in the box. Some are red and some are yellow. How many of each could you have? Find all the different combinations." To investigate this problem, students may then manipulate five two-color counters to explore the various, possible combinations.

Another activity involves having students put five counters in their hand or a cup and drop them onto their desk. Students then count up the number of counters of each color and repeat to practice working with combinations of a specific number. The system of least prompts can be used when students are practicing composing and decomposing sets.

Comparing Quantities

Comparing quantities, such as sets of objects, is another important EN skill that often develops prior to formal schooling. When presented with two sets of objects with obvious differences in quantities, young children may easily identify which set has more. If a student has not mastered this skill, explicit instruction can be used to teach the concept (see Figure 8.4). The concept of *less* often is more challenging for students and should be introduced after they understand the concept of *more*. Teachers can use the same approach when teaching the concept of *same*. It is recommended to avoid teaching opposing concepts at the same time to prevent confusion.

Once a student understands the concepts of *more, less*, and *same*, progress to concepts of *greater than, less than*, and *equal to*. This can be very challenging for students with disabilities, so one suggestion is to introduce these using money and the terms *more than enough* (greater than), *not enough* (less than), or *enough/same*.

Model script

Materials needed: Various quantities of manipulatives or pictures of different quantities

Directions: Tell the student, "Watch me first." Present two different quantities of manipulatives (or pictures). Point to the set with more and say, "This is more." Perform several examples of ***more*** and ***not more*** while pointing and stating, "This is more/not more" (see pictures below). Be sure to randomize the order to prevent memorization.

Compare

Lead script

Materials needed: Various quantities of manipulatives or pictures of different quantities

Directions: Tell the student, "Do it with me." Repeat directions from the model script, but the student should point to the quantity simultaneously and state verbally, "more/not more" if possible (see pictures below). Be sure to randomize the order to prevent memorization.

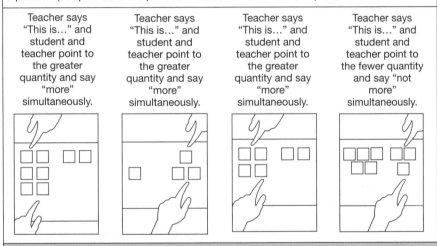

Test script
Student responses (randomize order of trials)

Materials needed: Various quantities of manipulatives or pictures of different quantities

Directions: Tell the student, "Now it's your turn." Assess student using different quantities for comparison each time by saying, "Show me more" and waiting for student to respond. Vary the side with more at random. For a correct response, provide praise (e.g., "Yes! That is more."). For an incorrect response, provide error correction (e.g., point to the greater set and state, "More. Repeat after me...more." Then repeat 3 trials of the teacher demonstrating more/not more before moving to the next trial [not scored]).
Special Note: Challenge the student to see if he or she also can identify ***not more***. Once mastery is reached, introduce the concept of ***less***. Use this script as a model.

Figure 8.4. Sample explicit instruction script for teaching the concept of *more* using tiling squares and examples and nonexamples.

Patterns

Experiences with patterns help to build algebraic thinking and reasoning. It is important for students to identify and extend patterns. Students may begin using physical objects, such as color tiles, connecting cubes, pattern blocks, or shapes. If students need assistance with spatial organization, create a pattern maker by drawing or printing off a strip of cells large enough for the student to fit objects inside. Always say the pattern aloud for the student. This will help students be able to predict what comes next in the pattern and extend the pattern.

Once students understand patterns, number patterns can be introduced. Examples include alternating schemes (e.g., 3, 4, 3, 4, 3...), increasing by a certain number (e.g., 1, 4, 7, 10, 13...), and doubling the previous number (e.g., 1, 2, 4, 8, 16...). Skip counting is also included in patterning. Begin by teaching skip counting by 5s, 10s, and then 2s. Explicit instruction can be used to teach skip counting. Visual supports, such as a hundreds chart for teaching 5s and 10s, can also be used when introducing the skill, but should be faded as students learn the skill.

GETTING STARTED

Rather than working on each of the aforementioned skills in isolation, one approach is to combine them into a lesson and use multiple trials to practice each skill (Browder et al., 2012). Figures 8.5 and 8.6 show how to combine skills into a lesson and embed them into a mathematics story to provide a meaningful context for the skills.

Another approach is to embed the skills in games or activities throughout the school day (Van de Walle & Lovin, 2006). Not only will students get multiple opportunities for practicing the skills but this will also help build generalization by practicing the skills in multiple contexts, with different people, and using different materials.

Instructional and assistive technology can be used to improve motivation, attending, and EN acquisition in students with disabilities (Chen & Bernard-Opitz, 1993; Whalen et al., 2010). Several free Internet-based activities can support students' development of EN skills, such as the NCTM Illuminations Activities (http:// illuminations.nctm.org/ActivitySearch.aspx), specifically the Five Frame and Ten Frame activities. The National Library of Virtual Manipulatives (http://nlvm.usu .edu/en/nav/vlibrary.html) also has several activities for teaching EN skills, including counting and composing numbers. As interactive whiteboards and tablets become more widely available in classrooms, programs and applications will continue to emerge for teaching and practicing EN skills.

Other low-tech examples, such as graphic organizers and manipulatives, can also aid in the conceptual understanding of problems. Figure 8.7 shows an example of a set maker mat that students can use to practice combining sets.

SUMMARY

EN skills help build mathematical competence and are indicative of mathematical success later in life. Students with severe disabilities tend to enter elementary school lacking a sound foundation in EN skills, and the gap widens as students progress through grades. Through sound instructional practices, including sys-

LESSON 3
Gardening with Math

Objectives

1 Count 1–5 movable objects in a line.
2 Count 1–5 nonmovable objects in a line.
3 Rote count from 1–5.
4 Make sets of 1–3.
5 Add premade sets with sums to 5.
6 Compare sets for same/equal.
7 Identify the symbol for equals (=).
8 Identify an ABAB pattern.
9 Use a nonstandard unit of measurement to measure 1–5.
10 Identify dates from 1st to 5th on a calendar.
11 Identify 1–5 days later in a week using a calendar.
12 Identify numerals 1–5.

> Incidental learning: Recognizing shapes, understanding ordinal numbers, subitizing

Materials
- Work Board (1 per S)
- Number line (1 per S)
- Number tiles 1–5 (1 set per S and T)
- **Math Stories**, Gardening with Grandpop, pp. 14–18
- Calendar 3 overlay (1 per S)
- Green magnetic stars
- **Student Response Book**, pp. 21–28
- 3 strawberries
- Symbol tiles: +, =, > (1 set per S and T)

- 10 worms of 2 colors
- Set Maker overlay; 1 per S
- Counting cubes (6 per S)
- Set Maker poster
- Paperclips (or other nonstandard unit of measurement)
- Pattern Maker poster
- **Math Fun**, pp. 19–24
- Embedded Instruction Planning Form (Appendix E)
- Optional: AAC device
- Optional: Water-based marker

Prepare Ahead
- Preprogram an AAC device to help nonverbal Ss count 1–5 aloud.
- Add the word *March* to the calendar overlays.

Repeated Lessons
- When teaching this lesson the first time, model each objective before requesting Ss to perform it. Fade your model prompt across days 2–4 of instruction, so by the 5th day you have taught the lesson, no model is provided, and Ss respond independently.
- To build generalization, vary the numbers (1–5) you focus on when you repeat the lesson.
- To add variety, vary the items (e.g., fruits and vegetables) Ss use for counting.

Lesson Plan ■

1 **Provide an anticipatory set.** Say, Have you ever planted a garden? Have Ss raise their hands to show how many have planted a garden. Count aloud the number of Ss with their hands raised and ask the Ss to count with you. Ask, What is your favorite vegetable or fruit to eat? Let Ss share their favorites (e.g., strawberries, tomatoes).

2 **Provide a warm-up with rote counting.** Let's get ready for math by counting to 10. Ready? Count with me. Hold up one finger as

you say each number 1–10. (Optional: use the manual sign for each number.) Count again to 10; this time quickly. Then choose a student to count to 5. For example, Eric, it's your turn. You count to 5 to get us ready for gardening. Have everyone say, It's time for math! It's time to garden.

3 **Use the time-delay procedure to review numerals.** Give each S a Work Board, number line, and number tiles 1–5. Have Ss place the number line and the number tiles on their Work

(continued)

Figure 8.5 Reprint of excerpt from an Early Numeracy math lesson. (From Jimenez, B., Browder, D.M., & Saunders, A. [2013]. *Early numeracy curriculum.* Verona, WI: Attainment Company, reprinted by permission.)

Figure 8.5 *(continued)*

Board. Great! For our next warm-up you will need your number line. I want to see how many numbers you can remember.

Round 1 (0-second delay). When I say a number, show me that number by pointing to it on your number line. If you are not sure, look at the number I am holding. Ready? Hold up a number tile while saying the number. Have Ss point to the number on their number line at the same time. Repeat for numerals 1–5 in random order.

Give praise to Ss who touch the correct number quickly and without help. For example, Yes. Quinn remembers the number 5. Go through numbers 1–5 as a very rapid drill. Be sure to name the number and hold it up at the same time to use 0-second delay prompting. OPTION: Skip Round 1 when Ss begin to recognize the numbers.

Prompt: If the S does not point, or points to an incorrect number, provide a prompt (see Appendix A).

Round 2 (4-second delay). Do you think these numbers are ready to plant a garden? Well, let's get them ready for some digging and planting. When I say a number, pick up the number tile and show it to me. If you are not sure which number to hold up, wait, and I will show you. Ready? Say each number in random order and have each S hold up the number tile. Give praise to the Ss who find the number with no help by saying, for example, Jessie's number 4 is ready to garden.

Prompt: If the S does not hold up the correct number tile, or holds up an incorrect number tile, provide a prompt (see Appendix A).

4   **Read the math story.** Before reading the story, decide which numbers (1–5) you will focus on for the lesson and insert the numbers where the red text occurs in the story.

Say, Now that we have our numbers ready, it's time for our story. Read the story, Gardening with Grandpop.

5   **Apply numeracy objectives to the math story.** Say, Yuck, I don't like worms either, but I sure do love to garden. Now it's time to have some fun with math and to read the story. I'll read the story again and this time we'll use our numbers. Read parts of the story and practice the numeracy skill.

Objective 6	**Compare sets for same/equal.**

Eva and Grandpop compared the amounts. Eva picked 3 strawberries. Let's see if you can find the group of pumpkins that is the same amount, or equal to, her strawberries. Show a page from the Student Response Book and hold 3 strawberries in your hand.

Cue	Materials needed	Wait for independent response	Provide a model	Assist and correct
Find the group of pumpkins that is the same amount or equal to Grandpop's strawberries. *Note: Vary the quantity (1–5) for each S, and vary the pages (26–27) each time you teach the lesson.*	■ Student Response Book, pp. 26–28 ■ 3 strawberries	S points to the option with an equal amount. If correct, give praise, Wow! That is the same amount as Eva's strawberries. They are equal. If no response or an error, provide a model.	Eva picked 3 strawberries. This set has the same amount of pumpkins. See, there are 3 pumpkins. They are equal. Your turn. Show me which set has the same or an equal amount of pumpkins. If correct, give praise, Good job finding the set that is equal! If no response or an error, assist and correct.	If an error, say, Next time, wait, and I will help if you are not sure. Don't guess. Point to the set with the same amount of pumpkins. This is the same amount of pumpkins. Point with me. The amount of pumpkins and the strawberries are the same. They are equal.

Objective 10

Identify dates from 1st to 5th on a calendar.

Objective 11

Identify 1–5 days later in a week using a calendar.

Last year, we planted our garden on March 1st. After only 4 days, we could already see the sprouts popping up from the soil. Can you believe it? Only 4 days later!

Distribute the calendar overlay and 2 magnetic stars to each S. Let's put your calendars on your Work Boards and add a star to March 1. That's March 1st. Starting with March 1, let's count forward 4 days. 1, 2, 3, 4. Using one S's overlay, move the star forward 4 days as you count. Point to the 5th. The sprouts came up on this date. That is 4 days later. Now it is your turn. Put a star on March 1. Show me 4 days later on the calendar.

Cue	Materials needed	Wait for independent response	Provide a model	Assist and correct
Put a star on March ____. Show me ____ days later. *Note: Choose numbers 1–5 for each blank. Do not have Ss move across weeks.*	■ For each S: Work Board, March calendar, 1 or 2 magnetic stars *Note: S can use fingers to count, or if needed, S can use a star to mark the starting point and move another star forward to count the number of days.*	S puts star on the correct date and counts forward for the designated number of days. If correct, give praise, Wow! You found the date and counted forward by yourself! If no response or an error, provide a model.	Here's March 1. Place the star. Now count 4 days like this: 1, 2, 3, 4. Move the star forward 4 days. Now you do it. If correct, give praise, Terrific finding the date and counting forward with some help! If no response or an error, assist and correct	If an error, say, Next time, wait, and I will help if you are not sure. Don't guess. Here's March 1. Place the star on the 1. Now count 4 days like this: 1, 2, 3, 4. Move the star forward 4 days. This is 4 days later.

Gardening with Grandpop

My name is Eva. Every spring, my grandpop and I plant a garden. There's nothing better than fresh carrots, lettuce, and onions from our garden. I think carrots are my favorite vegetable so Grandpop and I plant carrots. Grandpop said it takes 5 days to see the sprouts.

Last year, we planted our garden on March 1st. After only 4 days, we could already see the sprouts popping up from the soil. Can you believe it? Only 4 days later!

When Grandpop and I planted the seeds, we planted them in rows, with all the carrots together, all the green beans together, and all the onions together.

Then, we marked each row with a sign to remind us what was planted there. All of the signs were different shapes.

Grandpop let me pick vegetables. First, he let me pick heads of lettuce. Grandpop picked 3 pumpkins, and he let me pick 3 strawberries. Wait, 3 equals 3. That's the same amount. Grandpop and I picked the exact same number.

14 ■ UNIT ONE ■ Lesson 3

Figure 8.6. Reprint of a sample story excerpt from the Early Numeracy mathematics curriculum. (From Jimenez, B., Browder, D.M., & Saunders, A. [2013]. *Early numeracy curriculum*. Verona, WI: Attainment Company, reprinted by permission.)

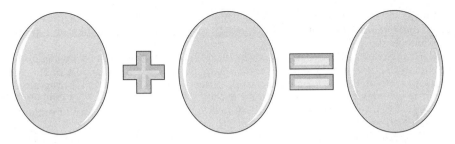

Figure 8.7. Sample graphic organizer for combining sets.

tematic instruction and explicit instructional methods, students with severe disabilities can be taught these skills. Although EN skills are typically thought of as precursor skills, they can be taught concurrently with grade-aligned mathematics and be embedded when teaching lessons aligned to the Common Core State Standards in mathematics (National Governors Association Center for Best Practices, Council of Chief State School Officers, 2010). This is encouraged so that students with severe disabilities get exposure to the general curriculum in mathematics while simultaneously building foundational skills.

REFERENCES

Akmanoglu, N., & Batu, S. (2004). Teaching pointing to numerals to individuals with autism using simultaneous prompting. *Education and Training in Developmental Disabilities, 39*, 326–336.

Birkan, B. (2005). Using simultaneous prompting for teaching various discrete tasks to students with mental retardation. *Education and Training in Developmental Disabilities, 40*, 68–79.

Browder, D.M., & Grasso, E. (1999). Teaching money skills to individuals with mental retardation: A research review with practical applications. *Remedial and Special Education, 20*, 297–308.

Browder, D.M., Jimenez, B.A., Spooner, F., Saunders, A., Hudson, M., & Bethune, K.S. (2012). Early numeracy instruction for students with moderate and severe developmental disabilities. *Research and Practice for Persons with Severe Disabilities, 37*, 1–13.

Browder, D.M., Spooner, F., Ahlgrim-Delzell, L., Harris, A.A., & Wakeman, S. (2008). A meta-analysis on teaching mathematics to students with significant cognitive disabilities. *Exceptional Children, 74*, 407–432.

Chen, S.H., & Bernard-Opitz, V. (1993). Comparison of personal and computer-assisted instruction for children with autism. *Mental Retardation, 31*, 368–376.

Cihak, D.F., & Foust, J.L. (2008). Comparing number lines and touch points to teach addition facts to students with autism. *Focus on Autism and Other Developmental Disabilities, 23*, 131–137. doi:10.1177/1088357608318950

Clements, D.H. (1999). Subitizing: What is it? Why teach it? *Teaching Children Mathematics, 5*(7), 400–405.

Collins, B.C. (2007). Teaching students with moderate and severe disabilities: Systematic instruction. In B.C. Collins (Ed.), *Moderate and severe disabilities: A foundational approach* (pp. 118–145). Upper Saddle River, NJ: Pearson Education.

Collins, B.C., Hager, K.L., & Galloway, C.G. (2011). Addition of functional content during core content instruction with students with moderate disabilities. *Education and Training in Autism and Developmental Disabilities, 46*, 22–39.

Colyer, S.P., & Collins, B.C. (1996). Using natural cues within prompt levels to teach the next dollars strategy to students with disabilities. *The Journal of Special Education, 30*, 305–318.

Denton, K., & West, J. (2002). *Children's reading and mathematics achievement in kindergarten and first grade.* Retrieved from http://nces.ed.gov/pubsearch/pubsinfo .asp?pubid=2002125

Fickel, K.M., Schuster, J.W., & Collins, B.C. (1998). Teaching different tasks using different stimuli in a heterogeneous small group. *Journal of Behavioral Education, 8,* 219–244.

Fletcher, D., Boon, R.T., & Cihak, D.F. (2010). Effects of the TOUCHMATH program compared to a number line strategy to teach addition facts to middle school students with moderate intellectual disabilities. *Education and Training in Autism and Developmental Disabilities, 45,* 449–458.

Fuson, K.C. (2004). Pre-K to grade 2 goals and standards: Achieving 21st century mastery for all. In D.H. Clements, J. Sarama, & A.-M. DiBiase (Eds.), *Engaging young children in mathematics: Standards for early childhood mathematics education* (pp. 105–148). Mahwah, NJ: Lawrence Erlbaum Associates.

Gersten, R., Beckmann, S., Clarke, B., Foegen, A., Marsh, L., Star, J.R., & Witzel, B. (2009). *Assisting students struggling with mathematics: Response to Intervention (RtI) for elementary and middle schools* (NCEE 2009-4060). Washington, DC: National Center for Education Evaluation and Regional Assistance, Institute of Education Sciences, U.S. Department of Education. Retrieved from http://ies.ed.gov/ncee/wwc/publications/ practiceguides

Gersten, R., & Chard, D. (1999). Number sense: Rethinking arithmetic instruction for students with mathematical disabilities. *The Journal of Special Education, 33,* 18–28.

Gursel, O., Tekin-Iftar, E., & Bozkurt, F. (2006). Effectiveness of simultaneous prompting in small group: The opportunity of acquiring nontarget skills through observational learning and instructive feedback. *Education and Training in Developmental Disabilities, 41,* 225–243.

Hiebert, J.C. (1986). *Conceptual and procedural knowledge: The case of mathematics.* Mahwah, NJ: Lawrence Erlbaum Associates.

Jimenez, B.A., Browder, D.M., & Courtade, G.R. (2008). Teaching an algebraic equation to high school students with moderate developmental disabilities. *Education and Training in Developmental Disabilities, 43,* 266–274.

Jimenez, B.A., Browder, D.M., & Saunders, A. (2013). *Early numeracy.* Verona, WI: Attainment Company.

Jordan, N.C., Glutting, J., & Ramineni, C. (2010). The importance of number sense to mathematics achievement in first and third grades. *Learning and Individual Differences, 20,* 82–88. doi:10.1016/j.lindif.2009.07.004

Jordan, N.C., Kaplan, D., Ramineni, C., & Locuniak, M.N. (2009). Early math matters: Kindergarten number competence and later mathematics outcomes. *Developmental Psychology, 45,* 850–867. doi:10.1037/a0014939

Judge, S., & Watson, S.M.R. (2011). Longitudinal outcomes for mathematics achievement for students with learning disabilities. *The Journal of Educational Research, 104,* 147–157. doi:10.1080/00220671003636729

Kilpatrick, J., Swafford, J., & Findell, B. (Eds.). (2001). *Adding it up: Helping children learn mathematics.* Washington, DC: National Research Council.

Krajewski, K. (2005, April). *Prediction of mathematical (dis-)abilities in primary school: A 4-year German longitudinal study from kindergarten to grade 4.* Paper presented at the Biennial Meeting of the Society for Research in Child Development, Atlanta, GA.

Kroesbergen, E.H., & Van Luit, J.E.H. (2003). Mathematics interventions for children with special educational needs: A meta-analysis. *Remedial and Special Education, 24,* 97–114.

Leinwand, S. (2012). *Sensible mathematics: A guide for school leaders in the era of the Common Core State Standards* (2nd ed.). New York, NY: Heinemann.

McIntosh, A., Reys, B.J., & Reys, R.E. (1992). A proposed framework for examining basic number sense. *For the Learning of Mathematics, 12,* 2–8.

Morgan, P.L., Farkas, G., & Wu, Q. (2009). Five-year growth trajectories of kindergarten children with learning difficulties in mathematics. *Journal of Learning Disabilities, 42,* 306–321. doi:10.1177/0022219408331037

National Council of Teachers of Mathematics. (2000). *Principles and standards for school mathematics*. Reston, VA: Author.

National Governors Association Center for Best Practices, Council of Chief State School Officers. (2010). *Common Core State Standards (mathematics)*. Washington, DC: Authors. Retrieved from http://www.corestandards.org/

National Mathematics Advisory Panel. (2008). *Foundations for success: The final report of the National Mathematics Advisory Panel* (No. ED04CO0082/0001). Washington, DC: U.S. Department of Education. Retrieved from http://www2.ed.gov/about/bdscomm/list/mathpanel/report/final-report.pdf

No Child Left Behind Act of 2001, PL 107-110, 115 Stat. 1425, 20 U.S.C. §§ 6301 *et seq.*

Rao, S., & Kane, M.T. (2009). Teaching students with cognitive impairment chained mathematical task of decimal subtraction using simultaneous prompting. *Education and Training in Developmental Disabilities, 44*, 244–256.

Rao, S., & Mallow, L. (2009). Using simultaneous prompting procedure to promote recall of multiplication facts by middle school students with cognitive impairment. *Education and Training in Developmental Disabilities, 44*, 80–90.

Richardson, K. (2011). *How children learn number concepts: A guide to the critical learning phases*. Bellingham, WA: Math Perspectives.

Sarama, J., & Clements, D.H. (2009). *Early childhood mathematics education research: Learning trajectories for young children*. New York, NY: Routledge.

Skibo, H., Mims, P., & Spooner, F. (2011). Teaching number identification to students with severe disabilities using response cards. *Education and Training in Autism and Developmental Disabilities, 46*, 124–133.

Snell, M.E., & Brown, F. (2011). Selecting teaching strategies and arranging educational environments. In M.E. Snell & F. Brown (Eds.), *Instruction of students with severe disabilities* (pp. 122–185). Upper Saddle River, NJ: Pearson Education.

Stigler, J., & Hiebert, J. (1999). *The teaching gap*. New York, NY: The Free Press.

Test, D.W., Howell, A., Burkhart, K., & Beroth, T. (1993). The one-more-than technique as a strategy for counting money for individuals with moderate mental retardation. *Education and Training in Mental Retardation, 28*, 232–241.

Van de Walle, J.A., & Lovin, L.A.H. (2006). *Teaching student-centered mathematics: Grades K-3* (1st ed.). Boston, MA: Pearson Education.

Waugh, R.E., Alberto, P.A., & Fredrick, L.D. (2011). Simultaneous prompting: An instructional strategy for skill acquisition. *Education and Training in Autism and Developmental Disabilities, 46*, 528–543.

Whalen, C., Moss, D., Ilan, A.B., Vaupel, M., Fielding, P., MacDonald, K.,...Symon, J. (2010). Efficacy of TeachTown: Basic computer-assisted intervention for the intensive comprehensive autism program in Los Angeles Unified School District. *Autism, 14*, 179–197. doi:10.1177/1362361310363282

Wolery, M., Ault, M.J., & Doyle, P.M. (1992). *Teaching students with moderate to severe disabilities: Use of response prompting strategies*. New York, NY: Longman.

FOR FURTHER INFORMATION

Books on Teaching Early Numeracy Skills

Clements, D.H., & Sarama, J.A. (2009). *Learning and teaching early math: The learning trajectories approach*. New York, NY: Routledge.

Discusses learning progressions for each early numeracy skill in a teacher-friendly manner.

Stein, M., Kinder, D., Silbert, J., & Carnine, D.W. (2005). *Designing effective mathematics instruction: A direct instruction approach*. Upper Saddle River, NJ: Pearson.

Provides in-depth information on how to teach individual mathematical skills using direct instruction to students with disabilities.

Van de Walle, J., Lovis, L.H., Karp, K.H., & Bay-Williams, J.M. (2013). *Volume 1: Teaching student-centered mathematics: Developmentally appropriate instruction for grades pre K-2* (2nd ed.). Upper Saddle River, NJ: Pearson.
Provides information on mathematical content and instructional practices for teaching prekindergarten to Grade 2 skills.

Early Numeracy Curricula

Griffin, S., & Clements, D.H. (2008). *Number worlds.* Columbus, OH: SRA/McGraw-Hill.
Provides a comprehensive mathematics curriculum for numeracy skills in a progressive pattern to students at least one grade level below average.

Jimenez, B.A., Browder, D.M., & Saunders, A. (2013). *Early numeracy.* Verona, WI: Attainment Company.
A mathematics curriculum to teach early numeracy skills designed specifically for students with severe disabilities.

Interactive Math Software

Clements, D.H., & Sarama, J. (2007). *Building blocks: SRA real math, grade preK.* Columbus, OH: SRA/McGraw-Hill.
The *Building Blocks* curriculum contains interactive software to teach early numeracy skills.

Web Sites

National Council of Teachers of Mathematics: Illuminations
http://illuminations.nctm.org
This web site provides interactive online activities for preK through second grade to practice mathematical skills, including early numeracy skills.

The National Library of Virtual Manipulatives
http://nlvm.usu.edu/en/nav/category_g_1_t_2.html
This web site provides interactive games and activities using virtual manipulatives to practice early numeracy skills, such as color patterns.

CHAPTER 9

Teaching Grade-Aligned Math Skills

Julie L. Thompson, Keri S. Bethune,
Charles L. Wood, and David K. Pugalee

Joneé is a third-grade student with cerebral palsy and severe intellectual disability. She is nonvocal and has an inconsistent point response, but she is able to use a rocker switch to choose between two items. Joneé's teacher, Ms. Goldstein, had concerns about the feasibility of teaching Joneé higher level concepts aligned to grade-level, Common Core State Standards (CCSS) for mathematics (National Governors Association Center for Best Practices, Council of Chief State School Officers, 2010) while continuing to help her achieve her individualized goals. Her individualized education program (IEP) goals included using one-to-one correspondence to count up to 10 items, comparing two sets of items to determine which is larger or smaller, and identifying numerals 0–10. At a math workshop Ms. Goldstein learned strategies to incorporate counting and cardinality into advanced mathematical concepts and was excited to use them with Joneé. When teaching a grade-aligned unit on perimeter and area, Ms. Goldstein taught that length is the larger side of the rectangle and width is the shorter side. Joneé was provided repeated opportunities identifying larger and smaller while completing calculations to determine perimeter and area. She practiced one-to-one correspondence by using a 10-level switch programmed to count numbers consecutively from 1 to 10 with each press of the switch. She learned one-to-one correspondence by pressing the switch to count tiles when a peer pointed to the next tile to determine length, width, or area. In addition, she practiced numeral identification by selecting the numeral corresponding to the number of tiles counted. Joneé not only enjoyed participating in math and engaging with her peers but also showed progress on her individualized goals. In fact, by the end of the unit, Joneé consistently identified perimeter and area situations using picture symbols attached to her rocker switch. Ms. Goldstein was encouraged with how Joneé could seamlessly provide opportunities for improving numeracy skills while teaching grade-aligned CCSS for mathematics.

Brian is a sixth-grade student with autism who is also deaf. He is nonvocal and communicates through picture symbols and sign language, mostly in single words or short phrases, to request preferred items and activities. In addition to the support of his special education teacher, Brian has a dedicated sign language interpreter who works with him throughout the day. In the beginning of the school year, Brian worked on using sign language to complete one-to-one correspondence counting and could write his numbers independently. Brian also had many challenging behaviors when changes were made to his routine. His teacher, Ms. Walker, understood that Brian needed to learn grade-aligned math skills. One skill his class worked on was increasing knowledge of fractions, including equivalent fractions and adding fractions with like denominators. Ms. Walker also used scripted lessons aligned to the CCSS for mathematics to provide systematic instruction and visual supports to teach Brian how to draw pictures representing fractions, identify equivalent fractions, and use his drawings to complete addition of fractions with like denominators. She modified all lessons to include additional visual cues to help Brian understand the vocabulary. After using these lessons with Brian, Ms. Walker saw far fewer challenging behaviors and reported a dramatic increase in his math skills. She used the same approach across a range of math units, and Brian made so much progress that by the end of the year, he was signing numbers up to 100, using a calculator to solve equations, and identifying geometry vocabulary such as *area* and *perimeter* (e.g., when a teacher shows the student a photograph and says, "Show me area/perimeter," Brian can point to the area or the perimeter).

Macy is a 10th-grade student with autism and moderate intellectual disability. She communicates vocally by using short phrases. Macy's special education teacher, Mr. Everett, has observed strengths in Macy's ability to remember facts and learn to follow the sequence of steps in completing tasks/assignments, but he has also noticed that Macy struggles with application and comprehension. Mr. Everett knew that Macy could learn some math skills but worried about whether Macy would be able to understand the math concepts or apply the skills in real-life situations. Mr. Everett used scripted lessons that taught the grade-aligned standards in the context of themes such as planting a garden. He used systematic instruction embedded in age-appropriate, functionally relevant activities. Macy gained proficiency of math calculations but also learned to apply the skills to relevant situations. For example, one lesson focused on calculating area and volume to select an appropriate box to ship a package. Macy showed progress across each of the six lessons and began learning not only the steps to completing various problems but also showed growth in demonstrating an understanding of the concepts involved, such as probability, transformations, and volume.

Several literature reviews have demonstrated that students with severe disabilities can learn academics (Browder, Jimenez, & Trela, 2012; Hudson & Test, 2011; Spooner, Knight, Browder, & Smith, 2012) including mathematics (Browder, Spooner, Ahlgrim-Delzell, Harris, & Wakeman, 2008). Other studies have shown that students with severe disabilities can learn grade-aligned academics (Browder et al., 2007; Jimenez, Browder, & Courtade, 2009; Knight, Smith, Spooner, & Browder, 2012; Mims, Hudson, & Browder, 2012) including higher level mathematics (Browder, Jimenez, & Trela, 2012). The vignettes describing Joneé, Brian, and Macy refer to specific students (pseudonyms used for anonymity) who received instruction via General Curriculum Access Projects at the University of North Carolina at Charlotte and experienced some success with mathematics instruction aligned to their age/grade level. Researchers previously asked, "Can students with severe disabilities learn grade-aligned academics?" Over the past several years, research has confirmed that these students can learn grade-aligned content, so researchers are now asking, "To what extent?" (Ayres, Lowrey,

Douglas, & Sievers, 2011; Courtade, Spooner, Browder, & Jimenez, 2012). Although there continues to be controversy on the extent to which time spent on advanced academic skills, including mathematics, is necessary, one cannot deny that mathematical learning will enhance quality of life for students with severe disabilities. For example, knowledge of mathematics supports independence for individuals with severe disabilities by allowing them to identify the correct bus to catch, read a transportation timetable, take an accurate dosage of medication, keep score when playing a game, measure quantities when cooking, maintain a password on their electronic tablet, dial a number to call a friend, and decide which store has the best sale.

The focus for teaching students with severe disabilities has historically been to teach the numeracy, money, and time concepts critical to successfully navigate life after school (Browder et al., 2008). Although still a primary goal, the requirements of the No Child Left Behind Act of 2001 (PL 107-110) and the Individuals with Disabilities Education Improvement Act (IDEA) of 2004 (PL 108-446) have led to a greater focus on a broader range of mathematical concepts (e.g., statistics, probability, geometry, algebra). The current challenge is to create learning experiences that promote acquisition of more advanced concepts while continuing to emphasize practical mathematical skills. How much students can learn will depend largely on the effectiveness of instruction. Students with severe disabilities benefit from repeated opportunities to practice (Polychronis, McDonnell, Johnson, Riesen, & Jameson, 2004), systematic prompting and feedback (Browder, Ahlgrim-Delzell, Spooner, Mims, & Baker, 2009; Levingston, Neef, & Cihon, 2009), graphic organizers and task-analytic instruction (Browder, Jimenez, & Trela, 2012; Jimenez, Browder, & Courtade, 2008; Rockwell, Griffin, & Jones, 2011), and Direct Instruction (Cihak & Foust, 2008; Thompson, Wood, Test, & Cease-Cook, 2012) to master skills. These instructional strategies may also be applied to develop more advanced conceptual knowledge.

In general education there has been a shift away from instruction focused solely on the product of doing mathematics (i.e., obtaining the correct answer) to instruction that helps students think like mathematicians and understand mathematical processes (Boyd & Bargerhuff, 2009). For example, rather than just being able to calculate area as length times width, it is more important that students understand the concept of area. Understanding the underlying concept is the goal for all areas of mathematics.

Conceptual knowledge in mathematics is also important for students with disabilities. Harniss, Carnine, Silbert, and Dixon (2010) stressed that explicit instruction allows students with disabilities to obtain a deep understanding of mathematical concepts. They suggested teaching an explicit strategy that students can apply to several related concepts. In a practice guide published by the Institute of Education Sciences on helping students who struggle with mathematics, Gersten and colleagues (2009) concluded that explicit and systematic instruction has strong research support according to standards developed by the What Works Clearinghouse, established by the U.S. Department of Education to review research using rigorous standards and identify "what works" in education. They recommended "providing models of proficient problem solving, verbalization of thought processes, guided practice, corrective feedback, and frequent cumulative review" (Gertsen et al., p. 6). Teachers can use these strategies to enhance mathematics instruction for students with disabilities and help them develop deeper knowledge and skills.

WHAT DO WE TEACH? BIG IDEAS FROM COMMON CORE STATE STANDARDS FOR MATHEMATICS

Chapter 3 provides a comprehensive description of the CCSS for mathematics. This section provides a brief description of the big ideas from the CCSS, discusses how counting and cardinality can be imbedded into the advanced mathematics topics, and describes how the standards for mathematical practice apply to students with disabilities. Because mathematics is based on conceptual progressions, we begin our discussion with the end in mind.

The focus of high school mathematics is modeling with mathematics in five content domains: statistics and probability, functions, number and quantity, algebra, and geometry. The purpose of instruction in elementary and middle school is to provide the foundational knowledge to support modeling with mathematics in these domains during high school and beyond. Table 9.1 illustrates the big ideas of the five content domains of mathematics and provides examples of real-world applications.

Table 9.1. Big ideas in mathematical domains and real-world applications

Statistics and probability
- Big ideas
  - Developing questions
  - Collecting data
  - Organizing data into graphical representations
  - Analyzing data
  - Interpreting results
  - Determining the probability of an event
- Real-world examples
  - Interpreting weather
  - Making predictions about sports
  - Making medical decisions
  - Determining the odds in a lottery

Functions
- Big ideas
  - Analyzing two sets of numbers that are related
  - Plotting number sets on a coordinate plane
  - Identifying proportional relationships
  - Using equations to demonstrate proportional relationships
  - Defining functions
  - Comparing functions
  - Analyzing a graph to describe functions
  - Understanding slopes
  - Identifying rates of change
  - Graphing functions

- Real-world examples
  - Calculating miles per gallon
  - Paying taxes
  - Understanding discounts
  - Determining savings over time with compound interest
  - Determining monthly or weekly salary based on dollars/hour

Number and quantity
- Big ideas
  - Completing operations (addition, subtraction, multiplication and division)
  - Understanding place value
  - Completing operations with fractions and decimals
  - Understanding rational and irrational numbers
  - Identifying absolute value
- Real-world examples
  - Counting money
  - Balancing a checkbook
  - Calculating how much food to make for a large group of people
  - Keeping tabs of stock in a grocery store

Algebra
- Big ideas
  - Understanding expressions and equations
  - Solving equations with and without an unknown variable
  - Determining whether two expressions are equal or unequal
  - Understanding properties of operations to solve equations
  - Understanding the connections between linear equations and lines on a coordinate plane
  - Identifying relationships between functions and linear equations
- Real-world examples
  - Deciding how much to tip
  - Developing a budget
  - Calculating how long it will take to save up to get an iPad
  - Deciding how much wallpaper is needed to cover the wall

Geometry
- Big ideas
  - Identifying and describing properties of two- and three-dimensional shapes
  - Describing locations and representations of shapes
  - Modeling and identifying transformations (rotations, translations, and reflections)
  - Demonstrating visualization and spatial reasoning
- Real-world examples
  - Understanding video game programming
  - Understanding astronomy
  - Measuring amount of toppings for a pizza based on area
  - Determining amount of packing foam needed to protect fragile items to be mailed in a box

For many years, counting and cardinality have been the main focus when teaching academics to students with severe disabilities. In the CCSS for mathematics this topic is taught only in kindergarten. The objectives for this topic are to "know number names and count the sequence", "count to tell the number of objects", and "compare numbers" (National Governors Association Center for Best Practices, Council of Chief State School Officers, 2010). In the mandate to teach grade-aligned academics to students with severe disabilities, it would be inappropriate to focus only on teaching these skills to students in grades beyond kindergarten. Yet, these skills are the foundation on which success in the other content domains is built. Therefore, it is important to provide opportunities to achieve mastery of these concepts. Fortunately, counting and cardinality practice can be easily embedded into all the mathematical content domains. Table 9.2 provides examples of ways to include counting and cardinality skills in each content domain at the elementary, middle, and high school levels. (For more recommendations on teaching early numeracy, see Chapter 8.)

In addition to standards teaching mathematical skills and concepts, the CCSS has introduced Standards for Mathematical Practice. These standards include

> 1) making sense of problems and persevering in solving them, 2) reasoning abstractly and quantitatively, 3) constructing viable arguments and critiquing the reasoning of others, 4) modeling with mathematics, 5) using appropriate tools strategically, 6) attending to precision, 7) looking for and making use of structure, and 8) looking for and expressing regularity in repeated reasoning. (National Governors Association Center for Best Practices, Council of Chief State School Officers, 2010)

The purpose of these standards is to promote mathematical thinking and prepare students for college and career readiness. Many have questioned what college and career readiness looks like for individuals with severe disabilities. Kearns and colleagues (2011) perceived this as students with severe disabilities achieving the skills needed to be successful in their environment during life after school. Kearns and colleagues maintained that although mastery of some of the skills associated with college and career readiness may be out of reach for students with severe disabilities, practice toward the standards offers meaningful learning for students with disabilities. They described five goals for students with disabilities that would support students in achieving readiness for life after school: 1) developing communicative competence; 2) achieving fluency in reading, writing, and math; 3) demonstrating age-appropriate social skills; 4) establishing independent work behaviors; and 5) attaining skills in accessing support systems. These goals complement the standards for mathematical practice. Table 9.3 describes these goals and pinpoints how they align to the Standards for Mathematical Practice. When developing lessons for students with severe disabilities, teachers should look for ways to incorporate these goals and practices to prepare students for life after high school.

RESEARCH-BASED PRACTICES ON TEACHING MATHEMATICS TO STUDENTS WITH SEVERE DISABILITIES

Although there remains a relatively small amount of research specific to teaching mathematics to students with severe disabilities, the research base is emerging. Browder and colleagues (2008) conducted a literature review and meta-analysis examining 14 group-design and 54 single-case studies to examine teaching mathematics to students with severe disabilities. All studies included at least one individual with a significant cognitive disability and had to include an intervention and data on teaching a mathematics skill. They found that 40.3% of studies focused on numbers and operations skills (e.g., counting, number matching), 53.7% focused on measurement skills (e.g., money, time), 3.0% focused on algebra skills (e.g., solving word problems, determining equivalence), 3.0% focused on geometry skills (e.g., recognizing and matching shapes), and 3.0% focused on data analysis and prob-

Table 9.2. Examples of ways to embed counting and cardinality across domains and grade band

	Statistics and probability	Functions	Number and quantity	Algebra	Geometry
Elementary school	Use one-to-one correspondence to count the number of votes Write the number of votes on a data sheet Compare the number of votes to determine who wins	Count the number of wheels on a car Given more than one car, calculate the total number of wheels Place points on a line graph for number of wheels for one, two, and three cars	Given a multiplication problem, count out the total number of groups Then count out the total number in each group Place sets together and count the total number of items Identify corresponding numeral	Given two addition expressions (e.g., 2 + 3 and 1 + 4) use manipulatives to count the total Compare the total numbers of the expressions and identify if they are the same	Count the number of sides of shapes Identify length and count up to that number on a ruler to draw the length and width of a rectangle Compare numbers of area and identify which shape is bigger
Middle school	Given a table of plant growth comparisons, identify the numbers in the table Use one-to-one correspondence to color the number of spaces representing each unit of plant growth for each plant to create a bar graph	Identify the numbers in a proportional relationship of ingredients for soil mix Given a graph of ingredients needed per pot, identify the number of pots on the graph Count in sequence and stop at the corresponding point on the graph to determine the unit amount of ingredients needed	Given a recipe that includes fractions, identify the numbers in the numerator and denominator Place the fraction in the correct place by counting on the number line When told to double a recipe use the number line to count to determine the total amount of ingredients needed	Given a subtraction equation with an unknown variable, use the number line to count on to determine the quantity of the variable (e.g., $9 - x = 1$; start at 9 and count "hops" to 1; $x = 8$)	Given a shape drawn on a coordinate plane, count to identify the ordered pairs for each of the points on the shape
High school	Given the odds of winning for the two football teams in the Super Bowl, put the odds on a number line Compare numbers to determine who has the best odds to win	Given two different unit rates of dollars/hour, identify numbers Count numbers and plot points on graphs for 1, 2, and 3 hours of work Compare graphs to see who makes more money	Given a rational number, start at 0 and count to the point on number line that corresponds with the number (moving to the left if negative and to the right if positive)	Given a linear equation where y is known, use a calculator to solve for x. Then count to plot the ordered pair on a graph	Given the ordered pairs for a shape in the constellations, count to identify the stars that form the shape (e.g., Big Dipper)

Table 9.3. College and career readiness goal descriptions and alignment to Standards for Mathematical Practice

---

"Communicative competence": Developing fluency with common vocabulary and increased mastery of novel vocabulary.
- Standards for Mathematical Alignment: "Construct viable arguments and critique the reasoning of others."

"Fluency in reading, writing, and math": Developing fluency with numeracy, common sight words, and comprehension.
- Standards for Mathematical Alignment: "Attend to precision, look for and express regularity in repeated reasoning."

"Age-appropriate social skills": Engaging in reciprocal communication, working collaboratively, and taking turns.
- Standards for Mathematical Alignment: "Construct viable arguments and critique the reasoning of others, attend to precision."

"Independent work behaviors": Solving real-life problems that could lead to employment, including knowing who to ask for help, recognizing when something is missing or needed and taking steps to get it, completing to-do lists.
- Standards for Mathematical Alignment: "Reason abstractly and quantitatively, look for and make use of structure, model with mathematics, make sense of problems and persevere in solving them."

"Skills in accessing supports": Asking for assistance when needed, recognizing and using tools.
- Standards for Mathematical Alignment: "Use appropriate tools strategically, make sense of problems and persevere in solving them."

Sources: Kearns et al. (2011); National Governors Association Center for Best Practices, Council of Chief State School Officers (2010).

ability skills (e.g., graphing); some studies taught more than one mathematics skill. They analyzed the studies to determine the extent to which teaching mathematics to students with severe disabilities could be an evidence-based practice. They found that 19 of the single-case studies met all of quality indicators suggested by Horner and colleagues (2005), and 30 of the single-case studies met most of the quality indicators. They found that none of the 14 group-design studies met all of criteria suggested by Gersten and colleagues (2005), and 4 studies met most of the criteria. The authors found moderate to strong support for the use of systematic instruction to teach mathematics to students with severe disabilities, and concluded that these students can learn specific mathematics skills.

Systematic instruction is a behavior-analytic approach to teaching functional, social, and academic skills to students with disabilities. In general, systematic instruction 1) targets observable and measureable skills that are socially meaningful, 2) uses strategies (e.g., prompting, fading, chaining, differential reinforcement) based on behavioral concepts and principles (e.g., motivating operations, positive reinforcement, stimulus control), 3) uses ongoing data collection to guide instruction, and 4) produces behavior change that can be maintained and generalized to other skills and contexts (Collins, 2006; Snell, 1983; Spooner et al., 2012; Stokes & Baer, 1977; Wolery, Bailey, & Sugai, 1988). The following sections include descriptions of research-based systematic instructional strategies for teaching mathematics to students with severe disabilities. Figure 9.1 provides a brief definition and example of each of the practices.

Systematic Prompting and Feedback

Several recent studies have examined systematic prompting and feedback to teach students with severe disabilities (Browder et al., 2012; Jimenez et al., 2008;

Research-based practices	What it is	When to use it	Example
System of least prompts	This is an errorless instructional strategy that uses a prompting hierarchy. First the student is given a chance to independently perform the skill and then the least intrusive prompt is given in the hierarchy until the student performs the skill correctly. Assistance is faded over time until the student performs the skill independently.	When learning simple facts, completing operations, or completing multistep processes	Student is given a data set (e.g., 4, 5, 5, 5, 5, 5, 6, 7, 8, 9, 10, 11, 11). Teacher says, "Show me mode." Teacher waits 3 seconds for the student to indicate 5 independently. If correct, the teacher praises the student. If the student provides no response or is incorrect, the teacher provides the least intrusive prompt. Verbal: "The mode is the number that shows up the most in a data set." Teacher repeats, "Show me mode." Teacher waits 3 seconds for the student to indicate 5 independently. If correct, the teacher praises the student. If the student provides no response or is incorrect, the teacher provides the next least intrusive prompt. This continues until the student demonstrates a correct response. Prompt hierarchy for this skill includes the following: Verbal: Teacher says, "The mode is the number that shows up the most in a data set." Model: Teacher says, "The mode is 5." Gesture: Teacher points to the number 5. Hand over hand: Teacher takes the student's hand and assists the student in pointing to the number 5. Aligns to CCSS: HS.DPS.1c1: Use descriptive stats; range, median, mode, mean, outliers/gaps to describe the data set (S.ID.4, S.ID.5).

(continued)

Figure 9.1. Research-based practices, definitions, and examples. *Key: CCSS:* Common Core State Standards.

Figure 9.1. *(continued)*

Research-based practices	What it is	When to use it	Example
Time delay	This is an errorless instructional strategy in which a prompt giving the correct answer is provided immediately (0-second delay) and then after a brief delay (e.g., 3 seconds). The prompts are faded as the student begins to perform the correct response.	When learning simple facts such as number identification, symbol identification, shapes, and money	During focus and review the student practices the prerequisite skill of identifying the symbol for *percent*. Teacher presents the following symbols: <, %, $ 0-second delay: Teacher says, "Show me percent," points to percent, and waits for the student's response (e.g., point, eye gaze). If the student responds correctly, the teacher provides praise. If the student does not respond, the teacher repeats, "Show me percent." Teacher repeats this process until the student correctly responds two consecutive times. Then the teacher moves to a 3-second delay. 3-second delay: Teacher says, "Show me percent," points to percent, and waits 3 seconds for the student's response (e.g., point, eye gaze). If the student responds correctly, the teacher provides praise. If the student responds incorrectly, the teacher says, "No, this is percent," and points to the percent symbol. If the student does not respond, the teacher repeats, "Show me percent." Teacher repeats this process until the student correctly responds two consecutive times. If the student makes several mistakes in a row during the 3-second delay trials, the teacher should return to the 0-second delay trials. Aligns to CCSS: 6RP3: Find a percent of a quantity as a rate per 100.

Research-based practices	What it is	When to use it	Example
Graphic organizer	This instructional strategy uses a visual template to help the student group, organize, and solve problems.	When completing operations, formulas, and multistep processes	Equation: 1st number / variable / total Aligns to CCSS: 6EE7: Solve real-world and mathematical problems by writing and solving equations of the form $x + p = q$ and $px = q$ for cases in which p, q, and x are all non-negative rational numbers. 7EE4: Use variables to represent quantities and construct simple equations to solve problems. Use variables to represent quantities in a real-world or mathematical problem, and construct simple equations and inequalities to solve problems by reasoning about the quantities. 8EE7: Solve linear equations in one variable.

(continued)

Figure 9.1. *(continued)*

Research-based practices	What it is	When to use it	Example
Task analysis	This instructional strategy breaks down skills into smaller, more achievable steps.	With any multistep skill being taught	Student is told to find the range of a data set. Task analysis: 1. Selects range using a graphic organizer (____ - ____ = ____ range) 2. Locates largest number in the data set 3. Writes (places) largest number in the first blank 4. Locates smallest number in the data set 5. Writes (places) largest number in the second blank 6. Enters first number in a calculator 7. Enters "-" in the calculator 8. Enters second number in the calculator 9. Pushes "=" 10. Writes (places) answer in third blank Aligns to CCSS: 6SP5: Giving quantitative measures of center and variability. HS:S-ID2: Use statistics appropriate to the shape of the data distribution to compare center and spread of two or more different data sets.

Research-based practices	What it is	When to use it	Example
Model-lead-test	This instructional strategy uses scaffolding that begins with teacher modeling, is followed by the teacher leading the students in completing the step or skill, and ends with the teacher testing the students by having them independently demonstrate the skill. It also includes a systematic error correction.	When teaching simple facts, vocabulary, and/or skills with multiple steps, such as using the Pythagorean Theorem or completing a graphic organizer	Student is told to demonstrate surface area of a box.

Model: "My turn to show surface area." (Teacher traces palm over all surface of box.)

Lead: "Do it with me. Show me surface area." (Teacher and student trace palm over all surface area of box.)

Test: "Your turn. Show me surface area." (Student traces palm over all surface of box.)

If the student makes an error, the teacher completes the sequence again until the student demonstrates the correct response independently during the test.

Aligns to CCSS:

6GA4: Represent three-dimensional figures using nets made up of rectangles and triangles, and use the nets to find the surface area of these figures. Apply these techniques in the context of solving real-world and mathematical problems.

7GB6: Solve real-world and mathematical problems involving area, volume, and surface area of two- and three-dimensional objects composed of triangles, quadrilaterals, polygons, cubes, and right prisms. |

Levingston et al., 2009; Polychronis et al., 2004). Browder and colleagues taught early numeracy skills to third- through fifth-grade students with autism and/or moderate intellectual disability using four key components: 1) focusing on early numeracy skills (i.e., counting and cardinality, composing sets, adding with sets, comparing sets, completing patterns, linear measurement, and calendar skills), 2) using systematic instructional techniques, 3) varying the presentation of the instruction and story-based lessons while keeping the numeracy skills consistent, and 4) promoting generalization to grade-level content by embedding instruction into inclusive settings. The packaged intervention was taught during small-group instruction in the students' self-contained classrooms and included a story about a familiar event to provide context to the mathematics skills, instructional supports (i.e., graphic organizers and number lines), and systematic instruction on the specific mathematics skills. In addition, students attended their grade-appropriate general education mathematics classes with paraprofessionals providing embedded instruction of the numeracy skills during mathematics lessons. All of the numeracy skills except number identification were taught using a system of least prompts. The system of least prompts involves providing the least intrusive prompt to support completion of the skill (Collins, 2012). First the student is provided a brief time to respond, usually 3–5 seconds, and if an incorrect or no response is given, the teacher provides the least intrusive prompt (e.g., a gesture cue) and waits for a response. If the student does not respond or responds incorrectly, then the next least intrusive prompt (e.g., a model) is given. Typically the prompting hierarchy from least to most includes verbal, model, gesture, partial physical prompt, and hand over hand.

Time delay also was used to teach number identification (Browder et al., 2012). Time delay is an errorless prompting strategy in which a skill is taught by first introducing the concept and providing a 0-second delay controlling prompt to teach the concept. A controlling prompt is the prompt level needed to ensure that a correct response occurs (Collins, 2012). In the Browder and colleagues' study, the controlling prompt was pointing to the correct number. Once the student consistently demonstrates the skill with 0-second delay, prompting the skill is introduced, and the student receives prompting after a predetermined pause, usually 3–5 seconds. The instructor attempts to interrupt a student error and provide prompting for the correct response during the pause. If the student makes an error or does not respond, the instructor uses the controlling prompt to solicit a correct answer and then repeats the skill again. Polychronis and colleagues (2004) also used time delay and error correction. They taught number identification and telling time to students with moderate intellectual disability and/or autism using a 0-second and then 3-second time delay. Error correction consisted of the instructor identifying the correct answer and then repeating the skill.

Levingston and colleagues (2009) used systematic instruction to teach multiplication and division skills to a 10-year-old student with autism and a 10-year-old typically developing student by providing a teacher model to complete multiplication and division, verbal prompting, and feedback via self-checking.

Graphic Organizers and Task Analytic Instruction

Graphic organizers and task analytic instruction also have shown promise for teaching grade-aligned mathematics to students with severe disabilities (Browder et al., 2012; Browder, Jimenez, & Trela, 2012; Jimenez et al., 2008; Levingston et al., 2009; Rockwell et al., 2011). Jimenez and colleagues (2008) taught students with moderate intellectual disability to solve for x in a simple equation (e.g., $4 + x = 9$). They developed a nine-step task analysis and a graphic organizer (___ + x = ___), then used time delay to teach the steps. Levingston and colleagues (2009) also used graphic organizers and task analytic instruction to teach multiplication and division. Given a word problem and a graphic organizer (i.e., ___ ☐ ___ = ___), the students were taught prerequisite skills that included identifying the label of the answer, whether the problem required multiplication or division, the larger number (placed on the first blank line), and the smaller number (placed on the second blank line). The prerequisite skills were taught one at a time. Students were given a word problem with everything but the prerequisite skill and the answer left blank. During instruction, first the solution for the prerequisite skill and the answer were modeled and then a verbal prompt was provided to guide the student to complete the step. For each consecutive step, the student completed the previously mastered step plus received instruction on the new prerequisite step. This was completed until the students achieved mastery on all of the steps.

Rockwell and colleagues (2011) used schema-based strategy instruction (SBI) to teach a student with autism to read word problems, discriminate what type of operation was required to solve the problem, and use a schematic diagram for the problem type as a guide to solve the problem. The authors explain that SBI "is an intervention that uses visual representations, heuristics, and Direct Instruction to teach students to solve word problems" (Rockwell et al., 2011, p. 26). The purpose of the visual representations is to support understanding of the strategy necessary to solve the problem. For example, the student was taught to identify a "compare" problem. The diagram showed a larger amount, a smaller amount, and the difference. This type of graphic organizer assists students in understanding the underlying process, whereas most graphic organizers assist with taking steps to arrive at the solution.

Two studies (Browder et al., 2012; Browder, Jimenez, & Trela, 2012) taught multiple topics (geometry, algebra, data analysis, and measurement) to middle and high school students with severe disabilities using task analysis and graphic organizers. Students were taught to find points on a plane, solve a one-step equation, interpret two bar graphs, and complete purchasing problems. They used story-based problems to add context and created an average of eight stories per skill to provide opportunities for repeated practice and generalization. In addition, they provided graphic organizers, such as a one-step equation template, for each skill taught.

Direct Instruction

Direct Instruction focuses on the big ideas of concepts, uses unambiguous instruction, involves ongoing assessment of student performance, and promotes a high level of active student response (Watkins & Slocum, 2004). One technique used in Direct Instruction is model-lead-test (MLT). MLT is a form of scaffolding and systematic error correction (Watkins & Slocum, 2004). When introducing a new skill, the teacher models the skill, then leads the students in the skill, and finally has the student complete the skill independently. For example, the teacher might say, "Watch me circle the larger number. Let's do this next one together. Now, it's your turn to circle the larger number in the next problem." When stu-

use with H.S. easily

task analysis + graphic organizers

dents make an error, MLT can be used to immediately correct the error. Cihak and Foust (2008) taught students to complete addition using MLT. The purpose of their study was to investigate whether a number line or touch point strategy was more effective in supporting students with autism to learn addition skills. They taught both strategies using MLT. Students in the study demonstrated greater accuracy with addition using MLT plus touch points. The touch point strategy uses circles and dots on numerals 0–9 that students can tap with their pencil or finger to count on when adding.

The use of Direct Instruction curriculum to teach literacy and communication to students with moderate and severe disabilities has shown promising results (Flores & Ganz, 2007, 2009; Flores, Shippen, Alberto, & Crowe, 2004; Ganz & Flores, 2009; Kinder, Kubina, & Marchand-Martella, 2005). Thompson and colleagues (2012) investigated the effects of using *Connecting Math Concepts* (Engelmann, Carnine, Kelly, & Engelmann, 2003) to teach telling time to students with autism and moderate intellectual disability. The students not only learned to tell time but also performed as well as or better than their same-age peers. This indicates that the use of Direct Instruction to teach telling time may be effective in teaching students with moderate disabilities. The authors suggested that future research investigate the effects of Direct Instruction curriculum to teach other mathematic standards to students with moderate disabilities.

GENERAL GUIDELINES FOR GETTING STARTED TEACHING MATHEMATICS TO STUDENTS WITH MODERATE AND SEVERE DISABILITIES

The goal of the Browder and colleagues (2012) study was to provide a template for teaching standards-based mathematics. They suggested writing a story, developing or selecting a graphic organizer, and then creating a step-by-step task analysis to teach the skill. Saunders, Bethune, Spooner, and Browder (2013) suggested a six-step approach to teach mathematics to students with moderate and severe disabilities. These steps include 1) determining the standard to teach; 2) choosing a real-life activity that involves application of the standard; 3) identifying evidence-based practices to teach the skills; 4) selecting and/or developing manipulatives, graphic organizers, and/or technology to support skill acquisition; 5) incorporating progress monitoring; and 6) planning for generalization. Based on these guidelines the authors of this chapter have developed a lesson plan template to support instruction of students with severe disabilities, as shown in Figure 9.2. The lesson plan template includes

1. Common Core State Standards: Focusing on the big ideas in mathematics to identify a grade-aligned standard to teach. If you are teaching students in multiple grades (e.g., Grades 3–5), select standards in each grade level that align well.

2. Alternate achievement standards: Some states have already developed alternate achievement standards that align to the CCSS. If so, include these.

Common Core State Standard(s):	Alternate achievement standard(s)	Student(s) measureable objective(s):

Research-based instructional procedure(s)		Task analysis of steps to solve problem	Progress monitoring
☐ Time delay ☐ Prompting – **Type:** _____ ☐ Model-lead-test ☐ Graphic organizer (attach) ☐ Embedded instruction – **When:** _____ **Where:** _____		1.	
		2.	
		3.	
		4.	
Materials	**Technology**	5.	
		6.	
		7.	
		8.	
		9.	
		10.	
		11.	
		12.	

Focus and review

Story problem

Follow-up activity (if worksheet, attach)

Figure 9.2. Sample lesson plan template.

Good Chart!

3. Student measureable objectives: Determine the skill that you would like your student(s) to demonstrate by the end of the lesson, and write a clear measurable objective that aligns to the CCSS.

4. Research-based instructional procedure(s): Select the procedures that you will use during your instruction.

5. Task analysis: Write a task analysis of the steps the student(s) will need to complete in order to demonstrate the skill. Check with a math expert or general education math teacher to verify the accuracy of the steps required to complete the skill.

6. Progress monitoring: Frequent and ongoing data collection should be used during instruction to determine the accuracy of student(s) responses in completing the steps. You might put checks and minuses to indicate correct or incorrect, or you could indicate the prompting level required to elicit the correct response.

7. Materials: List the materials, including manipulatives, which will be used during the lesson.

8. Technology: Identify the technology that you will incorporate during the lesson. This may include individualized communication systems, electronic tablets, and an interactive white board, for example.

9. Focus and review: Indicate how you will introduce the topic and what prerequisite skills may need to be reviewed prior to the lesson. This is a good place to incorporate counting and cardinality fluency building activities.

10. Story problem: Write a brief story or word problem that relates the math skill to a real-world activity (e.g., a story about a student needing to make change when working at the school store). Use this to guide instruction. If the lesson is taught in multiple sessions, the amounts, shapes, volumes, and so forth can be interchanged to provide opportunities for repeated practice of the skill.

11. Follow-up activity: List activities you will use to promote generalization of the skill. These may include community-based activities, homework, or other opportunities for practice in a different setting, situation, or context.

Figures 9.3 and 9.4 are examples of lesson plans created from the template for middle and high school students. Wisconsin alternate achievement descriptors aligned to the CCSS were used as example alternate achievement standards (Wisconsin Department of Public Instruction, 2012). Figure 9.3 is a middle school number and quantity lesson plan teaching students to compare, add, and subtract fractions. Figure 9.4 is a high school geometry lesson plan teaching students to predict a measure for the volume of an object and determine the accuracy of their predictions.

SUMMARY

Mathematics provides an important foundation of knowledge and skills for individuals with severe disabilities. Aligning instruction to grade-level CCSS, although potentially challenging for teachers, offers varied opportunities for individuals

Common Core State Standard(s):

- 6.NS.1: Interpret and compute quotients of fractions, and solve word problems involving division of fractions by fractions, e.g., by using visual fraction models and equations to represent the problem.
- 7.NS.1: Apply and extend previous understandings of addition and subtraction to add and subtract rational numbers; represent addition and subtraction on a horizontal or vertical number diagram.
- 8.NS.1: Know that numbers that are not rational are called irrational. Understand informally that every number has a decimal expansion; for rational numbers show that the decimal expansion repeats eventually, and convert a decimal expansion into a rational number.

Alternate achievement standard(s):

- EE6.NS.1: Compare the relationships between two unit fractions.
- EE7.NS.1: Add fractions with like denominators (halves, thirds, fourths, and tenths) so the solution is less than or equal to 1.
- EE8.NS.1: Subtract fractions with like denominators (halves, thirds, fourths, and tenths) with minuends less than or equal to 1.

Student(s) measureable objective(s):

- Students will compare the relationship between two fractions by identifying the concepts of *more/less* when presented with visual fractions.
- Students will add two fractions with like denominators so that the solution is less than or equal to 1.
- Students will subtract two fractions with like denominators when the minuend is less than or equal to 1.

Research-based instructional procedure

☒ Time delay

☒ Prompting – **Type**: Least-to-most (independent, verbal, gesture, physical)

☐ Model-lead-test

☐ Graphic organizer (attach)

☐ Embedded instruction – **When**: _____ **Where**: _____

Task analysis of steps to solve problem	Progress monitoring			
1. Student looks at each class's pie and predicts who sold the most.				
2. Student counts/identifies the number of pieces that come in a pie.				
3. Student counts/identifies the number of pie pieces Ms. Anderson's class had left.				
4. Student subtracts this number from the total number of pieces using a graphic organizer.				
5. Student identifies total number of pieces Ms. Anderson's class sold.				
6. Student counts/identifies the number of pie pieces Mr. Newton's class has left.				

Figure 9.3. Sample middle school number and quantity lesson plan.

(continued)

Figure 9.3. (continued)

Materials	Technology	
• Visual fraction representing each class's leftover pie (laminated and cut apart) • Fraction addition/subtraction graphic organizer	Can be completed on an interactive whiteboard, computer, electronic tablet, or other device.	7. Student subtracts this number from the total number of pieces using a graphic organizer.
		8. Student identifies total number of pieces Mr. Newton's class sold.
		9. Student counts/identifies the number of pie pieces Ms. Wood's class has left.
		10. Student subtracts this number from the total number of pieces using a graphic organizer.
		11. Student identifies total number of pieces Ms. Wood's class sold.
		12. Student compares each class's total and identifies who sold the most pie.
		13. Student compares answer to prediction.
		14. Student adds each class's leftover pie amount and identifies total number of pieces leftover.

Focus and review

Teacher says, "Today we are going to learn to complete math problems that use fractions. We are going to work with fractions. We are going to share something with our friends. For example, if we were going to share a big piece of construction paper, we would need to use fractions to split it up. Today, we are going to be talking about pieces of pie. Have any of you had pie before? What's your favorite kind of pie?" The concepts of more, less, and equal are used in this lesson. If your students have mastered these concepts, move on to the story problem. If not, use constant time delay and the following script to review more, less, and equal.

Story problem

Butler Middle School is having a pie-selling contest to raise money for the spring dance. Each class is selling pieces of pie for $2 per slice. Each pie was divided into eight slices. After the first day, Mrs. Anderson's class had 1/2 a pie left, Mr. Newton's class had 1/4 of a pie left, and Ms. Wood's class had 1/8 of a pie left. How many slices of pie did each class sell? Who sold the most slices?

Follow-up activity (if worksheet, attach)

Students can practice this activity by dividing up/sharing different items in the classroom. For example, students can use fractions to practice dividing a large piece of construction paper, or share a class pizza.

Common Core State Standard(s):	Alternate achievement standard(s):	Student(s) measureable objective(s):
Explain volume formulas and use them to solve problems. • G-GMD.1: Give an informal argument for the formulas for the circumference of a circle, area of a circle, volume of a cylinder, pyramid, and cone. • G-GMD.3: Use volume formulas, pyramids, cones, and spheres to solve problems.	EEG-GMD.1-3: Make a prediction based on knowledge of volume to identify volume of common containers (cups, pints, gallons, etc.).	• Students will select an appropriate measurement tool to fill a volume. • Students will make a prediction on the number of gallons, pints, cups needed to fill a given volume of space. • Students will determine the accuracy of their predictions.

Research-based instructional procedure		Task analysis of steps to solve problem	Progress monitoring			
☐ Time delay		1. Student selects a gallon.				
☒ Prompting – **Type:** <u>System of least prompts</u>		2. Student hypothesizes how many gallons it will take to fill the bucket.				
☐ Model-lead-test		3. Student fills the bucket and counts the number of gallons used.				
☐ Graphic organizer (attach)		4. Student identifies whether or not his or her prediction was correct.				
☐ Embedded instruction – **When:** _____ **Where:** _____		5. Student selects a pint.				
Materials	**Technology**	6. Student hypothesizes how many pints it will take to fill the pitcher.				
• Pictures of people washing cars • Empty gallon jug • Empty pint container • Empty one-cup measurement • 2–3 different-sized buckets • 2–3 different-sized pitchers • 2–3 different-sized drinking cups • Note: If the lesson is repeated over a few days, use different-sized materials for subsequent lessons.	Can be completed on an interactive whiteboard, computer, electronic tablet, or other device	7. Student fills the pitcher and counts the number of pints used.				
		8. Student identifies whether or not his or her prediction was correct.				
		9. Student selects a cup.				
		10. Student hypothesizes how many cups it will take to fill the glass.				
		11. Student fills the glass and counts the number of cups used.				
		12. Student identifies whether or not his or her prediction was correct.				

Figure 9.4. Sample high school geometry lesson plan.

(continued)

Figure 9.4. *(continued)*

Focus and review

Teacher says, "Today we are going to be learning about volume. Volume means how much space a three-dimensional object occupies. Another way of explaining volume is how big an object is." (Show different-sized objects.) "We are going to read a story to help Mrs. Dunning's class plan for a car wash to raise money for a field trip." (Show pictures of student car washes.) The measurements used in this lesson include a gallon, a pint, and a cup. Check for mastery. If your students have mastered identifying these measurements, move on to the story problem. If not, use constant time delay to review gallon, pint, and cup measurements.

Story problem

Mrs. Dunning's class is going on a field trip to the science museum. They need to raise money to help pay for their tickets and for lunch. The class decided to have a car wash to raise money. They will need buckets of water, liquid soap, and lemonade to drink. Sam is in charge of getting the water to wash the cars, Lucy is in charge of getting the soap, and Ruthie is in charge of getting the lemonade. The buckets, pitchers, and glasses are outside in the parking lot, but the supplies and sink are in the work closet inside, so we'll need to plan a way to get the supplies outside.

Follow-up activity (if worksheet, attach)

Students could help prepare for an actual car wash and gather needed materials in the appropriate volumes. Students could work on identifying various volumes during academic and functional activities throughout their day (e.g., preparing lunch items, measuring various volumes in science class).

with severe disabilities to build fluency in fundamental skills and concepts. The least dangerous assumption maintains that individuals with severe disabilities can learn higher level mathematical concepts (Donnellan, 1984). Research over the past few years indicates that this assumption is warranted, as students have demonstrated acquisition of higher level mathematical skills (e.g., Browder, Jimenez, & Trela, 2012; Rockwell et al., 2011).

Several resources are available to help teachers gain more knowledge of CCSS and mathematics concepts. Some online resources include Illustrative Mathematics (http://www.illustrativemathematics.org), Common Core Math Tools (http://commoncoretools.me/tools/), and North Carolina Math Unpacking Standards (http://www.ncpublicschools.org/acre/standards/common-core-tools/#unmath).

REFERENCES

Ayres, K., Lowrey, K., Douglas, K., & Sievers, C. (2011). I can identify Saturn but I can't brush my teeth: What happens when the curricular focus for students with severe disabilities shifts. *Education and Training in Autism and Developmental Disabilities, 46,* 11–21.

Boyd, B., & Bargerhuff, M.E. (2009). Mathematics education and special education: Searching for common ground and the implications for teacher education. *Mathematics Teacher Education & Development, 11,* 54–67.

Browder, D., Ahlgrim-Delzell, L., Spooner, F., Mims, P.J., & Baker, J.N. (2009). Using time delay to teach literacy to students with severe developmental disabilities. *Exceptional Children, 75,* 343–364.

Browder, D.M., Jimenez, B.A., Spooner, F., Saunders, A., Hudson, M., & Bethune, K.S. (2012). Early numeracy instruction for students with moderate and severe developmental disabilities. *Research and Practice for Persons with Severe Disabilities, 37,* 308–320.

Browder, D.M., Jimenez, B., & Trela, K. (2012). Grade-aligned math instruction for secondary students with moderate intellectual disability. *Education and training in autism and developmental disabilities, 47*(3), 373–388.

Browder, D.M., Spooner, F., Ahlgrim-Delzell, L., Harris, A.A., & Wakeman, S. (2008). A meta-analysis on teaching mathematics to students with significant cognitive disabilities. *Exceptional Children, 74,* 407–432.

Browder, D.M., Wakeman, S.Y., Flowers, C., Rickelman, R.J., Pugalee, D., & Karvonen, M. (2007). Creating access to the general curriculum with links to grade-level content for students with significant cognitive disabilities: An explication of the concept. *The Journal of Special Education, 41,* 2–16.

Cihak, D.F., & Foust, J.L. (2008). Comparing number lines and touch points to teach addition facts to students with autism. *Focus on Autism and Other Developmental Disabilities, 23,* 131–137.

Collins, B.C. (2006). *Moderate and severe disabilities: A foundational approach.* Upper Saddle River, NJ: Merrill/Prentice Hall.

Collins, B.C. (2012). *Systematic instruction for students with moderate and severe disabilities.* Baltimore, MD: Paul H Brookes Publishing Co.

Courtade, G., Spooner, F., Browder, D., & Jimenez, B. (2012). Seven reasons to promote standards-based instruction for students with severe disabilities: A reply to Ayres, Lowrey, Douglas, & Sievers (2011). *Education and Training in Autism and Developmental Disabilities, 47,* 3–13.

Donnellan, A.M. (1984). The criterion of the least dangerous assumption. *Behavioral Disorders, 9,* 141–150.

Engelmann, S., Carnine, D., Kelly, B., & Engelmann, O. (2003). *Connecting math concepts: Level B presentation book 1.* Columbus, OH: SRA/McGraw-Hill.

Flores, M.M., & Ganz, J.B. (2007). Effectiveness of direct instruction for teaching statement inference, use of facts, and analogies to students with developmental disabilities and reading delays. *Focus on Autism and Other Developmental Disabilities, 22,* 244–251.

Flores, M.M, & Ganz, J.B. (2009). Effects of direct instruction on the reading comprehension of students with autism and developmental disabilities. *Education and Training in Developmental Disabilities, 44,* 39–53.

Flores, M.M., Shippen, M.E., Alberto, P., & Crowe, L. (2004). Teaching letter-sound correspondence to students with moderate intellectual disabilities. *Journal of Direct Instruction, 4,* 173–188.

Ganz, J.B., & Flores, M.M. (2009). The effectiveness of direct instruction for teaching language to children with autism spectrum disorders: *Identifying materials. Journal of Autism and Developmental Disorders, 39,* 75–83.

Gersten, R., Beckmann, S., Clarke, B., Foegen, A., Marsh, L., Star, J.R., & Witzel, B. (2009). *Assisting students struggling with mathematics: Response to Intervention (RtI) for elementary and middle schools* (NCEE 2009-4060). Washington, DC: National Center for Education Evaluation and Regional Assistance, Institute of Education Sciences, U.S. Department of Education. Retrieved from http://ies.ed.gov/ncee/wwc/publications/practiceguides

Gersten, R., Fuchs, L.S., Compton, D., Coyne, M., Greenwood, C., & Innocenti, M.S. (2005). Quality indicators for group experimental and quasi-experimental research in special education. *Exceptional Children, 71,* 149–164.

Harniss, M.K., Carnine, D.W., Silbert, J., & Dixon, R., (2010). Effective strategies for teaching mathematics. In M. Coyne, E. Kameenui, & D. Carnine (Eds.), *Effective strategies that accommodate diverse learners* (4th ed., pp. 139–170). Columbus, OH: Merrill.

Horner, R.H., Carr, E.G., Halle, J., McGee, G., Odom, S., & Wolery, M. (2005). The use of single-subject research to identify evidence-based practice in special education. *Exceptional Children, 71,* 165.

Hudson, M.E., & Test, D.W. (2011). Evaluating the evidence base of shared story reading to promote literacy for students with extensive support needs. *Research and Practice for Persons with Severe Disabilities, 36,* 34–45.

Individuals with Disabilities Education Improvement Act (IDEA) of 2004, PL 108-466, 20 U.S.C. §§ 1400 *et seq.*

Jimenez, B.A., Browder, D.M., & Courtade, G.R. (2008). Teaching an algebraic equation to high school students with moderate developmental disabilities. *Education and Training in Developmental Disabilities, 43,* 266–274.

Jimenez, B.A., Browder, D.M., & Courtade, G.R. (2009). An exploratory study of self-directed science concept learning by students with moderate intellectual disabilities. *Research and Practice for Persons with Severe Disabilities, 34,* 33–46.

Kearns, J., Kleinert, H., Harrison, B., Sheppard-Jones, K., Hall, M., & Jones, M. (2011). *What does "college and career ready" mean for students with significant cognitive disabilities?* (pp. 24–25). Lexington: University of Kentucky.

Kinder, D., Kubina, R., & Marchand-Martella, N.E. (2005). Special education and direct instruction: An effective combination. *Journal of Direct Instruction, 5,* 1–36.

Knight, V., Smith, B., Spooner, F., & Browder, D. (2012). Using explicit instruction to teach science descriptors to students with autism spectrum disorder. *Journal of Autism and Developmental Disorders, 42,* 378–389. doi:10.1007/s10803-011-1258-1

Levingston, H.B., Neef, N.A., & Cihon, T.M. (2009). The effects of teaching precurrent behaviors on children's solution of multiplication and division word problems. *Journal of Applied Behavior Analysis, 42,* 361–367.

Mims, P.J., Hudson, M.E., & Browder, D.M. (2012). Using read-alouds of grade-level biographies and systematic prompting to promote comprehension for students with moderate and severe developmental disabilities. *Focus on Autism and Other Developmental Disabilities, 27,* 67–80. doi:10.1177/1088357612446859

National Governors Association Center for Best Practices, Council of Chief State School Officers. (2010). *Common Core State Standards (mathematics).* Washington, DC: Authors. Retrieved from http://www.corestandards.org/

No Child Left Behind Act of 2001, PL 107-110, 115 Stat. 1425, 20 U.S.C. §§ 6301 *et seq.*

Polychronis, S.C., McDonnell, J., Johnson, J.W., Riesen, T., & Jameson, M. (2004). A comparison of two trial distribution schedules in embedded instruction. *Focus on Autism and Other Developmental Disabilities, 19,* 140–151.

Rockwell, S.B., Griffin, C.C., & Jones, H.A. (2011). Schema-based strategy instruction in mathematics and the word problem-solving performance of a student with autism. *Focus on Autism and Other Developmental Disabilities, 26,* 87–95.

Saunders, A., Bethune, K., Spooner, F., & Browder, D. (2013). Solving the common core equation: Teaching mathematics CCSS to students with moderate and severe disabilities. *TEACHING Exceptional Children, 45*(1), 24–33.

Snell, M.E. (Ed.). (1983). *Systematic instruction of the moderately and severely handicapped* (2nd ed.). Columbus, OH: Merrill.

Spooner, F., Knight, V.F., Browder, D.M., & Smith, B.R. (2012). Evidence-based practice for teaching academics to students with severe developmental disabilities. *Remedial and Special Education, 33,* 374–384. doi:10.1177/0741932511421634

Stokes, T.F., & Baer, D.M. (1977). An implicit technology of generalization. *Journal of Applied Behavior Analysis, 10,* 349–367.

Thompson, J.L., Wood, C.L., Test, D.W., & Cease-Cook, J. (2012). Effects of direct instruction on telling time by students with autism. *Journal of Direct Instruction, 12,* 1–12.

Watkins, C.L., & Slocum, T.A. (2004). The components of direct instruction. In N.E. Marchand-Martella, T.A. Slocum, & R.C. Martella (Eds.), *Introduction to direct instruction* (pp. 28–65). Boston, MA: Pearson.

Wisconsin Department of Public Instruction. (2012). Common core essential elements and alternate achievement descriptors for mathematics. Retrieved from http://dpi.wi.gov/sped/assmt-ccee.html

Wolery, M., Bailey, D.B., & Sugai, G.M. (1988). *Effective teaching: Principles and procedure of applied behavior analysis with exceptional students.* Boston, MA: Allyn & Bacon.

FOR FURTHER INFORMATION

Books

Browder, D.M., & Spooner, F. (2011). *Teaching students with moderate and severe disabilities.* New York, NY: Guilford Press.

This is a methods textbook on teaching skills, including academics, to students with severe disabilities. It includes a comprehensive chapter on teaching mathematics.

Collins, B.C. (2012). *Systematic instruction for students with moderate and severe disabilities.* Baltimore, MD: Paul H. Brookes Publishing Co.

This practitioner-friendly resource explicitly teaches how to use systematic instruction to teach skills to students with severe disabilities.

Reys, R.E. (2009). *Helping children learn mathematics.* Hoboken, NJ: John Wiley & Sons.

This is a methods textbook on teaching elementary mathematics. It includes helpful illustrations and example lessons and activities.

Stein, M., Kinder, D., Silbert, J., & Carnine, D.W. (2005). *Designing effective mathematics instruction: A Direct Instruction approach* (4th ed.). New York, NY: Prentice Hall.

This is a methods textbook on teaching mathematics using Direct Instruction. It uses a practitioner-friendly approach and provides scripts and visuals for how to explicitly teach the majority of mathematics concepts.

Curricula

Engelmann, S., & Engelmann, O. (2012). *Connecting math concepts: Comprehensive edition.* Columbus, OH: McGraw-Hill.

This is a Direct Instruction curriculum teaching K–5 mathematics skills aligned to the Common Core State Standards.

Trela, K., Jimenez, B., & Browder, D. M. (2007). *Teaching to the standards: Math.* Verona, WI: Attainment Co.

This is a middle and high school curriculum developed specifically for students with severe disabilities and aligned to National Council of Teachers of Mathematics (NCTM) standards.

Web Sites

Autism Internet Modules

http://www.autisminternetmodules.org

This teacher and family friendly web site was developed to provide resources for evidenced-based practices for students with autism. It provides modules, checklists, videos, and materials for implementing practices including task analysis, time delay, visual supports, and prompting. While the site was specifically developed for those working with individuals with autism, many of the practices are research-based for students with severe disabilities also. Note: The site requires registration but is a free resource.

Illustrative Mathematics

http://www.illustrativemathematics.org

This web site provides activities and illustrations aligned to the Common Core State Standards.

North Carolina Department of Public Information

http://www.ncpublicschools.org/acre/standards/common-core-tools/#unmath

This teacher-friendly resource provides guidance and explanations of the Common Core State Standards for mathematics. It includes visuals and definitions of key vocabulary.

Tools for the Common Core Standards

http://commoncoretools.me/tools

This web site was developed by one of the authors of the Common Core State Standards for mathematics. It includes documents demonstrating progressions of the big ideas for mathematics from kindergarten to high school, with examples of activities and in-depth explanation of concepts.

CHAPTER 10

Science as Inquiry

Bree A. Jimenez and Heidi B. Carlone

Today when Elijah woke up to get ready for school, he looked outside and noticed that the patio table was wet. He figured it must have rained last night and went to get dressed and eat his breakfast. Elijah's father takes him to school each day. Today on their way outside, Elijah noticed that the family car was wet too; however, the driveway was not. Elijah wasn't able to ask his dad why the car was wet even though the driveway wasn't. Elijah doesn't communicate verbally, he uses an assistive device to communicate his needs and wants; however, his communication system doesn't include a system to pose questions (yet!). At school during morning routine his teacher did mention that today's weather was warm and sunny. Elijah's teacher indicated that they had not received rain in the past week and wouldn't for several more days. Elijah was confused, he wondered "Why was the car wet if it hadn't rained last night?"

All children (or adults for that matter) experience the world around them. Inquiry is the practice in which people investigate the world, ask questions of it, communicate about it, and begin to find answers. There is a balancing act in teaching science within the classroom that juggles student's use of inquiry and their content knowledge. The act of inquiry is much more than a set of skills done the same way each day; inquiry is "habit of mind." Engaging in scientific inquiry should be the focus of all science instruction to better prepare students to engage in the world, school activities, and everyday lives. As students acquire skills within the practice of inquiry, they will better understand how to participate and communicate in their community to the greatest extent possible.

THE LATEST IN SCIENCE EDUCATION SCHOOL REFORM

Since their release in 2010, the Common Core State Standards (CCSS; National Governors Association Center for Best Practices, Council of Chief State School Officers, 2010) have swept through the majority of the United States, providing common standards to be used to teach English language arts and mathematics to students in kindergarten through high school (K–12). With this initiative came an opportunity for the field to consider adoption of updated common standards in K–12 science education. Although there already were existing national documents on science content for Grades K–12 (developed in the early to mid-1990s), this recent focus on new state standards has provided the field of science education a chance to strengthen and improve standards created more than 15 years ago. The National Science Education Standards (NSES; National Research Council [NRC], 1996) provided educators with guidelines to use when developing science curricula across the nation. However, the call for updated standards has been greatly needed, not only because science has progressed over the past several decades but also because with the implementation of standards-based educational reform, there is a new and growing body of research on learning and teaching that can inform a revision of the standards and revitalize science education.

A FRAMEWORK FOR K–12 SCIENCE EDUCATION: PRACTICES, CROSSCUTTING CONCEPTS, AND CORE IDEAS

In 2012, the NRC developed a conceptual framework to guide the next set of science standards specifically addressing the need for science education that develops students' engagement in experiencing science throughout their entire school career. Differing from the previous standards (NRC, 1996), the Next Generation Science Standards (NGSS; Achieve, Inc., 2013a) refine and clarify *scientific inquiry* by establishing the following eight science and engineering practices:

1. Asking questions

2. Developing and using models

3. Planning and carrying out investigations

4. Analyzing and interpreting data

5. Using mathematics and computational thinking

6. Constructing explanations

7. Engaging in argument from evidence

8. Obtaining, evaluating, and communicating information

The shift from describing the teaching and learning of science from *"scientific inquiry"* to *"engagement in scientific and engineering practices"* (NRC, 2012) accomplishes multiple goals. First, sociocultural learning theory literature has prompted a "practice turn" in the learning sciences literature, which challenges the notion that learning can be understood solely in terms of behavioral skills or mental structures. Instead, sociocultural theory views learning as participation in practice (Ford & Forman, 2006) or, more specifically, as a process of socialization of students into science's norms and practices (Forman, 2003). Teaching science as engagement in a set of disciplinary practices integrates the mental processes of learning the science content with the physical and social engagement in science's practices. As students participate in scientific practices, they engage intellectually, socially, and physically. Doing so helps students understand the diversity of approaches that scientists use to investigate, model, and explain the natural world (NRC, 2012). See Figure 10.1 for a comparison of the old and new science frame-

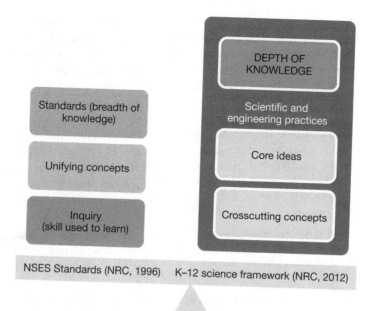

Figure 10.1. Comparison of the old and new science frameworks with a new emphasis on depth of knowledge through scientific and engineering practices.

works. For students with severe disabilities, this approach to science instruction aligns well with the need to develop *in vivo* learning experiences that not only teach new content or rote skills but also allow students to build generalization and problem-solving skills while *living* the lesson. For this population of students, it is often most useful to teach in context, building fluency over repeated practice.

Second, the emphasis of science as a set of practices integrates the "sense-making" part of learning with the "language-use" part of learning (Achieve, Inc., 2013b, p. 2). Engagement in all scientific practices is language intensive, requiring students to speak, read, write, and/or visually represent their ideas to others as they develop scientific models and explanations, engage in argumentation, and revise and refine their ideas to reach shared conclusions (Achieve, Inc., 2013b, p. 2). Good science instruction, in this view, provides opportunities for all students to simultaneously develop scientific understanding, ways of viewing the world, and language proficiency. Making the language demands of science more explicit benefits students with disabilities because it specifically addresses students' communication needs within the natural context of the science lesson. Previous research on teaching science to students with severe disabilities has noted the specific communication and language needs of the population within the context of science instruction, with attention given to explicit concept instruction to build language skills for science communication (Knight, Smith, Spooner, & Browder, 2012). Although communication is often a direct area of support for students with severe disabilities, the opportunity and acknowledgement of the language-use component of the new framework highlights the connectedness of how *all* students need support to successful and fully engage in science inquiry practices.

Third, the focus on science as a set of practices may pique students' curiosity, cultivate their motivation to learn more, and help them understand the creative aspects of doing science. It is a more holistic, realistic view of science that emphasizes aspects of science beyond experimentation to include other practices such as modeling, critique, and communication (NRC, 2012). The practices are not meant to be viewed as steps, but as aspects of doing science that are engaged sometimes on their own, and sometimes in concert with other practices to construct knowledge about the natural world. For students with severe disabilities, becoming self-determined, lifelong learners is often the greatest goal in preparation for transitioning to postschool life. The NRC framework begins with the unified principle that all children are born investigators, sustained in the development of understanding over time (long after formal schooling), and that all students bring a personal touch to their journey in learning science.

> The framework is designed to help realize a vision for education in the sciences and engineering in which students, over multiple years of school, actively engage in scientific and engineering practices and apply crosscutting concepts to deepen their understanding of the core ideas in these fields. (NRC, 2012)

In the NRC framework, scientific practices are organized among three spheres of activity: 1) investigation and empirical inquiry (e.g., asking questions, observing, experimenting measuring, collecting data), 2) developing explanations (e.g., reasoning, creative thinking, modeling), and 3) evaluating explanations (analysis, argumentation, critique). There is an assumption that scientists move back and forth among these spheres of activity and that a given activity may involve one or more of these spheres.

PROVIDING A PERSONALLY RELEVANT CURRICULUM

With a focus on teaching to the general curriculum content standards for all students—including those with moderate and severe disabilities—it is essential to take a moment to ask *why* it is important to teach specific content and practices. Curricula for students with severe disabilities have evolved since the early 2000s. With the focus of science education for students with severe disabilities now aligned to grade-level standards, a spotlight on science practices aligns with what the field of severe disability has long valued: self-determination, communication, and curriculum based on individualized support needs fostering productive citizenship. Trela and Jimenez (2013) described *personal relevant curriculum* as person-centered adaptations made to both access grade-appropriate curriculum and receive individualized support. Personal relevance within science instruction promotes inclusive practices by signaling common curriculum that is differentiated, not different, for students with intellectual disability.

As noted earlier in this chapter, science inquiry is not just a set of steps to complete to get to the finish line (science lesson done), it is a practice that students learn to use and embed in their everyday lives. The notion of personal relevance signifies the need for individualized meaning in the practices and content taught within the science classroom. When examining the use of inquiry to teach science, lessons should promote students' use of their own wants, needs, and self to investigate, communicate, and build content knowledge throughout the lesson itself, over multiple units of instruction, or even over years.

In 2007, the NRC reviewed research on teaching young children and found that even before entering school, children have sophisticated ways of making sense of their worlds. The review also noted that although most students do not have deep understandings, they all (regardless of background) develop ideas while experiencing everyday activities, such as hobbies, watching TV, and being with friends and family. With Elijah in the opening vignette, inquiry is happening at a very self-directed level. Elijah is a student with a severe disability who would benefit greatly from explicit language instruction within the context of a science lesson and throughout the school day as a mode to help him *experience* science. Whether the act of wonder is stated as a question (verbally, through an augmentative device, or not at all), all students should be given the support necessary to build their ability to pose questions onto building explanations.

Inquiry itself is described as a practice, rather than a process or skill within the NRC framework. For Elijah, the process has begun naturally through experiencing life; he now needs the guidance and support of a science-rich context to learn how and what it really means to inquire and engage in scientific practices. What is more personally relevant for Elijah than to gain the communication and self-directed problem-solving skills to answer his own questions about the world in which he lives every day?

MODEL FOR INQUIRY WITHIN THE NEW NRC FRAMEWORK

For students with severe disabilities, the emphasis for science education should be focused on the investigation, evaluation, and explanations of science (see Figure 10.2). There is not a single approach to science, nor one specific process to inquiry. Activities should be integrated so that all students, including those with severe disabilities, experience inquiry-based learning as they participate. The focus of inquiry is on its practices encumbering the dynamic learning that occurs when engaged in the content (e.g., learning about land formations through models, communication, questioning, discussions, arguing, predicting, imagining).

Inquiry was previously taught using rigid models that did not allow for movement within the lesson. For example, the lesson poses a question, students watch an experiment unfold, and then they answer the question (often based on the teacher's guided efforts to form understanding of the concept). The core ideas of inquiry practices use individual student's perceptions, critiques, and communication. For students with severe disabilities, these core ideas align nicely with historically valued educational emphases, such as self-determination, language development, and community involvement. It is worth noting the framework's additional focus on engineering practices; however, this chapter only focuses on the science practices for this population.

Research-Based Practices

Since the early 2000s the field of severe disability has greatly expanded the research in teaching academics to include most areas of instruction aligned to academic standards (e.g., English language arts, mathematics, science). In response to federal mandates, such as the No Child Left Behind Act of 2001 (PL 107-110), educators must base their practices within research (empirical evidence) to support the strat-

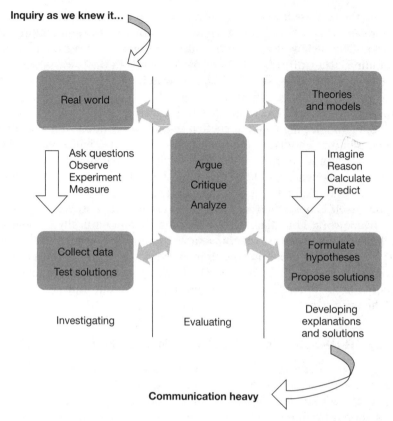

Figure 10.2. Scientific practices for students with severe disabilities. *Source:* National Research Council (2012).

egies and curricula employed in the classroom. This has been a challenge in the field of severe disability due to the scarcity of research focused on grade-aligned academics. Specific to the content area of science education, a literature review conducted by Spooner, Knight, Browder, Jimenez, and DiBiase (2011) found only 17 total studies examining science education for students with severe disabilities. Of those studies, only 14 met standards to deem them adequate or high-quality research, meaning that the research was conducted with high levels of fidelity, research methods, and impact. Most importantly the review highlighted specific components of science education (based on the NSES, e.g., physical science) that had a good deal of research to support *how* to teach them. In addition, the review dissected each research study to determine what instructional strategies were most prominently used to teach science (e.g., time delay, peer-mediated instruction). Based on the findings of Spooner and colleagues (2011), systematic instruction was found to be an evidence-based practice to teach science concepts (e.g., chemistry) and content (e.g., vocabulary). See Chapter 1 for more on how research is used to support instruction.

Over the past several years there has been an even greater emphasis on science education in schools. With this focus, several new studies have been conducted to investigate how to teach content-specific science skills within the context of inquiry for students with severe disabilities. For example, science lessons that focus on concept and vocabulary attainment across physical, life, and Earth and space science within an inquiry-based task analysis have found great success in teaching students with disabilities, including those with autism and the most intensive support needs (Jimenez, Lo, & Saunders, 2012; Smith, Spooner, Jimenez, & Browder, 2013).

Science research for this population began based on the need to investigate how to teach special education teachers to use inquiry within their own science lessons. In a study conducted by Courtade, Browder, Spooner, and DiBiase (2010), four special education teachers of students with severe disabilities were trained to embed components of inquiry, based on the suggestions of NSES, into science instruction for their students. Findings indicated that not only were all teachers able to embed a 12-step inquiry task analysis following the four inquiry components of *Engage, Investigate & Describe, Explain and Report* in the 4 E Learning Cycle, but also their students increased the number of science responses within each lesson (see Figure 10.3). In 2012, Browder and colleagues used the same task analysis

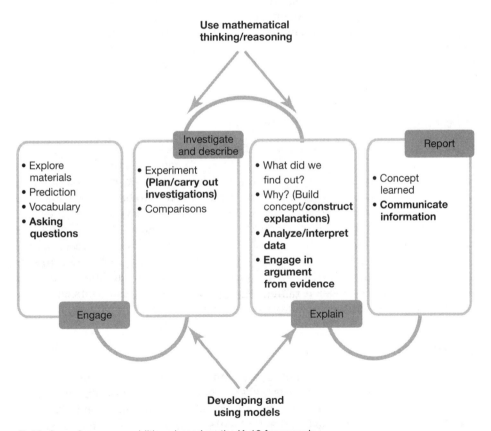

Bolded words are new additions based on the K–12 framework.

Figure 10.3. Summary of inquiry process used with the 12-step task analysis linked to practices emphasized in the NRC framework.

and investigated its effect when delivered by the special education teachers across four units of grade-aligned instruction (i.e., Earth's history, biology, Earth's waters, chemistry) on student mastery of new grade-aligned science concepts and vocabulary. Students who participated in the science inquiry lessons learned new science concepts and vocabulary aligned to their grade-level standards across units of instruction.

Students with moderate intellectual disabilities also have demonstrated that they can acquire concepts through an inquiry process. In Jimenez, Browder, Spooner, and DiBiase (2012), students in inclusive science classes were taught grade-aligned science concepts (e.g., kinetic energy is energy in *motion*) by their same-age peers during an inquiry-based lesson. The students used the problem-solving–based lessons to generalize the concepts to various examples (e.g., kinetic energy: moving swing, speeding motorcycle, windmill). In addition, Smith and colleagues (2013) found that students with severe disabilities also could learn concepts during inquiry lessons. In these lessons, three students with multiple disabilities engaged in the inquiry process through a teacher-delivered inquiry task analysis by asking questions of materials, making predictions, investigating, developing explanations, and building concept understanding. Concept attainment is an important component in building science understanding. As students gain understanding of science standards, vocabulary, concept understanding, and problem-solving skills (inquiry) should be built in unison to provide all students the knowledge and skills needed to understand the natural world around them. See Chapter 11 for more examples and specific instructional tools that can be used to teach crosscutting science concepts and core ideas.

Building on Research for Practice

As noted earlier in this chapter, scientific practices are extremely important in teaching all students science. As the field of science continues to evolve, and with the development and implementation of the NRC framework, it is imperative to take a look at what has been successful in the past and how to bring those practices into the next phase of science instruction for students with severe disabilities.

In the Spooner and colleagues (2011) review, only one study was found that investigated science inquiry; however, even more recently (2009 to present), multiple research studies have investigated the use of systematic instruction to specifically teach inquiry practices with students with severe disabilities. Table 10.1 provides a quick review of some of the research conducted with students with moderate to severe intellectual disability to teach inquiry.

GETTING STARTED

Building a science community in the classroom is important for all students. Gaining the knowledge of *what* science is and *how* the standards support problem solving and learning for students with severe disability is also important. The next step to success is planning instruction that will support students' complex learning needs and personally relevant grade-aligned instruction.

Table 10.1.   Research-based practices to support scientific inquiry with students with moderate and severe disabilities

Graphic organizers to promote inquiry

- **Study:** Jimenez, B.A., Browder, D.M., & Courtade, G.R. (2009). An exploratory study of self-directed science concept learning by students with moderate intellectual disabilities. *Research and Practice for Persons with Severe Disabilities, 34,* 1–14.

    ○   *Who? What?* Three students with moderate intellectual disability were taught to self-direct themselves through secondary science lessons (Precipitation; Solutions) using a KWHL chart (Know, Want to know, How to find out, what is Learned) and response boards.

    ○   *A glimpse inside the study:* The teacher would give a verbal cue during a science lesson, such as, "What do you KNOW about the materials?" Students would then find the K on their own graphic organizer and place a picture symbol in the blank (from a choice of 3–4 options). Students were taught to use the KWHL chart using a constant time-delay procedure. Once students mastered use of the chart with one set of materials, they were asked to demonstrate mastery across new materials and in the inclusive science classroom.

- **Study:** Jimenez, B.A., Browder, D.M., Spooner, F., & DiBiase, W. (2012). Inclusive inquiry science using peer-mediated embedded instruction for students with moderate intellectual disabilities. *Exceptional Children, 78,* 301–317.

    ○   *Who? What?* Five middle school students with moderate intellectual disability were taught to direct their cooperative learning groups in using a KWHL chart during inclusive inquiry-based science lessons.

    ○   *A glimpse inside the study:* Students with and without disability were given a KWHL chart to use to guide daily lessons. The teacher would give a verbal cue during a science lesson, such as, "How can we find out more about the topic or materials?" Students with moderate disability would then point to the correct portion of the graphic organizer to guide their peers to fill in the chart. Peers without disability taught students with moderate disability to use the chart using constant time-delay procedures.

Building inquiry across the years

I wonder . . . My mom has blue eyes and my dad has brown eyes. My eyes are brown too. I wonder why my eyes are not the same color as my mom's?

- **Study:** Smith, B.R., Spooner, F., Jimenez, B.A., & Browder, D. (2013). Using an early science curriculum to teach science vocabulary and concepts to students with severe developmental disabilities. *Education & Treatment of Children, 36,* 1–31. doi: 10.1353/etc.2013.0002.

    ○   *Who? What?* One teacher of three elementary students with multiple disabilities used a task-analysis approach to guide inquiry science lessons linked to the grade-level standards. All three students made significant gains in content learned while engaging in these inquiry lessons.

    ○   *A glimpse inside the study:* The task analyses used to teach the lessons included "wonder" stories to build and link students' prior knowledge, as well as steps to guide predictions, KWHL questions, and evaluations of learning. Three units of science were taught, with each unit expanding on inquiry skills learned in the previous. For example, in Unit 1, the teacher modeled making a prediction and guided students toward possible choices to complete the L step of the KWHL chart. Unit 2 lessons allowed students to make their own predictions (teacher provided support using a least-to-most prompting system), and students completed the W and L of the KWHL chart.

- **Study:** Browder, D.M., Trela, K., Courtade, G.R., Jimenez, B.A., Knight. V., & Flowers, C. (2012). Teaching mathematics and science standards to students with moderate and severe developmental disabilities. *The Journal of Special Education, 46,* 26–35.

    ○   *Who? What?* Ten middle and high school students with moderate and severe disabilities were taught new science vocabulary and concepts during inquiry science lessons. The lessons were taught by five classroom special education teachers using a 12-step inquiry task analysis.

    ○   *A glimpse inside the study:* Middle and high school students learned new grade-aligned science vocabulary and concepts in the context of the inquiry lesson with systematic instruction. The inquiry lessons focused on teaching the students to ask questions, analyze materials and data, compare materials pre- and postexperiments and report their results.

Select and Understand the
Appropriate Scientific Core Ideas and Practices

The NGSS are

> Built on the notion of learning as a developmental progression. It is designed to
> help children continually build on and revise their knowledge and abilities, starting
> from their curiosity about what they see around them and their initial conceptions
> about how the world works. The goal is to guide their knowledge toward a more
> scientifically based and coherent view of the natural sciences and engineering, as
> well as of the ways in which they are pursued and their results can be used. (NRC,
> 2012, pp. 10–11)

So, when choosing the content that educators want to teach, in addition to
the scientific practices they want to focus on, the NRC framework provides a helpful overview of the learning progressions that break down the content and practices from least to most sophisticated (Achieve, Inc., 2013c, 2013d). For example,
in examining a core disciplinary idea of "earth materials and systems" in earth
science, students learn that "wind and water change the shape of the land" early on
and then learn, in later grades, to understand that "rainfall helps to shape the land
and affects the types of living things found in a region" and that "water, ice, wind,
organisms, and gravity break rocks, soils, and sediments into smaller pieces and
move them around" (Achieve, Inc., 2013c, p. 2). In examining the learning progressions for scientific practices, students learn early to ask questions (one of the eight
practices) that build "on prior experiences and [progress] to simple descriptive
questions that can be tested" and, in later grade levels, they also may ask questions that "specify qualitative relationships" and, even later, specify "relationships
between variables, and [clarify] arguments and models" (Achieve, Inc., 2013d, p. 4).
Again, when applying these learning progressions to teaching students with severe
disabilities, teachers may need to reconsider the grade-level demarcations recommended by the NRC framework and revisit skills and concepts taught in earlier
grades to build connections.

Collaboration with general education science teachers is necessary when
developing and identifying standards, core concepts, and grade-appropriate ways
in which inquiry practices will take place in the classroom. The next chapter provides strategies and tools to build collaborative networks for lesson planning and
co-teaching within the inclusive science classroom. This chapter will get readers
started by including a list of helpful web sites teachers can use as resources for (re)
learning scientific content in the major scientific areas of the NGSS: earth/space
sciences, life sciences, and physical sciences (see For Further Information at the
end of this chapter).

Select and Embed Multiple Ways to Engage Students

The practice of inquiry is typically engaging for students; however, it may be necessary to embed specific tools within daily science practice to provide students
with support to engage and make generalizations within the core ideas and crosscutting concepts taught. One example of a research-based strategy to engage students in the process of inquiry is the use of a wonder story (see Table 10.1). This
story is usually an engaging story written by the teacher to provide some back-

ground information students may or may not have, offer a meaningful context (e.g., a rainstorm that made the sand in the sandbox look different), and serve as an "attention-getter" for the lesson. Table 10.2 reviews the eight scientific practices outlined by the NRC framework (2012) and provides several examples of what these practices may look like for this population of students. Student engagement is highlighted within these examples through teaching students to ask questions (e.g., Why does the sandbox look different?), engage in arguments (e.g., I *do/do not* think the rain will change the sand), and using data/observations to support their questions. The use of assistive technology, graphic organizers, and technology are

Table 10.2. A Glimpse into Science Practices for Students with Severe Disabilities

Practice 1: Asking Questions and Defining Problems: Science begins with questions, such as, "What is happening to frog populations in North Carolina? Why are we seeing a decrease in population in certain ecological regions?" and "What is the effect of exercise on lifespan?" Scientists seek to provide explanatory answers to their questions by collecting empirical data. A part of formulating good scientific questions is understanding what is already known about a topic.

- What this may look like for students with severe disabilities
   - Asking *why* questions about everyday occurrences (e.g., Elijah's story).
   - Reading a wonder story and identifying or developing the question(s) to guide a lesson(s).

Practice 2: Developing and Using Models: Science involves constructing, testing, and revising models. Models are "abstract, simplified representations that facilitate prediction and explanation" (Manz, 2012, p. 1072). Models are helpful when scientists want to study something that is too small, too old, or too big to collect data empirically. They make it possible to reduce the natural world's complexity to focus in on specific aspects of natural phenomena. Models facilitate an "if/then/therefore" kind of thinking.

- What this may look like for students with severe disabilities
   - Using a representational model to understand and investigate (e.g., developing the layers of the Earth with different familiar "land" materials; rocks, gravel, sand).
   - Using and constructing simulation models to predict and explain happenings. For example, if these plates move ... then they will either fold (canyon) or pop up (mountain) . . . therefore . . . land formations occur.

Practice 3: Planning and Carrying Out Investigations: Scientific investigations occur in the laboratory or field. When a scientist plans and carries out a scientific investigation, she or he identifies a question, determines what information is needed to answer that question (e.g., what kinds of data need to be collected), what variables need to be controlled, and how data will be recorded. Data are used to create explanations and to test and/or revise predictions.

- What this may look like for students with severe disabilities
   - Identify what type of data are needed to answer questions.
   - Identify scientific materials needed to create explanations ("What tool will help me take the data I need to answer my question?" [e.g., thermometer, microscope]).
   - Predict, review prediction, make changes to it, then possibly predict again based on the next step of the question.
   - Self-direct practices through the use of a KWHL chart during lessons.

Practice 4: Analyzing and Interpreting Data: Data do not speak for themselves. Scientists must analyze and interpret data so they understand the patterns and relationships. This analysis process is creative, logical, and evidence-based. When scientists analyze data, they use many different tools, including tables, graphs, and statistical analysis to understand the trends and patterns in the data.

- What this may look like for students with severe disabilities
   - Identify what could be done differently during the experiment.
   - Give examples (using evidence) of what was discovered (e.g., When the water was dirty with pollution and oil, the bird's feathers didn't get clean).

(continued)

Table 10.2.   *(continued)*

 ° Use evidence-based reasoning and argumentation (e.g., oil-based paint would be bad for the fish in the pond behind the school too because I noticed...!).

 ° Record data in tables, graphs, and charts. Interpret data to make arguments.

Practice 5: Using Mathematics and Computational Thinking: Scientists have to figure out how to represent physical variables and their relationships. To do so, they use mathematics and computational tools. Statistical analysis allows scientists to assess the significance of patterns or relationships in the data. Computational tools allow for calculations that cannot be carried out analytically, to develop simulations to model complex systems, and to make predictions.

- What this may look like for students with severe disabilities

 ° Formulate predictions based on probability and inferences (e.g., the more destruction to buildings, the greater the tectonic shock).

 ° Use basic algebraic equations to predict and evaluate questions (e.g., use an algebraic equation to determine the allowable weight [# of cars] a bridge should be able to handle).

 ° Argue findings based on numerical or visual representations of data.

Practice 6: Constructing Explanations: Scientists produce theories that provide explanations to describe the nature of phenomena and to make predictions and inferences. Scientific theories are based on a lot of evidence, revised in light of new evidence, and undergo significant scrutiny by other scientists before they are accepted. Scientific explanations, then, are accounts of natural phenomena that link scientific theory with specific observations. Scientific explanations should be logical, coherent, and evidence-based.

- What this may look like for students with severe disabilities

 ° Building predictions from a guess into scientific hypothesis based on specific observations (e.g., generate prediction and articulate why; student is given choices for prediction and is able to move from random choice to predictions based on past experiences).

 ° Making inferences about the past (e.g., using fossils, tell who/what was in/on the environment).

 ° Identify gaps or weaknesses in current explanations (e.g., identify nonexample, then reconstruct explanations [e.g., magnets stick to *most* metals]).

Practice 7: Engaging in Argument from Evidence: Scientists look skeptically on one another's work. Is the evidence solid? Are the methods sound? Are the conclusions reasonable, logical, and based on evidence? Scientists must use reasoning and argumentation to make their case to other scientists and to the public that their claims are sound. The knowledge scientists produce goes through rigorous peer review by other scientists. They often collaborate with peers to gather additional evidence and to construct more comprehensive explanations for natural phenomena than could be achieved individually.

- What this may look like for students with severe disabilities

 ° Argue, using reasoning, to identify research questions, findings, and explanations (e.g., ask a question then defend it with peers by pointing out key elements of a wonder story that aligns to the question, or sequencing pictures to illustrate why the question now has a plausible explanation).

 ° Teachers may set up data in multiple formats, asking students to identify the best ways to record and/or analyze data (e.g., compare circle graphs or bar graphs to record magnitude of earthquake data).

 ° Identify flaws in their own theories (e.g., student identifies measurement of moisture in clouds could be taken by placing a ladder up to cloud; teacher or peer-directed challenge of why this is or is not a good measurement tool).

Practice 8: Obtaining, Evaluating, and Communicating Information: Scientists must communicate their ideas clearly if others are to be convinced of their findings. Scientists are fluent oral and written communicators and communicate in formal and informal ways. They use and produce tables, diagrams, and graphs. Additionally, they read, interpret, and produce other scientific texts (e.g., papers, online articles, lectures, videos) and are able to evaluate the scientific validity of the information.

- What this may look like for students with severe disabilities

 ° Use words, tables, diagrams, and graphs to show understanding or ask questions. For students with preliteracy and numeracy skills, this practice may include: 1) using a bar graph to ask scientific questions, 2) listening to an adapted newspaper article about social issues (e.g., News-2-You), asking questions, and reporting their findings, or 3) using data sources to which to compare their own findings.

Source: National Research Council (2012).

also great strategies to engage students by providing them a means to communicate and show what they know. (See Chapter 11 for ideas of how to use these tools to teach new science content.)

Setting Student Expectations for Science Practice

The eight distinguishing practices outlined by the NRC framework should be used to plan inquiry instruction for students with moderate and severe disabilities. All students, regardless of grade level or ability, can participate in all eight practices at some level. The idea is that students' abilities to use and engage in these practices grow over time. The goal is to help students engage in and use the practices to facilitate their understanding of science, appreciate the wide range of approaches used to create scientific knowledge, and pique students' curiosity and motivate their interest in learning about natural phenomena and the natural world. Although the practices are designed for K–12 education, it is not clear that students with severe disability were in mind when developing the framework.

When are they ever?

This chapter attempts to translate new practices in science education for this population of students, providing an initial model to essentially build on. Educators and researchers in the field of severe disability need to continue to use existing research-based practices on science education for students with severe disabilities and build on best practices in the field of science education. Again, Table 10.2 highlights the eight practices and provides examples of how students with severe disabilities may demonstrate understanding of these principles. The practice of science should be the focus of all instruction, and within this focal point students will gain skills to solve problems, communicate, and build a conceptual understanding of the world around them.

Planning Steps of the Lesson

Lesson plans come in many shapes and formats. They may include a planning guide that focuses on the core ideas and concepts to be taught, a task-analysis that outlines the questions to be asked during the lesson, or a curriculum-based lesson that highlights the main activities and ideas within the unit. Regardless of the format, science should always be taught in the context of building inquiry practices for all students. Students with severe disabilities may need additional supports added to science lessons, such as picture symbols, assistive technology for communication, or various response modes (e.g., verbal, eye-gaze, grasp response from choice board) to demonstrate science practices. The research in science for this population has demonstrated that teachers can use systematic instruction (i.e., task-analysis, time delay, and least-to-most prompting) to teach science; lesson plan implementation should use these strategies. Figure 10.4 illustrates a sample lesson plan using a task-analysis approach (research-based to teach science to this population) with suggested activities added to provide students opportunities to deepen their practice and in turn grow as scientists. The task analysis provided engages students in a process aligned with the eight science practices previously reviewed. Although typically task analysis may be used to teach rote chained responses, the steps outlined in Figure 10.4 provide the teacher with a format to build science processes within each lesson.

Science Strand: Earth Science—Water Cycle

Materials: Vocabulary word/picture cards, sponge, water, KWHL chart, assistive technology, concept statement on sentence strip with picture symbols for key vocabulary

Teacher will:	Extending science practices: Students will:	Science practice
Introduce lesson: Use a wonder story or brief video to build or link to prior knowledge of the topic. Sample video: (http://www.brainpop.com/science/earthsystem/watercycle/preview.weml)	Generate questions about the topic (e.g., Why are there clouds today but no rain?) Choose research question from options. Identify research question when presented in a story.	Asking questions and defining problems
Review target vocabulary using sight words/pictures/models Target words include *rain, precipitation, cloud, snow*	Identify and initiate communication using the language of science throughout lesson and in everyday activities. Build language through concept training (e.g., describing words such as *liquid, heavy*).	Developing and using models
Ask, "What do you know about _____." (Show materials).	Describe materials using picture symbols, GoTalk software on an iPad programmed with descriptor words (*wet/heavy*).	Developing and using models
Fill in the *K* (Know) on the KWHL chart. Response ideas: Students may self-direct use of the chart with naturally occurring prompts during the lesson (e.g., record K after class discussion). If presenting the KWHL chart on SMART Board technology, students/teacher can drag picture representations into appropriate box on the graphic organizer. Student uses his or her own iPad to touch the appropriate box in the KWHL graphic organizer, then uses text-to-speech option to fill the boxes.		
Ask, "What do you want to know?"	Ask questions based on wonder story and/or previous research or peer questions.	Asking questions and defining problems; engaging in argument from evidence
Fill in the *W* (Want to know) on the KWHL chart (see response ideas previously listed).		
Ask, "What do you think will happen in the experiment? What is your prediction?"	Make prediction based on previous knowledge (review pictures from other lessons in unit: condensation and evaporation).	Asking questions and defining problems; engaging in argument from evidence
Ask, "How can we start to answer our questions? What tools do you want to use today?"	Identify appropriate tools to collect data (e.g., which of the five senses are needed; a microscope can be used to see the rain). Respond to peers' choices of tools needed; backup choices with how tool will help.	Planning and carrying out investigations; engaging in argument from evidence
Fill in the *H* (How) on the KWHL chart (see response ideas previously listed).		
Conduct experiment	Make choices during experiment based on prior step of research (e.g., hold model of cloud [dry sponge = no rain; add water to sponge = rain]). Analyze what to do next; push on sponge.	Developing and using models; planning and carrying out investigations;

Figure 10.4.   Sample lesson plan task analysis highlighting science practices in action.

	Describe what would push on a cloud in the sky; not our hands. Using the representation model of a cloud and simulation of air pressure on the cloud, communicate what is happening.	using mathematics and computational thinking; obtaining, evaluating, and communicating information
Teacher will:	**Extending science practices:** **Students will:**	**Science practice**
Compare/contrast (same/different)	Use materials/models/numerical data to compare by matching pictures to materials, sorting, and/or completing a Venn diagram. Compare cloud without moisture versus cloud with moisture/no air pressure versus cloud with moisture/air pressure.	Developing and using models; analyzing and interpreting data; using mathematics and computational thinking; engaging in argument from evidence
Concept statement	Assist in building concept statement. Identify concept statement from choice of two to three options (When the liquid in clouds get heavy it falls as precipitation). Build first/then/therefore sequence with pictures (First: cloud ...Then: moisture in cloud/air pressure pushing on it ... Therefore: precipitation).	Using mathematics and computational thinking; constructing explanations; obtaining, evaluating, and communicating information
Review experiment results/ask, "Why?"	Review prediction; change if needed. Answer *why* questions by demonstrating the steps of the experiment that were essential to making it rain.	Analyzing and interpreting data; using mathematics and computational thinking; constructing explanations
Summarize concepts and next set of questions	Review prediction to identify why it was correct/incorrect (using evidence to support). Identify next question using pictures/words within a sequencing chart.	Developing and using models; constructing explanations; obtaining, evaluating, and communicating information
Fill in the *L* (Learn) on the KWHL chart (see response ideas previously listed).		

Three months in the future . . . Elijah's teachers have begun to use the NRC framework's eight practices to design science instruction. His teachers not only teach core ideas and concepts (e.g., condensation, the water cycle) to Elijah, but they also have been developing lessons that build Elijah's ability to ask questions with his assistive device, such as, "Why does that happen?" Elijah has always noticed things in his natural world; however, now he is taking an active role in investigating when, why, and how things occur. Last week Elijah's class was learning about rocks and how they change over time (with pressure, heat, and cooling). His teachers provided many opportunities for him to ask questions, take data about his observations, and use the data to form answers (that will eventually lead to the next set of questions). Although Elijah is learning new science content, the most exciting thing for Elijah, his family, and friends is that he is also starting to ask questions at home and in the community when he really wants to know something. Science practices built into his daily education provide him the skills needed to make personally relevant connections . . . today Elijah communicated with pride "Butterfly. Change. Rocks. Change."

SUMMARY

Inquiry is not something one does in a science lesson, it is science! Students with severe disabilities should engage in science practices through hands-on, thought-provoking experiences. Regardless of the big ideas being taught, all students are expected to actively participate and grow within their questioning, communicating, and depth of understanding of unifying concepts and core ideas over time.

REFERENCES

Achieve, Inc. (2013a). *The next generation science standards*. Retrieved from http://www .nextgenscience.org/next-generation-science-standards

Achieve, Inc. (2013b). *The next generation science standards: Appendix D: All standards, all students: Case studies*. Retrieved from http://www.nextgenscience.org/next-genera tion- science-standards

Achieve, Inc. (2013c). *The next generation science standards: Appendix E: Disciplinary core idea progressions*. Retrieved from http://www.nextgenscience.org/next-generation-science-standards

Achieve, Inc. (2013d). *The next generation science standards: Appendix F: Science and engineering practices*. Retrieved from http://www.nextgenscience.org/next-generation-science-standards

Browder, D.M., Trela, K., Courtade, G.R., Jimenez, B.A., Knight, V., & Flowers, C. (2012). Teaching mathematics and science standards to students with moderate and severe developmental disabilities. *The Journal of Special Education, 46*, 26–35.

Courtade, G.R., Browder, D.M., Spooner, F., & DiBiase, W. (2010). Training teachers to use an inquiry-based task analysis to teach science to students with moderate and severe disabilities. *Education & Training in Developmental Disabilities, 45*, 378–399.

Ford, M., & Forman, E.A. (2006). Learning and instruction in science: Elaborating the design approach. In C. Conrad & R.C. Serlin (Eds.), *Sage handbook for research in education: Engaging ideas and enriching inquiry* (pp. 139–155). Thousand Oaks, CA: Sage Publications.

Forman, E.A. (2003). A sociocultural approach to mathematics reform: Speaking, inscribing, and doing mathematics within communities of practice. In J. Kilpatrick, G. Martin, & D. Schifter (Eds.), *A research companion to the NCTM Standards* (pp. 333–352). Reston, VA: National Council of Teachers of Mathematics.

Jimenez, B.A., Browder, D.M., & Courtade, G.R. (2009). An exploratory study of self-directed science concept learning by students with moderate intellectual disabilities. *Research and Practice for Persons with Severe Disabilities, 34*, 1–14.

Jimenez, B.A., Browder, D.M., Spooner, F., & DiBiase, W. (2012). Inclusive inquiry science using peer-mediated embedded instruction for students with moderate intellectual disabilities. *Exceptional Children, 78*, 301–317.

Jimenez, B.A., Lo, Y., & Saunders, A. (2012). The additive effects of scripted lessons plus guided notes on science quiz scores of students with intellectual disabilities and autism. *Journal of Special Education*. Advance online publication:doi:10.1177/0022466912437 937

Knight, V.F., Smith, B.R., Spooner, F., & Browder, D. (2012).Using explicit instruction to teach science descriptors to students with autism spectrum disorders. *Journal of Autism and Developmental Disorders, 42*, 378–389.

Manz, E. (2012). Understanding the codevelopment of modeling practice and ecological knowledge. *Science Education, 96*, 1071–1105.

National Governors Association Center for Best Practices, Council of Chief State School Officers. (2010). *Common Core State Standards.* Washington, DC: Authors. Retrieved from http://www.corestandards.org/

National Research Council. (1996). *National science education standards.* Washington, NC: The National Academies Press.

National Research Council. (2007). *Taking science to school: Learning and teaching science in grades K–8.* Washington, DC: The National Academies Press.

National Research Council. (2012). *A framework for K-12 science education: Practice, crosscutting concepts, and core ideas.* Washington, DC: The National Academic Press.

No Child Left Behind Act of 2001, P.L. 107-110, 115 Stat. 1425, 20 U.S.C. §§ 6301 *et seq.*

Smith, B.R., Spooner, F., Jimenez, B., & Browder, D.M. (2013). Using an early science curriculum to teach science vocabulary and concepts to students with severe developmental disabilities. *Education & Treatment of Children, 36*, 1–31. doi:10.1353/etc.2013.0002

Spooner, F., Knight, V., Browder, D., Jimenez, B.A., & DiBiase, W. (2011). Evaluating evidence-based practices in teaching science content to students with severe developmental disabilities. *Research and Practice for Persons with Severe Disabilities, 36*, 62–75.

Trela, K., & Jimenez, B. (2013). From functional to personally relevant curriculum: A reflection on the shift from "different" to "differentiated curriculum for students with significant intellectual disabilities. *Research and Practice for Persons with Severe Disabilities, 38*, 117–119.

FOR FURTHER INFORMATION

Curricular Supports to Build Student Inquiry

Early Science Curriculum

http://www.attainmentcompany.com/early-science-curriculum

This research-based elementary curriculum was developed for students with significant developmental disabilities, including autism. It systematically teaches the process of inquiry through hands-on lessons.

Science Step by Step

http://www.attainmentcompany.com/science-step-by-step

This curriculum provides science lessons developed with picture-based directions for hands-on discovery activities.

Teaching to Standards: SCIENCE

http://www.attainmentcompany.com/teaching-standards-science

This research-based secondary curriculum was developed for students with moderate to severe intellectual disability. It uses an inquiry approach to teach new science concepts and vocabulary through experiments.

TcH: Teaching Channel

https://www.teachingchannel.org/videos?page=1&categories=subjects_ science,topics_common-core&load=1

This web site includes hundreds of short videos of real lessons, including sample science lessons using inquiry.

Inquiry Science and Students with Disabilities

Ahlgrim-Delzell, L., Knight, V.F., & Jimenez, B.A. (2009). *Research-based practices for creating access to the general curriculum in science for students with significant intellectual disabilities.* Retrieved from http://www.ksde.org/LinkClick.aspx?fileticket=oSN MPjmFS7M%3D&tabid=2384&mid=9027

Duran E., Duran L., Haney, J., & Scheuermann, A. (2011). A learning cycle for all students: Modifying the 5E instructional model to address the needs of all learners. *The Science Teacher, 78*(3), 56–60.

Online Professional Development Supports

Science Instruction: Students with Significant Intellectual Disabilities

http://mast.ecu.edu/modules/ssid_se

This web site provides free online professional development modules to support science instruction for students with severe disabilities. Modules are designed to provide research-based practices in academic instruction for students with intellectual disability, as well as video and lesson planning supports.

Web Sites

American Association for the Advancement of Science (AAAS) Science NetLinks

http://www.sciencenetlinks.com

This premier K–12 science education resource includes teaching tools, interactives, podcasts, and hands-on activities.

Annenberg Learner

http://www.learner.org

This web site contains teacher resources and videos directly related to core ideas in life sciences for K–6.

Brainpop

http://www.brainpop.com

This web site contains kid-friendly explanations of major science concepts.

National Aeronautics and Space Administration (NASA) Educator Resources

http://www.nasa.gov/audience/foreducators/index.html

This web site contains many videos, teacher resources, current events, and scientific information about space sciences.

National Oceanic and Atmospheric Administration (NOAA) Education Resources

http://www.education.noaa.gov/

This web site includes many videos, teacher resources, and scientific information about weather, climate, and oceans.

National Science Teachers Association (NSTA) Learning Center

http://www.learningcenter.nsta.org

This web site has a video archive for teachers to learn more about any content area necessary to teach core disciplinary ideas. Further, NSTA also has SciGuides (http://learningcenter.nsta.org/products/sciguides.aspx), which are a collection of thematically aligned lesson plans, simulations, and web-based resources for teachers to use with their students centered on standards-aligned science concepts.

Next Generation Science Standards

http://www.nextgenscience.org/next-generation-science-standards

This web site provides an outline of how the standards were developed, why they were developed, how to use the standards in everyday practice, and several resources to support educators align instruction to the Framework.

Smithsonian Science Education Center

http://www.ssec.si.edu/

This web site contains free resources for teaching science, including lesson ideas, interactive videos, and teacher preparation videos.

United States Department of Agriculture (USDA) Forest Service Conservation Education

http://www.fs.usda.gov/main/conservationeducation/educator-toolbox/ elementary

This web site contains resources for teaching conservation concepts.

CHAPTER 11

Teaching Science Concepts

Fred Spooner, Bethany R. McKissick,
Victoria Knight, and Ryan Walker

The teacher begins class by displaying a picture of the Grand Canyon and asks the class, "Does anyone know where this is?" One student answers, "It's the mountains," another student says, "It's the desert," and finally a student responds, "It's the Grand Canyon! I've been there." "You're right," replies the teacher, "It is the Grand Canyon." She then asks the class "Why does it look like that?" and students begin to call out answers. While the students provide a variety of responses, Rebekah, a student with autism spectrum disorder (ASD), continues to draw circles on a sheet of paper. The teacher then announces, "Today we are going to learn about erosion." When Rebekah finally looks up from her paper, the students have broken into groups and are gathering materials to create their own land models to investigate the process of erosion. After the teacher helps Rebekah find her group, Rebekah watches her group make a land model and complete the experiment of changing the model with wind and water. The teacher then asks the class, "What causes erosion?" Again, Rebekah goes back to drawing circles on her paper.

A problem with the traditional approach to teaching science (that of a content-, text-based approach) often used in the past, is that the facts that were taught were often unrelated terms and figures that were memorized and soon forgotten (Walker, 2012). The benefits of teaching science concepts with inquiry is that students gain ownership of the information and have the ability to tell a complete story using supporting information that cannot be separated from the process of science (see Chapter 10). Concepts and knowledge that are derived through scientific processes are tentative in nature yet durable. This means what scientists accept as a working understanding helps them continue their work, but as new information comes to the surface, scientists must continually reevaluate previously accepted theory to fit a new model. Thus, the scientific community is continuously evolving and scientific knowledge is ever changing, but the scientific

Support for this chapter was provided in part by Grant No. R324A080014 from the U.S. Department of Education, Institute of Education Sciences, awarded to the University of North Carolina at Charlotte. The opinions expressed do not necessarily reflect the position or policy of the Department of Education, and no official endorsement should be inferred.

induction process produces reliable information that is long-lasting in nature and replicable (McComas, 1996). They provide a foundation on which students can further their understanding of related concepts (McComas, 1996). It is this characteristic of science processes that makes scientific knowledge different from other types of knowing, adding value beyond random facts.

The Common Core State Standards (CCSS; National Governors Association Center for Best Practices, Council of Chief State School Officers, 2010) specifically address scientific literacy from a reading and writing perspective. The CCSS stress the importance for students to critically evaluate text by using reasoned judgment and speculation of supporting facts. The importance of teaching science concepts with inquiry or processes of science are also echoed within the American Association for the Advancement of Science (AAAS; 1989) and the Next Generation Science Standards (Achieve, Inc., 2013). These guidelines for science educators not only advocate for the teaching of concepts through inquiry but also require science teachers to teach the steps of the inquiry process explicitly.

As educators transition from a traditional approach to teaching science in which the emphasis is on vocabulary and general facts to a comprehensive, global process of teaching concepts through the process of science, the need for effective and research-based strategies to teach conceptual knowledge to students with severe disabilities, who may require repeated and systematic strategies in order to acquire content knowledge, is paramount.

WHAT WE KNOW ABOUT TEACHING SCIENCE TO STUDENTS WITH SEVERE DISABILITIES

Based on the emphasis to teach academic content—primarily literacy, mathematics, and science—to students with severe disabilities, as predicated by the Individuals with Disabilities Education Improvement Act (IDEA) of 2004 (PL108-446) and the No Child Left Behind Act of 2001 (PL 107-110), educators know more about teaching literacy than mathematics, and more about teaching mathematics than science. For example, in a literature review conducted by Spooner, Knight, Browder, Jimenez, and DiBiase (2011), only 17 studies were found in the area of science. Systematic instruction has been documented as an evidence-based practice for teaching academics in these content areas for students with severe disabilities (Smith, Spooner, Jimenez, & Browder, 2013; Spooner, Knight, Browder, & Smith, 2012). Specifically in the area of science, most of the content that has been taught is representative of Content Standard F in the National Science Education Standards (NSES; National Research Council [NRC], 1996).

Content Standard F: Science in Personal and Social Perspectives of the National Science Education Standards contains information related to personal health; populations, resources, and environments; natural hazards; benefits and risks; and science and technology in society. Until the early 2000s, teaching science content to students with severe disabilities has focused on teaching functional skills such as first aid skills. As a field, educators have been teaching safety-related skills to students with severe disabilities since the mid-1980s (e.g., Bannerman, Sheldon, & Sherman, 1991; Collins & Griffen, 1996; Katz & Singh, 1986; Spooner, Stem, & Test, 1989). Initial work in the area of science started with the Courtade, Spooner, and Browder (2007) review, which examined the literature for a 20-year period

(1985–2005). This review found that safety skills are legitimately science content (meaning although they are functional in nature, they fall under science content standards) that were validated by a science content expert (a science education researcher). Eight of the 11 studies focused on teaching some form of first aid and safety skills (e.g., Collins & Stinson, 1995; Winterling, Gast, Wolery, & Farmer, 1992); however, only three of the eight NSES standards (Content Standard B: Physical Science [teaching mobility when lost in the community], Content Standard D: Earth and Space Science [teaching weather words], Content Standard F: Science in Personal and Social Perspectives [teaching safety]) were being taught to students with severe disabilities (Browder & Shear, 1996; Taber, Alberto, Hughes, & Seltzer, 2002; Taber, Alberto, Seltzer, & Hughes, 2003). The Spooner and colleagues (2011) review extended the Courtade and colleagues (2007) review by addressing the *how*, *what*, and *why* of science instruction and by applying quality indicator criteria, quantity and dispersion requirements for single-case design research (Horner et al., 2005), and the National Secondary Transition Technical Assistance Center (2010; Test et al., 2009) guidelines for defining evidence-based practices for teaching science content for students with disabilities.

In defining an evidence-based practice, investigators analyze both the methodological quality and magnitude of available research on a practice (Cook, Tankersley, & Landrun, 2009; Gersten et al., 2005; Horner et al., 2005). Although there have been several quality indicator guidelines that have been proposed to document evidence-based practices for different research methodologies (e.g., qualitative [Brantlinger, Jimenez, Klingner, Pugach, & Richardson, 2005], quantitative [Gersten et al., 2005]), in the area of severe disabilities, there has been predominate use of single-case designs to answer research questions (McDonnell & O'Neill, 2003; ~~Riscarch~~ Spooner et al., 2011). From a single-case research design perspective, this means applying Horner and colleagues (2005) quality indicator guidelines (e.g., 20 variables across seven major areas, participants, settings, dependent variables, independent variables) to each study. Once quality indicator criteria have been met, then the total collection of studies is examined for quantity and dispersion requirements (i.e., 5 studies, 3 investigators, 3 geographic locations, and a minimum of 20 participants). When applying the Horner and colleagues quality indicator criteria to discern if there were evidence-based practices for teaching science content to students with severe disabilities, educators discovered that systematic instruction, as an overarching instructional package, was an evidence based-practice (Spooner et al., 2011).

RESEARCH-BASED PRACTICES FOR STUDENTS WITH MODERATE TO SEVERE DISABILITIES

Systematic instruction has been used as an overarching instructional strategy to teach students with severe disabilities beginning with the first applied investigation (Fuller, 1949), a variety of functional skills (e.g., dressing [Azrin, Schaeffer, & Wesolowski, 1976], safety [Bannerman et al., 1991]), and academic content (literacy, mathematics, and science; Spooner et al., 2012). In general, systematic instruction is a set of procedures used to teach socially important skills by 1) defining target skills that are detectable and quantifiable; 2) generating behavior change that can be generalized to other people, materials, contexts, and skills; 3) using data to demonstrate that skills were a function of the independent variable; and 4) using behavioral principles to promote transfer of stimulus control (Collins, 2007; Drascow, Wolery, Halle, & Hajiaghamohseni, 2011; Snell, 1983; Spooner et al., 2011; Stokes & Baer, 1977; Wolery, Bailey, & Sugai, 1988).

Time Delay to Teach Vocabulary Instruction

Time delay is one of the most supported practices in teaching vocabulary to students with severe disabilities (Spooner et al., 2011, 2012). Collins (2012) defined constant time delay as a systematic and errorless teaching strategy in which a controlling prompt is provided after a specific delay interval of time and naturally fades as the learner begins to perform the desired behavior (e.g., verbal identification of a word) before the delivery of the controlling prompt. At the beginning of instruction, the delay between presentation of the stimulus and the controlling prompt is 0 seconds. Following a set number of 0-second trials, the instructor inserts a designated delay interval (e.g., 3 seconds) between the presentation of the stimulus and delivering the controlling prompt. The time delay can either be progressive or constant. In progressive time delay, instead of moving immediately from a 0-second delay interval to a 3-second delay interval, the instructor may slowly increase the delay interval from 0 seconds to 1 second to 2 seconds at a predetermined pace over a number of sessions (Collins, 2012). Progressive time delay may be more effective for students who have difficulty waiting and who often make incorrect guesses before a controlling prompt is delivered.

Collins and Griffen (1996) used constant time delay to teach four elementary school students with severe disabilities to read product warning labels found on cleaning supplies. Johnson and McDonnell (2004) used constant time delay embedded within a general education setting to teach parts of an insect and plant cell. Jimenez, Browder, Spooner, and DiBiase (2012) used peer-mediated time delay to teach science vocabulary definitions and how to identify a picture to go along with the definition (e.g., a picture of a roller coaster in motion to represent kinetic energy) within an inclusive middle school science classroom.

When considering Rebekah from the opening vignette, the teacher could have provided flash cards with key words written on them (e.g., *mountain, water, wind*), possibly with accompanying pictures. Using these cards, the teacher could have implemented a few time-delay trials to teach Rebekah the vocabulary used in that day's lesson. This type of instruction may have increased her participation in the first part of the lesson, which was geared toward engagement and activating any previous background knowledge.

Task Analytic Instruction to Teach Chained Skills

A task analysis is a break down of a chained task (which is any task that has multiple steps) into smaller steps for instruction (Collins, 2012). For example, a task analysis for completing a science experiment may include steps for gathering materials, setting up the experiment, conducting the experiment, and analyzing results. The task of gathering materials could be one step or broken down into multiple steps, depending on the needs of the student. A student who requires extensive supports may need extra steps, for example.

Smith, Spooner, Jimenez, and Browder (2013) used a task analysis implemented by a special education teacher to provide content-rich science inquiry lessons to teach students with severe disabilities skills pertaining to the inquiry process (e.g., how to make a prediction, how to implement an experiment). Browder, Trela, Courtade, Knight, and Flowers (2010) provided special education teachers task analyzed science inquiry lesson plans along with materials for a hands-on experiment/activity. In both of these studies, the special education teacher used the system of least prompts procedure (Jimenez, Knight, & Browder, 2012; see Table 11.1). In this procedure, a learner is first given the opportunity to respond independently. If the student does not make an independent response, an instructor provides prompts

Table 11.1. Example task analysis from an early science curriculum

Teaching step 1: Read wonder story. Place question on the KWHL (Know, Want to know, How to find out, what is Learned) chart.
- *Student response:* Find the question
- *Lesson concept: Circle of life*

Teaching step 2: Teach new vocabulary with time delay.
- *Student response:* Point to picture at 0-second delay; point to picture at 5-second delay (out of an array of at least three choices)
- *Lesson concept: Dead, decay*

Teaching step 3: Review prior concept statements for the unit and fill in the *K* on the KWHL chart.
- *Student response:* Point to picture for each review concept statement (out of an array of at least 3 choices)
- *Lesson concept: Plants, plants and animals, life cycle, change, grow, living, need*

Teaching step 4: Engage students in activity.
- *Student response:* Engage with materials
- *Lesson concept: None*

Teaching step 5: Teach discrimination of concept (e.g., example/nonexample).
- *Student response:* Point to object for concept
- *Lesson concept: Living/dead* (Use pictures and real plants if you have them.)

Teaching step 6: INVESTIGATE: Ask students for a prediction.
- *Student response:* Select yes/no for prediction
- *Lesson concept: I think plants and animals are/are not always living*

Teaching step 7: Fill in the *H* on the KWHL chart.
- *Student response:* Pick appropriate sense
- *Lesson concept: Eyes to see*

Teaching step 8: Review safety rule.
- *Student response:* N/A
- *Lesson concept: #5*

Teaching step 9: Conduct experiment.
- *Student response:* Engage with materials
- *Lesson concept: Living/dead*

Teaching step 10: Present two concept statements at a 0-second delay.
- *Student response:* Point to picture to complete each statement
- *Lesson concept: (0-second delay) ___is a dead plant; dead plants and animals ____*

(continued)

Table 11.1. *(continued)*

Teaching step 11: DESCRIBE: Ask students what happened and give second trial on concept statements (0-second delay).
- *Student response:* Point to picture to complete each concept statement
- *Lesson concept: (0-second delay) ___ is a dead plant; dead plants and animals ___*

Teaching step 12: Give third trial with concept statement (5-second delay).
- *Student response:* Point to picture to complete each concept statement
- *Lesson concept: (5-second delay) ___ is a dead plant; dead plants and animals ___*

Teaching step 13: EXPLAIN: Review prediction.
- *Student response:* Select yes/no for prediction correct
- *Lesson concept: Yes/no*

Teaching step 14: REPORT: Point to materials during a fourth trial of concept statements (5-second delay).
- *Student response:* Point to picture to complete each concept statement; Put on KWHL chart under L
- *Lesson concept: (5-second delay) ___ is a dead plant; Dead plants and animals ___*

Teaching step 15: Discuss the learn statement.
- *Student response:* Put on KWHL chart under L
- *Lesson concept: I know this because....*

Teaching step 16: Complete the student report.
- *Student response:* Point to picture to be pasted into report
- *Lesson concept: Dead, decay*

From Jimenez, B., Knight, V., & Browder, D. (2012). *Early science curriculum.* Verona, WI: Attainment Company; adapted by permission.

from least to most intrusive using a predetermined prompt hierarchy (e.g., verbal prompt, verbal prompt with model, hand-over-hand prompt).

Within Rebekah's classroom, it is possible that including this task analysis for all students could have resulted in increased engagement and independence during the experiment. Instead of watching her group complete the experiment, Rebekah could have been assigned responsibility for completing one or more of the steps of the experiment. Participating in the experiment also may have helped Rebekah understand the abstract concepts of erosion and change.

Explicit Instruction Using Examples/NonExamples

Although explicit instruction has more than 30 years of empirical support for teaching students with high incidence disabilities (e.g., Engelmann & Carnine, 1991; Goeke, 2009; Rosenshine & Stevens, 1986), the research supporting its use for students with severe disabilities has just begun to increase (Flores & Ganz, 2007; Ganz & Flores, 2009; Knight, Smith, Spooner, & Browder, 2012; Smith, Spooner, & Wood, 2013). Explicit instruction is an active process that emphasizes the student's role within the learning process by focusing on how the information is presented and how the student processes/organizes that information. The support or scaffolds provided by explicit instruction are the cornerstones for making the process successful in teaching new skills or behaviors to a variety of learners (Rosenshine, 1987). These scaffolds or supports are typically delivered using some variation of a model-lead-test format (Engelmann & Carnine, 1991). This strategy follows a script that typically includes key phrases such as, "My turn, with me, and your turn" or "I do, we do, and you do." Other key features of explicit instruction are the inclusion of research-based elements such as active engagement or activation of background knowledge (Goeke, 2009). This could include the presentation of an object, video, or sound clip that helps introduce the lesson. For example, while learning about the life cycle, a teacher may present students with pictures of the life cycle of a butterfly, insect, or animal the students are familiar with.

Knight and colleagues (2012) examined the effect of explicit instruction using a model-lead-test format to teach science descriptors (e.g., *heavy, change, living, dead*) to three elementary students with severe disabilities. In this study, researchers taught the science descriptors using tangible objects to represent each descriptor that the students could touch and manipulate. For example, when teaching the concept *living*, students discriminated between live and dead crickets so that students could observe movement, which is a relevant feature of being alive. While teaching the concept *change*, students had the opportunity to squish balls of clay to demonstrate changing the overall shape of the clay. Results of this study showed that not only was explicit instruction effective in providing instruction on those science descriptors but also participants were able to maintain acquired skills over time and generalize this information using novel materials and during a general education inquiry lesson.

Referring back to Rebekah, the teacher could have supported the discrimination between *change* and *no change* by using explicit instruction and land models or pictures of eroded landforms. Through explicit instruction, using manipulatives or models could have focused on the relevant features of change (e.g., does it look different, feel different) and provided her another hands-on activity to help make the abstract concept more concrete.

Embedded Instruction

Embedded instruction is loosely defined as providing instruction on skills used in ongoing routines or activities within the performance setting versus massed trials in a special education setting (McDonnell, 2011). For example, embedded instruction could be used to teach a student with a disability the concept of *living* versus *dead* within a science general education class during a lesson about the plant and animal life cycle. These embedded trials might occur during a warm-up activity, independent practice, or during a hands-on experiment. One key feature of embedded instruction is the flexibility of the embedded trials. This practice is meant to enhance instruction occurring in the general education setting; therefore, students are not pulled out to a separate setting or another part of the room during embedded instruction trials, and trials do not interfere with the instruction already occurring. A student should not miss out on the opportunity to participate in an experiment or demonstration to engage in embedded systematic instruction. Instead, the person implementing the embedded trials should wait until a more appropriate time, as described previously (e.g., independent practice).

Graphic Organizers

A graphic organizer is a visual aid that shows the connections among facts, concepts, or ideas. Graphic organizers can be especially helpful in science, in which the text is often insufficient for facilitating student comprehension of the material.

Students can see the similarities, differences, and connections among the subject matter by using various types of graphic organizers. For example, T-charts (i.e., a table with two columns in the shape of the letter T) can be used for sorting, cyclical sequence organizers can be used to show a cycle, KWHL (Know, Want to know, How to find out, what is Learned) charts can be used throughout an inquiry lesson, Venn diagrams can be used to compare two entities, cause and effect organizers can be used to show relationships, and idea webs can show how concepts are connected (Figures 11.1 and 11.2).

The use of graphic organizers has also been shown to be a research-based method to promote conceptual development in science for students with moderate and severe disabilities. For example, Knight, Spooner, Browder, Smith, and Wood (2013) used a T-chart and a cyclical sequence organizer to facilitate student acquisition of the concept of *convection* (Figure 11.3). T-charts can be used to sort concepts into two columns (e.g., vertebrates, invertebrates; animals, plants; living, nonliving). In the Knight and colleagues study, the researcher first used constant time delay (CTD) to teach students the vocabulary and definitions related to convection. Then, she implemented explicit instruction (e.g., examples and nonexamples, model-lead-test procedure) using a T-chart with the word *Yes* on the left side of the chart and the word *No* on the right side of the chart (see Figure 11.3). After the model and lead phases (described previously), students were tested on whether or not a picture was an example or nonexample of a vocabulary word used in the convection cycle. For example, when a student was shown a picture of a cloud without rain, hail, or sleet, the researcher asked, "Is this an example of precipitation?

Figure 11.1. Example of a completed cyclical sequence organizer showing convection. (From Knight, V.F., Spooner, F., Browder, D., Smith, B.R., & Wood, C.L. [2013]. Using systematic instruction and graphic organizers to teach science concepts to students with autism spectrum disorders and intellectual disability. *Focus on Autism and Other Developmental Disabilities, 28*[2], 115–126; reprinted by permission.)

Graphic organizer 1

Graphic organizer 2

Graphic organizer 3

Graphic organizer 4

Figure 11.2. Multiple examples of graphic organizers for the concept of convection. (From Knight, V.F., Spooner, F., Browder, D., Smith, B.R., & Wood, C.L. [2013]. Using systematic instruction and graphic organizers to teach science concepts to students with autism spectrum disorders and intellectual disability. *Focus on Autism and Other Developmental Disabilities, 28*[2], 115–126; reprinted by permission.)

Why or why not?" The researcher provided both close-in (e.g., a cloud *without* rain, snow, or hail) and divergent (e.g., a picture showing evaporation) nonexamples. The student was asked to sort multiple examples and nonexamples to identify correct examples of the concept by placing the example under either the *Yes* or *No* column on the T-chart.

Once students could accurately place all examples and nonexamples of the vocabulary words related to convection on the T-chart, the instructor used multiple examples of a cyclical sequence organizer to teach students where the vocabulary word was placed on the graphic organizer. Cyclical sequence organizers can demonstrate various cycles that occur in nature (e.g., ATP cycle for cellular respiration, photosynthesis, life cycle). Some organizers showed the weather cycle with a beach scene, and in others there was a mountain scene with a river; the multiple examples ensured that the students were not simply memorizing where to place the definitions without an understanding of the concept (see Figures 11.1 and 11.2). Finally, the cyclic nature of convection was taught using CTD to connect the arrows between concepts. The examiner would say, "Heated water causes evaporation." As the examiner said, "causes," she put the arrow in between "heated" and "evaporation." At 0-second delay, the student then imitated this model of placing the arrow.

Another type of graphic organizer supported by research for students with moderate and severe disabilities is the KWHL chart (Figure 11.4). KWHL charts

Figure 11.3. Example of a completed T-chart showing examples and nonexamples of precipitation. (From Knight, V.F., Spooner, F., Browder, D., Smith, B.R., & Wood, C.L. [2013]. Using systematic instruction and graphic organizers to teach science concepts to students with autism spectrum disorders and intellectual disability. *Focus on Autism and Other Developmental Disabilities, 28*[2], 115–126; reprinted by permission.)

can be used throughout an inquiry lesson and can assist students with disabilities in general education settings and resource settings. KWHL charts help students organize information on what they know and what they want to learn about a particular topic before and after the research is completed. KWHL charts can increase participation in cooperative learning groups, attention to the inquiry lesson, and recording information from the lesson (Browder et al., 2010).

For example, Jimenez, Browder, and colleagues (2012) used a KWHL chart across lessons and units to teach and assess students' self-monitoring of the inquiry

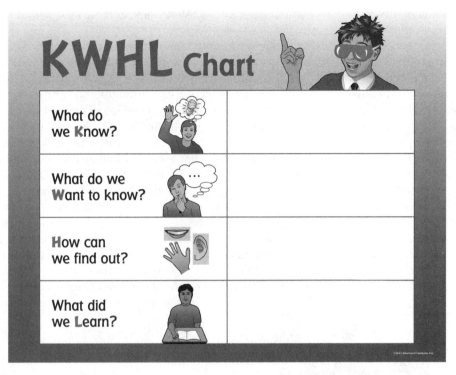

Figure 11.4.   KWHL (Know, Want to know, How to find out, what is Learned) chart. (From Jimenez, B., Knight, V., & Browder, D. [2012]. *Early science curriculum.* Verona, WI: Attainment Company, reprinted by permission.)

process throughout the lesson. In this study, all students with disabilities received new KWHL charts for each lesson, and the teacher used a poster-sized KWHL chart for the entire general education class.

Both of the visuals described in this section could have not only supported Rebekah's learning and engagement within the science classroom but also could have helped all students organize the information. The teacher addresses, at some level, what the students already know and includes an experiment (i.e., how will we find out?). Finally, reviewing what the students had learned would have given all of the students an opportunity to provide some deeper reflection.

Computer-Assisted Instruction

The Association for Educational Communications and Technology (1977) has defined computer-assisted instruction as a method in which a computer is used to teach, guide, and test the student until a desired level of proficiency is attained. This includes the application of any computer software to address a student's educational needs, often focusing on providing instruction to remediate deficits of facts and concepts (Edyburn, Higgins, & Boone, 2005; Hedges, Konstantopoulos, & Thoreson, 2000). Although computer-assisted instruction does not yet have enough research support to be called an evidence-based practice, it is an effective method for increasing conceptual knowledge in the content area of science for students with moderate and severe disabilities (Knight, McKissick, & Saunders, 2013; Pennington, 2010).

In one example of using computer-assisted instruction to teach science content, Smith, Spooner, and Wood (2013) used a PowerPoint slide show and an iPad to teach students with severe disabilities science terms (e.g., *chromosomes*) and applications of those terms representing concepts (e.g., threadlike structures in the nucleus are called _____). The researcher used a version of explicit instruction that included alternating model-test phases. The first slide included the phrase *My turn, this picture shows* _____, and the correct response option highlighted (Figure 11.5). In addition, the researcher recorded her own voice, which automatically read the statement and the correct response option (i.e., "This picture shows chromosomes"). The following slide included the statement *Your turn: This picture shows* _____ and the recorded voice read the statement and all of the response options (i.e., "This picture shows... a pizza, organ, chromosomes, or mitosis"). If the student touched the correct response, the slide advanced. If the student touched an incorrect response, the same highlighting feature that was used on the model slides appeared. Then, the student touched the correct response indicated by the highlighting and continued with the slideshow presentation.

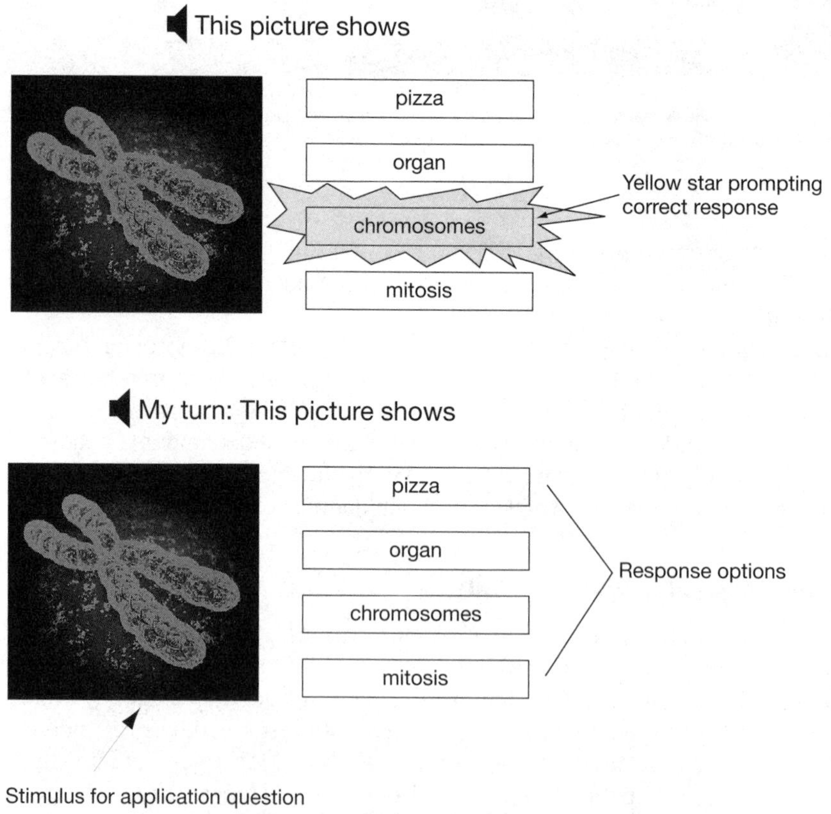

Figure 11.5. Sample probe and intervention slides. (Reprinted from Smith, B.R., Spooner, F., & Wood, C.L. [2013]. Using embedded computer-assisted explicit instruction to teach science to students with autism spectrum disorder. *Research in Autism Spectrum Disorders, 7,* 433–434. Copyright 2013 with permission from Elsevier.)

Science Instruction in the Inclusive Setting

Scientific literacy is a goal for all students, including students with disabilities (AAAS, 1989). Inquiry science also includes a hands-on process approach, which may benefit many students with severe disabilities versus traditional approaches. Systematic instructional procedures, such as CTD, task analysis, and embedded instruction can be used to teach science concepts (e.g., kinetic energy, homeostasis) within the inclusive setting (e.g., Jimenez, Browder et al., 2012; Smith et al., 2013). The use of computer-assisted instruction via portable devices can diminish common barriers to inclusion (e.g., the "hovering adult"), allowing students to interact with one another. In a content area in which working within scientific lab groups is key, being able to access the content in order to be an active member within a group is vital in learning the concepts.

BUILDING ON RESEARCH FOR PRACTICE

This section includes examples of the research- and evidence-based practices described in this chapter. Included within these examples are some helpful how-to tips as well as components teachers may need to consider when adapting science content for individual student abilities. Remember, it is important to consider a student's current mode of communication (e.g., does the student use pictures or require concrete objects?) and the types of responses a student already has in his or her repertoire of responding (e.g., does the student answer yes/no questions accurately, can the student generate a response independently or does he or she need options?).

How to Create Graphic Organizers

Teachers can easily create their own graphic organizers using a variety of approaches (e.g., Microsoft Word/Excel, Boardmaker, Inspiration software, IOS applications). In order to create a graphic organizer, the teacher must decide which concept(s) he or she wants to teach and then determine what type of graphic organizer to use. If a graphic organizer does not already exist for the content, the next step is to sketch out the graphic organizer by hand before trying to create it on the computer. Then the teacher should determine the best approach to creating the graphic organizer (e.g., which software/application to use) and search for possible applications for students who use iPads and iPods to complete schoolwork (e.g., Idea sketch, Popplet).

Creating Computer-Assisted Instruction

In order to be successful when creating computer-assisted instruction, teachers must consider 1) the abilities and needs of individual students, 2) the goal of the lesson, 3) the instructional design they will embed into the computer-assisted instruction, 4) the activities that the technology must support, and 5) how the nature of the technology will relate to the activities. Computer-assisted instruction interventions have demonstrated effectiveness when research- and evidenced-based practices are embedded within the intervention. Teachers should contemplate what aspects (e.g., stimulus prompting, error correction and feedback) might be beneficial for their students.

Creating Video Models

There are three types of models to use when creating video modeling interventions: 1) filming the target student doing the desired behavior/activity, 2) filming someone else doing the desired behavior/activity, and 3) filming the desired behavior/ activity from a personal perspective (i.e., it looks like you're actually doing it). When deciding which model would be most advantageous for their students, teachers must make several considerations.

When creating video models from the first perspective, teachers should remember that this model requires a high level of teacher attention and that the student must perform all of the steps in the skill. In addition, it may require advanced editing skills to paste clips together to create a finished project. As a final component of this model, teachers should remember students may behave differently simply because they are being filmed.

When considering the second model, teachers should remember that this model works best when the person filmed is familiar or highly motivating for the students to watch. Although this model may not require editing, a teacher may need an additional person available to record the entire model, and during filming a teacher will need to insert brief pauses if the skill is a chained behavior (e.g., using a microscope) to ensure a student has enough time to complete each step of the behavior chain.

If a teacher chooses to implement the third model for creating video modeling interventions, he or she must take into account that this model also requires an additional person to film the desired behavior/activity. When creating the video model, the teacher should ensure that the visible body parts (e.g., hands) are similar to the student to enhance the person-first experience. Finally, in this model, a teacher will not be able to address other behaviors during the activity (e.g., if the student should record observations from the microscope).

Slideshow Presentations

There are four key questions teachers should ask themselves when creating slideshow presentations to implement computer-assisted instruction. First, do students have the fine motor skills to use a computer and mouse or do they need a tablet PC? If tablets are required, it's important to make sure that the tablet software supports slideshow functions like hyperlinks and recorded audio. Second, should the slide show only advance if the student selects the correct response? If so, the teacher will need to program hyperlinks and turn off the "on mouse click option" under the Transitions menu. Third, will students require the information on the slides read to them? If so, the teacher will need to record his or her voice using the "record audio" option under the Insert menu. Finally, does the student easily memorize the order of correct response options? If so, the teacher will need to create different versions of each slide show presentation in which the order of stimuli and response options are varied.

Visual Aids

Similar to creating slide show presentations, there are several key considerations teachers must consider when creating visual aids. The first question is *why* use a visual aid? Determine if there is a better approach (e.g., multimedia, video, computer simulation) to present the material. Second, *what* should be taught? Teachers must not only determine the concept but also which visual aid will work the best. Third, *who* is being taught? The visual aid must match the symbolic level of communication the students use and how the students currently "show what they know." Fourth, *how* will the concept be taught and the visual aid used? Effective visual aids must highlight the salient aspects of the visual aid and eliminate the rest, limiting the amount of material (e.g., text, pictures) on any one aid. Finally, will the aid be used to teach, to test, or both?

Collaborating with Science Educators   *Big @ H.S.*

One of the first steps in collaborating with science educators is to identify the priority standards within the general education science curriculum for all students together. Second, whereas the special education teacher might define the alternate achievement for the students with disabilities, it is important to verify with the science educator that the alternate achievement is aligned with the core curriculum. The third step may be to use the inquiry task analysis designed by Browder and colleagues (2010) and determine the key vocabulary words and concept statements (or "big ideas" from the lesson) that will be used within the inquiry lesson. A science content expert can help to improve alignment to the science standards by verifying the vocabulary and concept statements, or he or she may be the one to determine the vocabulary words and concept statements. This will depend on the setting in which the instruction is delivered.

Research shows that grade-level content can be delivered in both self-contained and inclusive settings (e.g., Browder et al., 2010; Jimenez, Browder et al., 2012). Depending on the setting, both teachers and peers can be responsible for delivering systematic, embedded instruction. For example, in an inclusive setting, if the general education science teacher is responsible for embedding the numbers of trials needed for students to reach mastery, it may be cumbersome and could negatively impact the inquiry process for all students. One solution may be to use peers to deliver the trials. In some cases, special education teachers may need to provide additional trials beyond those given by the general education science teacher and/or peers. In addition, in an inquiry setting, it makes more sense for the science educator to use a universal design for learning approach to develop the key vocabulary and concept statements from the beginning for all of his or her students, rather than the special educator developing an alternate set of skills specifically for the students with disabilities after the lesson has been created. In thinking about the student vignette, strategies explained within this chapter would have supported many students, not just Rebekah.

SUMMARY

Science is part of the CCSS, and the recommendation is that it should be taught via the process of inquiry. Chapter 10 cogently outlines inquiry as an instructional process and provides a framework for its implementation in K–12 settings. Of the three academic areas (literacy, mathematics, and science) that have been the focus of instruction for IDEA 2004 and the No Child Left Behind Act of 2001, educators know the least about teaching science content to students with severe disabilities

(Spooner et al., 2011). This chapter has documented that students with severe disabilities can learn science concepts and vocabulary using evidence-based practices (e.g., task analysis, time delay), which are all part of the overarching package called systematic instruction. Additional work suggests that procedures such as explicit instruction, embedded instruction, graphic organizers, and computer-assisted instruction also have been successful at helping students with severe disabilities acquire science content.

REFERENCES

Achieve, Inc. (2013). *The next generation science standards.* Retrieved from http://www.nextgenscience.org/next-generation-science-standards

American Association for the Advancement of Science. (1989). *Science for all Americans.* New York, NY: Oxford University Press.

Association for Educational Communications and Technology. (1977). *Educational technology: Definition and glossary of terms (Vol. 1).* Washington, DC: Author.

Azrin, N.H., Schaeffer, R.M., & Wesolowski, M.D. (1976). A rapid method of teaching profoundly retarded persons to dress via a reinforcement-guidance method. *Mental Retardation, 14*(6), 29–33.

Bannerman, D.J., Sheldon, J.B., & Sherman, J.A. (1991). Teaching adults with severe and profound retardation to exit their homes upon hearing the fire alarm. *Journal of Applied Behavior Analysis, 24,* 571–577.

Brantlinger, E., Jimenez, R., Klingner, J., Pugach, M., & Richardson, V. (2005). Qualitative studies in special education. *Exceptional Children, 71,* 197–207.

Browder, D.M., & Shear, S.M. (1996). Interspersal of known items in a treatment package to teach sight words to students with behavior disorders. *The Journal of Special Education, 29,* 400–413.

Browder, D.M., Trela, K., Courtade, G.R., Knight, V.F., & Flowers, C. (2010). Teaching mathematics and science standards to students with moderate and severe developmental disabilities. *The Journal of Special Education, 46,* 26–35. doi:10.1177/0022466910369942

Collins, B.C. (Ed.). (2007). *Moderate and severe disabilities: A foundational approach.* Upper Saddle River, NJ: Pearson/Merrill/Prentice Hall.

Collins, B.C. (2012). *Systematic instruction for students with moderate and severe disabilities.* Baltimore, MD: Paul H. Brookes Publishing Co.

Collins, B.C., & Griffen, A.K. (1996). Teaching students with moderate disabilities to make safe responses to product warning labels. *Education & Treatment of Children, 19,* 30–45.

Collins, B.C., & Stinson, D.M. (1995). Teaching generalized reading of product warning labels to adolescents with mental disabilities through the use of key words. *Exceptionality, 5,* 163–181.

Cook, B.G., Tankersley, M., & Landrum, T.J. (2009). Determining evidence-based practices in special education. *Exceptional Children, 75,* 365–383.

Courtade, G., Spooner, F., & Browder, D.M. (2007). Review of studies with students with significant cognitive disabilities which link to science standards. *Research and Practice for Persons with Severe Disabilities, 32,* 43–49.

Drascow, E., Wolery, M., Halle, J., & Hajiaghamohseni, Z. (2011). Systematic instruction for students with severe disabilities. In J.M. Kauffman & D.P. Hallahan (Eds.), *Handbook of special education* (pp. 516–531). New York, NY: Routledge.

Edyburn, D., Higgins, K., & Boone, R. (2005). *Handbook of special education technology research and practice.* Whitefish Bay, WI: Knowledge by Design.

Engelmann, S., & Carnine, D. (1991). *Theories of instruction: Principles and applications.* Eugene, OR: ADI Press.

Flores, M.M., & Ganz, J.B. (2007). Effectiveness of direct instruction for teaching statement inference, use of facts, and analogies to students with developmental disabilities and reading delays. *Focus on Autism and Other Developmental Disabilities, 22,* 244–251.

Fuller, P.R. (1949). Operant conditioning of a vegetative human organism. *American Journal of Psychology, 62,* 587–590.

Ganz, J.B., & Flores, M.M. (2009). The effectiveness of direct instruction for teaching language to children with autism spectrum disorders: Identifying materials. *Journal of Autism and Developmental Disorders, 39,* 75–83.

Gast, D.L., Winterling, V., Wolery, M., & Farmer, J.A. (1992). Teaching first-aid skills to students with moderate handicaps in small group instruction. *Education & Treatment of Children, 15,* 101–124.

Gersten, R., Fuchs, L., Compton, D., Coyne, M., Greenwood, C., & Innocenti, M.S. (2005). Quality indicators for group experimental and quasi-experimental research in special education. *Exceptional Children, 71,* 149–164.

Goeke, J.L. (2009). *Explicit instruction: A framework for meaningful direct teaching.* Upper Saddle River, NJ: Merrill.

Hedges, L.V., Konstantopoulos, S., & Thoreson, A. (2000). *Computer use and its relation to academic achievement in mathematics, reading, and writing.* Retrieved from http://www.air.org/files/Hedges_computeruse.pdf

Horner, R.H., Carr, E.G., Halle, J., McGee, G., Odom, S., & Wolery, M. (2005). The use of single-subject research to identify evidence-based practice in special education. *Exceptional Children, 71,* 165–180.

Individuals with Disabilities Education Improvement Act (IDEA) of 2004, PL 108-466, 20 U.S.C. §§ 1400 *et seq.*

Jimenez, B.A., Browder, D., Spooner, F., & DiBiase, W. (2012). Inclusive inquiry science using peer-mediated embedded instruction for students with moderate intellectual disability. *Exceptional Children, 78,* 301–317.

Jimenez, B., Knight, V., & Browder, D.M. (2012). *Early science.* Verona, WI: Attainment Company.

Johnson, J.W., & McDonnell, J. (2004). An exploratory study of the implementation of embedded instruction by general educators with students with developmental disabilities. *Education & Treatment of Children, 27,* 46–63.

Katz, R.C., & Singh, N.N. (1986). Comprehensive fire safety training for adult mentally retarded persons. *Journal of Mental Deficiency Research, 30,* 59–69.

Knight, V.F., McKissick, B.R., & Saunders, A. (2013). A review of technology-based interventions to teach academic skills to students with autism spectrum disorder. *Journal of Autism and Developmental Disorders.* doi: 10.1007/s10803-013-1814-y

Knight, V.F., Smith, B.R, Spooner, F., & Browder, D.M. (2012). Using explicit instruction to teach science descriptors to students with autism spectrum disorders. *Journal of Autism and Developmental Disorders, 43,* 378–389. doi:10.1007/s10803-011-1258-1

Knight, V.F., Spooner, F., Browder, D., Smith, B.R., & Wood, C.L. (2013). *Using systematic instruction and graphic organizers to teach science consepts to students with autism spectrum disorders and intellectual disability. Focus on Autism and Other Developmental Disabilities, 28*(2), 115–126.

McComas, W. (1996). Ten myths of science: Re-examining what we think we know. *School Science & Mathematics, 96,* 10–16.

McDonnell, J.J. (2011). Instructional contexts. In J.M Kauffman & D.P. Hallahan (Eds.), *The handbook of special education* (pp. 532–543). New York, NY: Routledge.

McDonnell, J.J., & O'Neill, R. (2003). A perspective on single/within subject research methods and "scientifically based research." *Research and Practice for Persons with Severe Disabilities, 28,* 138–142.

National Governors Association Center for Best Practices, Council of Chief State School Officers. (2010). *Common Core State Standards.* Washington, DC: Authors. Retrieved from http://www.corestandards.org

National Research Council. (1996). *National science education standards.* Washington, DC: The National Academies Press.

National Secondary Transition Technical Assistance Center. (2010). *Decision rules.* Retrieved from: http://www.nsttac.org/sites/default/files/assets/pdf/pdf/ebps/LOEDecisionRules.pdf

No Child Left Behind Act of 2001, PL 107-110, 115 Stat. 1425, 20 U.S.C. §§ 6301 *et seq.*

Pennington, R.C. (2010). Computer-assisted instruction for teaching academic skills to students with autism spectrum disorders: A review of literature. *Focus on Autism and Other Developmental Disabilities, 25,* 239–248. doi:10.1177/1088357610378291

Rosenshine, B. (1987). Explicit teaching and teacher training. *Journal of Teacher Education, 38,* 34–36.

Rosenshine, B., & Stevens, R. (1986). Teaching functions. In M.C. Witrock (Ed.), *Handbook of research on teaching* (pp. 376–391). New York, NY: Macmillan.

Smith, B.R., Spooner, F., Jimenez, B., & Browder, D.M. (2013). Using an early science curriculum to teach science vocabulary and concepts to students with severe developmental disabilities. *Education & Treatment of Children, 36,* 1–31. doi:10.1353/etc.2013.0002

Smith, B.R., Spooner, F., & Wood, C.L. (2013). Using embedded computer-assisted explicit instruction to teach science to students with autism spectrum disorder. *Research in Autism Spectrum Disorders, 7,* 433–443. doi:10.1016/j.rasd.2012.10.01010

Snell, M.E. (Ed.). (1983). *Systematic instruction of the moderately and severely handicapped* (2nd ed.). Columbus, OH: Merrill.

Spooner, F., Knight, V., Browder, D.M., Jimenez, B., & DiBiase, W. (2011). Evaluating evidence-based practices in teaching science content to students with severe developmental disabilities. *Research and Practice for Persons with Severe Disabilities, 36,* 62–75.

Spooner, F., Knight, V.F., Browder, D.M., & Smith, B.R. (2012). Evidence-based practices for teaching academic skills to students with severe developmental disabilities. *Remedial and Special Education, 33,* 374–387. doi:10.1177/0741932511421634

Spooner, F., Stem, B., & Test, D.W. (1989). Teaching first aid skills to adolescents who are moderately mentally handicapped. *Education and Training in Mental Retardation, 24,* 341–351.

Stokes, T.F., & Baer, D.M. (1977). An implicit technology of generalization. *Journal of Applied Behavior Analysis, 10,* 349–367.

Taber, T.A., Alberto, P.A., Hughes, M., & Seltzer, A. (2002). A strategy for students with moderate disabilities when lost in the community. *Research and Practice for Persons with Severe Disabilities, 27,* 141–152.

Taber, T.A., Alberto, P.A., Seltzer, A., & Hughes, M. (2003). Obtaining assistance when lost in the community using cell phones. *Research and Practice for Persons with Severe Disabilities, 28,* 105–116.

Test, D.W., Fowler, C.H., Richter, S.M, White, J., Mazzotti, V., Walker, A.R., … Korting, L. (2009). Evidence-based practice in secondary transition. *Career Development for Exceptional Individuals, 32,* 115–128. doi:10.1177/0885728809336859

Walker, R. M. (2012). *The relationship between middle level school science programs and a residential environmental learning center.* (Doctoral dissertation). Retrieved from ProQuest LLC, (3522055).

Winterling, V., Gast, D.L., Wolery, M., & Farmer, J.A. (1992). Teaching safety skills to high school students with moderate disabilities. *Journal of Applied Behavior Analysis, 25,* 217–227.

Wolery, M., Bailey, D.B., & Sugai, G.M. (1988). *Effective teaching: Principles and procedures of applied behavior analysis with exceptional students.* Boston, MA: Allyn & Bacon.

FOR FURTHER INFORMATION

Computer-Assisted Instruction

Edyburn, D., Higgins, K., & Boone, R. (2005). *Handbook of special education technology research and practice.* Whitefish Bay, WI: Knowledge by Design.

Knight, V., McKissick, B., & Saunders, A. (2013). A review of technology-based interventions to teach academic skills to students with autism spectrum disorder. *Journal of Autism and Developmental Disabilities.* Advance online publication. doi:10.1007/s10803-013-1814-y

Pennington, R.C. (2010). Computer-assisted instruction for teaching academic skills to students with autism spectrum disorders: A review of literature. *Focus on Autism and Other Developmental Disabilities. Focus on Autism and Other Developmental Disabilities. 25*, 239-248. doi:10.1177/1088357610378291

Embedded Instruction

Jameson, J.M., McDonnell, J., Polychronis, S., & Riesen, T. (2008). Embedded, constant time delay instruction by peers without disabilities in general education classrooms. *Intellectual and Developmental Disabilities, 46*, 346–363.

McDonnell, J. (2011). Instructional contexts. In J.M Kauffman & D.P. Hallahan (Eds.), *The handbook of special education* (pp. 532–543). New York, NY: Routledge.

McDonnell, J., Johnson, J.W., & McQuivey, C. (2008). *Embedded instruction for students with developmental disabilities in general education classrooms.* Arlington, VA: Division on Developmental Disabilities of the Council for Exceptional Children.

Embedded Instruction for Early Learning

http://embeddedinstruction.net/what-embedded-instruction-early-learning

This web site focuses mostly on early childhood students but provides valuable information on how to use embedded instruction in the classroom.

Explicit Instruction Using Examples and Nonexamples

Goeke, J.L. (2009). *Explicit instruction: A framework for meaningful direct teaching.* Upper Saddle River, NJ: Merrill.

Jimenez, B., Knight, V., & Browder, D.M. (2012). *Early science curriculum.* Verona, WI: Attainment Company.

Early Science Curriculum

http://www.attainmentcompany.com/early-science-curriculum

Students learn about erosion in this video example.

Explicit Instruction

http://explicitinstruction.org/?page_id=317

This web site provides video vignettes, questions, and feedback.

Graphic Organizers

Knight, V., Spooner, F., Browder, D., Smith, B.R., & Wood, C. (2013). Using systematic instruction and graphic organizers to teach science concepts to students with autism spectrum disorders and intellectual disability. *Focus on Autism and Other Developmental Disabilities, 28*, 115–126. doi:10.1177/1088357612475301

EdHelper.com

http://edhelper.com/teachers/graphic_organizers.htm

This web site provides a variety of free, printable graphic organizers.

Inspiration

http://www.inspiration.com

This web site provides a free 30-day trial of Inspiration-based software. It allows students to create idea maps on the computer and to create presentations and papers from outlines.

Systematic Instruction to Teach Vocabulary and Chained Skills

Browder, D.M., & Spooner, F. (2011). *Teaching students with moderate and severe disabilities*. New York, NY: Guilford Press.

Collins, B.C. (2012). *Systematic instruction for students with moderate and severe disabilities*. Baltimore, MD: Paul H. Brookes Publishing Co.

Courtade, G., Jimenez, B., Trela, K., & Browder, D.M. (2008). *Teaching to science standards: An inquiry based approach for middle and high school students with moderate and severe disabilities*. Verona, WI: Attainment Company.

Systematic Instruction Plans

http://mast.ecu.edu/modules/sip/

This web site provides a brief online module for developing systematic instruction plans. It includes facilitators' resources, such as PowerPoint presentations.

Teaching Science in Inclusive Settings

Agran, M., Alper, S., & Wehmeyer, M. (2002). Access to the general curriculum for students with significant disabilities: What it means to teachers. *Education and Training in Mental Retardation and Developmental Disabilities, 37*, 123–133.

Agran, M., Cavin, M., Wehmeyer, M., & Palmer, S. (2006). Participation of students with moderate to severe disabilities in the general curriculum: The effects of the self-determined learning model of instruction. *Research and Practice for Persons with Severe Disabilities, 31*, 230–241.

Collins, B.C., Evans, A., Creech-Galloway, C., Karl, J., & Miller, A. (2007). Comparison of the acquisition and maintenance of the teaching functional and core content sight words in special and general education settings. *Focus on Autism and Other Developmental Disabilities, 22*, 220–233.

SECTION IV

Alignment of Curriculum, Instruction, and Assessment

The Curriculum, Instruction, and Assessment Pieces of the Student Achievement Puzzle

Rachel Quenemoen, Claudia Flowers, and Ellen Forte

Ms. Swift was looking forward to the teacher planning session with other area educators that was part of a research project the local university and her school district were conducting. As the only teacher of students with severe intellectual disabilities in her school, she really appreciated time to work with teachers who understood her challenges and successes. The extra work involved in a research project was a small price to pay for the chance to learn from other teachers who understood her students. At the first research team meeting 3 months ago, she had been very worried about the challenging assignments she had been given to try out with her students. The university researchers clearly did not understand who her students were. The content that they expected her to teach seemed completely out of reach and a waste of time for her students, and she told them so. Had they ever been in a classroom of students who truly have severe intellectual disabilities? Did they realize that many of these students also have other disabilities that affect what and how they learn?

Still, the research team gave her specific instructional strategies and curriculum models based on the new state content standards, including examples of how teachers in general education classrooms taught the new content. She supported inclusion of her students in grade-level general education classrooms to the extent appropriate. Some of these models would help her adapt the general education activities for her students. The researchers even taught her how to use evidence-based practices to teach specific skills that were targeted in the grade-level lessons. She had faithfully tried them all out, along with the progress monitoring tools that helped track student learning. Each teacher was given forms to describe the learning characteristics of each learner and to document which of the strategies worked best for each student based on his or her needs. If nothing else, Ms. Swift hoped that she could help these ivory tower researchers to understand better the challenges the students faced and why the new state standards were hopelessly out of reach.

The training they provided to her on classroom assessment was helpful. The idea that good classroom assessment went beyond standardized tests, and that multiple assessment tools were necessary to support learning, including structured systematic observations—now that made sense to her. The research forms were set up to gather data from these assessment tools of how each student was progressing toward grade-level benchmarks. These data were meant to document each student's path toward the content targets, to provide evidence of the student's learning. After that first meeting, she figured the forms should give her the data she needed to show them how off-base their expectations were. And she really appreciated their belief that the teacher is an active research partner to the university team—an action researcher. Yes, these data would show them what teaching these students is really like!

Now, as she prepared for the first quarterly meeting to share student work, she was really looking forward to showing them what she had discovered through her action research. There were "aha" moments to share, as she anticipated, but the aha moments were hers. Her students had really shown her.

As she came into the room full of teachers and university partners, she had her students' work in her binder—evidence gathered from classroom activities, progress monitoring tools, and even from the classroom assessment samples at the end of the grade-level lessons. As she opened the binder in anticipation, brimming with enthusiasm for what she had discovered her students could do, the teacher next to her turned to her and said, "You won't believe what my kiddos have been doing! And it isn't just what they are able to learn, it is how motivated by and proud they are of learning what other students their age learn. They are even more engaged in the lunchroom because they are actually part of the learning with their peers!" Ms. Swift laughed out loud, as did several of the other teachers. With that, they rolled up their sleeves, and began to share what they had learned.

Over the next years, these teachers worked together to review and discuss what they were learning. These small collegial study groups allowed them to learn from one another and, collectively with researchers, document the content pathways and tools that work well for students and for teachers. In turn, the teachers made use of what they learned in the study group as they returned to their classrooms to support and assess all their students' progress toward the desired content targets.

The university researchers used the teachers' action research results as well. By working with multiple groups of teachers over time, the university team was able to document the progress of hundreds of students who were having evidence-based opportunities to learn the new, challenging content. The researchers used these data in order to shape the design of additional classroom, progress monitoring, and summative assessments that are instructionally sensitive to support higher achievement for both teachers *and* their students.

Alternate assessments based on alternate achievement standards (AA-AAS) are large-scale summative assessments designed to measure attainment of state content knowledge and skills for students with the most significant cognitive disabilities. The ultimate goal of these assessments is to improve academic teaching and learning for students, but no single assessment given once a year can serve all users and purposes (Pellegrino, Chudowsky, & Glaser, 2001; Shepard, 2006). This is not to say that something is wrong with AA-AAS; rather, most summative assessments are administered near the end of the academic year when there is little instructional time remaining to affect student learning, and results from these assessments may not be available until after the school year has ended. Pellegrino and colleagues (2001) defined a quality assessment system as one that is coherent, comprehensive, and continuous. A coherent system is aligned with significant and common goals for student learning (i.e., important learning standards). A comprehensive system addresses the full range of knowledge and skills expected by academic content standards while providing districts, schools, and teachers with data to meet their decision-making needs. A system that is continuous provides ongoing data throughout the school year.

Assessments may be categorized into three types: 1) formative assessments, 2) interim (or benchmark) assessments, and 3) summative assessments. Distinguishing characteristics among these types include the frequency of use, the purpose, and the intended use of outcomes of the results (Table 12.1).

At the two ends of what might be considered a proximal-to-distal spectrum relative to instruction, formative and summative assessments reflect very different purposes and intended use of assessments. Formative assessments are methods typically used during and as part of instruction to help teachers adjust the immediate instructional process to meet students' needs. Summative assessments generate indicators of how much students have learned up to a particular point in time. It is possible for assessments to serve both formative and summative purposes, but the more purposes a single assessment addresses, the more each purpose is compromised (Pellegrino, Chudowsky, & Glaser, 2001).

Table 12.1. Schema for distinguishing types of assessments

Formative assessment

- *Frequency of use:* Daily and embedded in instruction
- *Purpose and intended use:* Student and teacher feedback toward ongoing learning toward specific learning standards
- *Example:* Teacher questioning, student self-assessments, observations, descriptive feedback, using peer feedback, progress monitoring, curriculum-based measures

Interim or benchmark assessments

- *Frequency of use:* Bi-weekly, monthly, or immediately following instruction on a specific set of academic goals
- *Purpose and intended use:* Identifying groups of struggling learners; determining professional development and programmatic needs; making adjustments to curriculum
- *Example:* Pre/posttests, writing samples, curriculum-based measures

Summative assessment

- *Frequency of use:* Annually
- *Purpose and intended use:* Accountability, rank, and school improvement goals
- *Example:* Alternate assessments based on alternate achievement standards

Source: Payne-Lewis and Kahl (2012).

FORMATIVE ASSESSMENTS

Although there is some disagreement on the definition (Bennett, 2011; Young & Kim, 2010), most experts define formative assessment as a process used by teachers and students during instruction that provides feedback to adjust ongoing teaching and learning to help students improve their achievement (Heritage, 2010a). The assessment must occur during the learning process while the student is working on tasks that directly embody the intended learning goal (Shepard, 2006). Formative assessments are not necessarily tests or artifacts, but could be a process that produces qualitative insight into student understanding (Shepard, 2008). For example, a teacher could closely observe a student or ask questions as the student solves a problem. Then, the teacher will understand the student's response process, rather than just the final response, to adapt instruction if needed.

Black and Wiliam's (1998) foundational review of the formative assessment literature indicated that focused efforts to improve formative assessment practices produced significant gains in student learning, and these practices were generally more effective than one-on-one tutoring, intensive reading instruction, or other instructional interventions. Although there is some debate about the strength of degree of effectiveness of formative assessment (Bennett, 2011), almost all educators agree that to support student learning, teachers must evaluate students' understanding in relation to instructional goals and processes on a continuous basis. Assessment and instruction should be conceptualized as one entity within the learning environment (Heritage, 2010b; Shepard, 2005).

Research studies suggest that the use of formative assessment methods with students with significant cognitive disabilities also can have a positive effect on students' learning. Progress monitoring techniques provide teachers with systems for measuring student progress, summarizing data, and making instructional decisions based on data patterns. In a study by Browder, Karvonen, Davis, Fallin, and Courtade-Little (2005), students of teachers who received progress monitoring training had higher alternate assessment scores than those teachers who did not receive training, which suggests that formative information can improve results on AA-AAS. Based on research conducted by Horn (2010), Hudson and Wakeman (2012) used response cards to gather data about student understanding. For example, teachers provided students with two response cards, one with a + symbol and one with – symbol. Students were asked a series of questions to distinguish between addition and subtraction properties (see Table 12.2 for examples of the questions). These results provided teachers with information to make immediate instructional decisions or plan future lessons to reteach the concepts of addition and subtraction.

For formative assessments to be integrated into instruction effectively, teachers need to understand the cognitive and conceptual connection that creates a foundation for learning. Formative assessment is of little use if teachers do not know what to do when students are not able to grasp important concepts (Heritage, Kim, Vendlinski, & Herman, 2009). Formative assessment professional development will be an important factor in building a coherent assessment system for students with significant cognitive disabilities.

Table 12.2. Series of questions for + and − response cards

"Show me *plus*.": Student points/eye gazes to the +.

"Again. Show me *plus*.": Student points/eye gazes to the +.

"Show me *minus*.": Student points/eye gazes to the −.

"Again. Show me *minus*.": Student points/eye gazes to the −.

"A story problem says 'in all.' Show me the symbol that tells us to put our sets together.": Student points/eye gazes to the +.

"A story problem says 'altogether.' Show me the symbol that tells us to put our sets together.": Student points/eye gazes to the +.

"A story problem says 'left.' Show me the symbol that tells us to take away.": Student points/eye gazes to the −.

"A story problem says, 'remain.' Show me the symbol that tells us to take away.": Student points/eye gazes to the −.

"A story problem says, 'difference.' Show me the symbol that tells us to take away.": Student points/ eye gazes to the −.

From Bethune, K., Thompson, J., Saunders, A., & Browder, D. (2012). *MASSI: Math Activities with Scripted Systematic Instruction.* Minneapolis, MN: National Center and State Collaborative; adapted by permission. Retrieved from http://www.ncscpartners.org.

INTERIM OR BENCHMARK ASSESSMENTS

Interim or benchmark assessments are new assessment terms that were introduced to fill the gap between classroom formative assessments and end-of-year summative assessments (Herman, Osmundson, & Dietel, 2010). Although formative assessments are embedded in ongoing classroom instruction and summative assessments provide an indication of how students are performing relative to annual learning standards, interim or benchmark assessments are strategically administered at the end of a specific set of academic goals. Perie, Marion, and Gong (2009) defined interim assessments as assessments that are administered during instruction to evaluate students' knowledge and skills relative to a specific set of academic goals in order to inform policy maker or educator decisions at the classroom, school, or district level. The key components of interim assessments are that they 1) provide for an evaluation of student's knowledge and skills relative to a specific set of academic goals, 2) are typically administered within a limited time frame, and 3) are designed to inform decisions at the classroom level and beyond. These assessments are used to serve a variety of purposes, including predicting a student's ability to succeed on a large-scale summative assessment, evaluating an educational program or intervention, and diagnosing gaps in student learning.

Although there are few examples of the use of interim assessments with students with significant cognitive disabilities, this will likely change as states develop a more coherent assessment system for this student population. Curriculum-based measures are approaches for assessing the growth of students in basic skills and are well-researched with students with disabilities (Deno, 2003), but they have rarely been used with students with significant cognitive disabilities. As the academic curriculum and understanding of how students acquire academic content knowledge matures, it is expected that curriculum-based measures will become an important measure for this student population.

The *Race to the Top Assessment Program* (U.S. Department of Education, n.d.) was designed to develop innovative and coherent assessment systems that support student learning. The development of curriculum and best practices for instruction for students with significant cognitive disabilities is part of the work with the National Center and State Collaborative (NCSC; http://www.ncscpartners .org). For example, mathematics activities with scripted systematic instruction (MASSI; Bethune et al., 2012) provide teachers instructional activities and assessment tools that are aligned to Common Core State Standards (CCSS; National Governors Association Center for Best Practices, Council of Chief State School Officers, 2010). At the end of the MASSI lessons, which typically take about 1–2 weeks to complete, tests are provided for teachers to evaluate student learning. Figure 12.1 displays some of the items that are administered to students after instruction on matching equation to representation.

SUMMATIVE ASSESSMENTS

Large-scale summative assessments are administered statewide once annually; results are used in state accountability systems to inform program and policy decisions. AA-AAS were first mandated within the Elementary and Secondary Education Act of 1965 (PL 89-10; as reauthorized in the Improving America's Schools Act of 1994 [PL 103-382]) and the Individuals with Disabilities Education Act Amendments (IDEA) of 1997 (PL 105-17) as a summative assessment for students with significant cognitive disabilities. Requirements for these assessments were later strengthened in the ensuing reauthorizations of these laws. Initial AA-AAS test designs were typically portfolio assessments that incorporated a collection of functional curricula evidence (e.g., leisure, daily living, vocational, self-help skills). In addition to functional curricula, indicators of best practice with this student population, such as generalization, self-determination, and inclusion, were included in the assessment (Karvonen, Wakeman, Ahumada, Bowman, & Turner, 2012).

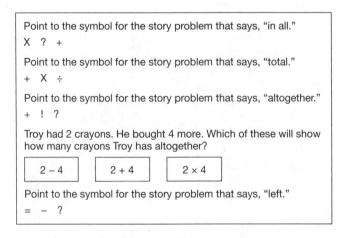

Figure 12.1. Example of items administered to students with significant cognitive disabilities after instruction on specific goals in addition and subtraction.

In the past decade, AA-AAS have evolved to become more aligned with academic content standards and resemble more traditional standardized test designs. AA-AAS formats have broadened to include rating scales, performance assessments, and multiple choice on-demand tests (Cameto et al., 2010; Thompson, Johnstone, Thurlow, & Altman, 2005). Thompson and colleagues (2005) reported that most states were using a portfolio or body of evidence (30 states) followed by performance events/tasks (21 states), a rating scale or checklist (13 states), and multiple-choice constructed responses (6 states). By 2008, there was a blurring of format boundaries as portfolios added more standardization of required evidence, and checklists/rating scales and performance assessments added more collected evidence of student achievement (Quenemoen, 2008). In a 2009 survey, all states reported using academic content standards as the basis for assessment (Altman et al., 2010).

Evidence suggests that some teachers are able to use AA-AAS for formative purposes. When AA-AAS are designed by teachers and evidence is collected as part of the curriculum-embedded assessment, teachers are able to determine individual students' needs and modify instruction and student learning. Still other AA-AAS systems require students to reflect on their learning and determine methods for improving their performance. Building and improving AA-AAS to support putting the pieces of the puzzle together is a high priority.

COHERENT ASSESSMENT SYSTEMS AND THE NATIONAL CENTER AND STATE COLLABORATIVE APPROACH

Improving the assessment of students with significant cognitive disabilities begins with the conception of a coherent assessment system using multiple measures for multiple purposes. Although the previous sections have focused on the different types of assessments that are used for different purposes, the backbone for instruction and assessments is that both must share the same underlying models of learning and shared curriculum (Shepard, 2006). One promising area for strengthening instruction and assessment is the use of learning progressions. Learning progressions provide a picture of the path students typically follow as they learn, and provide a description of skills, understandings, and knowledge in the sequence in which they typically develop (Masters & Forster, 1996). When teachers begin with possible learning progressions, they are able to use assessments more strategically and more frequently (Hess, 2011).

The NCSC is a consortium of states and national organizations (NCSC, 2012) that is building a comprehensive system of curriculum, instruction, and assessment—formative and summative—based on a common model of learning. The NCSC approach to designing curricula, instructional supports, and assessments builds on an informed articulation of the content model, an understanding of the learner characteristics, and a model of learning that brings the content and learner together. These features inform principled design decisions that come from the concept of the Assessment Triangle, first presented in Pellegrino, Chudowsky, and Glaser (2001), then modified under the New Hampshire Enhanced Assessment Initiative (NHEAI), and ultimately documented in Marion and Pellegrino (2006). The Assessment Triangle is described by Pellegrino and colleagues as the three foundations on which every assessment must rest: "a model of how students represent knowledge and develop competence in the subject domain, tasks or situations that allow one to observe students' performance, and an interpretation method for drawing inferences from the performance evidence thus obtained" (2001, p. 2).

TRANSLATING THE COMMON CORE STATE STANDARDS INTO A FOUNDATION FOR THE NATIONAL CENTER AND STATE COLLABORATIVE PUZZLE PIECES

As described in Chapter 2, the Common Core State Standards Initiative, a coalition coordinated by the National Governors Association (NGA) and the Council of Chief State School Officers (CCSSO), released the CCSS in English language arts (ELA) and mathematics in June 2010. The content experts convened by the NGA and the CCSSO to create the CCSS characterized the focus for this new set of standards as the 21st century knowledge and skills students need to be college- or career-ready when graduating from high school. The knowledge and skills inherent to the CCSS are challenging for all students. Teachers of students with moderate to severe disabilities will need significant support to translate these important new standards into instructional practice for their students, in their design of curriculum, in understanding of the evidence-based instructional practices that support student learning, and in design of assessments.

With this in mind, NCSC has organized the development of curriculum, instruction, and assessment resources and supports such that, from the outset, each component aligns with the CCSS, is accessible for the range of students with moderate to severe disabilities, and is based on a common understanding of how students acquire the knowledge, skills, and abilities defined in the CCSS. These three components of a comprehensive system of curriculum, instruction, and assessment—a content model, a clear understanding of learner characteristics, and a learning model—form the foundation of the NCSC approach to implementation of the CCSS.

To address alignment with the CCSS as well as with a common understanding of academic learning, NCSC first adopted the learning progression frameworks (LPFs) developed through a project sponsored by the National Alternate Assessment Center (NAAC) at the University of Kentucky. The NAAC LPFs represent, for ELA and mathematics CCSS-defined content areas, descriptions of "successively more sophisticated ways of thinking about a topic that can follow one another as students learn about and investigate a topic over a broad span of time" (National Research Council [NRC], 2007, p. 219; Hess, 2011). Building on work done by the Committee on Assessments (Pellegrino et al., 2001), the LPFs are intended to "offer a coherent starting point for thinking about how students develop competence in an academic domain and how to observe and interpret the learning as it unfolds" (Hess, 2011, p. 3). These are built on the pathways educators have seen for typical students and not specifically for students with moderate to severe disabilities, but they reflect the grade- and age-appropriate pathways that can be expected as all students—including those with moderate to severe disabilities—progress through the grade levels.

The second step in NCSC's approach to aligning curriculum, instruction, and assessment with one another and with the CCSS is the development of Core Content Connectors (CCCs), which link the content targets defined in the CCSS with the progress indicators described in the LPFs. The CCCs represent the most important content for instruction and assessment for students who participate in AA-AAS as identified through literature reviews and the joint moderated judgment of experienced teachers in mathematics and ELA, as well as teachers of students with moderate to severe disabilities (NCSC, 2012). They are not extended from the content in the CCSS, but instead break priority standards from the CCSS into teachable and assessable content targets. These targets provide more frequent, smaller benchmarks as students with moderate to severe disabilities move through the core content in the CCSS.

Within the NCSC system, all CCCs are addressed through curriculum professional development supports, and 10 prioritized CCCs have been identified in each grade for each of the mathematics and ELA content areas for representation on the NCSC assessments. The CCCs, then, represent a sampling of the CCSS that connects standards-level goals to the progress indicators defined in the LPFs and allow for meaningful instructional planning and for aligned classroom assessments meant to inform instruction directly (e.g., formative and interim assessments), as well as at the summative assessments used for other purposes.

The crucial feature of the CCCs is the identification of concrete targets that allow educators to first teach the challenging content in the CCSS and then to observe and make inferences about student performance.

Principled-Design Practices Related to the National Center and State Collaborative Assessment

NCSC builds on the approach of evidence-centered design (ECD; Mislevy, Almond, & Lukas, 2003) to guide the development of assessments and assessment items. In developing an ECD-based assessment, one first identifies the knowledge, skills, and abilities that are to be assessed. The NCSC approach to the content model supports this work. The next step, in very simple terms, involves the detailed specification of content to be assessed in relation to the model of learning as well as what evidence of student learning can be observed as the students build their skills and knowledge. The outcomes of this step are design patterns that describe the conditions under which the learning can be observed that, in turn, are used to generate task templates that describe potential observations specifically. That is, they provide an example of what tasks or items look like and how they are to be presented and scored. These task and item examples are informed by the nature of learner characteristics and a model of learning in the academic domain for the students.

By using this principled approach to assessment development, NCSC strengthens system alignment and integrity. In addition to establishing this evidence as part of the design and development process for the assessment, the curricular and instructional materials are built on the same content model, understanding of learner characteristics, and model of student learning. In this type of system, there is no disconnect between best practice in teaching the content and best practice in assessing student learning, whether formative or summative. They are cut from the same cloth, if you will, built on a common model of student cognition in the academic content areas.

Translating the Pieces of the Puzzle into Instructional Practice for Students with Moderate to Severe Disabilities

The model of student cognition described previously—the content model, an understanding of learner characteristics, and the model of learning—is the foundation of the NCSC instruction and curriculum resources as well. The NCSC instructional resources provide support for teachers to address the CCSS when teaching students with moderate to severe disabilities in two areas, first in understanding the content, and then in teaching the content.

Understanding the Content   Many teachers of students with moderate to severe disabilities have limited understanding of the academic domains themselves. In a survey of teachers in 18 states, researchers concluded that

> Resources that provide teachers with basic academic content knowledge in a user friendly format are absolutely necessary. Teachers also need the prioritization of content within the Common Core State Standards, so that those with limited access to collaboration with general education teachers or whose experiences and teaching priorities have only focused on functional skills will see academic instruction as feasible and appropriate. (Lee et al., 2013, p. 34)

Two sets of NCSC resources are being developed to help teachers gain a deeper understanding of the content. The Content Modules are an online multimedia resource that provides teachers with a deeper understanding of complex concepts. For example, the Fractions and Decimals Content Modules outlines mathematical concepts that provide a deep understanding of the content that helps teachers support learning in the classroom. The Curriculum Resource Guides (see Figure 12.2 for example) show how the content is taught in general education and provides ideas for teaching across content areas, assessment examples, ideas for real-life use, examples of modifications and adaptations for students with specific learning needs, and ways to promote college and career readiness. They were developed by special educators with extensive experience in adapting general curriculum for students with significant cognitive disabilities and validated by mathematics content experts for accuracy and by special education teachers for clarity.

Teaching the Content   NCSC resources provide a range of instructional tools for meeting all students' needs, and are grounded in the assumption of the least restrictive environment for learning, in both the context of grade-level peers and the content. The NCSC Units and Lesson Plans provide models of universally designed instruction based on the CCSS for that grade level. They model how to teach the prioritized CCCs from the NCSC content model in the context of general education lessons. The Units and Lesson Plans incorporate multiple means of engagement, representation, and expression into the lesson designs. They also include formative classroom assessments that help teachers understand where students may need more intensive supports as they work in the context of the grade-level curriculum.

For students who need more intensive supports to be successful in the grade-level curriculum, the NCSC project offers additional resources for teachers to build intensive instruction based on evidence-based practices. These MASSIs (or in the case of English language arts, LASSIs) provide instructional resources for the pri-

Curriculum Resource to Prepare Students for AA-AAS Mathematics Content: Equations

---

The purposes of the Curriculum Resource Guides are:

- To provide guidance for teaching the Common Core State Standards (CCSS) to students with Significant Cognitive Disabilities (SWSCD) that both aligns with these standards and provides differentiation for individual student needs

- To provide examples for differentiating instruction for a wide range of SWSCD. These examples can be used in planning specific lessons, alternate assessment items, and professional development

- To serve as a companion document to the Progress Indicators for the CCSS found in the NCSC Learning Progressions Progressions

- To help educators build knowledge of the essential content reflected in these Progress Indicators of the CCSS

- To delineate the necessary skills and knowledge students need to acquire to master these indicators

---

1. What are "equations" and how are they taught in general education settings?

1a.1 The essential knowledge in this content area

Equations are a statement that the vales of two mathematical expressions are equal. Expressions can be thought of as a phrase while an equation is a complete sentence.

Comparison of Terms	
Expression	Equation
mathematical phrase: × + 3	mathematical sentence: × + 3 = 9
word phrase: a number plus three	word sentence: a number plus three is nine
number, operation, variable	number, operation, variable, equal sign
evaluate: 1. substitute 2. simplify	solve for/ isolate the variable
	one solution

$$4 \times 7 = \underbrace{28}_{\text{expression}}$$
$$\text{equation}$$

$$4 \times 7 = 2 \times 14$$
$$\underbrace{\text{expression}}\ \underbrace{\text{expression}}$$

Students can use models (objects or drawings) to represent expressions or equations.

$4 \times 7 \rightarrow$

Figure 12.2. Example from the NCSC Curriculum Resource Guides. Curriculum Resource Guides include content, tables with core content connectors and performance examples, general education activities, real world applications, ideas for promoting career and college readiness, and accessibility for all learners. (From National Center and State Collaborative. [n.d.]. *NSCS curriculum resource to prepare students for AA-AAS: Mathematics content: Equations* [p.7]. Minneapolis, MN: Author; reprinted by permission.

oritized content for the NCSC Summative Assessment at increasing levels of difficulty. The entry points are appropriate for students with little to no understanding of the content, but they continue through to higher levels of full understanding of the targeted skills and knowledge. They incorporate real-life applications and hands-on activities. Data sheets are provided for monitoring progress as well as a skills test for practicing responding in a testing context. To help support teachers in using these effective teaching strategies, an instructional resource guide provides guidance for teachers by explaining and providing examples of how to use these evidence-based prompting and instructional strategies.

Neither the Units and Lesson Plans nor MASSIs/LASSIs provide everything a teacher needs to address all of the content at each grade level. Instead, they provide models and examples for how to teach the content that teachers can apply and use to generate resources for other areas of instruction. To support teachers' development of additional resources based on these models, NCSC provides additional content tools to show how the CCSS and CCC systems work together across and within the grade levels and content areas, as part of a system of professional development support. The comprehensive system of curriculum, instruction, and professional development tools and support are introduced on the NCSC web site (http://www.ncscpartners.org) under the Resources tab as Dissemination Materials.

Instructional resources are developed, reviewed, field tested, and revised until the team considers them to meet all of the following criteria:

- Promote CCSS by using the CCCs, dually aligned with learning progressions and CCSS

- Set high expectations for all students

- Apply principles of universal design for learning

- Apply evidence-based teaching practices for students with significant cognitive disabilities

- Use general curriculum resources and general education content experts' review

- Offer options for all students with the most significant cognitive disabilities

- Reflect the model of cognition being used for assessment

- Provide a teacher-friendly resource that promotes effective instruction

Using key principles to guide development and gathering expert and practitioner input through field testing helps to ensure that the NCSC resources are immediately useful and effective once in teachers' hands.

Educator Effectiveness and the National Center and State Collaborative System

The NCSC project will identify promising data sources for a comprehensive approach to program and educator effectiveness in part based on the collective curriculum, instruction, and assessment resources the project is developing. There are not good models yet available that incorporate recent research on academic instruction for students with significant cognitive disabilities. Principals regularly report a lack of understanding of what teachers serving this population should know and do (Towles-Reeves, Kleinert, & Anderman, 2008). Similarly, teachers report that principals have low expectations of achievement from these students and a lack of resources for effectively providing access to the general curriculum (Flowers, Ahlgrim-Delzell, Browder, & Spooner, 2005). A multiple-measures approach to evaluating teacher and principal effectiveness may include, but is not limited to, 1) a teacher self-assessment, 2) school/program assessment, 3) principal walk-through tools, and 4) coaching processes. The NCSC tools and resources should be helpful in defining these and other measures that can support educator effectiveness.

COMMUNICATING WITH TEACHERS ABOUT ACADEMIC INSTRUCTION AND THE ALTERNATE ASSESSMENTS BASED ON ALTERNATE ACHIEVEMENT STANDARDS

NCSC's approach is predicated on the notion that teachers teach better when they have a deep understanding of the content and its acquisition as well as of their students and challenges they face individually in learning and performance contexts. Teachers do not teach better simply because they are content experts or because they know a student's score on an AA-AAS. They teach better because they understand long-term and short-term instructional goals in relation to one another and what it takes to process and respond correctly to a question or to perform a requested task or skill in general and for individual students in their classrooms. The curriculum, instructional strategies, and assessment tools must all come from the same expectation vision and development models (Pellegrino, Chudowsky, & Glaser, 2001; Shepard, 2006).

Furthermore, just as students must practice and internalize skills to learn them effectively, teachers need to work collaboratively to gain this interpretive ability because they must have access to others' experiences and to hear, see, and try over and over to internalize—proceduralize—their ability to connect performance to expectation, make informed decisions about next steps, and take those steps.

As underscored in the previous section, coherence among the achievement targets, the knowledge and skills targeted for instruction, the knowledge and skills targeted for assessment, and the learning model that underlies how one teaches and assesses is critical to how a learning system functions. But, what does that mean for real teachers in real classrooms in real time?

Consider what a teacher represents in the student learning system: the intersection of the students with the content they are meant to be acquiring. The teacher must create the general instructional context and specific opportunities for his or her students to interact with the content, based on both the target knowledge and skills and his or her students' individual characteristics; make inferences about what each student understands based on his or her observations; adjust instruction based on those inferences; and make summative judgments based on a body of evidence.

This critical and complex role can be rather simply conveyed when talking with teachers about assessment by using the notation C-T-S to represent content, teacher, and student, respectively. Hold a large letter C in one hand and a larger letter S in the other; standing with both arms outstretched to the sides, naturally form a letter T with your body and arms. You are the teacher (T). You connect content (C) with students (S) and vice versa. You relate them to one another. You bring them together.

This simple image may help teachers to see how central they are in a system that may often feel imposing and overwhelming. As described in this chapter, standards can provide excellent overall goals for a year's worth of instruction, but unless and until they are translated into a language and form that connects to everyday practice in the classroom, they serve little purpose in supporting student achievement. Likewise, the only assessments that serve instruction are those that align with not only the same standards-based targets but also the same learning progressions that guide teachers in supporting students' growing mastery of academic content.

Recall the experience of Ms. Swift, the teacher from our vignette at the beginning of this chapter. She was presented with visions of instruction and of the possibilities for her students that were so unlike her own that she could not initially see the connections between her current world and the new one offered by the researchers. She could not accept a new way of seeing her students because her own experience gave her evidence to the contrary. She so firmly believed in the wrong-headedness of the researchers' methods that she sought to implement them for the purpose of proving them wrong, that is, until her students showed her otherwise.

Ms. Swift had to come to see herself as a connector rather than an arbiter. She had to take her expert understanding of her students' multifaceted skills and abilities and relate those to the knowledge, skills, and abilities in the academic learning progressions she was just beginning to understand. Although some of the CCSS themselves seemed beyond the reach of her students, she began to recognize in her own students' progressions how students build knowledge and skills over time. She began to see how to support those progressions through her instruction. The pieces began to fit together for her and, thus, for her students.

SUMMARY

The NCSC system is firmly rooted in the aligned interplay of curriculum, instruction, and assessment. Still, at its heart it is dependent on teachers internalizing this model by applying it in their daily practice. Then, all of the pieces will fit together in ways that contribute, over time, to students' readiness for full participation in their communities as well as in college and career settings. This coherence, along with teachers' central role in connecting their students with the expectations that lead to community, college, and career readiness, forms the core of the NCSC system.

REFERENCES

Altman, J.R., Lazarus, S.S., Quenemoen, R.F., Kearns, J., Quenemoen, M., & Thurlow, M.L. (2010). *2009 survey of states: Accomplishments and new issues at the end of a decade of change.* Minneapolis: University of Minnesota, National Center on Educational Outcomes.

Bennett, R.E. (2011). Formative assessment: A critical review. *Assessment in Education: Principles, Policy and Practice, 18*, 5–25.

Bethune, K., Thompson, J., Saunders, A., & Browder, D. (2012). *MASSI: Math Activities with Scripted Systematic Instruction.* Minneapolis, MN: National Center and State Collaborative. Retrieved from http://www.ncscpartners.org/resources-cop-presentations

Black, P., & Wiliam, D. (1998). Assessment and classroom learning. *Educational Assessment: Principles, Policy and Practice, 5*(1), 7–74.

Browder, D.M., Karvonen, M., Davis, S., Fallin, K., & Courtade-Little, G. (2005). The impact of teacher training on state alternate assessment scores. *Exceptional Children, 71*, 267–282.

Cameto, R., Bergland, F., Knokey, A.-M., Nagle, K.M., Sanford, C., Kalb, S.C., ... Ortega, M. (2010). *Teacher perspectives of school-level implementation of alternate assessments for students with significant cognitive disabilities. A report from the National Study on Alternate Assessments.* (NCSER 2010-3007). Menlo Park, CA: SRI International.

Deno, S.L. (2003). Developments in curriculum-based measures. *The Journal of Special Education, 37*, 184–192.

Elementary and Secondary Education Act of 1965, PL 89-10, 20 U.S.C. §§ 241 *et seq.*

Flowers, C., Ahlgrim-Delzell, L., Browder, D., & Spooner, F. (2005). Teachers' perceptions of alternate assessments. *Research and Practice for Persons with Severe Disabilities, 30*, 81–92.

Heritage, M. (2010a). *Formative assessment and next-generation assessment systems: Are we losing an opportunity?* Washington, DC: Council of Chief State School Officers. Retrieved from http://www.ccsso.org/Documents/2010/Formative_Assessment_Next_Generation_2010.pdf

Heritage, M. (2010b). *Formative assessment: Making it happen in the classroom.* Thousand Oaks, CA: Corwin.

Heritage, M., Kim, J., Vendlinski, T., & Herman, J. (2009). From evidence to action: A seamless process in formative assessment? *Educational Measurement: Issues and Practice, 28*(3), 24–31.

Herman, J.L., Osmundson, E., & Dietel, R. (2010). *Benchmark assessments for improved learning* (AACC Policy Brief). Los Angeles: University of California.

Hess, K. (Ed.). (2011, November). *Learning progressions frameworks designed for use with the Common Core State Standards in English language arts and literacy K-12.* National Alternate Assessment Center at the University of Kentucky and the National Center for the Improvement of Educational Assessment. Retrieved from http://www.nciea.org

Horn, C. (2010). Response cards: An effective intervention for students with disabilities. *Education and Training in Autism and Developmental Disabilities, 45*(1), 116–123.

Hudson, M., & Wakeman, S.Y. (2012). *Using formative assessment data to make instructional decisions and increase student engagement for students with intellectual disability.* Manuscript in preparation.

Improving America's Schools Act of 1994, PL 103-382, 20 U.S.C. §§ 630 *et seq.*

Individuals with Disabilities Education Act Amendments (IDEA) of 1997, PL 105-17, 20 U.S.C. §§ 1400 *et seq.*

Karvonen, M., Wakeman, S., Ahumada, A., Bowman, T., & Turner, L. (2012, June). *An examination of change over time within alternate assessments items and student performance.* Presentation at the National Conference on Student Assessment for the Council for Chief State School Officers, Minneapolis, MN.

Lee., A., Towles-Reeves, E., Flowers, C., Hart, L., Kearns, J., Kerbel, A., ... Thurlow, M. (2013). *Teacher perceptions of students participating in AA-AAS: Cross-state summary* (A product of the NCSC validity evaluation). Minneapolis: University of Minnesota, National Center and State Collaborative.

Marion, S.F., & Pellegrino, J.W. (2006). A validity framework for evaluating the technical quality of alternate assessments. *Educational Measurement: Issues and Practice, 25*(4), 47–57.

Masters, G.N., & Forster, M. (1996). *Progress maps.* (Part of the *Assessment Resource Kit.*) Melbourne, Australia: The Australian Council for Educational Research.

Mislevy, R.J., Almond, R.G., & Lukas, J. (2003). *A brief introduction to evidence-centered design.* CSE Technical Report 632, The National Center for Research on Evaluation, Standards, Student Testing (CRESST), 2004. Also ETS Research Report RR-03-16.

National Center and State Collaborative. (n.d.). *NSCS curriculum resource to prepare students for AA-AAS: Mathematics content: Equations.* Minneapolis, MN: Author.

National Center and State Collaborative. (2012). *About the NCSC.* Retrieved from http://www.ncscpartners.org/about

National Research Council. (2007). Learning progressions. In Duschl, R.A., Schweingruber, H.A., Shouse, A.W. (Eds.), *Taking science to schools. Learning and teaching science in grades K–8* (pp. 213–250). Washington, DC: The National Academies Press.

National Governors Association Center for Best Practices, Council of Chief State School Officers. (2010). *Common Core State Standards.* Washington, DC: Authors. Retrieved from http://www.corestandards.org/

Payne-Lewis, J., & Kahl, S.R. (2012, April). *Impacting learning through the use of formative assessment.* Training session presented at the National Council on Measurement in Education, Vancouver, British Columbia, Canada.

Pellegrino, J.W., Chudowsky, N., & Glaser, R. (2001). *Knowing what students know: The science and design of educational assessment.* Washington, DC: National Academy of Sciences.

Perie, M., Marion, S., & Gong, B. (2009). Moving toward a comprehensive assessment system: A framework for considering interim assessments. *Educational Measurement: Issues and Practice, 28*(3), 5–13.

Quenemoen, R. (2008). *A brief history of alternate assessments based on alternate achievement standards* (Synthesis Report 68). Minneapolis: University of Minnesota, National Center on Educational Outcomes.

Shepard, L.A. (2005). Curricular coherence in assessment design. *Yearbook of the National Society for the Study of Education, 103*, 239–249.

Shepard, L.A. (2006). Classroom assessment. In R.L. Brennan (Ed.), *Educational measurement* (4th ed., pp. 623–646). Westport, CT: American Council on Education/Praeger.

Shepard, L.A. (2008). Formative assessment: Caveat emptor. In C.A. Dwyer (Ed.), *The future of assessment: Shaping teaching and learning* (pp. 279–303). Mahwah, NJ: Lawrence Erlbaum Associates.

Thompson, S.J., Johnstone, C.J., Thurlow, M.L., & Altman, J.R. (2005). *2005 special education outcomes: Steps forward in a decade of change.* Minneapolis: University of Minnesota, National Center on Educational Outcomes. Retrieved from http://www.cehd.umn.edu/NCEO/OnlinePubs/2005StateReport.htm

Towles-Reeves, E., Kleinert, H., & Anderman, L. (2008). Alternate assessments based on alternate achievement standards: Principals' perceptions. *Research and Practice for Persons with Severe Disabilities, 33*, 122–133.

U.S. Department of Education (n.d.). *Race to the top assessment program.* Retrieved from http://www2.ed.gov/programs/racetothetop-assessment/index.html

Young, V.M., & Kim, D.H. (2010). Using assessments for instructional improvement: A literature review. *Education Policy Analysis Archives, 18*, 19. Retrieved from http://epaa.asu.edu/ojs/article/view/809

FOR FURTHER INFORMATION

Alternate Assessments Based on Alternate Achievement Standards (AA-AAS)

Quenemoen, R., Kearns, J., Quenemoen, M., Flowers, C., & Kleinert, H. (2010). *Common misperceptions and research-based recommendations for alternate assessment based on alternate achievement standards* (Synthesis Report 73). Minneapolis: University of Minnesota, National Center on Educational Outcomes.

National Alternate Assessment Center (NAAC), University of Kentucky

www.naacpartners.org

Although federal funding for NAAC has ended, research, publications, and training resources are still available on this site.

National Center and State Collaborative

http://www.ncscpartners.org

This web site includes resources specifically related to the Common Core State Standards and alternate assessments.

National Center on Educational Outcomes (NCEO), University of Minnesota

http://www.cehd.umn.edu/NCEO/TopicAreas/AlternateAssessments/altAssess Topic.htm

This web site provides resources on specific topics, including academic standards, accommodations, accountability, alternate assessments, graduation requirements, participation, and reporting.

Books Focused on Assessment

Kleinert, H.L. & Kearns, J.F. (Eds.). (2010). *Alternate assessment for students with significant cognitive disabilities.* Baltimore, MD: Paul H. Brookes Publishing Co.

Russell, M., & Kavanaugh, M. (Eds.). (2011). *Assessing students in the margins: Challenges, strategies, and techniques.* Charlotte, NC: Information Age Publishing.

Books Focused on Curriculum and Instruction

Browder, D.M., & Spooner, F. (Eds.). (2006). *Teaching reading, math, and science to students with significant cognitive disabilities.* Baltimore, MD: Paul H. Brookes Publishing Co.

Browder, D.M., & Spooner, F.H. (2011). *Teaching students with moderate and severe disabilities.* New York, NY: Guilford Press.

Web Sites

Dynamic Learning Maps (DLM)

http://dynamiclearningmaps.org

DLM is funded by the Federal Office of Special Education Programs for research and development of an AA-AAS, along with the NCSC project.

edCount

http://www.edcount.com

EdCount works with educators in aligning instructional systems and building teacher and leader capacity, building quality assessment systems that support teaching and learning, and gathering data and sharing knowledge so that policy and practice may inform one another.

Moving Your Numbers

http://www.movingyournumbers.org

Moving Your Numbers provides examples of real districts—from small rural communities to large urban centers—that are positively affecting the performance of all children, including students with disabilities, through collective and focused actions of adults.

The National Center for the Improvement of Educational Assessment (NCIEA)

http://www.nciea.org

The Center's mission is to contribute to improved student achievement through enhanced policies and practices in educational assessment and accountability by working with states and other educational agencies to design and implement effective assessment and accountability policies and programs.

National Center for Research on Evaluation, Standards, & Student Testing (CRESST)

http://www.cse.ucla.edu

CRESST has long contributed to the development of scientifically based evaluation and testing techniques, vigorously encouraged the development, validation and use of sound data for improved accountability and decision making, and aggressively explored technological applications to improve assessment and evaluation practice.

National Center on Student Progress Monitoring

http://www.studentprogress.org

Although federal funding for this center has ended, research, publications, and training resources are available at this site.

SWIFT

http://www.swiftschools.org

SWIFT is a national K–8 center that provides academic and behavioral support to promote the learning and academic achievement of all students, including those with the most extensive needs.

University of Louisville, Formative Assessment-Autism/Moderate and Severe Disabilities

http://louisville.edu/education/abri/primarylevel/assessment/autism_msd

The videos focus on the application of the entire range of primary level strategies to students with behaviors and needs typical of autism spectrum disorders and/or moderate and severe disabilities. The videos represent a cross section of student ages, group sizes, and instructional focus.

CHAPTER 13

Promoting Learning in General Education for All Students

Cheryl M. Jorgensen, Jennifer Fischer-Mueller,
and Holly Prud'homme

Theresa was a ninth-grade student who had been included in general education classes throughout elementary and middle school. When she entered high school she was enrolled in heterogeneous general education classes with the support of her classmates, a part-time instructional assistant, a speech-language pathologist, an occupational therapist, and a highly skilled building-based inclusion facilitator. Theresa was a member of her school's community service and drama clubs. With sensory supports, adapted materials, and assistive technology, Theresa mastered academic content based on her state's general academic standards reduced in depth, breadth, and complexity, and she participated in alternate assessments based on alternate achievement standards (AA-AAS).

Theresa's school was one of an increasing number around the United States that have adopted the philosophy and practice of inclusive education. That is, the school enrolls all students, including those with significant intellectual disability and/or other developmental disabilities, in heterogeneous general education classes where they participate fully in general education instruction based on general education learning standards. Despite successes such as Theresa's and research showing the benefits of inclusion, there are still many people who believe that some students are just "too disabled" to benefit from inclusion. They ask, "What about students who do not currently show communicative intent? Students who have great difficulty moving any part of their bodies? Those who have very short attention spans? Those who are judged to have such significant intellectual disabilities that participation in an academically based curriculum seems to make little sense?"

This chapter describes the rationale for and strategies that support the inclusion of all students, including those with the most significant disabilities, in general education classrooms. The chapter concludes by presenting nine action steps for schools just beginning to include students and for those that are committed to continuous improvement. Quotations from co-authors Fischer-Mueller and Prud'homme are presented throughout the chapter to illustrate the commitment to and strategies employed by general educators to promote students' membership, participation, and learning.

RATIONALE FOR INCLUSIVE EDUCATION

The introductory Congressional findings of The Individuals with Disabilities Education Improvement Act (IDEA) of 2004 (PL 108-446; Sec. 601 [c][1] and [5]) reflect the values-and evidence-based rationale for inclusive education:

> Disability is a natural part of the human experience and in no way diminishes the right of individuals to participate in or contribute to society...Almost 30 years of research and experience has demonstrated that the education of children with disabilities can be made more effective by having high expectations for such children and ensuring their access to the general education curriculum in the regular classroom, to the maximum extent possible.

I do truly believe that to be the best educator that you can be it is imperative to do whatever you can to meet the needs of each and every student in your class. It is essential that you view differentiating for each student as your job.

–Holly Prud'homme

Using theory, historical research, and empirical literature, Jackson, Ryndak, and Wehmeyer (2008/2009) made a case for inclusive education as a research-based practice and concluded that

> Placement in age- and grade-appropriate general education contexts and having special and general educators team to provide supports and modifications for all students are first-order research based practice, and that the benefits of proven methods of instruction are realized in the long run only when this first step is implemented in the life of a child. (p. 190)

In addition to these reasons for providing inclusive education, this practice is also supported by strong science. Research findings on the effect of inclusive education on students with significant disabilities include, for example, 1) higher expectations for student learning (Jorgensen, McSheehan, & Sonnenmeier, 2007); 2) heightened engagement, affective demeanor, and participation in inclusive social activities (Hunt, Farron-Davis, Beckstead, Curtis, & Goetz, 1994); 3) improved communication and social skills (Beukelman & Mirenda, 2005; Fisher & Meyer, 2002; McSheehan, Sonnenmeier, & Jorgensen, 2009; Soto, Muller, Hunt, & Goetz, 2001); 4) more satisfying and diverse social relationships (Guralnick, Connor, Hammond, Gottman, & Kinnish, 1996); 5) optimal access to the general education curriculum (Jorgensen, McSheehan, & Sonnenmeier, 2010; Wehmeyer & Agran, 2006); 6) improved academic outcomes (Cole, Waldron, & Majd, 2004; Ryndak, Alper, Ward, Storch, & Montgomery, 2010; Ryndak, Morrison, & Sommerstein, 1999); 7) improved adult outcomes in the areas of postsecondary education, employment, and independence (White & Weiner, 2004); 8) better quality individualized education programs (IEPs; Hunt & Farron-Davis, 1992); 9) fewer absences from school and referrals for disruptive behavior (Helmstetter, Curry, Brennan, & Sampson-Saul, 1998); and 10) achievement of more IEP goals (Brinker & Thorpe, 1984).

Amro[1] was a nonverbal student with a significant cognitive disability who was a member of my 10th-grade science class. He had a role in a student-written "Lives of a Cell" skit and took center stage. This performance-based assessment vividly displayed what Amro was learning. He was learning how to be a member of a team, how to be responsible for his part, how to listen, and how to cooperate.

–Jennifer Fischer-Mueller

Research has also shown benefits of inclusion for students without disabilities, including 1) improved attitudes toward diversity (Finke, McNaughton, & Drager, 2009), 2) unique opportunities for learning about prejudice and equity (Fisher, Sax,

---

[1]For more information about Amro see Jorgensen (1998).

& Jorgensen, 1998), and 3) improved educational outcomes for all students when inclusion was the primary
school reform (Theoharis & Causton-Theoharis, 2010).

The rationale for inclusion is also supported by the
fact that no studies conducted since the late 1970s have
shown an academic advantage for educating students
with intellectual and other developmental disabilities
in separate settings (Falvey, 2004). In fact, studies have
shown some negative effects of separate special education placement (Causton-Theoharis, Theoharis, Orsati, &
Cosier, 2011; Fisher, Sax, Rodifer, & Pumpian, 1999; Hunt
& Farron-Davis, 1992).

And finally, the performance of students without disabilities is not compromised by the presence of students with disabilities in their classrooms (Baker,
Wang, & Walberg, 1994/1995; Cole et al., 2004; Staub & Peck, 1994).

> We talked a lot about the value for Amro of being in our school and learning from others. However we also discovered that students and adults learned much from him. We learned what it meant to be inclusive and how to find value in everyone.
>
> –Jennifer Fischer-Mueller

QUALITY INDICATORS OF INCLUSIVE SCHOOLS

Several researchers and inclusive education organizations have described the quality indicators of inclusive education—the "how do you know it when you see it"—
helping parents and professionals differentiate true inclusion from its imitators
(e.g., part-time inclusion, reverse inclusion, 50/50 classrooms; Florida Department
of Education, 2007; Jorgensen, McSheehan, Schuh, & Son-
nenmeier, 2009; Maryland Coalition for Inclusive Education, 2011). These indicators reflect student, team, school,
and district variables.

A truly inclusive education means that students are
1) members of age-appropriate general education classrooms in their neighborhood schools and participate in
inclusive academic, social, and extracurricular activities;
2) presumed competent to communicate about and learn
general education curriculum content; 3) provided with
augmentative and alternative communication (AAC) systems and supports if they do not communicate in ways
that are commensurate with their same-age typically
developing peers; 4) provided with supplementary aids
and services (e.g., emotional and behavioral, accessible
materials, technology, sensory, instruction, physical and
environmental adaptations) that enable them to learn the
general education curriculum and to accomplish their
IEP goals; 5) taught self-advocacy and self-determination skills; 6) provided with
intentional facilitation of their social relationships; and, 7) involved in making
choices about their learning and in decisions about their educational experience
and future.

> I believe that social growth is as important, if not more important, than academic growth. Knowing all the facts in the world will not help you if you have not learned how to work with others. I believe that often times my students learn more valuable skills from ac- cepting and believing in each other than I will ever be able to teach them through text books and lesson plans.
>
> –Holly Prud'homme

Teams of general educators, special educators, related service providers
and others 1) work collaboratively to design culturally responsive and accessible
instruction, teach, evaluate the fidelity of instruction and supports, and measure
student learning and other important educational outcomes; 2) provide instruction

and support primarily within general education instruction and other inclusive activities and settings; 3) work in partnership to support students' inclusive education; and 4) use person-centered planning to design students' graduation plans and assist in their transition from school to postsecondary education, career, and an inclusive adult life.

Schools provide professional development to general and special educators to enhance the quality of inclusive education; and leadership teams support the inclusive education mission by providing resources, hiring qualified staff, and using data to inform continuous improvement.

> My team and I take advantage of professional development opportunities to keep abreast of new strategies and techniques that enhance our practice. We attend workshops on differentiation, creating measurable IEP goals that support general education curriculum, effective team planning, sensory awareness, behavior management, and AAC.
>
> –Holly Prud'homme

COLLABORATIVE TEAMING AND NEW ROLES

Changing team member roles and working effectively in a collaborative team are essential for successful inclusive education. Table 13.1 illustrates differences among a few key team member roles in inclusive versus non-inclusive schools. Although introducing the idea of changing roles is relatively straightforward, implementing those changes often challenges many educators' long-held beliefs and practices that were learned during initial personnel preparation programs, as well as more than 30 years of distinct disciplinary identities.

> Collaboration was a core value at our high school. We believed that our collective intelligence was greater than any one of us alone. Over time, our teaching team expanded to include students, who became Amro's friends. I believe they were his real teachers.
>
> –Jennifer Fischer-Mueller

Jorgensen and colleagues (2010) synthesized the essential communication skills, structures, and processes that promote effective team collaboration in inclusive schools. (Disciplinary skills related to general and special education professional standards and conduct are beyond the scope of this chapter.) Their work draws on that of Thousand and Villa (1992); Garmston and Wellman (1999); Hunt, Soto, Maier, and Doering (2003); Jorgensen, Schuh, and Nisbet (2006); and others.

Communication Skills

Skilled collaborative team members use a variety of effective communication skills including pausing, paraphrasing, probing for specificity, knowing when to put ideas "on the table" and when to take them off, paying attention to self and others, and pursuing a balance between advocacy and inquiry. The person serving as the primary team facilitator possesses skills in the areas of managing people and resources; collecting, analyzing, and synthesizing data; promoting recommended practices; facilitating meetings; presenting information clearly and accurately; consulting; modeling; coaching; and mediating. These facilitator skills are reflected in a newer role and job title for special education teachers known as inclusion facilitators (Jorgensen et al., 2006).

Table 13.1. Key team member roles in inclusive versus noninclusive schools

Team member	Inclusive school role	Noninclusive school role
General education teacher	Welcomes all students as members of heterogeneous general education classrooms	Determines class membership of students with disabilities based on "teacher deals" with special educators
	Uses universal design for learning principles to design accessible curriculum and instruction for all students	Designs instruction only for students without disabilities
	Shares in the creation of accessible materials for all students	Creates instructional materials only for students without disabilities
	Participates in formal and frequent team meetings to plan instruction and supports	Participates only in formal IEP and progress report meetings
	Collaborates with special educators to grade students with disabilities	Sees grading students with disabilities as the responsibility of the special education teacher
Special education teacher	Serves in the role of co-teacher or inclusion facilitator for students with disabilities	Teaches in a classroom composed only of students with disabilities
	Develops students' IEP goals based on general education standards and functional skills needed for full participation in school and transition to an inclusive life in the community	Bases students' IEP goals only on functional academic or community living skills, not general education standards
	Facilitates regular instructional planning meetings to design supports for students' full participation in general education instruction	Plans instruction in isolation
	Shares the responsibility for the design of instructional materials for all students	Assumes primary responsibility for designing instructional materials for students with disabilities
Speech-language pathologist	Follows Beukelman and Mirenda's (2005) Participation Model and recommendations from the National Joint Committee for the Communication Needs of Persons with Severe Disabilities (1991) in designing goals, supports, and services	Espouses a "prerequisites" model regarding candidacy for AAC or other communication supports
	Writes goals and objectives that prioritize skills needed for students to fully participate in general education instruction and typical social relationships	Values spoken language over communication using AAC methods and devices
	Integrates services within typical general education instructional routines and typical social activities	Writes IEP goals and objectives disconnected from general education standards
		Provides most services using a pull-out model

Note: IEP, Individualized education programs; AAC, Augmentative and alternative communication.

Meeting Structures

Effective meeting structures are essential for the efficient use of time and the generation of good ideas by instructional teams. The following five teaming structures achieve these results: 1) establishing a clear purpose and desired outcomes for meetings, 2) using a meeting space that facilitates collaboration without interruptions, 3) having an agenda appropriate to the meeting purpose that includes time limits for each discussion item (a downloadable template is available in Jorgensen et al., 2010, pp. 155–157), 4) identifying who needs to attend the meeting and ensuring their presence, and 5) rotating meeting process roles (e.g., facilitator, notetaker, timekeeper). (Figures 13.1 and 13.2 present planning forms to guide these discussions).

I work with a team of dedicated professionals that meets weekly to plan for our students. We incorporate the speech, sensory, motor, behavior, and specific educational goals into upcoming units of study and activities. When new worksheets, procedures, AAC programing, or preteaching need to occur we "divide and conquer" so that the work doesn't always fall onto one person.

–Holly Prud'homme

For students with significant disabilities, the authors recommend a weekly hour-long instructional planning meeting in which upcoming units and lessons are described and specific student supports are planned. Some teams allocate one meeting per week to instructional planning for 3 weeks during the month and use the final meeting of the month for general service coordination issues such as transportation, medical updates, technology discussions, and so forth.

Team Processes

With a strong foundation of effective communication skills and structures that promote harmonious and efficient meetings, team members also need to use a variety of teaming processes that lead to high-quality decisions. These processes include 1) building community and team identity, 2) setting and maintaining group norms, 3) building and carrying out sustainable agreements, 4) reflecting on practice, 5) resolving conflicts, 6) maintaining records and sharing meeting minutes, and 7) collaborating in the actual delivery of instruction and supplemental aids and services.

CURRICULUM, INSTRUCTION, AND ORGANIZATIONAL STRUCTURES THAT ACCOMMODATE THE LEARNING NEEDS OF ALL STUDENTS IN GENERAL EDUCATION

In the 1980s inclusion began one student at a time, and that is still how it happens in most schools. Several school reform models and initiatives exist, however, that use inclusion as the driver of efforts to align the separate systems of general and special education into one inclusive system for all students (Causton-Theoharis & Theoharis, 2008; Jorgensen, 1998; Sailor, 2010). Sailor and Roger (2005) described an approach—the Schoolwide Applications Model (SAM)—that melds elements of response to intervention (RTI) and positive behavior interventions and supports (PBIS) in a fully inclusive educational model. Although the hope is that all schools will adopt this model, because educators cannot wait for these reforms

Routines-Based Planning Form

Student: _____ Grade: _____ Date: _____

State the name of the instructional routine.	Specify what the students without disabilities are doing.	Indicate if the student can participate in the same way or if he or she needs an alternate way to participate in the same routine.	List the supports the student will need to fully participate.	Specify the team member who will prepare the supports.

Figure 13.1. Routines-based planning form. (From Jorgensen, C.M., & Lambert, L. [2012]. Inclusion means more than just being "in:" Planning full participation of students with intellectual and other developmental disabilities in the general education classroom. *International Journal of Whole Schooling, 8*[2], 25; reprinted by permission.)

Unit name: Class:

Dates of unit: Teacher:

Instructions: The team should discuss and record the most important learning objectives for the student in this unit in Question 1 and in Column 1 of Questions 2–5. In Question 6 Column 1, the team records the supports necessary for the student to participate and learn. In Question 6 Column 2, the team indicates who will prepare each support. After the unit is completed, the team revisits the form and records the team's qualitative assessment of the student's performance in Questions 2–5 and the fidelity with which supports were provided in Question 6. Low fidelity ratings mean that the team ought to have low confidence that the student's performance is an accurate representation of the student's capabilities and the quality of supports needs to be improved. The number of learning objectives and supports can be individualized to each student. The team leader loads this form onto a laptop and fills it in as the team plans. Each unit plan is saved with a file name specifying the subject area, the unit name, the student's initials, and a date. Example: History_CivilWar_JR_010113

1. What standards will the student pursue?

   a.

   b.

   c.

2. What enduring understandings/big ideas the student will acquire?

Enduring understandings	No progress	Some progress	Mastered	Exceeded
1.				

3. What prioritized vocabulary will the student learn?

Vocabulary	No progress	Some progress	Mastered	Exceeded
1.				

4. What prioritized knowledge or content will the student acquire?

Knowledge	No progress	Some progress	Mastered	Exceeded
1.				

5. What IEP objectives will be targeted during this unit?

IEP objectives	No progress	Some progress	Mastered	Exceeded
1.				

6. What supports will be necessary? With what fidelity were the planned supports provided?

Supports	Who will plan or prepare	Consistency (how *often* provided)				Accuracy (how *correctly* provided)			
		Rarely	Sometimes	Usually	Always	Rarely	Sometimes	Usually	Always
1.									

Note: Rarely, 0%–25%; sometimes, 25%–50%; usually, 50%–75%; always, approaching 100%; IEP, individualized education program.

Figure 13.2. Inclusive general education unit-based planning and feedback form for students with complex support needs.

before including students with significant disabilities, the remainder of this section describes the features of universally designed curriculum and instruction, and individualized supports for students with significant disabilities.

Universally Designed Curriculum and Instruction

Regardless of whether a school is fully inclusive or is a traditional school, teachers can use the principles of universal design for learning (UDL; Rose & Meyer, 2002) to promote all students' learning by providing 1) multiple means of knowledge representation (i.e., presenting information and content in different ways), 2) multiple means of action and expression (i.e., differentiating the ways that students can show what they know and can do), and 3) multiple means for engagement (i.e., using varied means for stimulating learning and motivation).

> When I create differentiated lesson plans I take many things into consideration. There are students who need to be challenged, students who need to have extra visuals or easier text, students who need vocabulary programmed into their AAC devices so that they can fully participate in the lesson, and students with individualized IEP goals that must be addressed.
>
> –Holly Prud'homme

High school teacher Dan Bisaccio used UDL principles to design an environmental science unit around New Hampshire science process skills such as "apply scientific theories and laws to new situations to generate hypotheses" and content standards such as "describe the type of impact certain environmental changes, including deforestation, invasive species, increased erosion, and pollution containing toxic substances, could have on local environments" (New Hampshire Department of Education, 2006). Mr. Bisaccio wanted to kick off the unit with a "grabber" activity that would engage each and every student in his class; some students who had a lot of prior knowledge, and some who didn't, some students who had a difficult time reading, and those whose attention span was short (Jorgensen, 1998, 2005). He wanted to avoid the stultifying, but all too common, scenario in which the teacher previewed the unit by "talking at" students and asking them to read the main and subordinate headings of a book chapter.

For this activity Mr. Bisaccio organized his 30 students into groups of 10. Each group was given a partially decomposed tree branch, and he first asked them to describe the stick. After ten minutes or so, spokespeople for each team described the stick's bark, its size and weight, its smell and taste, and so forth. Then Mr. Bisaccio asked the students to tell a plausible "story of the stick" using the creative talents and learning styles of all their group members. After giving the students about 20 minutes of preparation and rehearsal time, group performances included narrative stories, skits, poems, charts and diagrams, and even a rap song that depicted their hypotheses.

> Amro's presence in my class heightened the importance of presenting information in a way that would reach him, and by extension, all the other students in my heterogeneous, inclusive classroom. My job was to make Amro's learning of science visible.
>
> –Jennifer Fischer-Mueller

This kick-off activity set the stage for a unit that engaged all students. It had an overarching essential question: Are the New Hampshire forests healthy? Mr. Bisaccio presented information in multiple ways, including text and videos. Although he presented a short lecture every day that aligned with the reading or homework, the students took an active part in their own learning by doing library research, conducting observations in the nearby woods, hearing a first-hand account from a New Hampshire forester, and engaging in small-group discussions and debates. At the conclusion of the unit there was a traditional multiple-choice test in addition to a performance exhibition in which groups presented arguments supporting their answer to the essential question.

Where are students w/ MSD

Supports for Students with Significant Disabilities

Even when curriculum, instruction, and assessment are universally designed, there are some students who need more intensive or personalized supports in order to learn alongside their classmates without disabilities.

Many authors have developed schema for categorizing supports, but most include the following: 1) physical supports, 2) sensory supports, 3) emotional/behavioral supports, 4) adapted materials, 5) assistive technology, 6) personalized instruction, 7) communication supports, and 8) individualized means for demonstrating learning (Jorgensen et al., 2006). These support categories are not mutually exclusive, and for many students, full participation requires the use of several supports simultaneously. Leslie was just such a student in Mr. Bisaccio's class. Her IEP team used a routines-based planning process and format (see Figure 13.1) to design support plans for the teaching routines that Mr. Bisaccio frequently used. For example, during the teaching routine in which students read from a handout and took notes (this is written in Column 1), the students had to decode and comprehend the text, determine which information was important to write in their notebooks, highlight key words or other information, and ask questions to clarify their understanding (entered in Column 2). Leslie needed individualized supports for all aspects of participating in this routine, so the phrase *alternate ways of participating* was written in Column 3, corresponding to each of the typically developing student behaviors listed in Column 2. It is important to note that Leslie would not participate in an alternate activity, but rather the same activity with supports. In Column 4 the team specified those supports: 1) enlarged text written at a first- or second-grade level containing the key vocabulary and concepts of the topic (special education teacher), 2) aided language boards or graphic organizers to enhance both receptive understanding and expressive communication (speech language pathologist), and 3) a notetaking template on her laptop. In Column 5 they wrote the names of the team members who would be responsible for preparing the supports and facilitating Leslie's use of them during the notetaking activity.

> I am in my 10th year of teaching first and second grade and I have not once been able to pull out the lesson plans and differentiated work from a year before and feel comfortable that I had everything I needed to meet the needs of the current year's students. The routines, supports, modifications, expectations, sensory needs, use of AAC devices, and goals for each student make each class each year a completely different experience.
>
> Holly Prud'homme

Students helped

Leslie's team used a second planning process to identify her priority learning objectives for each unit of instruction (see Figure 13.2). They determined that she would focus on the same essential question as the other students (i.e., Are the New Hampshire forests healthy?) She was expected to master core vocabulary such as *ecological system*, *bio-diversity*, *pollution*, and *environmentalist*. The team prioritized learning standards that were similar to those for students without disabilities, but reduced in depth, breadth, and complexity. So instead of the knowledge standard "describe the type of impact certain environmental changes, including deforestation, invasive species, increased erosion, and pollution containing toxic substances, could have on local environments," Leslie's knowledge standard was "describe the impact that two ecological threats have on trees and animals in the New Hampshire forest." Prioritized IEP goals included managing her materials, taking notes of key information in an informational text, asking and answering questions, and fulfilling a meaningful role in group activities. Finally, the last section of the unit planning form was a summary of the individualized supports that Leslie needed throughout the whole unit, informed by the previous routines-based planning discussions.

> Students in my classroom challenge each other by asking thought-provoking questions, helping without giving the answer, encouraging each other to try their best, reminding one another of expectations, and including each other to promote everyone's growth.
>
> –Holly Prud'homme

One of the most important guidelines for the provision of support is to use that which is "only as special as necessary" (Giangreco, Edelman, Luiselli, & MacFarland, 1998, p. 3).

Direct instruction benefits all students, but care must be taken not to create "islands in the mainstream" (Biklen, 1985, p. 18) by pulling students with disabilities aside or taking them out of the room for one-to-one instruction for the majority of the class period. Particularly when schools have adopted multitiered systems of support (e.g., RTI), there are ample opportunities throughout a typical school day for all students to receive direct instruction without being removed from core, inclusive general education lessons (Collins, Evans, Creech-Galloway, Karl, & Miller, 2007; Polychronis, McDonnell, Johnson, Riesen, & Jameson, 2004). In Leslie's case, she benefitted from the UDL principles Mr. Bisaccio used to design his unit, deliver instruction, and assess student learning. He differentiated his questions to target Leslie's learning objectives. As students worked in cooperative groups, he circulated throughout the classroom and spent a few minutes of each class period with Leslie. Leslie's peers were taught how to provide support to her without giving her the answer. The special education teacher came into the classroom several times a week to co-teach a lesson, facilitate a small group of which Leslie was a part, provide her with direct instruction, or model for and coach her paraprofessional. Leslie also went to a noncategorical academic support center daily where she was tutored by an upper class peer.

NINE ACTION STEPS TO GET STARTED
OR IMPROVE CURRENT INCLUSIVE PRACTICE

Although the organizational structures that support inclusive education have been recognized for more than 20 years (Salisbury, Strieker, Roach, & McGregor, 2001), progress has been uneven from school to school and state to state, and has been highly dependent on the advocacy of individual parents or professionals. The following nine action steps address the organizational structures and processes that may help accelerate the pace of changes toward effective inclusion and more importantly, sustain it over time (Ferguson, Kozleski, & Smith, 2005; Fixsen, Naoom, Blase, Friedman, & Wallace, 2005; Knoster, Villa, & Thousand, 2000).

1. Establish an inclusive education leadership team that includes parents of students with and without disabilities, general and special education administrators and teachers, related service providers, Title I teachers and reading specialists, instructional technology staff, and paraprofessionals. This team's responsibilities include

   a. Creating a vision and mission statement for inclusive education

   b. Modeling inclusive values and practices

   c. Developing a plan for building consensus for change

   d. Creating infrastructures that support inclusion

   e. Developing an implementation plan with benchmarks of achievement for students and staff

   f. Identifying and using data management systems to monitor student learning in light of changing practices

   g. Planning and providing job-embedded professional development

   h. Communicating with staff members, families, school board members, and other community members regarding inclusive education

2. Use an inclusive education quality indicator tool (Jorgensen, McSheehan, & Sonnenmeier, 2010, p. 227) to conduct an assessment of a school's current state of inclusive education and use the results to inform the inclusion implementation plan.

3. Start a professional learning community to learn about inclusive education by reading books such as

   a. *Differentiated Activities and Assessments Using the Common Core Standards* (Coil, 2011)

   b. *Including Students with Severe and Multiple Disabilities in Typical Classrooms* (Downing, 2008)

   c. *Joyful Learning: Active and Collaborative Learning in Inclusive Classrooms* (Udvari-Solner & Kluth, 2008)

   d. *Peer Support Strategies for Improving All Students' Social Lives and Learning* (Carter, Cushing, & Kennedy, 2009)

   e. *Practically Speaking: Language, Literacy, and Academic Development for Students with AAC Needs* (Soto & Zangari, 2009)

    f.   *Self-Determination: Instructional and Assessment Strategies* (Wehmeyer & Field, 2007)

    g.   *The Beyond Access Model: Promoting Membership, Participation, and Learning for Students with Disabilities in the General Education Classroom* (Jorgensen et al., 2010)

    h.   *The Inclusion Facilitator's Guide* (Jorgensen et al., 2006)

    i.   *The Paraprofessional's Handbook for Effective Support in Inclusive Classrooms* (Causton-Theoharis & Kluth, 2009)

    j.   *You're Going to Love This Kid! Teaching Students with Autism in the Inclusive Classroom, Second Edition* (Kluth, 2010)

4.   Provide professional development on inclusive evidence-based practices by, for example, sending IEP team members to conferences such as PEAK (http://www.peakparent.org), TASH (http://www.tash.org), or summer institutes sponsored by the School of Education at Syracuse University (http://soe.syr.edu/centers_institutes/schools_of_promise) or the Institute on Disability at the University of New Hampshire (http://iod.unh.edu).

5.   Create a chart of team roles comparing and contrasting current responsibilities with those needed for successful inclusion (see Table 13.1).

6.   Design a master school schedule that prioritizes common planning time. Absent this up-front design, use other creative ideas to enable team members to plan together regularly, including

    a.   Hire a part-time, permanent substitute teacher who covers general education teachers' classes while they participate in instructional planning meetings.

    b.   Hold meetings during students' recess or lunch periods and assign team members to cover those duties on a rotating basis.

    c.   Ensure that related service providers are able to participate in instructional planning meetings by designating one unit of their service time per week to collaboration.

    d.   Bring two classes together for a curriculum-related film, freeing one teacher for a planning meeting.

7.   Use instructional planning forms. Teams that make a commitment to use the instructional planning forms presented in Figures 13.1 and 13.2 usually find that students' participation and learning show signs of improvement.

8.   Complete an environmental survey to assess the physical and sensory accessibility of the whole building and then address barriers to students' full participation in the academic and social life of the school.

9.   Purchase and provide training in the use of instructional and assistive technology. Identify a person who is responsible for cataloging and maintaining all equipment and software.

SUMMARY

Mara Sapon-Shevin said

> Inclusion is not about disability, nor is it only about schools. Inclusion demands that we ask, what kind of world do we want to create? What kinds of skills and commitment do people need to thrive in diverse society? By embracing inclusion as a model of social justice, we can create a world fit for all of us. (2003, p. 26, 28)

> I believe a classroom teacher's job is to differentiate every day to meet the incredibly diverse needs of each and every student in the class, and if you are unwilling to do this then you are in the wrong profession. I know that it is not an easy task or one that can be done quickly. But I also know that with hard work, teamwork, and a positive classroom community it is certainly possible, and the benefits are undeniable.
>
> Holly Prud'homme

> I've come to appreciate that we are all made up of layers of strengths and needs, and that teaching and learning require interdependence and common core beliefs. I now understand what really matters, thanks to Amro and the entire community that supported his learning and my teaching.
>
> Jennifer Fischer-Mueller

Realizing inclusion requires adoption of this philosophy; presuming all students' competence; strong administrative leadership; a collaborative school culture; ongoing professional development based on evidence-based inclusive practices; use of data to drive decision-making; restructuring of spaces and staff roles; curriculum and instruction based on the principles of UDL; and, when necessary, providing individualized supports for students with the most significant disabilities.

History has shown that the abilities of students with significant disabilities have been grossly underestimated; all students have valuable contributions to make; all students develop into better citizens when they learn in inclusive communities; and change takes commitment, leadership, time, and resources.

REFERENCES

Baker, E.T., Wang, M.C., & Walberg, H.J. (1994/1995). Synthesis of research: The effects of inclusion on learning. *Educational Leadership, 52*, 33–35.

Beukelman, D., & Mirenda, P. (2005). *Augmentative and alternative communication: Management of severe communication disorders in children and adults* (3rd ed.). Baltimore, MD: Paul H. Brookes Publishing Co.

Biklen, D. (1985). *Achieving the complete school: Strategies for effective mainstreaming.* New York, NY: Teachers College Press.

Brinker, R.P., & Thorpe, M.E. (1984). Integration of severely handicapped students and the proportion of IEP objectives achieved. *Exceptional Children, 51*, 168–175.

Carter, E.W., Cushing, L.S., & Kennedy, C.H. (2009). *Peer support strategies for improving all students' social lives and learning.* Baltimore, MD: Paul H. Brookes Publishing Co.

Causton-Theoharis, J., & Kluth, P. (2009). *The paraprofessional's handbook for effective support in inclusive classrooms.* Baltimore, MD: Paul H. Brookes Publishing Co.

Causton-Theoharis, J., & Theoharis, G. (2008). Creating inclusive schools for all students. *School Administrator, 65*(8), 24–25.

Causton-Theoharis, J., Theoharis, G., Orsati, F., & Cosier, M. (2011). Does self-contained special education deliver on its promises? A critical inquiry into research and practice. *Journal of Special Education Leadership, 24*(2), 61–78.

Coil, C. (2011). *Differentiated activities and assessments using the common core standards.* Marion, IL: Pieces of Learning.

Cole, C.M., Waldron, N., & Majd, M. (2004). Academic progress of students across inclusive and traditional settings. *Mental Retardation, 42*, 136–144.

Collins, B.C., Evans, A., Creech-Galloway, C., Karl, J., & Miller, A. (2007). Comparison of the acquisition and maintenance of teaching functional and core content sight words in special and general education settings. *Focus on Autism and Other Developmental Disabilities, 22*, 220–233.

Downing, J.E. (2008). *Including students with severe and multiple disabilities in typical classrooms.* Baltimore, MD: Paul H. Brookes Publishing Co.

Falvey, M. (2004). Towards realizing the influence of "Toward realization of the least restrictive environments for severely disabled students." *Research and Practice for Persons with Severe Disabilities, 29*, 9–10.

Ferguson, D.L., Kozleski, E.B., & Smith, A. (2005). *On…transformed, inclusive schools: A framework to guide fundamental change in urban schools.* Retrieved from http://www.niusileadscape.org/docs/FINAL_PRODUCTS/LearningCarousel/TransformedInclusive Schools.pdf

Finke, E.H., McNaughton, D.B., & Drager, K.D. (2009). "All children can and should have the opportunity to learn": General education teachers' perspectives on including children with autism spectrum disorder who require AAC. *Augmentative and Alternative Communication, 25*, 110–122.

Fisher, D., Sax, C., & Jorgensen, C. (1998). Philosophical foundations of inclusive, restructuring schools. In C. Jorgensen (Ed.), *Restructuring schools for all students: Taking inclusion to the next level* (pp. 29–47). Baltimore, MD: Paul H. Brookes Publishing Co.

Fisher, D., Sax, C., Rodifer, K., & Pumpian, I. (1999). Teachers' perspectives of curriculum and climate changes: Benefits of inclusive education. *Journal for a Just and Caring Education, 5*, 256–268.

Fisher, M., & Meyer, L. (2002). Development and social competence after two years for students enrolled in inclusive and self-contained educational programs. *Research and Practice for Persons with Severe Disabilities, 27*, 165–174.

Fixsen, D.L., Naoom, S.F., Blase, K.A., Friedman, R.M., & Wallace, F. (2005). *Implementation research: A synthesis of the literature.* Tampa: University of South Florida, Louis de la Parte Florida Mental Health Institute, The National Implementation Research Network (FMHI Publication #231).

Florida Department of Education. (2007). *Best practices for inclusive education.* Tallahassee, FL: Author.

Garmston, R.J., & Wellman, B.M. (1999). *The adaptive school: A sourcebook for developing collaborative groups.* Norwood, MA: Christopher-Gordon Publishers.

Giangreco, M.F., Edelman, S., Luiselli, T.E., & MacFarland, S.C.Z. (1998). Reaching consensus about educationally necessary support services: A qualitative evaluation of VISTA. *Special Services in the Schools, 13*(1/2), 1–32.

Guralnick, M.J., Connor, R., Hammond, M., Gottman, J.M., & Kinnish, K. (1996). Immediate effects of mainstreamed settings on the social interactions and social integration of preschool children. *American Journal on Mental Retardation, 100*, 359–377.

Helmstetter, E., Curry, C.A., Brennan, M., & Sampson-Saul, M. (1998). Comparison of general and special education classrooms of students with severe disabilities. *Education and Training in Mental Retardation and Developmental Disabilities, 33*, 216–227.

Hunt, P., & Farron-Davis, F. (1992). A preliminary investigation of IEP quality and content associated with placement in general education versus special education classes. *The Journal of the Association for Persons with Severe Handicaps, 17*, 247–253.

Hunt, P., Farron-Davis, F., Beckstead, S., Curtis, D., & Goetz, L. (1994). Evaluating the effects of placement of students with severe disabilities in general education versus special classes. *Journal of the Association for Persons with Severe Handicaps, 19*, 200–214.

Hunt, P., Soto, G., Maier, J., & Doering, K. (2003). Collaborative teaming to support students at risk and students with severe disabilities in general education classrooms. *Exceptional Children, 69*, 315–332.

Individuals with Disabilities Education Improvement Act (IDEA) of 2004, PL108-446, 20 U.S.C. §§ 1400 *et seq.*

Jackson, L.B., Ryndak, D.L., & Wehmeyer, M.L. (2008/2009). The dynamic relationship between context, curriculum, and student learning: A case for inclusive education as a research-based practice. *Research and Practice for Persons with Severe Disabilities,* *33-34,* 175–195.

Jorgensen, C.M. (1998). *Restructuring high schools for all students: Taking inclusion to the next level.* Baltimore, MD: Paul H. Brookes Publishing Co.

Jorgensen, C.M. (2005). An inquiry based instructional planning model that accommodates student diversity. *International Journal of Whole Schooling, 1*(2), 5–14.

Jorgensen, C.M., McSheehan, M., Schuh, M., & Sonnenmeier, R. (2009). *Essential best practices in inclusive schools.* Durham: Institute on Disability, University of New Hampshire.

Jorgensen, C.M., McSheehan, M., & Sonnenmeier, R. (2007). Presumed competence reflected in the educational programs of students with IDD before and after the Beyond Access professional development intervention. *Journal of Intellectual and Developmental Disabilities, 32,* 248–262.

Jorgensen, C.M., McSheehan, M., & Sonnenmeier, R.M. (2010). *The Beyond Access Model: Promoting membership, participation, and learning for students with disabilities in the general education classroom.* Baltimore, MD: Paul H. Brookes Publishing Co.

Jorgensen, C.M., Schuh, M.C., & Nisbet, J. (2006). *The inclusion facilitator's guide.* Baltimore, MD: Paul H. Brookes Publishing Co.

Kluth, P. (2010). *You're going to love this kid! Teaching students with autism in the inclusive classroom* (2nd ed.). Baltimore, MD: Paul H. Brookes Publishing Co.

Knoster, T.P., Villa, R.A., & Thousand, J.S. (2000). A framework for thinking about systems change. In R.A. Villa & J.S. Thousand (Eds.), *Restructuring for caring and effective education: Piecing the puzzle together* (2nd ed., pp. 93–128). Baltimore, MD: Paul H. Brookes Publishing Co.

Maryland Coalition for Inclusive Education. (2011). *Quality indicators for inclusive building-based practices.* Hanover, MD: Author.

McSheehan, M., Sonnenmeier, R.M., & Jorgensen, C.M. (2009). Membership, participation, and learning in general education classrooms for students with autism spectrum disorders who use AAC. In P. Mirenda & T. Iacono (Eds.), *Autism spectrum disorders and AAC* (pp. 413–442). Baltimore, MD: Paul H. Brookes Publishing Co.

National Joint Committee for the Communication Needs of Persons with Severe Disabilities. (1991). *Guidelines for meeting the communication needs of persons with severe disabilities.* Retrieved from http://www.asha.org/docs/html/GL1992-00201.html

New Hampshire Department of Education (2006). *K-12 Science Literacy. New Hampshire Curriculum Framework.* Retrieved from http://www.education.nh.gov/instruction/curriculum/science/documents/framework.pdf

Polychronis, S.C., McDonnell, J., Johnson, W., Riesen, T., & Jameson, M. (2004). A comparison of two trial distribution schedules in embedded instruction. *Focus on Autism and Other Developmental Disabilities, 19,* 140–151.

Rose, D.H., & Meyer, A. (2002). *Teaching every student in the digital age: Universal design for learning.* Alexandria, VA: Association for Supervision and Curriculum Development.

Ryndak, D.L., Alper, S., Ward, T., Storch, J.F., & Montgomery, J.W. (2010). Long-term outcomes of services in inclusive and self-contained settings for siblings with comparable significant disabilities. *Education and Training in Autism and Developmental Disabilities, 45,* 38–53.

Ryndak, D.L., Morrison, A., & Sommerstein, L. (1999). Literacy before and after inclusion in general education settings: A case study. *Journal of the Association for Persons with Severe Handicaps, 24,* 5–22.

Sailor, W. (2010). Access to the general curriculum: Systems change or tinker some more? *Research and Practice for Persons with Severe Disabilities, 33,* 249–257.

Sailor, W., & Roger, B. (2005). Rethinking inclusion: Schoolwide applications. *Phi Delta Kappan, 86,* 503–509.

Salisbury, C., Strieker, T., Roach, V., & McGregor, G. (2001). *Pathways to inclusive practices: Systems oriented, policy-linked, and research-based strategies that work.* Alexandria, VA: Consortium on Inclusive Schooling Practices.

Sapon-Shevin, M. (2003). Inclusion: A matter of social justice. *Educational Leadership, 61*(2), 26, 28.

Soto, G., Muller, E., Hunt, P., & Goetz, L. (2001). Critical issues in the inclusion of students who use augmentative and alternative communication: An educational team perspective. *Augmentative and Alternative Communication, 17,* 62–72.

Soto, G., & Zangari, C. (Eds.). (2009). *Practically speaking: Language, literacy, and academic development for students with AAC needs.* Baltimore, MD: Paul H. Brookes Publishing Co.

Staub, D., & Peck, C.A. (1994). What are the outcomes for nondisabled students? *Educational Leadership, 52*(4), 36–40.

Theoharis, G., & Causton-Theoharis, J. (2010). Include, belong, learn. *Educational Leadership, 68*(2). Retrieved from http://www.ascd.org/publications/educational-leadership/oct10/vol68/num02/Include,-Belong,-Learn.aspx

Thousand, J., & Villa, R. (1992). Collaborative teams: A powerful tool in school restructuring. In R.A. Villa, J.S. Thousand, W.C. Stainback, & S.B. Stainback (Eds.), *Restructuring for caring and effective education: An administrative guide to creating heterogeneous schools* (pp. 73–108). Baltimore, MD: Paul H. Brookes Publishing Co.

Udvari-Solner, A., & Kluth, P. (2008). *Joyful learning: Active and collaborative learning in inclusive classrooms.* Thousand Oaks, CA: Corwin Press.

Wehmeyer, M., & Agran, M. (2006). Promoting access to the general curriculum for students with significant cognitive disabilities. In D.M. Browder & F. Spooner (Eds.), *Teaching language arts, math, and science to students with significant cognitive disabilities* (pp. 15–37). Baltimore, MD: Paul H. Brookes Publishing Co.

Wehmeyer, M.L., & Field, S. (2007). *Self-determination: Instructional and assessment strategies.* Thousand Oaks, CA: Corwin Press.

White, J., & Weiner, J.S. (2004). Influence of least restrictive environment and community based training on integrated employment outcomes for transitioning students with severe disabilities. *Journal of Vocational Rehabilitation, 21*(3), 149–156.

FOR FURTHER INFORMATION

Augmentative and Alternative Communication

Beukelman, D.R., & Mirenda, P. (2013). *Augmentative and alternative communication: Supporting children and adults with complex communication needs* (4th ed.). Baltimore, MD: Paul H. Brookes Publishing Co.

This book provides strategies for assessment, selecting augmentative and alternative communication (AAC) devices, choosing vocabulary, and using AAC within inclusive classrooms and other natural contexts.

Autism

Kluth, P. (2012). *"You're going to love this kid!" A professional development package for teaching students with autism in the inclusive classroom* (2nd ed.). Baltimore, MD: Paul H. Brookes Publishing Co.

This book discusses creating a welcoming classroom climate, teaching to student strengths, and fostering cooperative learning, and provides a host of teaching strategies in all curricular areas.

DVDs

Class of '96: An Inclusive Community of Learners

http://www.iodbookstore.org/products/Class-of-%2796%3A-An-Inclusive-Community-of-Learners-%28DVD%29.html

This DVD describes Souhegan High School in Amherst, New Hampshire, where all students were fully a part of heterogeneous mainstream general education classes. Features administrators, teachers, and students talking about their school where both equity and excellence are valued.

Including Samuel

http://www.includingsamuel.com/home.aspx

This DVD chronicles Samuel Habib's family's efforts to include him in every facet of their lives. This award-winning film honestly portrays his family's hopes and struggles as well as the experiences of four other individuals with disabilities and their families.

We Thought You'd Never Ask: Voices of People with Autism

http://shop.landlockedfilms.info/We-Thought-Youd-Never-Ask-Voices-of-People-with-Autism-1.htm

This is a short documentary film of people with autism talking about how they see the world and themselves.

Inclusive Education Models and Recommended Practices

Jorgensen, C. (1998). *Restructuring high schools for all students: Taking inclusion to the next level.*
Originally published by Paul H. Brookes Publishing Company, this book is now available directly from the author at cheryl.jorgensen@unh.edu. It discusses a whole-school restructuring approach that includes all students, with chapters on philosophy, organizational structures, new staff roles, curriculum and instruction, social relationships, self-determination, and transition.

Jorgensen, C.M., McSheehan, M., & Sonnenmeier, R.M. (2010). *The Beyond Access Model: Promoting membership, participation, and learning for students with disabilities in the general education classroom.* Baltimore, MD: Paul H. Brookes Publishing Co.
This book focuses on team-based instructional planning that supports learning of the general education curriculum. It includes fillable forms for each step in the process.

Rapp, W.H., & Arndt, K.L. (2012). *Teaching everyone. An introduction to inclusive education.* Baltimore, MD: Paul H. Brookes Publishing Co.
Written as a college text, this book is a comprehensive resource for administrators and educators who are new to inclusive education.

National Organizations and Projects

I am Norm

http://www.iamnorm.org/home.aspx

I am Norm is an initiative designed by young people to promote the acceptance, respect, and full inclusion of youth with disabilities in schools and communities.

Its work is driven by a Youth Inclusion Taskforce and supported by a coalition of youth-serving partner organizations.

SWIFT

http://www.swiftschools.org

SWIFT is a project funded by the U.S. Department of Education Office of Special Education Programs that supports K–8 schools to promote the academic achievement of all students, including those with the most extensive needs, within restructured general education.

TASH

http://www.tash.org

TASH is committed to equity, opportunity, and inclusion for people with disabilities and hosts webinars and an annual conference featuring sessions on inclusive education for individuals with disabilities, families, and professionals.

New Roles for Staff in Inclusive Classrooms

Causton-Theoharis, J. (2009). *The paraprofessional's handbook for effective support in inclusive classrooms.* Baltimore, MD: Paul H. Brookes Publishing Co.
This book provides strategies for veteran or new paraeducators that encourage students' self-reliance, full participation in the general education classroom, and social relationships.

Jorgensen, C.M., Schuh, M.C., & Nisbet, J. (2008). *The inclusion facilitator's guide.* Baltimore, MD: Paul H. Brookes Publishing Co.
This book presents recommended practices in inclusive education and a new role for special educators as facilitators of instructional planning teams.

Potts, E.A., & Howard, L.A. (2011). *How to co-teach: A guide for general and special educators.* Baltimore, MD: Paul H. Brookes Publishing Co.
This book addresses both educators' perspectives and strategies for maximizing the benefits of a co-teaching partnership.

Universal Design and Differentiating Instruction

Schwartz, P., & Kluth, P. (2007). *You're welcome: 30 innovative ideas for the inclusive classroom.* Portsmouth, NH: Heinemann.
This book includes three teacher-friendly booklets with strategies for differentiating instruction, collaborative teaming, and positive behavior supports.

CAST

http://www.cast.org

CAST's web site has hundreds of resources and tools for designing universally accessible instruction, including links to more than 3,500 adapted books.

CHAPTER 14

What We Know and Need to Know About Teaching Academic Skills

Fred Spooner and Diane M. Browder

What educators know as a field about teaching academic skills to students with severe disabilities has substantially increased and changed over the last 30 years, and our knowledge about what to teach (content), has grown significantly in the last decade. Conversely, instructional strategies that have been used to train people who find learning difficult, beginning with the first application of operant procedures with humans (Fuller, 1949), have, for the most part, remained static with the use of procedures derived from the experimental analysis of behavior (Skinner, 1938, 1953) employed in real-world environments to improve socially significant behavior with human participants known as applied behavior analysis (Morris, Altus, & Smith, 2013). In the specific case of instructional practices that have yielded the acquisition of domestic and community skills to academic skills (e.g., tooth brushing [Horner & Keilitz, 1975], toileting [Azrin & Foxx, 1971], dressing [Azrin, Schaeffer, & Wesolowski, 1976], public telephone use [Test, Spooner, Keul, & Grossi, 1990], riding a bus [Neef, Iwata, & Page, 1978], crossing a street [Vogelsburg & Rusch, 1979], reading for daily living [Lalli & Browder, 1993], following job sequence [Browder & Minarovic, 2000]) for students with severe disabilities, the particular subset of behavior analytic techniques called systematic instruction (Browder & Spooner, 2011; Collins, 2007; Snell, 1983; Snell & Brown, 2006; Wolery, Bailey, & Sugai, 1988) has been utilized. Systematic instruction incorporates 1) instruction of socially meaningful skills by defining target skills that are observable and measureable; 2) using data to demonstrate that skills were acquired as a result of the intervention; 3) using behavioral principles to promote transfer of stimulus control including differential reinforcement, systematic prompting and fading, and error correction; and 4) producing behavior change that can be generalized to other contexts, skills, people, and/or materials. Realizing what we know influences what we continue to need to know as we move forward in improving the lives of students with severe disabilities and their families.

This closing chapter presents what educators know by describing shifts in curricular philosophy; delineation of evidence-based practices; focus on the Common Core State Standards (CCSS; National Governors Association Center for Best Practices, Council of Chief State School Officers, 2010); and some of the known challenges, concerns, and controversy in teaching academic skills to students with severe disabilities. The chapter then focuses on what educators still need to know.

For the rest of this chapter, the authors will use *we* to refer to educators in general, and what is *known* will be based on what is available in the published literature at the time of this writing.

WHAT WE KNOW

Over the course of the last three decades, we know that our understanding of training skills (content), both of a functional and academic nature, has extensively increased while at the same time the instructional procedures used to allow students to acquire that content have remained relatively constant. Shifts in curricular philosophy are occurring with evidence-based practices guiding the choice of preferred instructional procedures. Academic content needs to be grade-aligned and there are challenges, concerns, and controversy in moving the field forward.

Shifts in Curricular Philosophy

Since the official founding of the field of severe disabilities (technically a subdiscipline of Special Education) in 1974, in which Sontag and Haring (1996) chronicled the creation of TASH and the professionalization of teaching students with severe disabilities, we have seen the focus of curriculum for this population shift. In the 1970s there was a developmental focus, moving in the 1980s to a functional focus with an emphasis on the criterion of ultimate functioning (e.g., Brown, Nietupski, & Hamre-Nietupski, 1976). In the 1990s the curricular focus shifted somewhat, keeping the attention on functional skills and adding a focus on inclusion and self-determination. Beginning around 2010 the emphasis became general curriculum access (Browder et al., 2003; Browder, Spooner, & Meier, 2011). The attention on access to the general curriculum for students with severe disabilities was first made possible by mandates from the Individuals with Disabilities Education Act Amendments (IDEA) of 1997 (PL 105-17), the No Child Left Behind Act of 2001 (PL 107-110), and the Individuals with Disabilities Education Improvement Act IDEA of 2004 (PL 108-446). The message was that all children, including those with severe disabilities, would have access to and the opportunity to make progress in the general curriculum. With this new focus, most educators have not forgotten what they already knew about the importance and practice of teaching functional life skills, as evidenced by continuing coverage in the most recent textbooks (e.g., Browder & Spooner, 2011; Collins, 2007; Snell & Brown, 2011). In contrast, there was increasing emphasis on teaching academic skills (literacy/reading, mathematics, and science) with evidence-based practices to impart learning (Spooner, Knight, Browder, & Smith, 2012). As described in Chapter 1, students with severe disabilities demonstrated that they could meet this increasing expectation.

Evidence-Based Practices

The documentation of evidence-based practices was an important component that was brought to the forefront by the National Research Council (2002), as Shavelson and Towne articulated the gold standard of randomized control trials (large studies with participants assigned randomly to control and treatment conditions). A special issue of *Research and Practice for Persons with Severe Disabilities*

(Spooner, 2003) was dedicated to delineating and discussing scientifically based research and students with low-incidence disabilities. Spooner and Browder (2003) and McDonnell and O'Neill (2003) made the argument for the appropriate use of single-case design methodology to answer questions about instructional effectiveness for this population. Soon after, Horner and colleagues (2005) delineated a prototype for using single-subject designs to validate evidence-based practices. With the publication of the special issue of *Exceptional Children* ("Criteria for Evidence-Based," 2005), and the cogent description of quality indicators and criteria for single-case methodology by Horner and colleagues, researchers established a starting point to chronicle and evaluate what the field knew about teaching academic skills to students with severe disabilities.

In three overarching analytic reviews, Browder and colleagues (Browder, Spooner, Ahlgrim-Delzell, Harris, & Wakeman, 2008; Browder, Wakeman, Spooner, Ahlgrim-Delzell, & Algozzine, 2006; Spooner, Knight, Browder, Jimenez, & DiBiase, 2011) sought to establish the knowledge base for teaching academic skills to students with severe disabilities. Based on the number of experiments delineated in these reviews, we know more about teaching literacy/reading (128 experiments; Browder, Wakeman, et al., 2006) than we know about teaching mathematics (68 experiments; Browder et al., 2008), and we know more about teaching mathematics than we do about teaching science (17 experiments; Spooner et al., 2011). With the application of the Horner and colleagues (2005) quality indicator criteria and the quantity and dispersions requirements (5 articles, 3 investigators, 3 geographic locations, and a minimum of 20 participants), systematic instruction was found to be an evidence-based practice. More specifically, subsets of systematic instruction were found to be evidence-based practices for teaching science (task analysis for chained tasks and time delay for discrete responses; Spooner et al., 2011) and literacy (massed trial instruction and systematic prompting; Browder, Wakeman, et al., 2006). Two additional reviews focused on evidence for using time delay as an instructional procedure to teach literacy to students with severe disabilities (Browder, Ahlgrim-Delzell, Spooner, Mims, & Baker, 2009) and the degree to which evidence-based practices were documented for teaching academics (Spooner et al., 2012).

From a review, we also now know that these systematic instructional procedures are evidence-based practices for general education settings (Hudson, Browder, & Wood, 2013). Hudson and colleagues (2013) found 17 experimental studies that applied procedures such as embedded time delay instruction to teach academic content in general education settings. Paraeducators, peers, and teachers have been able to apply these procedures in this context.

What also is emerging is that these systematic instruction procedures can be used concurrently with technology. For example, in a review of 21st Century portable electronic devices (e.g., media players with audio playback, smartphones, handheld computers), Mechling (2011) commented on the potential benefits with studies supporting their use across work, school, and community settings and discussed directions for future research. In a synthesis of literature from 1987 to 2005, Bellini and Akullian (2007) found video modeling and video self-modeling to be evidence-based practices, as evaluated by the guidelines devised by Horner and colleagues (2005) for children with autism spectrum disorders (ASDs). In another study that used technology in conjunction with systematic instruction, Smith, Spooner, and

Wood (2013) used explicit embedded computer-assisted instruction (CAI) to teach science terms and applications of those terms to students with ASDs and intellectual disability. In general, outcomes suggested 1) a functional relationship between introduction of CAI and the number of assessment items answered correctly; 2) the study participants, teachers, and peers without disabilities strongly agreed that the intervention was effective and appropriate; and 3) all three participants were able to generalize the targeted science terms at high levels to the science terms activity sheet completed in the inclusive science setting.

Grade-Aligned Academic Learning

For the last decade researchers in the area of severe disabilities have been exploring grade-aligned academic tasks and the instructional strategies used to facilitate the acquisition of more difficult content (e.g., Browder & Spooner, 2006, 2011; Browder, Spooner, Wakeman, Trela, & Baker, 2006; Spooner, Dymond, Smith, & Kennedy, 2006). The term *grade-aligned* refers to academic content that has been prioritized and adapted for students with severe disabilities but is the same content being learned by peers of the same chronological age in the student's assigned grade. What we now know is that the same set of instructional procedures that has been implemented for the last 60 years—those procedures derived from Skinner's operant analysis (1938) and more cogently articulated for this population of learners by Snell (1983) and known as systematic instruction—continue to be effectively used for ensuring acquisition, fluency, generalization, and maintenance of this more advanced academic content. Through systematic instruction, students have learned language arts (Browder, Trela, & Jimenez, 2007; Shurr & Taber-Doughty, 2012), mathematics (Browder, Jimenez, & Trela, 2012), and science (Knight, Spooner, Browder, & Smith, 2012; Smith, Spooner, Jimenez, & Browder, 2013; Smith, Spooner, & Wood, 2013) that is aligned to their grade-level standards.

Challenges, Concerns, and Controversy

We also know that there have been some challenges, concerns, and controversy in the area of access to the general curriculum and teaching academic skills to students with severe disabilities. Even though access to the general curriculum was first written into part of IDEA of 1997, as a field we have made slow progress in increasing the degree to which students with severe disabilities have access to and make progress in general curriculum. As access to the general curriculum has continued to advance, opportunities for these students have varied greatly from one state to another (Ryndak, Moore, Orlando, & Delano, 2008–2009).

Jackson, Ryndak, and Wehmeyer (2008–2009) challenged the field to view general curriculum access as having three components: 1) context (general education), 2) content, and 3) learning. As described in the previous sections of this chapter, there has been excellent progress demonstrating that students can learn the content. There even is evidence of learning in inclusive settings (Hudson et al., 2013). In contrast, the movement toward inclusive opportunities has been disappointing. Ten years after the first mention of access in the law, Smith's (2007) perspective was that we had made some headway, but still had a long, long, road ahead. His analysis was based on a national sample taken in 2002–2003 (the most current data available at the time) and suggested that less than 11% of students with intellectual disability—ALL levels of intellectual disability, including students who function at higher levels—were included in general education classrooms. In this analysis, inclusion in general education classes was defined as spending more than 79% of school time in that setting. Smith went on to speculate about possible barriers (e.g., money, policy) to increasing the number of students with intellectual disability who were fully included. A reasonable assumption, based on Smith's analysis, is the students with more severe disabilities are included in the general education to a much lesser degree. Our view is that since the publication of Smith's cogent analysis about progress, things likely are at a similar or somewhat increasing level, but we are not where the field would like to be or should be on access.

One of the issues of debate is whether research on teaching grade-aligned standards in self-contained settings promotes understanding of access to general curriculum. Ryndak and colleagues (2008–2009) proposed that research in self-contained settings may promote polices that contradict access to general curriculum. Although this hypothesis merits further research and discussion, the authors advocate not dismissing any research that demonstrates that students can learn more than once thought possible. One of the most important contributions of the experimental research in self-contained settings is that it has offered a sufficient body of work to meet criteria for evidence-based practice for teaching academic content to students with severe disabilities (i.e., set of quality indicators plus quantity and dispersion requirements). For example, synthesis of the experimental research used to provide evidence of academic learning (Spooner et al., 2012), reading (Browder et al., 2009; Browder, Wakeman, et al., 2006), mathematics (Browder et al., 2008), and science (Courtade, Spooner, & Browder, 2007; Spooner et al., 2011) would not have been possible without considering research across contexts. For example, in a review of studies on students with severe disabilities that link to science standards, a total of 11 studies were identified from 1985 to 2005 (Courtade et al., 2007). None of the 11 studies were conducted in inclusive classrooms. Fortunately, this statistic is changing as researchers find ways to apply interventions in general education, including science, classes (Jimenez, Browder, Spooner, & DiBiase, 2012).

Another controversy is the degree to which access to general curriculum content positively impacts postschool outcomes. For example, Ayres, Lowrey, Douglas, and Sievers (2011) commented that teaching functional skills had a higher probability of leading to a more independent life for students with severe disabilities. In doing so, they take issue with the use of a standards-based curriculum and suggested that working on grade-level content seizes time that could be allocated to teaching skills for adult life such as getting a job, choosing where to live, or actively participating in the community. Courtade, Spooner, Browder, and Jimenez (2012), in supporting access, emphasized seven reasons why a standards-based curriculum is appropriate (e.g., right to a full educational opportunity, relevancy of a standards-based curriculum, unknown potential of students with severe disabilities, standards-based curriculum is not a replacement for functional curriculum, and students creating their own changing expectations through achievements). Ayres, Lowrey, Douglas, and Sievers (2012) countered with comments about overarching differences between the two positions, emphasizing the need for promoting independence in adult living.

A third area of contention is who the best person is to deliver specialized instruction. Zigmond and Kloo (2011) suggested three primary reasons why general and special education are and should remain different. They suggested that special education teachers are prepared to impart instruction to individuals or small groups of individuals with disabilities who have specific learning needs, whereas general education teachers are prepared to teach the content to a large group of students. Second, general education is a place, special education is a service. Third, highly qualified general education teachers are not, and should not be, the same as a qualified specialist or special education teacher. Outcomes of investigations over the past few years (Browder, Trela, et al., 2012; Courtade, Browder, Spooner, & DiBiase, 2010; Smith, Spooner, Jimenez, & Browder, 2013) support the view that academic content can be delivered with high fidelity by teachers who do not meet the "highly qualified" standard as defined by the No Child Left Behind Act of 2001.

Although there is controversy (impact of postsecondary outcomes, context of instruction, who delivers service) in discussions about accessing the general curriculum for students with severe developmental disabilities, all educators have a vested interest in advancing the quality of life for people with severe developmental disabilities in school, community, and postschool settings. This chapter is based on our belief that providing effective instruction in general curriculum content enhances future opportunities for all students. Although each planning team must make the decision about how best to meet the needs of an individual student, we hope providing a summary of evidence-based practices for teaching academic content will encourage setting more ambitious goals and promote greater opportunities for learning in an inclusive setting.

WHAT WE NEED TO KNOW

Since the phrase *access to the general curriculum* was included in IDEA of 1997, accessing the general curriculum has been a major focus of researchers attempting to create more effective instructional systems for students with severe developmental disabilities. In an effort to more clearly understand the phenomenon of access, the Office of Special Education Programs (Federal Register, 2002) initiated a funding priority to, in part, describe and define *access to the general curriculum*, as well as analyze and address how to meet obstructions and challenges in professional development. Spooner and colleagues (2006) summed up what we knew and needed to know about access at that time by commenting on documented approaches (e.g., peer supports, self-determination, teaching and accessing content standards), as well as benefits and pitfalls (e.g., broadening curriculum options, increasing expectations, divergent definitions, little known about the impact of general curriculum on postschool outcomes). Many of these areas still need much more exploration. In particular, we need to know more about broadening curricular options to include the CCSS, evaluating the impact on postschool outcomes through looking at social validity measures now, and promoting inclusive options.

How to Teach the Common Core State Standards

Nearly all states have now adopted the CCSS. These same standards also are forming the foundation for the next generation of alternate assessments that will be used with students with severe disabilities. Although recent research has provided some new directions for teaching grade-aligned standards, the CCSS will demand much more be known. For example, both Browder and colleagues (2007) and Shurr and Taber-Doughty (2012) have demonstrated how to adapt and teach grade-aligned literature to students with severe disabilities. In contrast, the CCSS sets expectations for students to go far beyond the levels of comprehension reflected in earlier studies.

Some authors have begun to provide guidelines for adapting the CCSS. For example, Saunders, Bethune, Spooner, and Browder (2013) used research-based strategies to create a set of steps that can be used on a daily basis in front-line instruction by teachers. The complicated process of understanding and applying the CCSS in mathematics has been simplified into a six-step process: 1) select a topic and create objectives, 2) identify a real-life activity in which the skills are used, 3) incorporate evidence-based practices for teaching mathematics, 4) include instructional supports, 5) utilize progress monitoring, and 6) plan for generalization. Although using a real-life activity is particularly germane in the content area of mathematics, seemingly these same six steps or a variation of them likely would work in other content areas (e.g., to develop background knowledge in English language arts).

What is not yet known are what outcomes to expect for students with severe disabilities in learning the CCSS. Although states will create new alternate assessments and set standards for adequate progress, there continues to be inadequate research to provide guidance for how to do so. This lack of research becomes especially critical when these outcomes also are used to consider teacher effectiveness. We can infer from past experience that students with severe disabilities will learn more when we teach better. What is critically needed is continued research to identify the evidence base for teaching more advanced academic content to students with severe disabilities.

How to Measure Meaningful Outcomes Now and Later

One of the concerns about investing so much in the academic learning of students with severe disabilities is the potential impact on postschool outcomes. As described in Chapter 1, three decades of intensive life skills instruction without much academics has produced disappointing outcomes. Increased academic learning could produce improved outcomes. Research is needed on the relationship between the level of academic competence of students with severe disabilities and their adult outcomes. There is research showing an overall positive relationship for academic competence and postschool outcomes for individuals with disabilities in general (Blackorby, Hancock, & Siegel, 1993; Heal & Rusch, 1994, 1995), but many of these individuals did not need help from school to master functional skills. What is needed now is to see if teaching both academic content and functional skills produces better outcomes for students with severe disabilities.

Because these outcomes will take years to generate and may be influenced by variables not related to schooling (e.g., lack of adult service providers), there also is the need to measure the impact of academic learning on students' quality of life at their current age. Social validation measures offer one option for assessing the applied value of changes in behavior and the interventions used to accomplish that change. Through this process of measuring the social validity of interventions and potential impact, we can assess the social importance of the goals, the acceptance of the interventions, and the social importance of the newly acquired skill (Cooper, Heron, & Heward, 2007; Kazdin, 1977; Wolf, 1978), and we can attempt to evaluate some of the measures underlying improvement in quality of life.

How to Increase the Number, Duration, and Quality of Inclusive Opportunities

When students with disabilities were learning a totally separate curriculum, educators could use this as justification for separate settings. For example, self-contained classrooms with built-in kitchens may have seemed ideal for educating students with severe disabilities. In contrast, all students should now have access to the general curriculum content of their grade level. The place where this content is typically offered to the fullest extent is the general education classroom. We now have models for how to teach academic content in inclusive settings to students with severe disabilities (e.g., embedded instruction, peer-mediated learning). The need exists for research on how to bring this to scale. We need to use the work that has been done (e.g., embedded instruction [McDonnell, Johnson, Polychronis, & Riesen, 2002], cooperative learning [Dugan et al., 1995], peer-mediated learning [McDonnell, Mathot-Buckner, Thorson, & Fister, 2001], heterogeneous small groups [Rankin et al., 1999]) and increase not only the number of students with intellectual disability but also those with severe disabilities who are receiving their education in inclusive environments. In bringing this effort to scale, we can improve Smith's (2007) baseline of 11% established in 2007.

What also is needed to make these inclusive opportunities more accessible to students with severe disabilities is to identify ways to promote learning in the instructional arrangements typical of general education, such as whole-class instruction, independent seatwork, inquiry-based learning, and cooperative learning groups. Nearly all of the research on ways to increase access to the general curriculum in inclusive settings has used systematic instruction embedded in the general education lesson (Hudson et al., 2013). Although there is the need for additional models of how to implement systematic instruction in general education, especially for the CCSS, there also is the need for models in which students learn in alternative formats. For example, the *Self-Determined Learning Model of Instruction* (SDLMI; Agran, Cavin, Wehmeyer, & Palmer, 2006; Wehmeyer, Palmer, Agran, Mithaug, & Martin, 2000) is a specific instructional strategy that can be implemented in general education classrooms for students with and without disabilities and has evidence of causal impact on self-determination, educational goal attainment, and access to the general education. The SDLMI is based on the component elements of self-determined behavior and research on student-directed learning, and is a model of instruction designed to enable front-line personnel to teach students to set and attain goals in multiple content areas—from academic to functional to behavioral—through setting goals, taking action, and then adjusting the goal or plan depending on the outcome of the action.

SUMMARY

As a field, we have come along way from the implementation and sole focus of developmental pinpoints for all individuals, regardless of their chronological age.

Curricular foci have shifted, and at this point in the continuum of attempting to provide a better quality of life for students with severe disabilities and their families, content instruction involves teaching academic skills with a balance of functional skills that are necessary for day-to-day living. Although curricular foci have shifted, the instructional strategies that we use to impart the content have held constant. Systematic instruction has been effective in changing behavior for the last 60 years. We know about evidence-based practices to teach reading, mathematics, and science to students with severe disabilities. We are understanding more and more about grade-aligned learning. We realize that not everyone in the field is in total agreement, as there continue to be challenges, concerns, and controversy. We also recognize that we still need to know more about teaching the CCSS, how to measure meaningful outcomes, and how to bring inclusive practices to scale.

REFERENCES

Agran, M., Cavin, M., Wehmeyer, M., & Palmer, S. (2006). Participation of students with moderate to severe disabilities in the general curriculum: The effects of the Self-Determined Learning Model of Instruction. *Research and Practice for Persons with Severe Disabilities, 31*, 230–241.

Ayres, K.M., Lowrey, K.A., Douglas, K.H., & Sievers, C. (2011). I can identify Saturn but I can't brush my teeth: What happens when the curricular focus for students with severe disabilities shifts. *Education and Training in Autism and Developmental Disabilities, 46*, 11–21.

Ayres, K.M., Lowrey, K.A., Douglas, K.H., & Sievers, C. (2012). The question still remains: What happens when the curricular focus for students with severe disabilities shifts? A reply to Courtade, Spooner, Browder, and Jimenez (2012). *Education and Training in Autism and Developmental Disabilities, 47*, 14–22.

Azrin, N.H., & Foxx, R.M. (1971). A rapid method of toilet training the institutionalized retarded. *Journal of Applied Behavior Analysis, 4*, 89–99.

Azrin, N.H., Schaeffer, R.M., & Wesolowski, M.D. (1976). A rapid method of teaching profoundly retarded persons to dress by a reinforcement guidance method. *Mental Retardation, 14*, 29–33.

Bellini, S., & Akullian, J. (2007). A meta-analysis of video modeling and video self-modeling interventions for children and adolescents with autism spectrum disorders. *Exceptional Children, 73*, 264–287.

Blackorby, J., Hancock, G.R., & Siegel, S. (1993). *Human capital and structural explanations of post-school success for youth with disabilities: A latent variable exploration of the National Longitudinal Transition Study.* Menlo Park, CA: SRI International.

Browder, D.M., Ahlgrim-Delzell, L., Spooner, F., Mims, P.J., & Baker, J.N. (2009). Using time delay to teach picture and word recognition to identify evidence-based practice for students with severe developmental disabilities. *Exceptional Children, 75*, 343–364.

Browder, D.M., Jimenez, B.A., & Trela, K. (2012). Grade-aligned math instruction for secondary students with moderate intellectual disability. *Education and Training in Autism and Developmental Disabilities, 47*, 373–388.

Browder, D.M., & Minarovic, T.J. (2000). Utilizing sight words in self-instruction training for employees with moderate mental retardation in competitive jobs. *Education and Training in Mental Retardation and Developmental Disabilities, 35*, 78–89.

Browder, D.M., & Spooner, F. (2006). *Teaching language arts, math, and science to students with significant cognitive disabilities.* Baltimore, MD: Paul H. Brookes Publishing Co.

Browder, D.M., & Spooner, F. (2011). *Teaching students with moderate and severe disabilities.* New York, NY: Guilford.

Browder, D.M., Spooner, F., Ahlgrim-Delzell, L., Flowers, C., Algozzine, B., & Karvonen, M. (2003). A content analysis of the curricular philosophies reflected in states' alternate assessment performance indicators. *Research and Practice for Persons with Severe Disabilities, 28*, 165–181. doi:10.2511/rpsd.28.4.165

Browder, D.M., Spooner, F., Ahlgrim-Delzell, L., Harris, A., & Wakeman, S. (2008). A meta-analysis on teaching mathematics to students with significant cognitive disabilities. *Exceptional Children, 74*, 407–432.

Browder, D.M., Spooner, F., & Meier, I. (2011). Introduction. In D.M. Browder & F. Spooner (Eds.). *Teaching students with moderate and severe disabilities* (pp. 3–22). New York, NY: Guilford.

Browder, D.M., Spooner, F., Wakeman, S., Trela, K., & Baker, J.N. (2006). Aligning instruction with academic content standards: Finding the link. *Research and Practice for Persons with Severe Disabilities, 31*, 309–321.

Browder, D.M., Trela, K., Courtade, G.R., Jimenez, B.A., Knight, V., & Flowers, C. (2012). Teaching mathematics and science standards to students with moderate and severe disabilities. *The Journal of Special Education, 46*, 36–48. doi:10.1177/0022466910369942

Browder, D.M., Trela, K., & Jimenez, B. (2007). Training teachers to follow a task analysis to engage middle school students with moderate and severe developmental disabilities in grade-appropriate literature. *Focus on Autism and Other Developmental Disabilities, 22*, 206–219.

Browder, D.M., Wakeman, S.Y., Spooner, F., Ahlgrim-Delzell, L., & Algozzine, B. (2006). Research on reading for students with significant cognitive disabilities. *Exceptional Children, 72*, 392–408.

Brown, L., Nietupski, J., & Hamre-Nietupski, S. (1976). Criterion of ultimate functioning. In M. A. Thomas (Ed.), *Hey, don't forget about me! Education's investment in the severely, profoundly, and multiply handicapped* (pp. 2–15). Reston, VA: Council for Exceptional Children.

Collins, B.C. (2007). Teaching students with moderate and severe disabilities: Systematic instruction. In B.C. Collins (Ed.), *Moderate and severe disabilities: A foundational approach* (pp. 118–145). Upper Saddle River, NJ: Pearson/Merrill/Prentice Hall.

Cooper, J.O., Heron, T.E., & Heward, W.L. (Eds.). (2007). *Applied behavior analysis* (2nd ed.). Upper Saddle River, NJ: Pearson Education.

Courtade, G., Browder, D.M., Spooner, F., & DiBiase, W. (2010). Training teachers to use an inquiry-based task analysis to teach science to students with moderate and severe disabilities. *Education and Training in Developmental Disabilities, 45*, 378–399.

Courtade, G.R., Spooner, F., & Browder, D.M. (2007). Review of studies with students with significant cognitive disabilities which link to science standards. *Research and Practice for Persons with Severe Disabilities, 32*, 43–49.

Courtade, G., Spooner, F., Browder, B., & Jimenez, B. (2012). Seven reasons to promote standards-based instruction for students with severe disabilities: A reply to Ayres, Lowrey, Douglas, & Sievers (2011). *Education and Training in Autism and Developmental Disabilities, 47*, 3–13.

Criteria for Evidence-Based (2005). [Special Issue]. *Exceptional Children, 71*(2).

Dugan, E., Kamps, D., Leonard, B., Watkins, N., Rheinberger, A., & Stackhaus, J. (1995). Effects of cooperative learning groups during social studies for students with autism and fourth-grade peers. *Journal of Applied Behavior Analysis, 28*, 175–188.

Federal Register 67 (118) Wednesday, June 19, 2002, pages 41792–41793.

Fuller, P.R. (1949). Operant conditioning of a vegetative human organism. *American Journal of Psychology, 62*, 587–590.

Heal, L.W., & Rusch, F.R. (1994). Prediction of residential independence of special education high school students. *Research in Developmental Disabilities, 15*, 223–243.

Heal, L.W., & Rusch, F.R. (1995). Predicting employment for students who leave special education high school programs. *Exceptional Children, 61*, 472–487.

Horner, R.H., Carr, E.G., Halle, J., McGee, G., Odom, S., & Wolery, M. (2005). The use of single-subject research to identify evidence-based practice in special education. *Exceptional Children, 71*, 165–180.

Horner, R.D. & Keilitz, I. (1975). Training mentally retarded adolescents to brush their teeth. *Journal of Applied Behavior Analysis, 8*, 301–309.

Hudson, M.E., Browder, D.M., & Wood, L. (2013). Review of experimental research on academic learning by students with moderate and severe intellectual disability in general education. *Research and Practice for Persons with Severe Disabilities, 38*, 17–29.

Individuals with Disabilities Education Act Amendments (IDEA) of 1997, PL 105-17, 20 U.S.C. §§ 1400 *et seq.*

Individuals with Disabilities Education Improvement Act (IDEA) of 2004, PL 108-466, 20 U.S.C. §§ 1400 *et seq.*

Jackson, L.B., Ryndak, D.L., & Wehmeyer, M.L. (2008-2009). The dynamic relationship between context, curriculum, and student learning: A case for inclusive education as a research-based practice. *Research and Practice for Persons with Severe Disabilities, 33-34,* 175–195.

Jimenez, B.A., Browder, D.M., Spooner, F., & DiBiase, W. (2012). Inclusive inquiry science using peer-mediated embedded instruction for students with a moderate intellectual disability. *Exceptional Children, 78,* 301–317.

Kazdin, A.E. (1977). Assisting the clinical or applied significance of behavior change through social validation. *Behavior Modification, 1,* 427–452.

Knight, V., Spooner, F., Browder, D.M., & Smith, B.R. (2012). Teaching science concepts using graphic organizers to students with autism spectrum disorder. *Journal of Autism and Developmental Disorders, 42,* 378–389.

Lalli, J.S., & Browder, D.M. (1993). Comparison of sight word training procedures with validation of the most practical procedure in teaching reading for daily living. *Research in Developmental Disabilities, 14,* 107–127.

McDonnell, J., Johnson, J.W., Polychronis, S., & Riesen, T. (2002). The effects of embedded instruction on students with moderate disabilities enrolled in general education classes. *Education and Training in Mental Retardation and Developmental Disabilities, 37,* 363–377.

McDonnell, J., Mathot-Buckner, C., Thorson, N., & Fister, S. (2001). Supporting the inclusion of students with severe disabilities in typical junior high school classes: The effects of class wide peer tutoring, multi-element curriculum, and accommodations. *Education & Treatment of Children, 24,* 141–160.

McDonnell, J., & O'Neill, R. (2003). A perspective on single/within subject research methods and scientifically based research. *Research and Practice for Persons with Severe Disabilities, 28,* 138–142.

Mechling, L.C. (2011). Review of twenty-first century portable electronic devices for persons with moderate intellectual disabilities and autism spectrum disorders. *Education and Training in Autism and Developmental Disabilities, 46,* 479–498.

Morris, E.K., Altus, D.E., & Smith, N. (2013). A study of the founding of applied behavior analysis through its publications. *The Behavior Analyst, 36,* 73–107.

National Governors Association Center for Best Practices, Council of Chief State School Officers. (2010). *Common Core State Standards.* Washington, DC: Authors. Retrieved from http://www.corestandards.org/

National Research Council. (2002). Scientific research in education. In R. Shavelson & L. Towne (Eds.), *Committee on scientific principles for educational research.* Washington, DC: The National Academies Press.

Neef, N.A., Iwata, B.A., & Page, T.J. (1978). Public transportation training: In vivo versus classroom instruction. *Journal of Applied Behavior Analysis, 11,* 331–344.

No Child Left Behind Act of 2001, PL 107-110, 115 Stat. 1425, 20 U.S.C. §§ 6301 *et seq.*.

Rankin, D.H., Logan, K.R., Adcock, J., Angelica, J., Pittman, C., Sexton, A., & Straight, S. (1999). Small group learning: Effects of including a student with intellectual disabilities. *Journal of Developmental and Physical Disabilities, 11*(2), 159–177.

Ryndak, D.L., Moore, M.A., Orlando, A., & Delano, M. (2008–2009). Access to the general curriculum: The mandate and role of context in research-based practice for students with extensive support needs. *Research and Practice for Persons with Severe Disabilities, 33–34,* 199–213.

Saunders, A., Bethune, K., Spooner, F., & Browder, D.M. (2013). Solving the common core equation. *TEACHING Exceptional Children, 45*(3), 24–33.

Shurr, J., & Taber-Doughty, T. (2012). Increasing comprehension for middle school students with moderate intellectual disability on age-appropriate texts. *Education and Training in Autism and Developmental Disabilities, 47,* 359–372.

Skinner, B.F. (1938). *The behavior of organisms: An experimental analysis.* New York, NY: Appleton-Century.

Skinner, B.F. (1953). *Science and human behavior.* New York, NY: The Free Press.

Smith, B.R., Spooner, F., Jimenez, B., & Browder, D.M. (2013). Using an early science curriculum to teach science vocabulary and concepts to students with severe developmental disabilities. *Education & Treatment of Children, 36,* 1–31. doi:10.1353/etc.2013.0002

Smith, B.R., Spooner, F., & Wood, C.L. (2013). Using embedded computer-assisted explicit instruction to teach science to students with autism spectrum disorder. *Research in Autism Spectrum Disorders, 7,* 433–443. doi:10.1016/j.rasd.2012.10.01010

Smith, P. (2007). Have we made any progress? Including students with intellectual disabilities in regular education classrooms. *Intellectual and Developmental Disabilities, 45,* 297–309.

Snell, M.E. (Ed.). (1983). *Systematic instruction of the moderately and severely handicapped* (2nd ed.). Columbus, OH: Merrill.

Snell, M.E., & Brown, F. (Eds.). (2006). *Instruction of students with severe disabilities* (6th ed.). Upper Saddle River, NJ: Merrill.

Snell, M.E., & Brown, F. (Eds.). (2011). *Instruction of students with severe disabilities* (7th Ed.). Boston, MA: Pearson.

Sontag, E., & Haring, N.G. (1996). The professionalization of teaching and learning for children with severe disabilities: The creation of TASH. *The Journal of The Association for Persons with Severe Handicaps, 21,* 39–45.

Spooner, F. (Ed.). (2003). Perspective on defining scientifically based research. *Research and Practice for Persons with Severe Disabilities* [Special issue], *28*(3).

Spooner, F., & Browder, D.M. (2003). Scientifically based research in education and students with low incidence disabilities. *Research and Practice for Persons with Severe Disabilities, 28,* 117–125.

Spooner, F., Dymond, S.K., Smith, A., & Kennedy, C.H. (2006). What we know about accessing the general curriculum for students with significant cognitive disabilities. *Research and Practice for Persons with Severe Disabilities, 31,* 277–283.

Spooner, F., Knight, V., Browder, D.M., Jimenez, B., & DiBiase, W. (2011). Evaluating evidence-based practice in teaching science content to students with severe developmental disabilities. *Research and Practice for Persons with Severe Disabilities, 36,* 62–75.

Spooner, F., Knight, V.F., Browder, D.M., & Smith, B.R. (2012). Evidence-based practice for teaching academics to students with severe developmental disabilities. *Remedial and Special Education, 33,* 374–387.

Test, D.W., Spooner, F., Keul, P.K., & Grossi, T. (1990). Teaching adolescents with severe disabilities to use the public telephone. *Behavior Modification, 14,* 157–171.

Vogelsburg, R.T., & Rusch, F.R. (1979). Training severely handicapped students to cross partially controlled intersections. *AAESPH Review, 4,* 264–273.

Wehmeyer, M.L., Palmer, S., Agran, M., Mithaug, D., & Martin, J. (2000). Promoting causal agency: The Self-Determined Learning Model of Instruction. *Exceptional Children, 66,* 439–453.

Wolery, M., Bailey, D.B., & Sugai, G.M. (1988). *Effective teaching: Principles and procedure of applied behavior analysis with exceptional students.* Boston, MA: Allyn & Bacon.

Wolf, M.M. (1978). Social validity: The case for subjective measurement or how applied behavior analysis is finding its heart. *Journal of Applied Behavior Analysis, 11,* 203–214.

Zigmond, N.P., & Kloo, A. (2011). General and special education are (and should be) different. In J.M. Kaufman & D.P. Hallahan (Eds.), *Handbook of special education* (pp. 160–172). New York, NY: Routledge.

Index

Page numbers followed by *f* or *t* indicate figures or tables, respectively.